The Stonewall Experiment

*The Cassell Lesbian and Gay Studies list
offers a broad-based platform to lesbian, gay
and bisexual writers for the discussion of
contemporary issues and for the promotion
of new ideas and research.*

COMMISSIONING:
Steve Cook
Roz Hopkins

CONSULTANTS:
Liz Gibbs
Keith Howes (Australia)
Christina Ruse
Peter Tatchell

Ian Young was born in London. His involvement in the gay movement, as activist, writer and publisher, began in the 1960s. His books include poetry, literary anthologies, bibliography and history. Director of a communications consultancy firm and a frequent contributor to the gay press, he lives with his partner Wulf in Toronto and Banff, Alberta.

The Stonewall Experiment

A Gay Psychohistory

Ian Young

CASSELL

Cassell
Wellington House
125 Strand
London
WC2R 0BB

215 Park Avenue South
New York
NY 10003

First published 1995

British Library Cataloguing-in-Publication Data
A catalogue record for this book is available from the British Library.

ISBN 0–304–33270–4 (hardback)
    0–304–33272–0 (paperback)

Typeset by York House Typographic Ltd, London
Printed and bound in Great Britain by Mackays of Chatham plc

The cover photograph shows a scene from *Dead Dreams of Monochrome Men*,
performed by DV8.

Contents

Acknowledgements

My thanks to the many people who helped me in the writing of this book most especially:

to my parents, Joan Young and the late George R. Young, for all their help;

to Gavin Dillard, Michael Saunders, James Shakley, M.J. Shakley, Dr Charles Silverstein, and the late Dr Casper Schmidt, for reading earlier versions of the manuscript and providing valuable comments and suggestions;

to John Balatka, Jim Bartley, John Bennett, Mike Campeau, Etienne Espinet, Richard George-Murray, Colman Jones, Joe Kadlec, Lawrence Lauzon, Ellen Lipsius, Danny Neudell, Jerry Rosco, John Scythes, Florence Sicoli, Bob Storm, Urania 235, John Wadey, Douglas G. Webb, Peter Lamborn Wilson, Bill Young, and the late Wallace Hamilton, for sharing their ideas and research materials with me;

to John Lauritsen, whose pioneering investigative writings on the AIDS crisis provided me with an invaluable guide;

to John Forbes, for sharing his knowledge of holistic medicine;

to Robert Wilson and Karsten Johansson, for their help with word processing;

to Fr Mark Sullivan, Gay Anarchists of New York and the Libertarian Book Club for providing me with a forum;

to Gallery Without Walls (Toronto) for exhibiting some of the illustrations;

to Charles St John, for reminding me of a key piece of the puzzle;

to the *New York Native*, *Torso*, *Just Out* (Portland, Oregon), *Steam* and *Rites* (Toronto) for publishing articles which evolved into sections of this book;

vii: Acknowledgements

to the Canadian Gay Archives, the AIDS Committee of Toronto Resource Centre, the Judith Merrill Collection, the Thomas Fisher Rare Book Library and the University of Toronto Science and Medicine Library for their research assistance;

to my agent, Norman Laurila;

to my brothers and sisters in the Hermetic Order of the Silver Sword, and to fellow members of the Toronto Science of Mind Study Group;

and most of all to my partner Wulf, for providing me with the time, encouragement and support I needed to write the book, and for learning with me.

I would also like to remember here some of those I knew whose lives were taken by AIDS: Steve Abbott, Bill 'Wolf' Agress, John Bannerman, Paul Bartlet, Don Bell, John Bodis, William Bory, Todd Brown, Wayne Bryant, Michael Callen, Robert Chesley, Sam D'Allesandro, Terry des Pres, Richard Dipple, Tim Dlugos, Robert Dove, Blaine Duncan, Sal Farinella, George Fisher, James Fraser, Don Garner, Ralph Hall, Richard Hall, Peter Higgins, Richard Horn, Jim Holmes, Erik Hughes, Ken Hutchinson, Mikhail Itkin, Tim Jocelyn, Jamie Joyce, Matthew Keating, Pat Kelley, Mike Kelly, Doug Knott, George Kreuse, Barry Laine, Guy Laprade, Denis Lemon, Stan Leventhal, Michael Lynch, T. J. MacEachern, Peter McGehee, Douglas McManus, Rick Maddocks, Geoff Mains, Rick Matucci, Joseph Modny, Marc Morin, Ron Neddow, Aaron Nixon, Alan Orenstein, Charles Pace, Harold Pickett, Michael Pitts, Vito Russo, Juris Silarajs, Herman Slater, Kevin Stevens, Michael Taylor, Michael Wade, Buddy Walker, Barry Way, George Whitmore, Alex Wilson, Doug Wilson, and – especially – Jamie Perry and Richard Phelan.

This book is also dedicated to them, and to all the others who did not survive the experiment.

To Wulf

*and to a new generation
of gay men*

*I wrote this book in order to satisfy my historical curiosity; in the words of a
more successful historian, 'to understand what happened, and why it
happened'. Historians often dislike what happened or wish that it had
happened differently. There is nothing they can do about it. They have to
state the truth as they see it without worrying whether this shocks or confirms
existing prejudices.*

— A. J. P. Taylor, *The Origins of the Second World War*

A Klee painting named **Angelus Novus** *shows an angel looking as though he is
about to move away from something he is fixedly contemplating. His eyes are
staring, his mouth is open, his wings are spread. This is how one pictures the
angel of history. His face is turned towards the past. Where we perceive a
chain of events, he sees one single catastrophe which keeps piling wreckage
upon wreckage and hurls it in front of his feet. The angel would like to stay,
awaken the dead, and make whole what has been smashed. But a storm is
blowing from Paradise. It has got caught in his wings with such violence that
the angel can no longer close them. The storm irresistibly propels him into the
future to which his back is turned, while the pile of debris before him grows
skyward . . .*

— Walter Benjamin, *Illuminations*

And every Natural Effect has a Spiritual Cause . . .

William Blake, *Milton*

Introduction

PSYCHOHISTORY is a study of human motivations. It involves the analysis of archival records and other cultural artefacts in an attempt to uncover the beliefs, fears, fantasies and desires of individuals and social groups. This book is a psychohistory of gay men. As it has been written from the perspective of the 1990s, it is also, necessarily, a cultural investigation into the origins of a plague.

In the unconscious mind – the realm of dreams, trance, intuition and prophecy – certain patterns of thought and belief are shared, to varying degrees, by society at large, and by members of specific social and psychic groups. These ideas exercise a profound influence on us, and on the consequences of our actions.

The Stonewall Experiment presents evidence for some of these ideas as they have inhabited the collective psyche of gay men during the past 125 years. It examines the myths, images, texts and behaviors of the 'gay culture', and explores their historical significance.

The mythographer James Hillman reminds us that historical events 'are not the primary facts of existence. Historical facts are secondary . . . senseless unless they point inward to central meanings. The historical "facts" may be but fantasies attached to and sprouting from central archetypal cores . . . .'[1] The sprouts, it seems, are our images of ourselves, and our modern uneasiness with history may reflect a fear of discovering who we are, or who we have been induced to imagine we are.

Self-images, and the patterns of behavior they influence, are strongly susceptible to manipulation by symbols, pictures, suggestions and covert signals. This manipulation can come directly from the self, or from others; its effects can be positive or negative. When positive, it can achieve the personal catharsis and transformation of magical or artistic creation. When negative, it can constitute psychological programming, subliminal propaganda or black magic.

As much as possible, I have tried to document what I have to say by reference to the public record, and particularly to what I call the gay archive – the store of gay history, lore, poetry, prophecy, imagery and imagination that is the psychic inheritance of what Christopher Isherwood called 'our tribe', and of every gay man who comes to awareness of himself.

My remarks are not a history of homosexuality, the gay movement, or the health crisis; they are not meant to be comprehensive or exhaustive. They are the notes and reflections of a poet who was involved in the gay liberation movement during the years between the Stonewall rebellion in 1969 and the onset of AIDS in 1981. As a poet, I have a particular interest in images, verbal messages and psychic undercurrents – the unconscious myths and motivations that are reflected by cultural phenomena, and that frequently determine events. The discovery and elucidation of this cultural evidence is what I mean by psychohistory.

My concern is to contribute something to our understanding of what occurred in the little more than a decade between Stonewall and AIDS and in the plague years that followed. What happened to the promise of the Stonewall revolution? Perhaps (like all revolutions, some would say) it was betrayed. If so, the nature of that betrayal was rooted both in the revolution itself and in the society that gave rise to it. As one philosopher put it, 'If [people] make their own history . . . they do not make it just as they please; they do not make it under circumstances chosen by themselves, but under circumstances . . . given and transmitted from the past.'[2]

As I write, the plague that descended on us in 1981 is still with us. A generation of young gay men has never known life without its presence. And though there are a number of developments, both hopeful and sinister, there is no end in sight. No one yet possesses the whole picture of this crisis. But we are now able to put some pieces of the puzzle together, and to begin to discern something of its general outline.

3: *Introduction*

What follows, then, is a poet's-eye view of the first 125 years of our visible existence – the years when gay men began to emerge as a people. It is written with a particular reader in mind: a young gay man (or whatever term he chooses for himself) of a future generation. Whoever he is, and whatever his circumstances, if he is to survive, thrive, and make his contribution, he will need to understand his history, and learn its lessons. This book is for him (speckled and dusty though it may be by the time it reaches him). Other readers, of course, are welcome, but they should remember that they are reading over his shoulder.

Notes

1.   James Hillman, 'Senex and puer: an aspect of the historical and psychological present', in James Hillman, ed., *The Puer Papers* (Dallas: Spring Publications, 1987), pp. 6–7.
2.   Karl Marx, 'The Eighteenth Brumaire of Louis Napoleon', quoted in David Rees, *Not for Your Hands: An Autobiography* (Exeter: Third House, 1992), unpaginated.

Prologue: A Walk down Christopher Street

How they had hoped and dreamed; now the sidewalks seemed to smell of blood.

— Geoff Mains (*Gentle Warriors*)

WE were standing, Wulf and I, at the intersection of Christopher and West Streets in Greenwich Village, on a chilly Thursday night in the autumn of 1987. The corner was deserted, and in the gusts of cool wind it seemed desolate and forsaken. Anticipating a nostalgic journey into the past, I had been confronted with the devastating reality of the present.

When I lived in New York, a decade earlier, the corner outside Badlands bar would have been alive with gay men, strolling, cruising, socializing, enjoying the one small area of that enormous city where we could talk with friends or pop in to buy an ice-cream or chat with a storekeeper without having to hide our gay souls, our gay feelings. Here we could be seen and known, appreciated or judged, for who we were, rather than for what we were not. That alone, that quite ordinary, and newly minted, honesty that elsewhere we were denied in peril of our lives, made Christopher Street (in spite of the smog) a breath of fresh air.

Wulf and I found a different Christopher Street in 1987. It was almost deserted. Some of the old businesses were gone, others that in the old days were always open late were now shut. Ty's, one of the few gay-owned bars, was open, doing a modest trade. But, on that particular evening, the few people on the street seemed disoriented, one or two of them muttering to themselves, self-involved and distracted. A chill breeze added to the eerie effect. We crossed Hudson Street and walked towards the river. In the old days, the corner at the end of Christopher Street, outside Badlands, was usually crowded. Especially late in the week, gay men would congregate there in groups or couples or singly, hanging out, checking out the talent, or just taking the air. There would be an electric feeling. A good feeling. Now, the corner was empty. Not a soul remained.

For gay men in New York City, the height of the Fear came at about that time, the years 1985–7. For several years, thousands of us had been dying – some quickly, some painfully slowly – of a frightening, mysterious and pitiless complex of diseases. The death toll continued to mount, with no abatement in sight. Everyone wondered whether it would strike him next. As one gay activist put it, 'We're all living in terror now.'

In olden days when plague swept through a city, you could smell it on the wind. And indeed, if anyone today could approach New York fresh from some medieval forest, he would certainly cough, his throat would constrict, his eyes water and his nostrils detect a certain burnt, sulphurous quality he would immediately recognize as a whiff of the Devil. But we have become accustomed to this atmosphere: it is merely the atmosphere of the modern world, the very air we breathe. It goes unnoticed, and we proceed unaware.

My own first day in Manhattan was hot and sunny, one summer in the heady, idealistic early years of gay liberation, the early 1970s. The next night, I followed my intuition through unfamiliar SoHo streets to the old Firehouse, headquarters of the Gay Activists Alliance, where I joined the celebration in progress – hundreds of dancing men and women. And I found a boyfriend, the only man who wasn't dancing and the last to leave – the coatcheck attendant. Where are you now, Craig Kennedy? Alive and well I hope.

For several years running I stayed in New York for long periods, living first with Craig, then with other friends. I went to the conventions of gay writers and scholars at Columbia University and NYU (which had such high energy and good spirits they seemed as much like festivals as conferences). And from 1975 to 1980 I lived in Manhattan, shuttling back and forth from my apartment on

Cleveland Place to the gay publishing house I ran from my parents' basement in the suburbs of Toronto.

Jamie Perry worked at the Anvil in those days, the notoriously raunchy gay bar located in an old, wedge-shaped building in the West Village near the river. For a seventeen-year-old runaway from Connecticut with a ninth-grade education, no matter how bright or how white, the city did not hold much prospect of employment. It came down to the Anvil or the streets. So, after a stint on the streets, Jamie tended bar or minded the door, ran the projector for the porno movies in the basement, and did three shows a night with the other dancers, strippers and drag artists. Jamie's speciality was lively dance impersonations of the popular stars of the day – Rod Stewart, Debbie Harry, Elton John.

In a program that usually included Mr Ruby Rims (female impersonator), Rafael and Eddie (young Puerto Rican strippers) and Yuba (a very tall, very black man with a unique fire act), Jamie stood out as a blond figure of joyous, knowing innocence. His hours were long, his pay was poor, the place was what is known in the business as 'a toilet' (though the dressing rooms were conspicuously without one). The working conditions were the pits and the management, it was assumed, were lower-echelon Mafia. It was a job. Jamie made a lot of money for the owners of the Anvil.

The Big Apple in the 1970s, any Friday night: the Anvil full of gay men, sweatily packed together dancing, buying drinks, snorting poppers, having fun, a large percentage of them 'ripped to the tits', for there were a great many drugs at the Anvil. In the cellar the flickering light of the projector (for this was B.V. – Before Video) illuminated dark puddles on the stone floor, and there were black rooms and cubby-holes for sex with improper strangers. The windows were sealed, the party timeless, human voices barely audible over the disco throb.

Jamie's first night on the job was his birthday. Next morning, when the crowd dispersed, a young black man was found lying on the wet cellar floor with a knife in his back.

I am not an especially superstitious person. But it did occur to me that if this was omen, it could scarcely be a worse one. From then on, for as long as the two of us lived in New York, I had an ominous feeling of impending danger that would float into my consciousness and subside again, but that was always lurking somewhere in the back of my mind. The feeling attached itself to Jamie. Late at night and in the mornings as I waited for him to walk home across town through Union Square to our apartment on Cleveland Place, I sometimes experienced a tightening anxiety which occasionally bordered on panic. When Jamie was late, or was mugged, or the time he blacked out on the street, I imagined our leaving New York. I had enjoyed being 'down there on a visit', but the world was waiting for Jamie and it was time he took a look at it.

It also became clear that Jamie's health was deteriorating. As I had no Green Card, I could not legally work. When a big enough cheque came – payment for a writing project - we left the gay ghetto for England's green and pleasant land, convalescence, and a view of horizons beyond that larger ghetto, Manhattan. As soon as we were on the plane, I felt an uncanny sense of relief. Born in London (during an air raid late in the war), now I was going home. And bringing someone with me.

Seven years later, on a Thursday night in 1987, I thought to take Wulf, my lover and partner of (then) four years, to see the old haunts, especially Christopher Street, where the Stonewall riots had so surprised everyone eighteen years before. As we passed the street sign at the corner of Christopher and Gay Streets I thought of Wallace, my old friend and mentor, who had died in a tumble downstairs the year I met Wulf. The sign had adorned the dustjacket of his first book, *Christopher and Gay*, a vivid, loving picture of the scene in the years just after Stonewall.

A few blocks later, we came to that deserted corner, and all the gay sounds of the past diminished into an eerie quiet, with only a cool breeze and the sounds of a few nearby cars to break the silence. I thought New York had never seemed so silent. We turned the corner, and walked the few steps to the Ramrod, the leather bar I sometimes used to go to. As we walked up to the storefront, I was shocked to see it closed and boarded up with unpainted planks, as though nailed into some flimsy coffin and abandoned. Wulf and I were the only people on the street. Only Wulf's presence, walking as usual a little ahead of me, kept me from drifting off into a world of memories and ghosts.

8: *The Stonewall Experiment*

That was the moment I felt the full impact of AIDS. Of course, I had lost friends, and friends of friends. I had begun a quest to understand what had happened. But I had to come upon that desolate corner, with its boarded-up bar, to feel in my gut for the first time the terrible magnitude of our loss. So many thousands of gay men, and others, had been taken away since the 1980s began, and many more would follow. My poet's mind, I suppose, needed to fix on an image, and I was given the image of an empty street.

It seemed far from the optimistic days of the early 1970s, when the gay movement had brought us a sense of freedom and hope. The natural affection and erotic feelings of man for man and woman for woman have been stifled for so long that all our human relationships have suffered for it. Civilization threatens to become more and more an emotional wasteland as the links between parent and child, husband and wife, friend and friend, deteriorate. But all the while, the incidence of overtly homosexual people has quietly increased. As one gay thinker remarked, 'at the turn of the century the estimate of one homosexual man in 200 was seen as amazingly high. Fifty years later, Kinsey concluded that one man in twenty was what we would term gay. After only ten years of the modern gay liberation movement, this figure again seems far too low.'[1]

But society is slow to adapt, and prejudice is much harder to kill than people. The new priesthood of science adapted the old priesthood's stigma on homosexuality, merely changing the terminology. Homosexuality was no longer seen as sin but as a symptom of sickness. Modern medicine forgets that symptoms are signs of self-healing. It scarcely occurred to anyone that homosexuals might be a healing force, and that to suppress us might have unforseen 'side-effects'.

Of course, some of us, in those early years, realized that our liberation might not last. As a New York journalist had said of an earlier period in the city's history, 'It was one of those heedless, luxury-glutted times that usually happens before a disaster.' But no one guessed what form a new disaster might take. An earlier attempt at emergence, in Europe in the 1920s and 1930s, had been cruelly aborted, the homosexual emancipation movement crushed and thousands of its followers stigmatized with pink triangles in the Nazi concentration camps. But the war against Nazism brought hope, and, as it happened, sowed the seeds of what was to become the homophile movement. After the riot at the Stonewall Inn in the early morning of 28 June 1969, during the last days of 1960s 'Flower Power', those seeds began to blossom. Yet by as early as 1973, many of the early, idealistic gay libbers had become disillusioned.[2] What followed was the time that Michel Foucault described as evolving 'a whole new art of sexual practice' that would turn the ghettos into 'laboratories of sexual experiment'.[3]

Preliminary experimental results began to appear on 5 June 1981, when the *Morbidity and Mortality Weekly Report* published case studies of five homosexual men who had contracted a rare form of pneumonia and a number of other 'opportunistic infections'. The decade of gay lib was over. The AIDies had begun.

Notes

1. David Fernbach, *The Spiral Path: A Gay Contribution to Human Survival* (London: Gay Men's Press, 1981), p. 199.
2. See, for example, Aubrey Walter, ed., 'Introduction' to *Come Together – The Years of Gay Liberation 1970–73* (London: Gay Men's Press, 1980); Bob Mellors, 'Gay Liberation' in *LSE: Magazine* (London), Summer 1990, p. 32; or almost any issue of the early movement 'gayzines' *Gay Post* or *Ain't It Da Truth*.
3. Quoted in Sylvère Lotringer, ed., *Foucault Live (Interviews, 1966–84)* (New York: Semiotext(e), 1989), p. 225.

Chapter one

The Myth of the Homosexual

*The homosexual must be entirely eliminated . . . . Just think . . .
how a people can be broken in nerve and spirit when such a plague
gets hold of it!*

— Heinrich Himmler

IN the beginning was the Word – or so they say. If to name a
thing is to create it, the modern creation of the homosexual must
have taken place sometime in 1867, by means of an anonymous
pamphlet published by one Karl Benkert, *alias* Karoly Maria
Kertbeny, a rather mysterious figure described in our history books
as either a Swiss physician or an Austro-Hungarian activist, or both.
Two years later, the word 'homosexual' appeared in English for the
first time.

Rabbi Loew of Prague (or was it Rabbi Elijah of Chelm?)
created the Golem out of mud and placed the Hebrew letter *aleph* on
his forehead; if it were removed, he would crumble into dust. Mary
Shelley and Baron Dr Frankenstein created Boris Karloff out of
lightning and graveyard scraps, and when the angry villagers came
after him, with torches, he perished as though mortal. The
homosexual, it seems, was from the beginning as much a creature of
the written – and printed – word as Golem or Monster.

We – or rather the homosexuals we used to be – have
something to do with changes brought about by the printed word
(that influential pamphlet!) and by the ideology of science, the
consequences of whose intrusion into human sexuality have been
illuminated by the most involving of all our cult classics, Richard

11: *The Myth of the Homosexual*

O'Brien and Jim Sharman's *The Rocky Horror Picture Show*. In this bisexual reworking of the Frankenstein myth, the mad scientist Dr Frank N. Furter, in operating gown and garter belt, shatters bourgeois sexual assumptions and awakens latent sexual desires while creating the innocent, vacuous stud Rocky as an experiment. A previous prototype, Eddie, a demented biker, has already run amok. Frank N. Furter's faustian bargain with other-worldly forces (who disguise themselves as his servants) leads him – and Rocky – to eventual ruin. Rocky expires carrying his creator on his back, and the two of them fall together into the great swimming pool of the unconscious. Whew!

So, who – what – are we? Why are we? Our psychohistory reflects our attempts to answer these vague but crucial questions, and as they seem to keep popping up in one form or another, we had better keep trying.

For a long time, we thought of ourselves as 'homosexuals'. Sometimes we still do. I have suggested that there is a myth involved with the idea of the homosexual, or rather, that the homosexual is involved in a myth. The word 'myth' is popularly taken – in spite of all Joseph Campbell's efforts – to mean an untruth. But it would be more accurate to say that myth is a psychological reality that we may experience, or experiment with, to determine what meaning and value it has for us. The myth of the homosexual is one of the myths of the religion of Science, and so tends to fulfil scientific laws and illustrate scientific lessons. If not the creation of science, the homosexual is – was – at least its adopted child. Science named him, and has been afraid of him ever since.

The new scientific terminology reflected the fact that the old religion of Christianity was being quickly overtaken as the arbiter of sexual behavior by the new religion of science. Traditional religious terminology was being replaced by newly minted jargon, but the stigmatized acts and thoughts remained for the most part the same.[1]

What through most of the Christian era had been the sin and heresy of Sodom, which might tempt any man in his moments of weakness, was now, in the age of technology, transformed into a special kind of 'sickness', with the afflicted placed in a distinct category of infected or mentally aberrant being. The notion of homosexuality as a kind of amputated and misdirected sexual function led inevitably to the creation of 'the homosexual' as a subspecies of humanity whose very identity was dependent on his unhealthy state – a kind of walking disease. Like Frankenstein's monster, the homosexual was stitched together out of disparate, rejected and salvaged human parts, and given, through science, a new life of his own.

The homosexual was thus installed in a rogues' gallery with other mythical creations of Western diabolism: the Vampire, the Leper, the Witch, the Gypsy, the Werewolf, the Jew – figures concocted out of the fears, folk memories and repressed desires of a civilization, aspects of Christian society's dark unconscious, its shadow side.

The homosexual was the first of this series of mythic creatures to arise not from the psychopathology of the Christian Church alone, but from the laboratories of the new medical and social sciences. (The drug addict or 'dope fiend' and, more recently, the Satanic child-abuser are later additions to this spectral menagerie of group fantasies.) When these scary and distorted shadows are projected onto real, living individuals, the results are disastrous.

The creation of the homosexual was especially suited to the rising new world of nationalism and technocracy. Virile 'normality' was the arsenal of every nation: Jews, homosexuals and other outsiders were considered weak, devious, effeminate, and threatening to the health and cohesion of the body politic. 'Jews and so-called sexual perverts', one scholar remarks, 'were often pictured as fragile, close to death, the victims of premature old age.'[2] The few brave souls who tried to counter such 'science' swam against a powerful tide. For example, Karl Heinrich Ulrichs, an early pioneer of homosexual emancipation, was pronounced insane on the basis of his ideas, the diagnosis published in an official textbook of forensic medicine.

As technological civilization became more and more unbalanced, characteristics regarded as feminine became all the more despised. Homosexuals, thought to share certain female traits, were viewed, like women, as inferior, flawed, defective, and a locus of infection. Unlike women, they were also seen as useless, even as a likely source of racial suicide. Better that they be cured, confined, limited, gheottoised, quarantined, eliminated.

As this shift in thinking from a Christian to a scientific paradigm took place, what had previously been seen as external punishment for sodomy – from God or the Church, and later from the state – now became, in addition, internalized. The punishments religion inflicted on the sodomite came to be seen as *internal* torments intrinsic to his diseased condition. As heterosexual relations became increasingly problematic, it became more and more necessary to ward off the possibility – the threat – of homosexual love, which was therefore pronounced a delusion, a mere simulacrum. The judicial death penalty was transformed into the conviction that the homosexual – diseased, incapable of love, and thus necessarily wracked with guilt and shame – was doomed to die young.

American psychiatry, and consequently the entire medical establishment, considered homosexuality a mental illness until the 1970s when intense pressure from the gay liberation movement forced a recantation.[3] As late as the 1990s the leading international medical body, the World Health Organization (in charge of co-ordinating anti-AIDS efforts world-wide) classified homosexuality as an illness, allotting it its own number in the bureaucratic catalogue of diseases, like typhus or chickenpox.

Vito Russo, in his study of homosexuality in the movies, included a 'necrology', a revealing catalogue of the untimely deaths of film gays and their causes: 'suicide (hanging)', 'suicide (poison)', 'murder', 'execution (electric chair)', and so on.[4] A similar list could be assembled from the plots of gay novels. The novelist Jack Fritscher observed that 'Whenever some man in the burgeoning gay population died unexpectedly, naturally, or from an overdose, or from murder, someone somewhere, sometime always said, with an oily laugh, "At least he didn't have to grow old." That, of course . . . was a fate worse than death.'[5]

The lasting irony of the scientific creation of the homosexual is that as soon as the monster was named, those who were being re-diabolized recognized the descriptions, distorted and grotesque though they were, as portraits nonetheless of themselves – and so began to realize that they were not alone! You cannot stigmatize without identifying. And so a tug-of-war began for whatever soul this synthetic creature might possess.

The myth of the homosexual has its origins deep in the history of Romanized Judaeo-Christianity. Created, anathematized, and kept artificially alive by science, the homosexual became a psychic magnet not only for forbidden sexual longings but for all manner of fears and obsessions, not least of which was the fear of death, which burgeoning secularism both fed and denied. And like other mythological creatures, the homosexual was said to embody numerous apparent contradictions: he was at once oversexed and impotent, infantile and cunning, self-hating and self-infatuated, vain and ashamed, delicate and brutal: a diseased and dangerous monster. Much of the early literature of modern homosexuality and its emancipation movement is given over to examinations and dissections of this myth, attempts to explicate it, apply it, rework it into less pathological forms and – finally – to supplant it.

Once gay-oriented people began seriously to question the myth of the homosexual and to act out their defiance and repudiation of it, it could only be a matter of time before, in new social circumstances, the inner contradictions of the myth would begin to tear it apart. By then, tremendous social and psychic damage had been done, and virtually every gay man had to some degree internalized the myth, identified with it, and become a part of it.

Any devotee of old movies knows it is not so easy to kill off a monster; just when you think he's finished, he may be at his most dangerous. Myths are as strong as monsters. After Stonewall, the assumption that the obsessive myth of the homosexual had been destroyed, turned out to be a dangerous illusion.

Obsessions have a tendency to incarnate, and one of the ways they do so is to bring about and manipulate social changes. The ghettoized gay 'lifestyle' that was conceded to gay men in the wake of Stonewall had the effect of releasing a socially created monster, to threaten liberated gays and frighten straights alike. Freed from its imprisonment in the social unconscious, but still confined by the ghetto's invisible walls, the monster was let loose in a labyrinth it could not escape.

15: The Myth of the Homosexual

In Mary Shelley's classic allegory of scientific hubris, the medical scientist creates a simulacrum of a human being, which lives briefly, is feared and persecuted, takes its terrible revenge, and dies. Had history taken a different turn, 'Homeros'[6] might have emerged as a modern god and not a monster at all. As it happened, it took little more than a century for the malign group fantasy behind the myth to make itself fully felt.

> Wasn't his flesh human flesh
> even made from the bodies of criminals,
> the worst the Baron could find?
>
> But love is not necessarily implicit in human flesh:
> Their hatred was now his hatred,
>
> so he set out on his new career
> his previous one being the victim,
> the good man who suffers.
>
> Now no longer the hunted but the hunter . . .
>
> His idea – if his career now had an idea –
> was to kill them all,
> keep them in terror anyway,
> let them feel hunted.
> Then perhaps they would look at others
> with a little pity and love.
>
> Only a suffering people has any virtue.
>
> (from 'The Return of Frankenstein' by Edward Field)[7]

The death of the sacred boy

And was not such beauty as his a thing destined for death?
— Yukio Mishima, *St Sebastian, a Prose Poem*

Respectable society in the nineteenth and twentieth centuries found the homosexual as menacing as Frankenstein's monster. Gay men lived the same myth, playing the part of the persecuted outsider who did not ask to be born and finds himself assailed by the slings and arrows of outrageous fortune. This self-image found its place in gay iconography in the form of the legendary St Sebastian, the martyred youth who by the end of the nineteenth century had become a sort of unofficial patron saint of male homosexuals. His characteristic image was described by Oscar Wilde as 'a lovely brown boy, with crisp, clustering hair and red lips, bound by his evil enemies to a tree and, though pierced by arrows, raising his eyes with divine, impassioned gaze towards the Eternal Beauty of the opening heavens'.[8]

Apart from the obvious erotic interest of a beautiful half-naked young man, St Sebastian offers the image of a youth who suffers and is sacrificed for his devotion to the spiritual life and his love of God (in the form of another young man, Jesus). Like Jesus, and other sacrificed gods before him, he is fastened to a tree, a pillar or a cross. The sado-masochistic eroticism of the image is intensified in the case of St Sebastian by his traditional depiction as suffering a kind of ecstasy as he is penetrated by a gang of men – Roman soldiers with arrows. Here is male beauty, oppressed, penetrated and transformed, a perfect icon for the homosexual in Christian culture, who is so often characterized as suffering, nobly or ignobly, and dying young. St Sebastian is a version of the sacrificial son – or sun.

After his release from prison, Oscar Wilde himself took the name of Sebastian Melmoth (the surname deriving from the hero of the novel *Melmoth the Wanderer* by Wilde's great-uncle Charles Maturin). Many other gay artists, before and since, have identified with the vulnerable, sexually ambiguous rebel, and played with the iconography.

Yukio Mishima, an eventual suicide, had himself photographed as St Sebastian. In Tennessee Williams' 1958 play *Suddenly, Last Summer*, we are told that the homosexual poet, Sebastian Venable, has been devoured by a gang of children on the beach. Ten years later, Michael, the dinner-party host in Mart Crowley's *The Boys in the Band*, tells his gay guests they have just eaten the body of Sebastian Venable. The rest of the play, with its theme of hidden love, sets out the consequences of this sacrificial feast.

17: The Myth of the Homosexual

James Dean is the perfect American St Sebastian. Each of his two most famous films has his tormented love for his inadequate father at its heart. In a well-known photograph taken during the shooting of his last movie, he assumes a sultry, crucified pose, with the Mother Figure, Elizabeth Taylor, kneeling at his feet. His autopsy revealed 'a pattern of keloid scars' where he had offered his chest to men's burning cigarettes. In Derek Jarman's 1976 film *Sebastiane*, the erotic undertones to the story are brought to the fore and the pictorial retelling becomes a sort of langorous S/M extravaganza.

Jarman's film notwithstanding, St Sebastian as a gay icon had largely fallen out of use by the post-Stonewall period. In the AIDS era, gay artists rediscovered him, and he made appearances in a number of AIDS-related presentations. It may be remembered that the legend involves a symbolic death and resurrection; Sebastian survived the Romans' target practice, only to be beaten to death – a fate suffered by many at the hands of gay-bashers over the centuries. Significantly, he is the official patron saint of those affected by plague, and affords protection against it.

During the Victorian era, St Sebastian became a central reverential icon for homosexuals, Christian legend reinforcing the myth of the homosexual as youthful sacrifice, a concept with its roots deep in the primeval rituals of the West.[9] After the homosexual had been discovered (or created) more or less jointly by the sexual emancipation movement and its treacherous ally, medical science, the new creature absorbed old sacrificial attributes, and the hybrid figure that resulted entered the emerging literature and popular mythology of homosexuality (*see plate 1*).

Two versions of this mythical figure – one light, one dark – can be seen in a pair of seminal homotexts of the late nineteenth century, familiar to our own age because of their status as classic novels of the period.

Herman Melville's *Billy Budd* was written in 1891 but not published until 1924, long after the author's death. Oscar Wilde's *The Picture of Dorian Gray* was first published in 1890, setting off a moralistic campaign against Wilde that culminated in his prosecution for homosexuality five years later. Many straight critics have displayed considerable obtuseness over these tales, especially *Billy Budd*, as its author, never having been prosecuted, is even now only reluctantly acknowledged as bisexual. Generations of gays, however, have recognized both books immediately as gay allegories. For Billy and Dorian represent contrasting versions of the mythical homosexual, conceived at a time when the creature was beginning to move into public consciousness.

The changeable sailor, or, why does Billy Budd stammer?

To Billy, God has one meaning – love; but as Melville presents him, the love he knows is the love of his fellow sailors . . .
— James Baird

A dazzling white sailor suit, and young Terence Stamp's winsome, windblown face, against an expanse of grey sky.

Billy Budd is the last of Melville's ruminations on the figure of the handsome innocent, usually depicted as a blond sailor or dark-skinned South Sea Islander. From the affectionate natives in his early travel narratives like *Typee* through Bulkington and Queequeg in *Moby Dick*, these totemic masculine figures provide contrast to Ishmael and the other wandering, lonely outcasts who are Melville's usual protagonists.

Melville's fiction can be seen as a pivot between the gloomy broodings of Nathaniel Hawthorne (for whom Melville felt an unrequited erotic affection) and the sunnier optimism of Emerson and Whitman, which the worldly Melville was unable to share. *Billy Budd* embodies the tension between the possibility of an all-male sexual paradise and the reality of civlization's traditional ritual sacrifice of male beauty, affection and innocence.[10]

Billy Budd tells the story of a handsome young sailor unfairly accused of disloyalty by the ship's Master-at-Arms, John Claggart. Unable to find words to defend himself, he strikes out, killing his accuser. He is executed by his captain, who then kills himself in remorse.

As the book begins, Billy has been transferred from a ship known as the *Rights-of-Man* to a less friendly one called the

Indomitable. The *Rights-of-Man* is alluded to as a kind of Whitman-esque male democracy, where the tender-hearted Billy was courted and treated with affection. The *Indomitable*, by contrast, suffers under Claggart's harsh regime, and many of its men have been pressed into service against their will. Into this repressively ordered society comes a young man who 'in the nude might have posed for a statue of young Adam before the fall' and whose beauty and loving nature fallen men find disturbing. 'Something about him provoked an ambiguous smile in one or two of the harder faces among the blue-jackets', Melville writes. By contrast, 'his person and demea-nor' have a 'particular favorable effect . . . upon the more intelligent gentlemen of the quarterdeck'.[11]

It is revealed too that Billy was a foundling, discovered in a pretty silk basket – an androgynous being of uncertain, even unnatural origins. Three times in the story's first two pages, the figure of the handsome sailor is linked to that of a sacred bull and to the constellation of Taurus, suggesting both earthy, masculine qualities and the pervasive, feminine influence of the star cluster's governing planet, Venus. The bull is also, of course, a traditional sacrificial animal.[12] All these meanings Melville conjoins with the image of the Handsome Sailor, a traditional figure of gay erotic folklore, whose darker aspect is the Changeable Sailor, a volatile creature, prone to sudden violence, even murder.

The arrival of the angelic sailor on board the *Indomitable* sets the tragedy into motion, as the repressive – and repressed – Claggart is torn between hate and desire, and tension and danger mount. It is Billy's beauty that first turns Claggart against him, and Melville compares Claggart's envy to the Biblical Saul's envy of David, beloved of Saul's son Jonathan. Melville provides a clue to the meaning of his allegory in his original subtitle, 'An Inside Narrative'. In the conflict among the three elements of society and personality represented by Billy, Claggart, and the well-meaning, intellectual bachelor Captain Vere, Billy (the innocent, erotic self, desiring liberation) is accused of disloyalty and strikes at Claggart (the repressive super-ego), killing him.

Billy is a stammerer – the one flaw in his saintly being. Unjustly accused of treason, he is unable to utter a defense; Melville compares his feeling of suffocation to that of a vestal virgin being buried alive! And it is Billy's silence that leads, inevitably, to his death. Melville even describes Billy at the moment of accusation as appearing 'leprous'; the angelic has suddenly become the unclean, the outcast. Vere, the representative of the ego, half in love with Billy and sympathetic to his cause, begins to waver, to 'vere' away from his true nature and towards the upholding of the law. Eventually, he acquiesces in Billy's execution. In the words of the literary scholar Georges-Michel Sarotte, 'Billy, instinct released from some immemorial past, has no place in our society. He agrees – he must agree – to his own sentence: "God bless Captain Vere." he announces, and the crew repeats it after him.'[13]

Vere, guilt-ridden, takes a 'magical drug' whose usual use is to 'soothe' and 'operate on the subtler element', freeing up the unconscious mind. But in ordering Billy's execution, Vere has repudiated his unconscious, and the drug kills him. The official report of the incident condemns Billy's 'extreme depravity' – a common description of sexual heresy.

In this last of Melville's novels, the tensions between affection and social guilt, between liberation and repression, underlie a version of the myth of the homosexual; the beautiful, essentially innocent young man goes willingly to his death to appease an oppressive society.

In his earlier works, Melville offered glimpses of innocent homoerotic love with dark-skinned, pagan men. In *Moby Dick*, Queequeg's tattooed body, resting like a shaman bridegroom on Ishmael's sleeping form, sires strange reveries before eventually metamorphosizing into the coffin, inscribed with magical markings, that buoys Ishmael to the ocean's surface, saving his life when the *Pequod* sinks.

Billy Budd also ends with the death of innocence, but here the magical transformation comes in the form of a drug which brings death to the grieving ego. With the deaths of Claggart, Billy and Vere, the three aspects of the personality have been destroyed by the harsh regime of the *Indomitable*. The myth of the homosexual has been played out to its final tragic chapter.

Dorian Gray and the werewolf

An inordinate passion for pleasure is the secret of remaining young.
— Oscar Wilde, *Lord Arthur Saville's Crime*

Oscar Wilde's *The Picture of Dorian Gray* is another story of a beautiful young man's involvement with two older male figures, two suitors who court him: one true, the other false. His true love, Basil Hallward, a painter and more or less open gay, paints Dorian's portrait at the same time as Lord Henry Wooton, a cynical aristocrat, is seducing the boy's soul. (In the 1945 movie directed by Albert Lewin, Lord Henry was played to perfection by George Sanders, an actor even more jaded and bored than his character.) As in *Billy Budd*, a struggle takes place among three men representing the three aspects of the psyche.

To begin with, Dorian Gray is an innocent. Basil, the maker of truthful images, captures on his canvas not only the truth of Dorian's innocent beauty but also the truth of his own love for his model. Lord Henry, on the other hand, fears love, and preaches its denial. He opposes suffering, which he sees as unnecessary, and he denies the soul, which he sees as an illusion. Posing as a detached critic of society, Lord Henry, married, closeted and successful, expresses society's cynicism toward people like Basil and Dorian. Fearful of Basil's love, Dorian is vulnerable to Lord Henry's worldly philosophy, and in his delusion, he makes a wish that he could remain unblemished and unaged, and that only the portrait, hidden away, would reveal the state of his soul. The novel's plot hinges on Dorian's wish coming terrifyingly true.

Wilde, it is important to remember, was in the grip of a disease the Victorians regarded with particular horror: syphilis, which one writer characterized as 'the werewolf of science'. This was why he had to discontinue sexual relations with his wife, and why, with his male sexual partners, he practiced what a century later came to be known as 'safe sex'. He was 'grievously ill' of a 'nervous fever' around the time of the book's composition. Perhaps, as his biographer Richard Ellman suggests, it was through learning of his venereal infection that 'the parable of Dorian Gray's secret decay began to form in his mind, as the spirochete began its journey up his spine to the meninges'.[14]

Thinking the magical portrait will enable him to avoid the consequences of his misdeeds, Dorian proceeds to lead a life of debauchery, betraying both male and female lovers, scandalizing everyone and frightening the horses. Eventually, Basil Hallward, discovering the secret of the portrait, urges Dorian to renounce his sinister pact and accept the consequences of his actions. But this would mean accepting the truth about himself, about life and death, and above all about love – which Dorian cannot do. Instead he murders Basil, and the hidden portrait grows even more hideous. By this point, Dorian is almost completely inured to remorse, and what little he does feel he alleviates with drugs.

Finally, driven to madness, he vandalizes the portrait, instinctively repudiating his corrupt life – and is transformed. Lying dead at the foot of the painting which he has destroyed with the same knife used to murder his lover, Dorian at last becomes diseased and prematurely aged, and the ghastly portrait changes again to disclose an innocent beauty.

One of *Dorian Gray*'s many levels of meaning is allegorical of the modern homosexual's dilemma. Wilde writes in the book – obviously with the oppression of homosexuals in mind – of looking back through history and being 'haunted by a feeling of loss. So much had been surrendered! and to such little purpose! There had been mad wilful rejections, monstrous forms of self-torture and self-denial, whose origin was fear, and whose result was a degradation infinitely more terrible than that fancied degradation from which, in their ignorance, they had sought to escape.'[15]

Dorian's 'exaggerated sense of conscience' suggests the socially-induced shame of the homosexual. The word 'shame' even became a code-word for male homosexuality during the *fin de siècle*.[16] 'In his attempt to kill conscience', Wilde writes, 'Dorian Gray kills himself.'[17] (We will encounter this pattern of narcissistic self-numbing – and its consequences – again, in Chapter 3, in a report by New York writer George Whitmore from the floor of the Mineshaft.)

Wilde's novel draws from a number of literary sources, including Huysmans, Maturin and Balzac, it is basically a modern version of the Narcissus myth: it is a tragic story of a young man's inability to love, and to accept love. The literary critic Mario Praz pointed out that the figure of Dorian was also influenced by the stories and essays of Wilde's mentor Walter Pater (who shared Wilde's sexual orientation). 'Pater', he wrote in *The Romantic Agony*, 'stresses beauty and sorrow as the dominant impressions in his portraits of youths, as we see him dwelling on the decay of beautiful things, either buildings or human beings . . . .' Praz quotes a representative passage: 'He would think of Julian, fallen into incurable sickness, as spoiled in the sweet blossom of his skin like pale amber, and his honey-like hair; of Cecil, early dead, as cut off from the lilies, from golden summer days, as from women's voices . . . .' He comments on 'the characteristic fate of all these youths (Marius the Epicurean, Flavian, Watteau, Duke Carl of Rosenmond), and of beauty devastated by cruelty.'[18]

The corruption and destruction of beauty and/or propriety was a popular theme in Victorian literature, reflecting the respectable era's fearful awareness of the half-hidden presence of syphilis and its frequent companion, tuberculosis. Four years prior to *Dorian Gray*, Wilde's contemporary Robert Louis Stevenson (who was tubercular) published his *Dr Jekyll and Mr Hyde*, which, like *Frankenstein*, is a thriller about a scientific experiment gone wrong. Stevenson's novella evokes a scientific version of the mythical werewolf figure and employs, like *Dorian Gray*, some dark homoerotic subtexts. One character refers to Dr Jekyll's residence as 'Black Mail House', believing that Mr Hyde lives there as Jekyll's companion. Some of Hyde's crimes, like Dorian's, are left unspecified as too horrible to discuss, homosexuality being, to the Victorians, 'the abominable crime not to be mentioned among Christians'. In the end, Jekyll – and Hyde – die by suicide.

The theme of the doomed young (homosexual) man, which reached a kind of over-ripe apogee in the minor literature of the *fin de siècle*, was to persist as a strongly dominant motif in a great deal of the homosexual literature that was to follow, from *A Shropshire Lad* and 'Anthem for Doomed Youth' through *Quatrefoil*, *Finistère* and *Giovanni's Room* to works by Genet, Purdy, Kirby Congdon and Dennis Cooper.

24: *The Stonewall Experiment*

Dorian Gray is Wilde's version of the myth of the homosexual. Where Melville gives us an innocent, Wilde gives us an innocent corrupted. Both young men are beautiful, sacrificial figures, nineteenth-century versions of St Sebastian. (Wilde referred to 'the note of Doom that like a purple thread runs through the gold cloth of *Dorian Gray*.[19]) Jeffrey Meyers, in his *Homosexuality and Literature 1890–1930* expresses it well: Dorian comes to 'love his own beauty and loathe his own soul, an impossible combination of homosexual narcissism and socially-conditioned self-hatred.'[20] But that 'impossible combination' has been the fate and dilemma of many gay men in this civilization, confronted with the decision whether to face the decaying reflection or flee it.[21] 'The danger', as Wilde wrote in *De Profundis*, 'was half the excitement.' It was as true in the 1970s, on the rotting piers and in the backrooms of the Mineshaft, as it was in Wilde's day.

Whereas *Billy Budd* has special resonance for the gay reader at any time, rereading *Dorian Gray* in the age of AIDS is an especially eerie experience. It is hard not to see the book as a kind of prophecy, not in the sense that Wilde 'foresaw' a health crisis, but in the sense that the social and psychological forces which Wilde saw as acting on gay men had, almost a hundred years later, so increased in intensity that their manifestation had become far more obvious.

In a hundred years, the tensions between homosexuality and modern society, brought to the surface in the Victorian era, became strained to breaking point. So tightly had the gap closed between the 'real' and the symbolic in the intervening century that the accuracy and appropriateness of the artistic imagery becomes shockingly evident. The psychosocial conditions Wilde had detected and fictionalized as he pondered his own venereal infection were now affecting large numbers of unambiguously gay men. For the contemporary reader, especially the gay reader, the image of waste and deterioration seen in Dorian's portrait inevitably suggests the ravages of AIDS.

During Wilde's trial for homosexuality, someone sent him a picture, apparently clipped from some natural history text, of a prehistoric lizard. No explanation was necessary. This is how Wilde, and his fellow homosexuals, were seen: primeval, predatory and doomed.

25: The Myth of the Homosexual

Democratic vistas

. . . I will establish in the Mannahatta and in every city of these states inland
and seaboard,
And in the fields and woods, and above every keel little or large that dents
the water,
Without edifices or rules or trustees or any argument,
The institution of the dear love of comrades.

— Walt Whitman, 'I Hear It Was Charged Against Me'

Once in a great while, at crucial junctures in the history of a culture, a visionary presence appears in the form of a poet–prophet who fulfils the dual role of religious mystic and social critic. Whatever his individual characteristics, he seems in a larger sense to have no significant antecedents, to have somehow burst through from another dimension in order to address the civilization in which he finds himself. William Blake was such a presence in the England of the early industrial revolution. Similarly, into the developing capitalist society of nineteenth-century America, came the figure of Walt Whitman.

Whitman had a Quaker background, and his writing is pervaded by the Quaker insight that personal and social redemption come through love, and that no problem can be solved without love. 'Affection', he wrote, 'shall solve every one of the problems of freedom.' He saw God as 'the loving bedfellow' and Jesus as 'the beautiful god'. Like an earthy visionary genius of a later time, John Cowper Powys, Whitman ranged in his work over a whole universe of spirit and nature in order to see the single individual clearly, as he really is.

A nurse during the American Civil War, tending and caring for wounded and dying young men, Whitman placed an erotic, compassionate vision of the continent's future at the heart of his prophetic message. There had been hints, and more than hints, of homoeroticism in earlier American literature – in the writings of James Fenimore Cooper, Herman Melville and Charles Warren Stoddard. Often, they were intertwined with the dream of reconciliation and love between the white man and his red, brown or black brother, who (unlike the white conqueror) maintained a measure of natural nobility and innocence in the face of slavery and genocide.

But the visions of spiritual innocence in Melville's and Stoddard's South Sea idylls had eventually to encounter the myth of the homosexual. We have seen the result in *Billy Budd*.[22] Into this clouded landscape, Whitman broke through like a shaft of clear light, as though from another place entirely, to state his brighter message as plainly as his times would allow.

In 1870, he wrote in *Democratic Vistas*:

> It is to the development, identification, and general preva-
> lence of that fervid comradeship ... that I look for the
> counterbalance and offset of our materialistic and vulgar
> American democracy, and for the spiritualization thereof.
> Many will say it is a dream, and will not follow my
> inferences: but I confidently expect a time when there will be
> seen, running like a half-wild warp through all the myriad
> audible and visibly worldly interests of America, threads of
> manly friendship, fond and loving, pure and sweet, strong
> and life-long, carried to degrees hitherto unknown – not only
> giving tone to individual character, and making it unprece-
> dently emotional, muscular, heroic and refined, but having
> the deepest relations to general politics.[23]

In the words of the Canadian Whitman scholar Robert K. Martin, Whitman saw his own sexual nature as 'the source of his art, the center of his book, and the foundation of his political theory. Prior to Whitman there were homosexual acts but no homosexuals. Whitman coincides with and defines a radical change in historical consciousness: the self-conscious awareness of homosexuality as an identity. "Calamus" is the heart of *Leaves of Grass* as well as the root.'[24]

Whitman realized that he was establishing 'new standards' and that what he saw as of central erotic, civic and spiritual importance, many others would interpret differently. For all his expansiveness and optimism, there would have to be, of necessity, an occult aspect to his teaching. He was leading his more sympathetic readers through 'paths untrodden / in the growths by margins of pond-waters', to the 'secluded spot' in either country or city, where friends can be together privately and express themselves fully. 'I will escape', he vows, 'from the sham that was proposed to me.'

Quite separate from the myth of the homosexual that was emerging in Whitman's time, the poet of 'Calamus' and 'Children of Adam' announced a democratic counter-myth (harking back to ancient Greek times and beyond) of 'adhesive' affections as both natural and politically essential. In Whitman's writings, the breast harboring feelings of male/male love is no longer riddled with arrows but fragrant with 'scented herbiage', a natural resting-place for the head of a comrade, or for a bound copy of *Leaves of Grass*.

The dust-jacket of Robert K. Martin's study of *The Homosexual Tradition in American Poetry*, published in 1979, shows Walt Whitman, pen in hand, seated at a desk in a closet with an open door. The image is appropriate; Whitman wrote at a time when the closet door was finally beginning to open on homosexual feelings, when they were at last emerging from being, in Lord Alfred Douglas' famous words, 'the love that dare not speak its name.' Whitman urged his readers to 'unscrew the locks from the doors! Unscrew the doors themselves from their jambs!'[25] A century later, 'Out of the closets and into the streets!' would become a gay rallying cry.

What is so extraordinary about Walt Whitman is his profound understanding of homosexuality – or 'adhesiveness' as he called it, adopting the jargon of phrenology – as central, rather than peripheral, to the future of America and the health of the body politic. Through 'a new ideal of manly friendship, more ardent . . . previously unknown', America's true destiny was to unfold. 'I say democracy infers such loving comradeship', 'as its most inevitable twin or counterpart', he wrote, 'without which it will be incomplete, in vain, and incapable of perpetuating itself.'[26]

For Whitman, the image of the fulfilled lover was the key to the social and spiritual redemption of America, with sexual experience the gateway to spiritual awakening, the male/male love the catalyst that would dissolve the barriers erected by a competitive and materialistic society. And – especially after his experiences in the Civil War – he knew how destructive such a society could be. In his great poem 'The Sleepers' he envisions the figure of a 'beautiful gigantic swimmer', a youthful, phallic figure venturing into the nourishing dangerous seas of the unconscious, and defiantly asks,

'Will you kill him in the prime of his middle age?'[27] Here, in the midst of Whitman's beatific vision, the myth of the homosexual, as well as the realities of war, intrude ominously in a sudden flash. Whitman's vision of early violent death was not a personal one; he survived the Civil War and lived to a ripe old age. His words, though, were echoed by a prophetic gay leader of another century who *was* 'killed in the prime of his middle age': Harvey Milk. Assassinated at age forty-eight, Milk had foreseen his own death by gunfire, and the lines he wrote a month before he died are reminiscent of Whitman: 'I can be killed with ease / I can be cut right down / But I cannot fall back into my closet / I have grown / I am not by myself / I am too many / I am all of us.'[28]

In the section of *Leaves of Grass* entitled 'Whispers of Heavenly Death', in his various war writings and intermittently throughout his work, Whitman made his peace with death not, as in so much homosexual literature, as 'the wages of sin' but rather as 'the harvest' of what life has tilled. 'Be not impatient', he admonished; 'Strong is your hold O mortal flesh, / Strong is your hold O love.' In his farewell poem 'So Long!' he 'concludes' by announcing firmly what will come after him: 'I announce adhesiveness', he says. 'I say it shall be limitless, unloosen'd . . . .' And he promises, 'I say you shall yet find the friend you were looking for.'[29]

Walt Whitman's poetic prophecy was the most radical vision of homosexual emancipation to appear in America until his namesake Carl Wittman's *A Gay Manifesto* in 1970. Many gay writers and activists took their inspiration from Whitman; translations of his work were especially important to the early gay movement in Germany. Oscar Wilde made his own pilgrimage to Whitman and the Renaissance scholar John Addington Symonds was among the Good Gray Poet's most prominent disciples. Like Wilde, a married man with children, Symonds disapproved of the 'decadence' of the Wilde circle and the aesthetic set grouped around *The Yellow Book*. Serious and tubercular, Symonds preferred the robust, self-consciously masculine Whitman to the fulsomely androgynous Wilde. But where Wilde's libertarian socialism, influenced by Ruskin, Kropotkin and William Morris, had a practical as well as an idealistic side, Symonds viewed Whitman's homo-democratic vistas through the protective stained glass of Greco-medieval fantasy:

> There shall be comrades thick as flowers that crown
> Valdarno's gardens in the morn of May;
> On every upland and in every town
> Their dauntless imperturbable array . . .
> Shall make the world one fellowship, and plant
> New Paradise for nations yet to be.
> O nobler peerage than that ancient vaunt
> Of Arthur or of Roland! Chivalry
> Long sought, last found! Knights of the Holy Ghost!
> Phalanx immortal! True Freemasonry,
> Building your temples on no earthly coast,
> But with star-fire on souls and hearts of man
> Stirred from their graves to greet your Sacred Host
> The Theban lovers, rising very wan,
> By death made holy, wave dim palms and cry:
> 'Hail, Brothers! who achieve what we began!' . . .
>
> . . . Thou dost establish – and our hearts receive –
> New laws of Love to link and intertwine
> Majestic peoples; Love to weld and weave
> Comrade to comrade, man to bearded man,
> Whereby indissoluble hosts shall cleave
> Unto the primal truths republican.[30]

Quoting Symonds in his anthology *Sexual Heretics*, Brian Reade remarks that knowing Symonds as we do, 'it is difficult not to repress a smile at the thought of clashing beards and tinkling watch-chains as the comrades become more and more republican'. Here a more martial version of the myth of the homosexual appears in the form of the martyrs of Thermopylae, adopted as inspirational forefathers of gay democracy.

Symonds, in his privately circulated monographs on homosexuality, expressed his belief that if his fellow Uranians were to find true freedom, they must address questions of morality and philosophy *in their own terms*. He championed naturalness and physical pleasure, 'moderated by reason, tact and aesthetic considerations.' He quoted Greek writers on the value of openness and loyalty in same-sex relationships and condemning furtiveness. 'There is no antagonism', he wrote, 'between our physical and spiritual constitution, but rather a most intimate connection.'

Even before *Leaves of Grass* and Symonds' fantasies, Edward Fitzgerald, adaptor of *The Rubaiyat of Omar Khayyam*, had published his *Euphranor: A Dialogue on Youth*, employing ideas of chivalry as ethical guides to male/male relationships.[31] But Symonds' and Fitzgerald's writings were essentially literary reveries, with little practical social dimension. That was provided by Whitman's most important philosophical disciple, the English poet, scholar of comparative religion and social reformer Edward Carpenter.

The god in his true light

A curious and interesting subject is the connection of the Uranian temperament with prophetic gifts and divination.

— Edward Carpenter

Ted Carpenter, who was born in 1844, knew Whitman personally, visiting him twice in America. Influenced by Christian socialism and the various reform movements of Victorian Britain, Carpenter adopted Whitman's mystical gospel and developed it into a comprehensive social vision. Among the causes he championed, wrote and lectured about were libertarian socialism, women's rights, workers' co-operatives, penal reform, ecological concerns, vegetarianism and market gardening, animals' rights, Oriental philosophy and the universal symbolism underlying all religions. Like Blake, he believed that 'all religions are one'. But where Whitman had defensively and cagily insisted on himself as an 'average man' and 'adhesiveness' as a universal component of all humanity, Carpenter adopted different tactics. Recognizing that some were more adhesive than others, he became an outspoken and prominent campaigner for homosexual emancipation.

31: *The Myth of the Homosexual*

Carpenter was the first public figure to live openly as a homosexual (or Uranian, to use his terminology). He and his companion, George Merrill, maintained a large cottage with an attached market garden at Millthorpe in the North of England, where as an openly gay couple they kept house and received friends, including many of the leading writers and progressive personalities of the day. 'Thus we settled down, two bachelors', wrote Carpenter in his autobiography, *My Days and Dreams*. 'Our lives had become necessary to each other so that what anyone said was of little importance.'[32]

In the same book, he tells a story about Merrill standing at the door of the cottage one day, 'looking down the garden brilliant in the sun, when a missionary sort of man arrived with a tract and wanted to put it in his hand. "Keep your tract", said George, "I don't want it." "But don't you wish to know the way to heaven?" said the man. "No. I don't", was the reply, "can you see that *we're in heaven here* – we don't *want* any better than this, so go away!" And the man turned and fled.' Carpenter and Merrill lived together until Merrill's death in 1928. Carpenter died a year later, at the age of eighty-five.

Carpenter was one of the most outstanding men of his era, ahead of his time in many ways. Charismatic and modest – a rare combination – he was also shrewd enough to manage to continue his campaign for the acceptance of sexually 'intermediate types' even in the wake of the Oscar Wilde debacle of 1895 which frightened so many homosexuals, sexual liberals and other intellectuals. Henry James and Thomas Hardy, among others, were profoundly jolted by it, and with very few exceptions such as Carpenter's disciple Reginald Underwood, gay writers did not again feel free to declare themselves or write openly until the 1960s. Carpenter was a strong influence on writers as diverse as D. H. Lawrence, Jack London, E. M. Forster and George Bernard Shaw, and on many other younger men who came to visit him and Merrill at Millthorpe; to them he was 'Ted' or sometimes (like Whitman) 'Dad'. In retrospect, it seems all the more remarkable that Carpenter avoided prosecution, or even any serious scandal. A kind of 'odour of sanctity' seems to have surrounded him. Indeed, many who knew him came to describe him as 'saintly'.

In his book *Civilisation, Its Cause and Cure*, Carpenter sees the latest stage of human social development as characterized by disease, law enforcement agencies, disrespect for nature, and the disruption of organic community. 'The civilized body of society is badly afflicted by parasites', he wrote, in a strikingly prophetic metaphor. He viewed science as increasingly estranged from reality, and with a growing potential for evil. He saw medicine as diverging further and further from the holistic concern with every person's 'central guide' to natural health. In such a state,

> not 20,000 doctors, each with 20,000 books to consult and 20,000 phials of different contents to administer, could meet the myriad cases of disease which would ensue, or bolster up into 'wholeness' the being from whom the single radiant unity had departed.
>
> Probably there has never been an age, nor any country (except Yankee-land?) in which disease has been so generally prevalent as in England today, and certainly there has never (with the same exception) been an age or country in which doctors have so swarmed, or in which medical science has been so powerful, in apparatus, in learning, in authority, and in actual organisation and number of adherents. How reconcile this contradiction – if indeed a contradiction it be?
>
> But the fact is that medical science does not contradict disease – any more than laws abolish crime. Medical science – and doubtless for very good reasons – makes a fetish of disease, and dances around it. It is (as a rule) only seen where disease is; it writes enormous tomes on disease; it induces disease in animals (and even men) for the purpose of studying it; it knows, to a marvellous extent, the symptoms of disease, its nature, its causes, its goings out and its coming in; its eyes are perpetually fixed on disease, till disease (for it) becomes the main fact of the world and the main object of its worship . . . . The same cause (infidelity and decay of the central life in men) which creates disease and makes men liable to it, creates students and a science of the subject.[33]

The meaning of man's loss of unity or exile from Paradise could only be, Carpenter felt, his abandonment of his true self. 'Man has to become conscious of his destiny – to lay hold of and realise his own freedom and blessedness – to transfer his consciousness from the outer and mortal part of him to the inner and undying.'[34]

In this quest, Carpenter saw the Uranian as a sort of facilitator of the evolution of the species. Homosexuality, so often conjoined with traits other than those of the stereotyped masculine man and feminine woman, acts to fuel necessary evolutionary changes, inhibiting destructive sexual polarization and stagnation, and urging humanity on to new adaptations and fresh approaches.

Carpenter felt that what he called 'intermediate types' of men and women had a special gift as 'reconcilers and interpreters of the two sexes to each other'.[35] In *The Intermediate Sex* he wrote:

I think perhaps of all the services the Uranian may render to society it will be found some day that in this direction of solving the problems of affection and of the heart he will do the greatest service. If the day is coming as we have suggested – when Love is at last to take its rightful place as the binding and directing force of society (instead of the Cash-nexus), and society is to be transmuted in consequence to a higher form, then undoubtedly the superior types of Uranians – prepared for this service by long experience and devotion, as well as by much suffering – will have an important part to play in the transformation. For that the [Uranians] in their own lives put Love before everything else – postponing to it the other motives like money-making, business success, fame, which occupy so much space in most people's careers – is a fact which is patent to everyone who knows them. This may be saying little or nothing in favor of those of this class whose conception of love is only of a poor and frivolous sort; but in the case of those others who see the god in his true light, the fact that they serve him in singleness of heart and so unremittingly raises them at once into the position of the natural leaders of mankind.[36]

Here was Whitman's gospel in *Leaves of Grass*, further extended and articulated: 'fervid comradeship' as the 'counter-balance and offset' of materialism; democracy's 'inevitable twin or counterpart, without which it will be incomplete, in vain, and incapable of perpetuating itself'. So at the time of the creation of modern homosexuality, its greatest spokesmen and prophets saw it not as a barren, meaningless variation, or as a minority taste to be confined in an officially prescribed alternative lifestyle, but as a necessary step in evolution, a means of development (and consequently, perpetuation) of the human species and the earth itself. This view recalls the Platonic and alchemical myth of the androgyne, symbol of reconciliation and wholeness.

In his *Intermediate Types Among Primitive Folk*, Carpenter stressed that homosexual men and women become 'the repositories and foci of new kinds of learning and skill, of new activities and accomplishments.' He gives as examples 'the priest or medicine-man or shaman', the prophet and diviner, the artist and craftsperson, and the true scientist, successor to the tribal observer of 'the stars and the seasons, medicine and the herbs.' And the god these 'intermediate types' worship 'combines in some degree the attributes of both male and female'. Decades later, Parker Tyler would name this gay god 'Homeros', which is the name I will use for him/her in this narrative.

The figure of the androgynous, nature-based teacher worshipping both god and goddess was Carpenter's benignly pagan answer to the mythical homosexual, alienated and doomed, that had been patched together by Pauline Christianity and its successor, materialistic science.[37] This Carpenterian idea of intermediate types as important to evolution was recapitulated by later thinkers, among them the English philosopher Gerald Heard, the eccentric transvestite theorist Charlotte Bach, and the gay liberationist David Fernbach.

By the early years of homosexual emancipation, between the identification of the homosexual in the 1860s and the Wilde trial of 1895, we can already see emerging two distinct attitudes to gays *among gays themselves*, and elucidated and encoded by leading writers of the time. On the one hand, the myth of the homosexual, whether as unnatural Frankenstein or beauteous Sebastian – alien, persecuted and doomed; and on the other, the mystical/radical vision of the New Man or New Woman, the evolutionary teacher, the androgyne, the modern shaman.[38]

For Christianity, Homeros could only be pagan, and therefore sinful. To the new scientific religion, intent on diagnostic explanations of old heresies and their categorization into proliferating disease states, it was monstrous, pathological. Like the savage customs of a newly discovered tribe, it had been delineated only so as to be done away with; the medicalization of Homeros occurred just at the time when scientific ideology was providing justifications for the continuing subjugation of non-European peoples and the natural world.

Carpenter's works continued to circulate quietly, especially among gay men, for decades. In the 1920s, the black American poet Countee Cullen wrote to his friend Alain Locke, 'I secured Carpenter's *Ioläus* from the library. I read it through at one sitting, and steeped myself in its charming and comprehending atmosphere. It opened up for me soul windows which had been closed; it threw a noble and evident light on what I had begun to believe, because of what the world believes, ignoble and unnatural. I loved myself in it.'[39]

By the 1970s, though, the mystical/political patrimony of Whitman and Carpenter had been largely forgotten.[40] Their inheritors fought with what few intellectual weapons remained to them, primarily left over from the black civil rights movement and the hippie counterculture. Gays faced a struggle not only against obvious social antagonists but also against a powerful, invisible adversary: our own self-identification with the myth of the homosexual, the unconscious image we held of ourselves as leprous outcasts and willing sacrificial victims. Appropriately, the health crisis struck first at those homosexuals (and others) whom scientific ideology and Christian civilization had most alienated, most segregated, and most mythologized.

Notes

1. See 'The sodomy delusion: a typological reconstruction', by Warren Johansson, in Wayne Dynes, *Homolexis: A Historical and Cultural Lexicon of Homosexuality* (New York: Gai Saber Monographs, 1985), p. 134.

2. George L. Mosse, *Nationalism & Sexuality: Respectability and Abnormal Sexuality in Modern Europe* (New York: Howard Fertig, 1985), p. 135.

3. See, for example, Thomas Szasz, *The Manufacture of Madness: A Comparative Study of the Inquisition and the Mental Health Movement* (New York: Harper & Row, 1970); Kenneth Lewes, *The Psychoanalytic Theory of Male Homosexuality* (New York: Simon & Schuster, 1988); and R. Bayer, *Homosexuality and American Psychiatry* (New York: Basic Books, 1981).

4. Vito Russo, *The Celluloid Closet: Homosexuality in the Movies*, rev. ed. (New York: Harper & Row, 1987), pp. 347–9.

5. Jack Fritscher, *Some Dance to Remember* (Stamford, CT: Knights Press, 1990), p. 304.

6. This name for the 'god of homosexuality' (who can take male or female form) was coined by Parker Tyler in his *Screening the Sexes: Homosexuality in the Movies* (New York: Holt, Rinehart & Winston, 1972).

7. In Edward Field, *Variety Photoplays* (New York: Grove Press, 1967), p. 39.

8. Quoted in Richard Ellman, *Oscar Wilde* (London: Penguin, 1988), p. 71.

9. The myth of St Sebastian may also be, in part, a Christianization of the story of Antinous, lover of the Roman Emperor Hadrian. Like the slaying of the English King William Rufus, who also had male lovers, Antinous' drowning in the Nile has been attributed to an accident, a political plot and a religious ritual embodying the sacrifice of the Sacred King – or his surrogate. The subject of Antinous has traditionally been taboo. When John Addington Symonds made some discreet inquiries at the British Museum in the 1870s, he 'received the chillingly unhelpful reply that "it is very courageous to ask even artistic questions about him"' (Royston Lambert, *Beloved and God: The Story of Hadrian and Antinous* (New York: Viking, 1984), p. 9). The Antinous/Sebastian identification was suggested by that scholar of the arcane, Montague Summers, in *Antinous and Other Poems* (London: Sisley's, 1907), in which preoccupation with the deaths of beautiful young men takes the form of a kind of icy gloating. For additional pertinent material on St Sebastian, see James M. Saslow, 'The tenderest lover: Saint Sebastian in Renaissance painting', *Gai Saber*, Spring 1977, p. 58, and Wayne Dynes' crotchety rejoinder, 'Putting St. Sebastian to the question', *Gai Saber*, Summer 1977, p. 150.

10. Herman Melville, *Billy Budd* (New York: Pocket Books, 1972).

11. Melville, *Billy Budd*, p. 13.

12. For another use of the bull as sacrificial virility symbol, see Chapter 3, pp. 102–12.

13. Georges-Michel Sarotte, *Like a Brother, Like a Lover: Male Homosexuality in the American Novel and Theater from Herman Melville to James Baldwin* (Garden City, NY: Anchor Press/ Doubleday, 1978), p. 81.

14. Ellman, *Oscar Wilde*, p. 91.

15. Oscar Wilde, *The Picture of Dorian Gray* (London: Penguin, 1973), p. 145.

16. See, for example, Lord Alfred Douglas' 'Two Loves' and 'In Praise of Shame' (both 1894) and Aleister Crowley's 'Dédicace' (1898), all three reprinted in Brian Reade's *Sexual Heretics* (London: Routledge & Kegan Paul, 1970).

17. Oscar Wilde, *Letters*, ed. Rupert Hart-Davis (London: Rupert Hart-Davis, 1962), p. 263.

18. Mario Praz, *The Romantic Agony* (Cleveland: Meridian, 1956), pp. 341–2, 472–5.

19. Quoted in Ellman, *Oscar Wilde*, p. 361.

20. Jeffrey Meyers, *Homosexuality and Literature 1890–1930* (London: Athlone Press, 1977), p. 28.

21. Yet another Victorian variation of the myth of the homosexual is suggested in Count Eric Stenbock's 'The Sad Story of a Vampire', first published in his *Studies of Death: Romantic Tales* (1894) and reprinted in *The Dracula Book of Great Vampire Stories*, ed. Leslie Shepard (Secaucus, NJ: Citadel Press, 1977). Set in Styria, 'a flat, uninteresting country' where 'vampires generally arrive at night, in carriages drawn by two black horses', Stenbock's short tale tells of one Count Vardalek who, in spite of his kindly nature, gradually drains the life from the narrator's faun-like young brother Gabriel, and then vanishes. The Estonian-born Stenbock (1860–1895), one of the more fascinating figures of the *fin de siècle*, still awaits a full biography. Rupert Croft-Cooke's *Feasting with Panthers* (London: W. H. Allen, 1967) provides a cameo portrait.

22. See also Leslie Fiedler, *Love and Death in the American Novel* (New York: Criterion Books, 1960) and 'Come back to the raft ag'in, Huck honey!' in *An End to Innocence: Essays on Culture and Politics* (Boston: Beacon Press, 1962).

23. From Whitman's *Democratic Vistas* (1871), quoted in Robert K. Martin, *The Homosexual Tradition in American Poetry* (Austin: University of Texas Press, 1979), p. 33.

24. Martin, *Homosexual Tradition*, p. 51. I am indebted to Robert K. Martin for invaluable insights into Whitman's poetry. Previous American critics have tended to distort and suppress Whitman's homosexuality and the importance of 'adhesiveness' (male/male

love) to his vision of a redeemed America. Even the poet's choice of the phallic calamus plant growing among the byways of America to symbolize male/male love was fatuously explained away. The rise of open gay scholarship in the wake of Stonewall made such tortured obscurantism seem antiquated and opened the way for healthier considerations of Whitman such as Martin's analysis and Charley Shively's biographical studies *Calamus Studies* (San Francisco: Gay Sunshine, 1987) and *Drum Beats* (San Francisco: Gay Sunshine, 1989).

25. Walt Whitman, *The Complete Poems* (London: Penguin, 1975), p. 86.

26. Martin, *Homosexual Tradition*, p. 100. Significantly, Whitman's homoerotic poem sequence 'Calamus' was first published in 1860, on the eve of the Civil War.

27. Whitman, *Complete Poems*, p. 443.

28. Quoted in Randy Shilts, *The Mayor of Castro Street* (New York: St Martin's Press, 1982), p. 287.

29. Whitman, *Complete Poems*, p. 511.

30. Quoted in Reade, *Sexual Heretics*, pp. 5–6.

31. Edward Fitzgerald, *Euphranor: A Dialogue on Youth* (privately printed, 1851).

32. Edward Carpenter, *My Days and Dreams* (London: George Allen & Unwin, 1916), p. 163.

33. Edward Carpenter, *Civilisation: Its Cause and Cure* (Boston: Tao Books, 1971), p. 23.

34. *Ibid.* p. 27.

35. Edward Carpenter (a namesake), *Edward Carpenter 1844–1929, Democratic Author and Poet: A Restatement and Reappraisal* (London: Dr Williams Trust, 1970), p. 17.

36. Edward Carpenter, *The Intermediate Sex: A Study of Some Transitional Types of Men and Women* (London, George Allen & Unwin, 1908), p. 122.

37. See Edward Carpenter, *Intermediate Types Among Primitive Folk: A Study of Social Evolution* (London: George Allen & Unwin, 1919).

38. Versions of both these attitudes can be seen throughout the work of the best-known homosexual of the era, Oscar Wilde. The tension between them is the tension between conflicting aspects of Wilde himself: the proud, pagan homosexual and the closeted, married man, deeply moved by the Christian myth. See, for example, *De Profundis* and the poems 'The Sphinx' and 'Hellas' in *Complete Works of Oscar Wilde* (London: Collins, 1966).

39. Quoted in Alden Reimonenq, 'Countee Cullen's Uranian "Soul Windows" ', in Emmanuel S. Nelson, ed., *Critical Essays: Gay and*

Lesbian Writers of Color (New York: Harrington Park Press, 1993), p. 144. *Ioläus* was Carpenter's gay anthology.

40.   One gay activist who attempted to keep Carpenter's memory and ideas alive was Bishop Mikhail Itkin, whose booklet *The Radical Jesus and Gay Consciousness: Notes for a Theology of Gay Liberation* (Long Beach, CA: Communiversity West, 1972) was dedicated 'to Edward Carpenter, prophet of gay freedom'.

Chapter two

Out of the Closets and into the Camps

I wanted for my perfect lover none other than the Wizard of Oz himself, and I was looking where he was least likely to be found: in the mirror of a dimly lit bar.

— Arnie Kantrowitz, *Under the Rainbow: Growing Up Gay*

EDWARD Carpenter died in 1929, the year the Great Depression brought an end to post-war optimism and began the inexorable build-up to World War II. While not exactly a forgotten man, he and his ideas had been eclipsed in the years following the Great War, though several of his books remained in print to inspire a scattered following and a small British homosexual emancipation movement.[1]

In 1908, Carpenter had written, 'It is possible that the Uranian spirit may lead to something like a general enthusiasm of Humanity, and that the Uranian people may be destined to form the advance guard of that great movement which will one day transform the common life by substituting the bond of personal affection and compassion for the monetary, legal and other external ties which now control and confine society. Such a part of course we cannot expect the Uranians to play unless the capacity for their kind of attachment also exists – although in a germinal and undeveloped state – in the breast of mankind at large.'[2] A tall order!

Before the Uranian people could even begin to come into their own, Europe would be laid waste and pink triangles would appear beside yellow stars in concentration camps. The Nazi regime took martial, hypermasculine values to their extreme. There is even a German word for it: *Mannerstaat*, the state as an expression of manliness. The ancient pagan gods, folk myths and runic symbols that Europe had tried to reject reappeared as an ideological nightmare. Charged with paranoia and spite, and incorporated into hypnotic rituals of mass hatred, they became part of an experiment in black magic on an unprecedented scale. Europe was quickly overcome by a thinly-disguised cult of evil, nihilism and death.

Once identified and isolated, the homosexual became a favorite sacrificial figure for nationalistic Europe. 'The image of the languid youth dying slowly but beautifully was hardly in tune with normative ideas of manliness' wrote the historian George L. Mosse, 'and homosexuals must die a lonely, ugly death because all beauty was strange to them. Vice must be punished and the outsider separated from the insider in death as in life.'[3] From the nineteenth century on, 'the outsider had to be clearly recognizable in order to be punished or excluded from society, hence the homosexual was condemned by law (and we remember the importance of forensic medicine in creating his stereotype), the insane committed, and the Jew isolated.'[4] These pseudo-scientific doctrines of racial and sexual inequality had grown intertwined with one another during the nineteenth and early twentieth centuries, giving rise eventually to the poisonous flowering of National Socialist science.

Male homoeroticism has provided much of the fuel for fascism, whether in the skinhead gangs of the 1990s or the European political movements of the 1930s. That eroticism must never be self-aware or overt but always repudiated and in a state of frustration and tension. Overt homosexuality – or even the suggestion of it – must be subject to ferocious punishment. It is paradoxical that Nazism in Europe was proceeded and nourished by the various branches of the German Youth Movement, with its nudism, idealization of classical beauty, and male camaraderie. This was a movement suffused with homoeroticism, which its leaders idealized, rationalized or denied.

Hitler's understanding of the intensely patriarchal nature of the German family contributed to his uncanny ability to manipulate the homoeroticism of German youth. His hypnotic hold over his people, as well as his ability to subvert Homeros to his own ends were both prefigured in Thomas Mann's political fable 'Mario and the Magician' in which a young man's hypnosis by an evil magician culminates in a kiss on the lips, which, in a dark reworking of the Sleeping Beauty legend, awakens him to his own shame.[5]

There was a considerable overlap between the homosexual movement and the different factions of the *wandervogel* youth. A number of prominent homosexual spokesmen of the time, such as Benedict Friedlander, Adolf Brand (publisher of the homosexual journal *Der Eigene*) and Hans Bluher (author of *The Role of the Erotic in the Male Community*) became racists, associating homosexuality with 'manly purity' and 'Aryan' superiority. Once the Nazis came to power, the diverse youth movements were absorbed into the Hitler Youth and their remaining idealistic elements dissolved in the 'blood and soil' of Nazi ideology.[6]

The way had been well prepared not only by protofascists within the homosexual and youth movements but by ideological prophets like the apostle of pagan aristocracy Stefan George[7] and the novelist Ernst Junger. Junger wrote of a 'new race of men', lean and muscular, with hard, flint-like faces, voices like machine-guns, and the desire for war in their blood. Bayonet thrusts were compared explicitly to orgasms, and the battlefield to the 'dishevelled bed'.[8] Troops of rosy-cheeked, lederhosen-clad Nazi youth marched through the countryside singing: 'When the Jew blood spurts under the knife, everything goes so much better!' War and social violence provided the outlet for pent-up sexual (especially homosexual) feelings. The attitude was captured perfectly by one of the most prominent artists of the Third Reich, the immensely talented sculptor Arno Brecker, in such official works as the famous bas-relief 'Kameraden', depicting two naked warrior-youths, one dying languidly in the arms of his more butch companion, whose features as he regards the enemy are contorted into a mask of grief, anger and hatred.[9]

In May 1933, a few months after Hitler came to power, the Institute of Sexual Science, headed by the prominent homosexual emancipationist Magnus Hirschfeld, was attacked by the Nazis and burned; its valuable books and archives were destroyed in a public bonfire and a bust of Hirschfeld was paraded on a pole through the streets. Luckily, Hirschfeld was abroad at the time. Many of his colleagues were arrested; few survived the war. Homosexual rights organizations were made illegal, their premises raided and their leaders interned. The death penalty was instituted for homosexual acts. Within a decade, even a kiss between men was subject to the same penalty. The 'Night of the Long Knives' on 30 June 1934 brought the murder of Hitler's old crony, the homosexual Ernst Rohm, and the rise to supreme power of the SS. The Nazi persecution of gays entered its most intense phase; in the hell of the concentration camps, a special place was prepared for them by the fanatically homophobic Reichsfuehrer, Heinrich Himmler. At the same time, public charges of homosexuality helped the Nazis curb the independence of the army and the Catholic Church.

Richard Plant's book *The Pink Triangle* provides an account of the fate of homosexuals in the Nazis' bureaucratic/pagan nightmare: the round-up of all identifiable homosexuals (their names obtained from police files and membership lists of pre-Nazi gay organizations) and their relegation to the camps, the vicious, usually fatal regimen, and the maniacal 'experiments' at the hands of a medical establishment that co-operated *en masse* with the Nazis.[10] Some gays, Plant himself among them, managed to escape. Others avoided detection, many serving in the armed forces. A few joined the anti-Nazi Resistance.[11]

In his 'Conclusion' to *The Pink Triangle*, Richard Plant writes, 'That homosexuals, by a series of laws, were treated as subhumans does not seem in retrospect particularly illogical or even unexpected. After all, their classification as heretical deviants boasted a long lineage . . . . In the course of European history, a vast number of bulls and mandates, pamphlets and tracts lumped together Jews, homosexuals, and other heretics, and linked them to witches, sexual deviants, and traitors . . . . From the thirteenth century to the twentieth, the hold of these anti-semitic and homophobic mythologies has never been broken among large parts of the population of Western Europe.' He adds that 'it is precisely technological progress that has made possible ever more refined techniques of brutalization, torture, and obliteration'.[12]

In the Nazi era, much of the propaganda against Jews, gypsies, homosexuals and those labelled mentally ill or retarded was couched in medical language. Social outsiders were seen as a threat to the physical and mental health of the German people; only by extinguishing them, 'snuffing them out as though they had never existed', in Himmler's words, could the body politic be cleansed. Homosexuals were referred to as a 'Jewish pestilence'. The rhetoric of medicine and hygiene justified the elimination of scapegoat populations. Heinrich Himmler was the first political figure to recognize gays as a people – a people that, in his eyes, was indistinguishable from a plague.

Dr Benway's casebook

Homosexuality is a dread dysfunction, malignant in character, which has risen to epidemic proportions.

— Dr Charles Socarides

By the end of World War II, the European gay movement lay in ruins with the rest of the continent. Those few homosexuals who had survived the horrors of the camps, instead of being freed with the other internees, were often jailed by the new authorities. As their wartime incarceration, even under such horrific conditions, was regarded as fully justified, they were refused all compensation. Unlike members of other interned groups, gays had little sense of themselves as part of a larger group; they remained isolated, stigmatized individuals, afraid to speak up for fear of another round of persecution. The history of gays in the Third Reich remained buried until the 1970s when German, and later American, researchers began to unearth the truth about the anti-gay holocaust.

In Britain, very little of the pre-war gay movement remained; America had never had one. What America did have was medical psychology. Pupils and followers of Freud and his colleagues, most of them Jewish, had fled Nazi-dominated Europe and established themselves in the United States. By the 1950s, an Americanized version of psychoanalysis had become popular and respectable by preaching adjustment and conformity, and it was this branch of the medical profession that took over the campaign against the 'illness' of homosexuality. From then until their last stand in the American Psychiatric Association referendum in 1974, it was psychiatrists, especially neo-Freudians, who spearheaded the social war against gay people.

The fanatical Dr Edmund Bergler (*Time* called him 'the final authority'), who believed that homosexuals were not discriminated against but were simply 'injustice collectors' and psychic masochists, and who regarded writers as mentally disturbed; Dr Irving Bieber, who believed that all homosexuals (and all bachelors!) were neurotics; Doctors Socarides, Hatterer, Oversey, Ellis, all fought a vehement medical war against gays, and were considered the 'experts' on the medical 'problem' of homosexuality. With very few isolated, usually female, exceptions, the rest of the medical profession concurred with their lucrative imprecations. Gay people hid their sexual orientation from their doctors, knowing that if it was discovered, their real illnesses would take second place to the pressing need to 'cure' their affections, and they could very well end up confined to an institution.

Don Jackson described one of these establishments in his 1973 article 'Dachau for queers'.[13] Most of the 'patients' at the Atascadero State Hospital in California were, as Jackson put it, 'plain ordinary homosexuals' who had the misfortune to be at the wrong place at the wrong time and fell into the hands of the police. The law provided that, as 'suspected sex criminals' gay men could be sent to Atascadero for up to ninety days without trial. Once you were committed, you lost all legal rights. Dr Paul E. Braumwell, the 'chief of research' at Atascadero summed up the attitude of the medical authorities to gay people as follows: 'These men have no rights: If we can learn something by using them, then that is a small compensation for the trouble they have caused society.'

The experiments in which gay men were 'used' included forcible injections of the drug succinylcholine or anectine which causes instant paralysis and a suspension of breathing. The prisoner is taken 'to the brink of death', then kept alive mechanically. The effect, according to the chief psychiatrist at another similar facility, Vacaville (among whose alumni were Charles Manson and police agent Donald DeFreeze of the Symbionese Liberation Army) is of a 'sensation of suffocation and drowning. The patient feels as if he had a heavy weight on his chest and can't get any air into his lungs.' Some of these experiments were funded by the Law Enforcement Assistance Administration, a domestic version of the CIA.

Another gay liberationist, Leo Dallas, wrote about his experiences in Atascadero after being convicted of 'lewd and lascivious conduct' for kissing another man on the street, a felony for which the maximum sentence was life imprisonment. His punishment included sessions of electric shocks to his genitals. Three weeks after his article was published, he was re-arrested on the same charge (another kiss observed by the police) and sent back to Atascadero for a further round of treatment.[14] Other experiments there involved painful electric shocks to destroy brain tissue.

Another of the medical profession's favorite 'treatments' for homosexuality was the drug prolixin, a personality-altering drug that acts on the hypothalamus, causing terrifying delusions, confusion, extreme pain and uncontrollable spasms. The purpose of the various 'exploratory studies', as these experiments were called, was to see what techniques were most effective in behavior modification, that is, in extinguishing homosexual impulses. The aim was to break down the natural responses of affection and pleasure and replace them with medically conditioned reflexes.

With the rise of medical psychiatry during and after World War II, the medical establishment had, by the 1950s, eclipsed the Church as the chief obstacle to the mental well-being of gay people. Of course, most homosexuals were able to avoid institutions like Atascadero and Vacaville. But there was almost nothing to counter the medical view of homosexuality, the myth that homosexuality is an illness, that homosexual stories end in early death, that mature homosexuality is an impossibility, and that 'nobody loves you when you're old and gay'. It was easy to believe the lies; evidence was censored and hidden from us. Claiming a paternal concern for homosexuals, the medical establishment happily staffed institutions like Vacaville, manipulating and deepening ingrained patterns of fear, self-hatred and illness. Many gay and lesbian adults, and even adolescents, despaired and succumbed to early deaths from alcoholism, drug abuse and suicide, fulfilling the prophetic myth.

The post-war period in North America saw the establishment of a close alliance between government and the medical establishment in programming gay people for self-destruction. As late as the 1970s, the American Psychiatric Association, the wing of the medical profession whose business it was to 'treat' homosexuals, was still fighting against the Gay Liberation movement's pressure to remove homosexuality from the list of mental illnesses. Forced by the militancy of the early movement to rescind its diagnosis, official medicine seethed for a few short years before gay men once again began falling into its hands, this time as AIDS patients, HIV 'carriers', victims of 'dementia' and AZT recipients.

The suffocating madness of the postwar years was dramatized by William S. Burroughs, in his prophetic novel *Naked Lunch*, published in France in the late 1950s and smuggled into the US by daring travellers. In the chapter titled 'The Examination', Burroughs invests a simple diagnostic session with the madness and menace of the time. Carl Peterson, homosexual, finds 'a postcard in his box requesting him to report for a ten o'clock appointment with Doctor Benway in the Ministry of Mental Hygiene and Prophylaxis . . . It would not have occurred to Carl to disregard the appointment even though failure to appear entailed no penalty . . . Freeland was a welfare state. If a citizen wanted anything from a load of bonemeal to a sexual partner some department was ready to offer effective aid. The threat implicit in this enveloping benevolence stifled the concept of rebellion . . . '

Having presented himself before Dr Benway, Carl is given a lecture on 'the matter of uh *sexual deviation*', which the doctor advises is no more to be censured or sanctioned than tuberculosis. Nevertheless, he adds, prophylactic measures must be imposed 'with a minimum of inconvenience and hardship to the unfortunate individual who has, through no fault of his own, become uh infected . . . We do not find obligatory vaccination for smallpox an unreasonable measure . . . Nor isolation for certain contagious diseases . . . I am sure you will agree that individuals infected with hurumph what the French call *les maladies galantes* heh heh heh should be compelled to undergo treatment if they do not report voluntarily.'

Carl 'suddenly felt trapped in this silent underwater cave of a room, cut off from all sources of warmth and certainty'. The doctor rambles on obsessively about cancer: 'Cancer, my first love!' He suggests 'the Kleinberg-Stanislouski semen flocculation test . . . a diagnostic too . . . indicative at least in a negative sense . . . '. Carl gives the nurse a specimen.

When the test results come back, Dr Benway refers to the 'Robinson Kleinberg flocculation test'. Carl asks about the discrepancy. The doctor titters. 'Oh dear no . . . You are getting ahead of me young man. You might have misunderstood. The Blomberg-Stanislouski, weeel that's a different sort of a test altogether. I *do* hope . . . not necessary . . . .' He titters again: 'But as I was saying before I was so charmingly interrupted . . . your KS seems to be . . . .' He held the slip at arm's length . . . 'completely uh negative.' Eventually, Carl tries to leave and begins to hallucinate. 'The doctor's voice was barely audible. The whole room was exploding out into space.'[15]

In its entirety the scene is hilarious and chilling; seen in retrospect, it seems not only a satire of the medicinal approach to homosexuality but also a grim foreshadowing of the AIDS consultations of twenty-five years later – even including the KS.

The future of the isophyl

'By . . . *learning to work with a devoted group that believes control and love are two aspects of the same thing, the isophyl can not only aid himself and his fellows, he can forward religion and help mankind.*

— Gerald Heard

It was during the conservative 1950s that the first stirrings of the gay movement began. The catalyst was the profound social dislocation brought about by World War II. By taking thousands of men and women away from their homes, farms and small towns and throwing them together in a common endeavor with others of their own sex, the war gave them for the first time a taste of freedom, a shared idealism about democracy and a recognition of their own affectional nature.[16] The movement for homosexual equality in America began with the returning veterans – male and female – of World War II. When they returned from the battlefields and nursing stations, they often ended up in port cities like San Francisco and New York, and the gay underworlds in those cities grew and took shape. California in the early 1950s was one of the centres of activity for the embryonic homophile movement. Among its leaders were Harry Hay, a former actor and Communist Party political organizer, and the British-born philosopher Gerald Heard, friend and spiritual mentor to a group of English expatriate mystics that included Aldous Huxley and Christopher Isherwood.

Born in 1912, Harry Hay was the moving force behind the founding of the Mattachine Society, the first real gay political organization in North America. During his youth, Hay lived for a time near a Washo Indian settlement in Nevada. He became interested in Indian culture and attended traditional dances. When he was thirteen, he was 'blessed by the elderly Paiute prophet Wovoka, whom Harry remembers as a very old man, blind and with a heavily wrinkled face. The . . . prophet touched the boy and said a prayer in his native language. Hay later recalled that the Indians told him Wovoka had said that "we should be good to this boy, for he will be a friend to us later".'[17]

Hay's lifelong fascination with sacred dance influenced his naming of the Mattachine Society, after a Renaissance fraternity of bachelors who performed ritual dances. He wanted, he said, to base the Mattachine Society on 'a great transcendent dream of what being Gay was all about. . . . Organizing the Mattachine was a call to me deeper than the innermost reaches of spirit, a vision-quest more important than life.'[18]

To Hay, being gay was not just a meaningless accident, much less an illness. He saw gayness as 'a gift', offering 'a different set of biological, social and spiritual receptors through which the world could be perceived and interpreted'. He believed that 'sexual energy not used by homosexuals for procreation . . . should be channelized elsewhere where its ends can be creativity'. And he asked of himself and the others who were drawn to the new society, three questions: 'Who are we gay people?', 'Where have we been throughout the ages?', and 'What might we be *for*?' These were, in essence, the same questions posed by Edward Carpenter, half a century before.[19]

Henry Fitzgerald Heard, novelist, philosopher and mystic, had lived in California since 1937. He was the possessor of a towering intellect, a wide range of knowledge and a sometimes quirky, always inquiring mind. A true prophet, Heard was born before his time, with the result that many (including most of his comrades in the homophile movement) were not up to his far-reaching speculations and prescriptions. 'Gerald Heard — but not understood!' was one friend's observant quip.

Heard knew then what we all know now – that the planet itself is in deep trouble, and that concerted efforts are necessary to rescue it. To do so, he felt we must acknowledge a pair of basics: the relationship between ethics and cosmology (the natural order), and the need for scientific and technological progress to be matched by psychological and spiritual development. 'History', said Heard, 'is a shadow cast by the evolving consciousness of man.' How, then, can we develop our consciousness in harmony with the Life Force, the all-inclusive spirit of which modern, technological man has become increasingly ignorant and destructive?

Heard directed his question in particular to fellow members of 'the human intergrade' – the gay men and lesbians he referred to as 'isophyls', a term he coined from Greek words meaning 'equal' and 'tribe'.

By the 1990s all fifty of Gerald Heard's books were out of print.[20] But his life and writings provide keys to understanding the Stonewall Experiment. In his posthumously published book *Training for the Life of the Spirit*, he wrote of the dilemmas of contemporary sexuality and the necessity of charting a path between 'amputation, grim repression' and its equally destructive, parasitic twin, compulsive promiscuity.

'Life has handed us the task of control', he wrote, 'and if we decline the gift and decide to act irresponsibly, no natural instinctive control will take over for us. Sexual appetite will not check itself and having given us pleasure leave us at ease. It will become an addiction, a feverish dream, a restless habit out of which no pleasure is any longer derived but the repetition of which cannot be checked. . . . Certainly promiscuity, or the constant excitement of wondering whether one might not have an adventure, these acts and thoughts set up a state of feeling which is fatal to a consistent balanced serene mind, let alone to an evolving consciousness.'[21]

Heard, like Carpenter, was disturbed by the increasing inability of civilized men to form close friendships: heterosexual and homosexual men alike, conditioned to fear the gay spirit, became incapable of true physical closeness and trust; the results were gay invisibility, male/male competition increasingly lacking in fellow-feeling, and sex progressively stripped of any personal component.

He saw in the growing countercultural movement some hope for change.

In a memoir of Heard, his friend Jim Kepner explicated some of the philosopher's ideas:

> To sustain creativity throughout a rising curve of life, with the sort of outgoing warmth Heard noted in hippies as early as 1958, the *neotenic* person (one who retains certain so-called immature qualities) is to develop by tantra-like exercises – a 'co-charging of bodies by bringing the two electric fields into contact along their specific zones.' This lining up of our hidden energy centers in such a way as to produce a synergistic burst of new energy was, he felt, what we were unconsciously attempting when we did what we called 'having sex'. He felt it was a dangerous misunderstanding to label such intimate play as *sexual*, a term he preferred to limit to action aimed at procreation. Somewhat like Whitman, he saw it as a physicospiritual sacrament, much in the manner of early Christian *agape*.[22]

Heard saw that gay people, in succumbing to what I have called the myth of the homosexual, had accepted society's diminution of them as nothing but walking sex acts. He urged a mental and psychological break with the myth and a discovery of our true energies, our true place in the cosmic harmony, and the possibility of close, trusting relations with one another. 'He saw a new kind of creativity in the erotic interplay of two or more persons who were not committed to breeding – but were truly committed to exploring one another's potentialities, to enjoying and to charging up one another.'[23]

Rejecting science's corruption of the figure of the androgyne, Heard saw the 'great hermaphrodite' as one of the aims of human development, and the increasing prolongation of childhood and adolescence, with their openness and creativity, as an important factor in evolution. 'Western economy', he wrote, 'can only escape fission and collapse if served by experts who must be concerned with and feel loyalty to the entire accelerating process. They must retain the brave curiosity of the child.'[24]

In proposing a future for the isophyl in society, Heard referred to the importance of what he called 'the deep mind', and that need for 'devotion to a beloved community' which arises as part of the original loving impulse underlying all religions. He foresaw the rapid growth of a new type of spirituality, citing as examples the Twelve Steps groups which since his death have spread so widely. This religious or spiritual quest, he felt, leads us back, as members of both the gay and the human communities, to some basic questions, of which the most important is: 'What is love?'

In one of his essays, Heard wrote that we are 'stalled' in trying to answer the question 'because those who believe in self-control don't believe in the up-to-date psychophysical scientific knowledge, while those who hold by scientific knowledge often look on self-control as a hangover from the blind inhibitions of superstition. This, then, is the key question that confronts modern man. By setting himself to solve it by learning to work with a *devoted* group that believes control and love are two aspects of the same thing, the isophyl can not only aid himself and his fellows, he can forward religion and help mankind.'[25]

Both Gerald Heard and Harry Hay had hoped the new homophile movement might produce such a 'devoted group'. But idealistic aspirations were soon smothered in the suspicious, conformist atmosphere of the 1950s. Only a tiny minority of gays were ready or able to listen to these new ideas, and after some initial successes, the Mattachine Society was seen as rocking the crowded boat of American conformity. A nation becoming increasingly paranoiac about communists began to associate sexual heresies with political ones. Joe McCarthy and Roy Cohn (bluntly characterized by the poet Harold Norse as 'two unsavory queers') fuelled and profited from the poisoned atmosphere. More conservative gays began to panic, and soon the Mattachine's original radical ideas were displaced by more timid and defensive impulses. The group began to be concerned, in Harry Hay's words, 'with being seen as respectable – rather than self-respecting'.

Hay left the gay movement, to re-emerge briefly in the 1960s with the Circle of Loving Companions. This small, countercultural gay group in Los Angeles involved itself in radical politics and street action and aligned with the hippies and an Indian organization called the Traditional Indian Land & Life Committee. Hay and his long-time lover John Burnside lived for a time among Indians, learning more of their customs and sharing ideas about gay liberation. Hay and Burnside rejoined white gay society in the 1980s when they acted as catalysts for the Radical Faerie movement. Gradually, Hay began to be regarded as an elder statesman and valued voice for gay spirituality. Gerald Heard died in 1971, and was largely forgotten by gays until Jim Kepner and Mark Thompson wrote about him in the 1987 anthology *Gay Spirit*.[26]

The small homophile movement made slow progress against political repression and medical ideology. But it was the rise of the black civil rights movement, the New Left, the women's movement and the hippie counter-culture of the 1960s that galvanized gay people to reassess their own position in American life and to act more militantly on their own behalf.

Gays had been active in all three of these movements; by the late 1960s, student homophile groups were springing up on a number of college campuses, and the Washington DC Mattachine Society had acquired a fiery and articulate leader in the person of astronomer Frank Kameny. It was Kameny who was largely responsible for turning the movement from a defensive one (inviting scientific 'experts' to speak to gay groups and asking for their support) to an aggressive one (coining the slogan 'Gay Is Good' and rejecting the myth of the homosexual as sick). Word quickly drifted down to the average queen on the street, and by 1969, the stage was set for Stonewall.

Tear down the Stonewall!

I've got rainbows up my ass, honey!
— Judy Garland

Judy Garland was buried the day before the Stonewall riot. Judy's persona held a special appeal for homosexuals of the old school, who identified her with a poignant mixture of vulnerability, defiance, yearning, self-pity and pills, and of course with the classic film *The Wizard of Oz*, a perennial gay favorite. The day of her funeral was sweltering and humid, and that night there was a full moon.

Most of the gay bars in New York's West Village were controlled by the Mafia organization run by Carmine Fatico, a protégé of the notorious Albert Anastasia. The Stonewall Inn was a scruffy little Mob-run place on Christopher Street, frequented by drag queens and a mixture of other gays (many of them young) and some lesbians. A little mix-up in the time-honoured system of payoffs between organized crime, the bar managers and the police resulted in a late-night police raid and a routine round-up of patrons. But for once (the heat, the moon, Judy's death – what a piss-off! – and the new atmosphere of militancy drifting down to street level) the patrons decided they were mad as hell and weren't going to take it any more. The police soon had a full-scale riot on their hands – one that lasted for several nights[27] *(see plate 2)*.

Though Stonewall is rightly regarded as the turning-point in gay attitudes, it left undisturbed far more than it changed. The authorities slowly realized their old tactics wouldn't work any more. But the infrastructure of the gay ghetto was only just being erected, and, like all ghettos, from certain angles it bore a disturbing resemblance to a prison.

Two leaders of the new Gay Activists Alliance explained the system that led to the raid this way: 'The police hit the bars at the prime hours, not so much so that they can give petty fines to the bar owners – it's for the effect of terrorizing the customers and sometimes physically abusing them. This drives the people away, alienates them, and forces the owner to either "up" the payoff or close down.' When word circulated that the owners were complying with the new protection rates, customers would return. 'The more successful a place becomes, it's a certain thing that harassment will step up. . . . It's happened to bars, it's happened to baths, it's happened to restaurants.'[28]

The criminal syndicate ensured that the police were properly paid off (in return for various favors) by both syndicate-owned businesses and others. If the others got too successful, the syndicate would take them over. And 'everyone who's been around any length of time knows you can't run a Queer bar in New York City without the blessings of the mob', editorialized the home-made 'gayzine' *Gay*

Post. 'Some have tried and ended up wearing cement shoes in the East River. (Remember the Salvation?)'[29]

In the nights that followed the Stonewall raid, the riots continued, and a second raid, on a bar called the Snakepit, caused one patron, Diego Viñales, a young immigrant, to try to escape by jumping from a window, impaling himself on an iron fence. (If this raid had preceded the one on the Stonewall, this book would have had to be called *The Snakepit Experiment.*) The *Village Voice*, covering the goings-on, reported that 'Sheridan Square this weekend looked like something from a William Burroughs novel as the sudden specter of "gay power" erected its brazen head and spat out a fairy tale the likes of which the area has never seen.' When Burroughs' old friend Allen Ginsberg appeared on the street, the *Voice* commented that his presence 'lent an umbrella of serenity to the scene with his laughter and quiet commentary on consciousness, "gay power" as a new movement, and the various implications of what had happened.'[30]

As it happened, for the past two months, Ginsberg and his lover Peter Orlovsky had been in New York recording William Blake's 'Songs of Innocence and Experience', poems written to show 'the Two Contrary States of the Human Soul'. Accompanied by a harmonium, they sang the haunting 'London':

> I wander thro' each chartered street,
> Near where the charter'd Thames does flow
> And mark in every face I meet
> Marks of weakness, marks of woe.
>
> In every cry of every Man,
> In every infant's cry of fear,
> In every voice; in every ban,
> The mind-forged manacles I hear.
>
> How the Chimney-sweepers cry
> Every blackning Church appalls,
> And the hapless Soldiers sigh
> Runs in blood down Palace walls
>
> But most thro' midnight streets I hear
> How the youthful Harlots curse
> Blasts the new-born Infants tear
> And blights with plagues the Marriage hearse.[31]

Leaving a recording session at Apostolic Studios to stroll through the Village, Allen and Peter walked right into the Stonewall riots. A little later, Ginsberg remarked, 'You know, the guys there were so beautiful – they've lost that wounded look that fags all had ten years ago.'[32]

Members of the Homophile Youth Movement circulated among the people on the streets on those nights, handing out a leaflet entitled 'Get the Mafia and the Cops Out of Gay Bars'. The leaflet exposed the 'unholy alliance' of police and Syndicate and the unwritten policy of consigning gays to degrading, unsafe hellholes. A lot of gay people were angry at the amount of drugs being pushed onto them; one member of the Gay Liberation Front, Bob Kohler, said plainly that 'the Stonewall is a dope drop, and should have been bombed three years ago!'[33]

The Stonewall riots were a watershed for gay people, and when the dam broke, a lot of idealism, anger and longing burst out of their social restraints, carrying with them the debris of deep repression, confusion and self-hatred. What Ginsberg called 'the wounded look' had been momentarily startled into awareness, but the wounds were too deep to be easily healed, the methods of healing were little known, and even such ideology as Gay Liberation possessed was largely left over from other movements. The ideas of earlier thinkers like Carpenter, Whitman and Heard, which could have provided inspiration and direction, were obscured or forgotten. Gay Liberation burst onto a North American society suffused with commercialism, organized crime, sexual neurosis and homophobia, a society which, as the fate of black civil rights and the hippies showed, had a cunning ability to co-opt radical movements.

Social stigmatization tends to produce a form of group trance. As James Baldwin wrote in *Notes of a Native Son*, 'It is the peculiar triumph of society – and its loss, that it is able to convince those people to whom it has given inferior status of the reality of this decree; it has the force and the weapons to translate its dictum into fact, so that the allegedly inferior are actually made so, insofar as the societal realities are concerned . . . . And escape is not effected through a bitter railing against this trap; it is as though this very striving were the only motion needed to spring the trap upon us.'[34]

Arson at the Firehouse

Everyone knows it was an inside job.
— *Ain't It Da Truth!*

Chief among the borrowed ideologies of Gay Liberation, and the borrowed mythologies behind them, were Marxism and Freudianism. These new 'sciences' (even in the Americanized versions ostensibly sympathetic to gays) saw homosexuals and homosexuality as a 'suppressed' or 'repressed' element in nature and society, the very terminology suggesting origins in a lower world. While some cultures have seen variant sexuality as linking its possessors to 'higher' spiritual worlds, indicating a connection upward, Judaeo-Christian society has traditionally viewed male/male love as narrowly sexual, devoid of redeeming emotions or spirituality, and in consequence closely identified with guilt, nakedness, the sin of pride ('Gay Pride') and the catastrophe of the Fall.

Homosexuality, whether rejected or liberated, has almost invariably been seen as a phenomenon of the lower reaches, the Nether World. New, ostensibly scientific perspectives could be embraced with no radical adjustment to the traditional view of same-sex eroticism as animalistic, subhuman or even demonic. This was reflected in the literature, attitudes and social activities of the gay subculture – and even in the word 'subculture' itself.

The first gay bar ever depicted on an American movie screen illustrated this virtually universal assumption. Don Murray plays Senator Brig Anderson – his very name suggesting his self-imprisonment – in Otto Preminger's *Advise and Consent*. As he enters the darkly glowing subterranean grotto, one of the patrons holds up a lit cigarette – the erect, smouldering phallic symbol of a gay hell so frightening the clean-cut young senator has no alternative but to head for home as fast as he can and take a cut-throat razor to his neck.

Much of the old, pre-Kameny, homophile movement had looked defensively inward, nail-biting endlessly about the medical diagnosis of homosexuality as an illness, or alternatively, seeing the gay cause as a kind of codicil to Marxist class-war (only to be repudiated by Marxism's official representatives). When Gay Lib came along, it replaced these attitudes with a new political activism. But belief in the old myth lingered. Without a solid foundation of self-understanding, most gays, no matter how caught up in the new movement, still lacked an essential self-confidence, still bought into the myth of the homosexual as merely a walking sexcrime, wounded and ultimately self-destroying. Harry Hay's three questions remained unanswered.

At the same time, the popular media remained focused on the question 'What *causes* homosexuality?' Two years after Stonewall, a feature in *Newsweek* preoccupied itself with this conundrum. On gays and the police, there was nothing. America was not yet permitted to know what was going on in that department. The attitude supplemented that of the psychotherapists, who told their desperate homosexual clients that they must avoid the company of other gays, overcome the sick urge to reveal their secret disease anywhere outside the consulting room, and make a heterosexual 'adjustment'. For many, this was a prescription for suicide.

Nevertheless, the word was finally out. The homosexual had officially arrived in America, and began to pop up in the press and even on television. A second wave of young gays from all over the continent began to arrive in the cities. Some came straight from the farm; as Wilde said, anyone can be good in the country! Others dropped out of university: 'Remember those college days when you never knew another gay person on campus and spent the entire first year looking for a friend?' wrote Bob 'Flash' Storm in an early issue of *Gay Post*.[35] I remember them well: I dropped out of college, left my straight, amiable, but friendless campus (appropriately named Victoria College), and headed for New York.

Most of us who were in New York City in the post-Stonewall period have fond memories of the Gay Activists Alliance Firehouse. An old firehall in SoHo had somehow been acquired by GAA and converted into office space, a coffee shop, literature shop, beer parlor and – one full floor – a huge dance hall, complete with Gay Lib mural the length of one wall. When I first arrived in Manhattan, I went to the gay bar nearest where I was staying, which turned out to be a dim, glitzy joint full of heavy drinkers and distant pretty-boys in expensive clothes. I didn't like it. I'd heard about the Firehouse and eventually made my way there. What a contrast to the commercial uptown bar! Here were hundreds of gay men and women (mostly men) dressed every which way, open, affectionate, laughing, mixing freely, talking quietly over coffee or beer or dancing up a storm. Here was something of what I had come down from the frozen North to find.

Shortly after I arrived on the scene, and after a number of GAA leaders had begun to play footsie with city government, the Firehouse burned down and a considerable amount of the gay community's money went missing. In the fall of 1974, the gay liberation magazine *Ain't It Da Truth!* (whose spies were everywhere) published an article on the demise of the Firehouse, revealing that in the attic of the building, videotape equipment purchased with funds from the GAA dances was being used to film porno movies featuring expensive call boys, paid by cheques from 'Lambda Club Limited' (the GAA's holding company). A few days after the article appeared, the president of GAA resigned. The following day, files and a great deal of equipment were removed; and that night the building was gutted by fire.

Ain't It Da Truth! fleshed out the common belief that the arson had served to cover up other transgressions; nevertheless, it reported, 'no arrests were ever made. Well politics makes strange bedfellows, and I guess if you have friends in City Hall, it's pretty easy to squash a police investigation.'[36] Up in flames with the Firehouse went Mario Dubsky's 8-foot-by-31-foot mural, a dynamic photomontage composed of scenes and slogans of gay rebellion, liberation and pride.

The fate of the Firehouse, like the shootings at the Ramrod and the fire at the Everard Baths years later, was a kind of ill omen. What had promised to be the beginning of a real gay community, run by our own people, independent of the crime syndicate and the ghetto mentality, had collapsed almost as soon as it had begun.

This chapter and the next look over some of the literature generated by the gay movement in the period between 1969 and 1981 and unearth a few clues to the movement's decline and its eventual extinction in the cataclysm of AIDS. There, amid the promising new light of liberation, we can spot the first small clouds of the gathering storm ahead. Re-examining these writings with the benefit of hindsight may give us a better understanding of the background to AIDS in the gay community. We may also be able to see, more clearly than was possible at the time, what our writers were telling us.

'Gerald Heard – but not understood!'

From community to commodity

A ghetto can be improved in one way only: out of existence.

— James Baldwin

A stalwart pillar of the community in those days was Wallace Hamilton, an urbane, earthy elder for many of the 'new free' gay youth in Manhattan's West Village. Wallace was fifty at the time of Stonewall, and for the next fifteen years, he acted as friend, advisor, lover, guru and father figure to many in what we called, often more in hope than in earnest, the gay community.

I first met Wallace in the mid-1970s when he lived on Sheridan Square in a cluttered apartment whose most prominent feature was a round table enormous enough to accommodate King Arthur and his boys, or a generous supply of friends, house-guests and drop-ins. When he hit the streets, Wallace inevitably wore a pea hat and navy surplus coat, in which outfit, combined with his swinging gait, he gave the impression of having just stepped off a tug-boat. Married twice and with a Harvard degree in, of all things, medieval history, he had worked in fields as diverse as town planning, medicine and religion. He knew his way around and was always prepared to point out the available routes or shine a little light on the path. His apartment soon became, in his words, 'a refuge against the outer chaos' of the ghetto. Wallace, to me and to many others, represented experience, wisdom and greatness of heart. He was one of the few elders who had 'come out' with Stonewall and joined the revolution early.

In his book about those days, *Christopher and Gay*, he describes a little of the scene outside the apartment walls. 'A soda joint called The Haven was in full operation in the neighborhood as probably the largest downtown retail distribution center for every known variety of drugs. Sunday mornings, going out to get the paper at nine or ten o'clock, I'd see the flotsam and jetsam of the night before strewn around Sheridan Square and West Fourth Street, kids barely able to walk, kids draped over fenders or nodding out in doorways, blank, lost looks on their faces. I had a sunlit vision of hell.'[37] These, it should be made clear, were young teenagers, some of them fresh into town from all points of the compass.

One story Wallace tells in his book is that of Fred, a rebellious blond kid with a taste for knives and brass knuckles. 'One evening he showed up, late and alone. He could barely stagger into the room, and stood there, staring at me through heavy-lidded, unfocused eyes. I assumed it was downs, a lot of downs . . . . His pulse was strange, his breathing light, his skin clammy, and once he hit the pillow, he seemed to pass out, eyes closed and mouth open . . . . He developed a cough that he couldn't seem to shake. From taking speed, he developed sores that wouldn't heal.' With help, Fred eventually got better – and 'went right back to the street-and-soda-joint life he'd left.'[38] Wallace comments: 'Considering the regimen some of those kids were on, sometimes speeding for days at a time, it's a wonder they didn't come down with the plague.'

Wallace lived to see the plague arrive, and I doubt he was as surprised as those whose knowledge of illness came solely from peering into microscopes. That persistent cough, those sores that wouldn't heal, became, after 1981, familiar symptoms. Wallace's observations give the lie to the contention that those who came down with AIDS were 'previously healthy'.

The last time I saw Wallace, we were sitting in what for both of us was a most unlikely place, the lounge area off the dance floor of Studio 54. Characteristically, he had taken me there to meet a magazine editor who he thought might publish my articles. He gestured sadly, sardonically, to the muscular young clones around us. 'This is the AIDS crowd', he told me. Even at that early stage, the syndrome had claimed at least one of his young lovers, and Wallace had begun to put some pieces of the puzzle together.

One piece he knew about was the central document of the early movement, Carl Wittman's *Refugees from Amerika: A Gay Manifesto*. It was first issued as a pamphlet to be distributed on the street in the gay Mecca of San Francisco in 1971 – just about the time Wallace was binding up the wounds of the young refugees on the other side of the continent. It came to be reprinted many times over 'in the initial flourish of a movement'.

A Gay Manifesto (it was usually known by its original subtitle) begins with the following declaration:

> San Francisco is a refugee camp for homosexuals. We have fled here from every part of the nation, and like refugees elsewhere, we came not because it is so great here, but because it was so bad there. By the tens of thousands, we fled small towns where to be ourselves would endanger our jobs and any hope of a decent life; we have fled from blackmailing cops, from families who disowned or 'tolerated' us; we have been drummed out of the armed services, thrown out of schools, fired from jobs, beaten by punks and policemen.
>
> And we have formed a ghetto, out of self-protection. It is a ghetto rather than a free territory because it is still theirs. Straight cops patrol us, straight legislators govern us, straight employers keep us in line, straight money exploits us. We have pretended everything is OK, because we haven't been able to see how to change it – we've been afraid.[39]

Carl Wittman believed that our first task was to free ourselves of 'the garbage' that's been poured into our heads for so many generations. 'Ghettos', he wrote, 'breed self-hatred. We stagnate there, accepting the status quo. The status quo is rotten. We are all warped by our oppression, and in the isolation of the ghetto, we blame ourselves rather than our oppressors.' He felt that ghettos breed exploitation, pointing out that the Tavern Guild, the organization of gay bars in the city, had refused to let gay liberationists collect defense funds or distribute literature in their establishments, seeing the new movement as a threat to their control over their patrons' lives and resources. (The English gay movement had to deal with police threats to landlords of any pubs serving people wearing gay badges. Gays who defied the police were charged with 'obstruction'.)

Towards the end of the *Gay Manifesto*, Wittman urged the setting up of gay institutions: communes, newspapers, food co-ops, schools, after hours places, rural retreats. In the years to follow, institutions would come and go, but straight society's commercial grip on the ghetto would tighten. Its isolation would remain more subtle, but just as restrictive, and many gays, including most of Wallace's neighborhood kids, would become trapped there, like orphans in the funhouse: 'no Mama, no Papa, no Uncle Sam' to come take them home. Most of those who survived the initial hazards found their way into the gay urban clone culture spotlighted by Larry Kramer's *Faggots* a few years later. Better-quality drugs. A step up!

Few of these refugees possessed the social skills essential for emotional equilibrium – or even survival – in the big city. Most of them had suffered abuse and ostracism because of their sexuality. The emotional, physical and sexual abuse many of them had been subjected to would have protracted and severe psychological effects. Isolated gay boys from small towns, they arrived in the Village or the Castro lacking the discernment and abilities necessary to maintain real friendships or meaningful ties. Alienated and adrift, they formed an excellent target group for the marketing of a new kind of urban lifestyle that was economically and culturally a lucrative expansion of the illegal drug market and the quasi-legal sex industry.

One young gay man's experience in the big city was fairly typical: 'My father drove me to New York', he recalled, 'where my first residence was the McBurney YMCA on Twenty-third Street near Seventh Avenue. My father left, and I unpacked my things and set up my stereo. At this point I knew not one person in New York. I had arrived on a Friday and had the weekend ahead of me. School would begin on Monday.'

Within two days, he had moved out of the Y, and discovered 'the whole gay thing', the lifestyle of the ghetto. 'So I fell into this whole thing very easily. . . . The scene was still that you went from bar to bar, and little by little I discovered where the interesting gay places were, including the back-room bars, like The Stud, where they had porno movies playing and a more or less dark room with people groping and having anonymous sex. In the beginning this was all strange to me, but ultimately it became a way of life – and it lasted for a long time . . . . It just became part of the nightly routine.'[40]

This was the experience of the teenaged Keith Haring, whose art would make him famous a few years later, before his death of AIDS in 1990. Haring's friend Kenny Scharf, added that Keith (an attractive and personable boy) 'thought he wasn't good looking and that he couldn't attract people. He had trouble with his self-image. So he made this scene of sex for the sake of sex, going to the bars, going to the baths.'[41]

For many young men in those days, sex became, in the words of London Gay Liberation Front founder Bob Mellors, 'a delicious compensation for not fitting in'.[42] Or, as Quentin Crisp put it, 'Sex is the last refuge of the miserable.'

For the first few years of gay liberation, the idealistic elements of the movement were kept alive by radical gay newspapers with strong cultural emphasis, run by small groups of committed people – papers like *Gay Liberator*, *Fag Rag*, *Gay Sunshine*, *Come Out*, the English *Come Together* and the Canadian *Body Politic*. These began partly as radical gay holdovers from the Flower Children era of the 1960s, a kind of street anarchism jostling against elements of the New Left, with a few suggestions of pagan and radical Christian spirituality peeping through here and there. These non-profit community papers put together on shoestring budgets struggled against the Mafia glossies for the attention of the gay public. But the glossies were distributed in smaller cities and even some outlying towns where *Gay Sunshine* could never penetrate. From their full-color pages, the ghettos of San Francisco and New York beckoned with the promise of a 'gay lifestyle' of instant acceptance and unlimited sex.

Mob-controlled 'gay' magazines – the slick glossy ones and the cheap ones blotchily inked on cheap newsprint – served as advertising flyers for the ultimate consumer product – a permanent sex holiday. If customers tended to vanish after a while, there were always plenty more to take their place.

At the other extreme, the most distinctive of all the gay publications of the day were a pair of home-made 'fagazines' of slightly old-fashioned psychedelic design, printed on heavy stock in a rainbow of bright colours. *Gay Post* and its sister publication *Ain't It Da Truth!* (which blew the whistle on the Firehouse arson) were printed on an erratic home copying machine in the West 102nd Street apartment of artist Ralph Hall and his lover Bob 'Flash' Storm, a locale which also served as crash space, Grand Central Station and home away from home for an ever-changing mix of gay street people, professional and amateur revolutionaries, and dark-skinned teenaged boys *(see plate 3)*.

Ralph, like Wallace, was a central figure of the Christopher Street scene in the 1970s. A natural anarchist, his combination of enthusiasm, indignation and sweetness was irresistible. He was very sexy. I first met him while walking down Christopher Street one evening. He was sitting on the pavement outside Ty's (one of the few gay-owned bars in the Village) with a small stack of copies of *Gay Post* in his hand. He was tall and very thin with long, hippyish hair, a sense of street style all his own, bright eyes and a gentle, mischievous smile. When, years later, I saw a photo of him taken a few years earlier, I realized how physically wasted he'd become by the time I met him. Were drugs responsible? Or improperly treated syphilis, as Ralph himself came to believe?

Ralph had been a writer for the early radical Gay Lib papers, but by the mid-1970s had become disillusioned with the gay press. It had been co-opted, he said, and was selling us not even half a loaf but just a few poisoned crumbs. Even the more independent gay media tended to be preoccupied with arcane matters of political rectitude or, in the case of the commercial *Advocate*, caught up with its own co-optation by dubious advertisers and a millionaire horse-breeder in search of a gay power base. The political nitty-gritty went unanalyzed, and as upwardly mobile gays moved into the halls of power, it was widely assumed that this would mean a distribution of bounty to the gay community. It was left to *Gay Post* and *Ain't It Da Truth!*, beholden to no one save their own customers on the street, to sound the alarm. A glance into their pages gives an idea of how things were going.

Issue No. 8 of *Gay Post* ('New York City's Own Gayzine of the Arts') includes contributions by Allen Ginsberg, Harvey Fierstein and street poet Jimmy Centola, and articles on the National Gay Task Force and the 1975 gay parade. 'N.G.T.F.: A profile in absurdity', by someone (probably Ralph or Flash) using the pen-name Clara Voyant, examines a new 'national' gay organization as representative of the new gay establishment. Oleaginous and fawning to City Hall and national politicians, thuggish and rude to gays who disagreed with them, the Task Force (a term borrowed from US military jargon) is seen as 'forever reassuring the establishment politicos, doctors, and what have you, that all gays want to be just like them (i.e. the maggot death culture: a society that manufactures war, jails, mental institutions, etc.).' The article has fun with the NGTF's executive director, Dr Bruce Voeller, and his efforts to have two *Gay Post* writers arrested.[43]

'N.Y.C. Gay Parade 1975: Which direction is it going', in the same issue, dealt with the literal change in direction of the annual parade marking the anniversary of the Stonewall rebellion. 'The assembly point of the parade has traditionally been Christopher Street', wrote *Gay Post*. 'However, Pastor Eckhard of St John's Evangelical Lutheran Church . . . pressured the police into enforcing an ambiguous section of the General Business Law to prevent "noisy, disruptive gay people who offend his parishioners" from gathering . . . . It is common knowledge his parish consists of . . . children bussed in from out of town whom he preaches to of the sin and degradation of Village folk.' The pastor also seems to have done a little moonlighting as chaplain to the Police Department.

The cops had gone even further than Pastor Eckhard's request; they demanded a hefty 'security bond' from the Christopher Street Liberation Day committee (supposedly as insurance against damage) and forbade the use of Fifth Avenue, the traditional Manhattan parade route. In the ensuing scuffles with City authorities, the seven-person gay negotiating team allowed themselves to be pressured into giving up Christopher Street, with only one dissenter, Rudy Grillo. For this, Grillo was denounced as a 'troublemaker' by the Village's congressman, Ed Koch, usually referred to by *Gay Post* as 'faggot congressman Krotch' who would later become notorious as a self-proclaimed heterosexual and mayor of New York.

Gay Post concluded, 'And so this year there will be another parade; but it will not be the same as before . . . . The conservative gay ethic had produced what is to some an affrontery and a great setback for gay liberation. Most who come will never know the changes and never care. For them liberation will never come; only self-perpetuating apathy and acquiescence.'[44]

The reversal of the annual gay walk from being a 'march' *out of* the ghetto to being a 'parade' *into* the ghetto with trinkets, souvenirs and bootleg beer hawked on all sides, symbolized the end of the radical phase of gay liberation and its replacement, in the mid-1970s, by nostrums more palatable but ultimately more noxious.[45]

Ain't It Da Truth! publicized other changes affecting the movement. One article, 'Clara Voyant on the sodomites and the pigs' begins with an account of the forcible ejection of gay reporters from the swearing-in as a civic official of a member of the National Gay Task Force. Once again Dr Bruce Voeller (known to Ralph and his colleagues as 'the fuehrer') was much in evidence. The article quotes a flyer handed out at the time alleging close links between the NGTF and 'the Mafia bars and publications with their numerous fund-raising fronts'. These 'businesses' co-ordinated campaigns to promote the NGTF as *the* 'gay spokespeople', discrediting and co-opting the Gay Liberation movement and drawing attention away from the most pressing gay social problems: the appalling treatment of lesbian and gay youth, prisoners and street people, poor and non-white gays and those incarcerated in mental institutions.

The magazine also criticized the abridgements of civil liberties proposed by NGTF-supported politicians. One article deals with a piece of investigative journalism entitled 'Where Is the Clubhouse?' by Lee Solomon, discussing 'how an elite group of about 40 closeted gays, most of whom are in high executive positions in the city, state or federal government, have been secretly manipulating the "gay movement" in New York for years.'

The basis for Solomon's report was a paper delivered to the American Political Science Association's 1975 convention in San Francisco. The paper, co-written by Ken Sherrill (a member of the élite group) details how the Clubhouse, a shadowy cabal of conservative white homosexuals (many of them married and closeted) was able to manipulate most of the gay organizations in New York and determine their agenda. A number of privileged gay activists were 'allowed' membership in the group which apparently had ties to a number of CIA think tanks. The article ties members of the group to both the burning of the Firehouse and the redirection of the gay parade.

Ain't It Da Truth! maintained that since the radical gay movement had been displaced by opportunistic groups like the Clubhouse, 'never has our community been more factionalized and apathetic'. The article ends with a suggestion that readers 'call Bruce Voeller at 431–3843 and find out what forms of biological warfare he helped develop for the CIA, when he was employed at Rockefeller University before he emerged as a "gay leader" . . . . Call Morty Manford at 691–3625. Get him to come clean with all he knows about the Firehouse arson . . . .'

It was obvious that unless all this was just Clara Voyant's feverish fantasy, the Stonewall Experiment had undergone some rapid and serious changes. Some of the lab assistants were still at their desks, but a whole new group was now directing the project. Clara Voyant concluded: 'Eight years after the Stonewall we are further away from freedom than ever.'[46]

Another poignant record of those days is contained in one of the best of the early gay liberationist tracts, *The Gay Mystique* by the novelist and movement activist Peter Fisher. Pete and his lover Marc Rubin were to become fixtures on the New York Gay Lib scene. In *The Gay Mystique* he describes his entry into the gay world as it was at about the time of Stonewall: 'When I first came out into the gay world, I hoped that I would find someone to love who loved me and settle down together.'

What he found was that 'no affair seemed to last for more than a week or two . . . . I remember waiting for phone calls that never came and the agony of hearing rumors or finding last week's lover in the bar with someone new. It wasn't long before I became cynical about the gay world and cynical about myself . . . . I heard myself repeating and believing things I had heard others say and had refused to believe. It was better not to become too deeply involved, because you would only get hurt in the end. You should never really open yourself up to another person – you were too vulnerable if you did. Sex was perfectly satisfying, anyway, and there was no need to waste your time looking for love . . . . I came to see myself as rather

odd for wanting a lover with whom I could settle down permanently
. . . . Why should I waste my best years when there was so much
going on, so many beautiful people to meet . . . . I felt enormously
guilty and cruel.'[47]

After this, the post-Stonewall gay movement came as a
personal liberation for Fisher as he broke free of his old attitudes,
came to greater understanding of himself and discovered his
capacity for love. In a moving passage, he describes meeting his lover
Marc through the Gay Activists Alliance, how as they 'sat on a
loading dock in the mist of a rainy evening', Marc gave him a ring.
Later, they exchanged simple vows in a chapel of the Cathedral of St
John the Divine. 'This was a place where many other people had
come in the past to join their lives, and although we had no service,
no family, no friends, no blessing but our own, we were part of that
spirit.'[48]

This kind of close emotional-erotic tie between man had
constituted the spiritual core of the gay tradition far back into history.
Male/male love was the sacred fire without which sex between men
was just a functional anomaly. Its rediscovery was at the centre of
the teachings of the gay prophets of the modern era: Whitman,
Carpenter, and their twentieth century exponents. But the repression of centuries had made it seem odd, embarrassing, suspicious,
tainted, somehow, by its emotional similarity to heterosexual
unions. Only furtive, anonymous sex, as one novelist put it
'something you do in the dark',[49] seemed characteristically gay.

Another important development of the 1970s was the sudden
rise in the amount of readily available gay male pornography. The
old semi-clandestine photos of smiling boys in posing straps and the
films of friendly wrestlers and innocent nude romps, produced by
artist–hobbyists like Pat Rocco or small firms like Athletic Model
Guild, were suddenly superseded by a deluge of crude, formulaic
porno films (and later, videos) whose production and distribution
were controlled almost entirely by organized crime. The few daring
independent erotic film-makers usually moved on to other genres or
were driven out of the country by selective law enforcement.

This Mafia porn is readily recognizable: the performers
seldom seem to be enjoying themselves and sometimes seem drunk

or drugged. Whenever a character or sequence of events begins to get interesting, the camera can usually be relied upon to cut away to giant close-ups of cocks and assholes, amputated from any human context. For many gay men and boys, these newly available commercial images constituted almost the only depictions of gay men in the public media. Apart from an occasional film or television episode in which a tormented homosexual constituted the central plot problem, gay people were virtually invisible in the mass media. Only in the context of pornography did they achieve visibility or identity.

Social institutions from psychiatry to pornography instilled into gay men the idea of sex without affection or committment as the essence of homosexuality. It is hardly surprising that many gays came to see any more intimate approach as a 'sell-out to the straight establishment . . . embarrassingly unliberated'. To be liberated could only be to carry on in the same manner as before – but without the penalties. Gay romance was condemned as nothing but an imitation of straight marriage; a word was even coined for it: 'heteromimetic'. Having a lover – or wanting one – had nothing to do with the heart's desire; you were merely 'identifying with your oppressors'. A pseudo-political veneer could conceal a great deal of loneliness, bitterness and self-disgust.

Seeing the narrow sexual patterns of most gay men as a direct result of years of isolation and oppression, gay liberationists urged the abandonment of 'self-destructive attempts to fit the warped roles given us by the male heterosexual system'. They identified fear as the main instrument of oppression; fear and rage were 'eating at our bowels'.[50]

To the cultural radicals of the gay movement, the alienation of anonymous sex had to be replaced by social visibility and new institutions that would validate gay sexuality while accommodating gays as whole people. 'The meat market stinks! Drink up and leave the racketeering bars!' one gay paper exhorted.[51] Steve Dansky in *Come Together* called for 'the complete negation of the use of gay bars, tearooms, trucks, baths, streets, and other traditional cruising institutions. These are exploitative institutions designed to keep gay men in the roles given to them by a male heterosexual system.'[52] And

Perry Brass, editor of New York's Gay Liberation Front newspaper *Come Out!*, urged his 'dear gay brothers' to 'please get out of the trucks, / the sun is rising, / before it is too late, / . . . when the sun rises / turn around and face each other . . . '.[53]

It was obvious that 'if we were to attract people from the gay community we had to create an alternative social scene to the existing gay pubs and clubs'.[54] But without a financial base, this would be a herculean labour, easily countered by the advertised allure of bars, bathhouses and backrooms, most of which were supported by the financial resources of organized crime.

Some years later, Dennis Altman, in an examination of 'why the movement failed to grow into a mass community of homosexuals prepared to assert their rights, as we hoped in those halcyon days of Stonewall and GAA zaps', identified the proliferation of the commercial gay male scene as the chief reason. 'The promise of endless gang-bangs available across the length and breadth of the country . . . [the] acceptance of gay sex as a commodity', he wrote, 'has done little to promote the sort of gay community that we innocently hoped for in the early days of the movement.' His remarks bore the sardonic title 'Fear and Loathing and Hepatitis on the Path of Gay Liberation'.[55]

A 1978 study by the Canadian sociologist John Allan Lee exemplifies the characteristic 1970s approach to gay sex. In *Getting Sex*, the consumer model prevails throughout.[56] Observing that 'Millions of North Americans go to bed every night sexually hungry', Lee draws the obvious conclusion: 'What our society needs is an adequate and reliable supply of risk-free, casual sex.' All that is needed, he says, is 'an effective system of sexual distribution' like the one developed by gay men. In *Getting Sex*, hunting and fishing metaphors predominate; potential sexual partners are 'prey', and are 'thrown back', like a bad, or undersized fish, if they turn out to be unacceptable.

Another factor affecting the direction of the Stonewall Experiment was the lack of awareness of gay history and ideas. Armchair Marxism converted into a procrustean bed for the militant gays who squeezed themselves into it. Sloganeering and dogmatism alienated more people than they attracted. As a result, many were simply turned off the gay movement and drifted, disappointed, into the faggot lifestyle. The English gay liberationist Aubrey Walter wrote of increasing conflicts in the London movement: 'The radical queen communards from Notting Hill would sweep into meetings and demand that people get into drag and make-up, haranguing anyone whom they considered too much of a "man". This sort of tactic had the opposite effect from what was intended, as it often drove gays back into their little butch moulds. Many men were also terrorized into bizarre and unproductive forms of drag.'[57]

With the streets and neighborhoods unsafe for gays and social institutions unwelcoming, the ghetto offered the only refuge, and especially in North America, bathhouses seemed to many like a zone of safety. Indeed, they were the only place where gays were allowed to feel safe. This was why the notorious police raids on the baths in Toronto in 1981 created such an uproar in the gay community there. The unwritten agreement – that baths were off-limits to the cops – had been breached. (From the police point of view, another term of the same agreement had already been broken, from the gay side, when a well-known bathhouse owner had the temerity to court respectability by running for city council!)

During my stay in New York in the late 1970s, almost every gay man I know went regularly or occasionally to the 'tubs' and enjoyed the raunchy mystique they cultivated. As the anonymous sex that was the baths' main draw didn't interest me, I never went: this was considered somewhat eccentric. As the gay community became more commercially oriented, the baths had become its central focus. Protected by the law as no other gay institution, they made millions for the financial powers behind them, and encouraged promiscuity on a scale that far exceeded anything in the past. Patrons of the baths were among the most frequent visitors to the VD clinics, and when the plague came, it was this group that was the hardest hit.

Among the gay men who recorded their impressions of the baths in those years were Dotson Rader, Dennis Rubini and Michael Rumaker. Their observations of the institutions that became epicenters of the epidemic deserve re-examination.

The sealed labyrinth

As deadly as they were sublime,
the tubs, though heaven for a spell,
turned out to be a steaming hell:
so many men, so little time.

— Robert Boucheron, *Epitaphs for the Plague Dead*

As the bath is a traditional symbol of healing and regeneration, it is not surprising that it became a central institution of post-Stonewall gay life. *The* book on the bathhouse scene as it was in the 1970s and early 1980s is Michael Rumaker's *A Day and a Night at the Baths*. At the beginning of his career, Rumaker had been associated with the Beat Generation; by the 1970s, he was in his forties. Written as an account of a first visit to New York's Eberhardt Baths (also known as Everard, Everhard and 'The Seventh Circle') his story covers a gamut of details, experiences and customers, the good, the bad and the ugly. One particularly evocative passage is a description of the dimly lit orgy room, its eerie, other-worldly atmosphere conveying a quality of repellent fascination. The 'sunlit vision of hell' that Wallace saw on the streets of the Village had moved indoors where 10-watt bulbs with broken shades now shed the only light.

Rumaker comments on the variety of physical and character types encountered, and continues:

> All prowl these dreary dim halls with the same purpose and search: to find, surprised, behind the monotonous row on row of cheap plywood doors, endlessly opening and closing, the heart's desire and the awakener of the heart; the miracle of a barely imagined paradise, here in this dingy, smelly place, heavy with stale body odors and decades-old perspiration of lust-sweat, and fear-sweat, and ashes of sperm-fire that encrust the walls and floors and ceilings from all the century-long years of those who have searched here in unspeakable pleasure and pain (for there is unspeakable pain here, too); searching patiently and tirelessly to discover, in sly and passionate ambush, in the litter and stink of this hidden away bathhouse in a floral market street of the city, a tiny

glint of the shy and elusive flower that enfolds the secret and the meaning.[58]

At one point, he notices an attractive Asian youth and offers him a cigarette:

> The spontaneous elfin grin he'd flashed at me just a few moments before now left no trace on his features, as if some totally different person, a stranger, had taken possession of the cubicle in the few seconds it had taken me to walk across the hall.
>
> He thanked me for the cigarette, and there was such a sound of weariness and indifference in his voice, that whatever initial desire, and hopes, I'd had, quickly evaporated. He regarded me briefly and in the narrowness of his eyes there was a flat, cold expression of embitterment, the tiny curl of his mouth in a smile giving a famished twist to his lips . . .
>
> He twitched his hips, grinding them into the mattress, throwing a look over his shoulder that was both defiance and challenge. Something curdled in me. I felt myself withdrawing, had already left the room, even though I remained fixed where I stood, held by the hypnotic poison of his eyes.[59]

For Rumaker, the Asian youth embodies an acceptance of objecthood and defeat, and so, of a kind of corruption. He keeps thinking about the boy, imagining him trapped against his will for the rest of his days. He envisions the boy's desire

> gone meaningless, only the spasms of habit remaining, returning him again and again to this spot; someone damned to haunt these hallways forever, even long after the building collapsed in decay and dust or burned to the ground in cinders, the aborted and beaten spirit of him prowling always – And how I have always felt myself like a person in exile; and other gay women and men to be in exile, anonymous in the cities, inconspicuous in the windowless cubicles of baths such as this; banned from the rural places – or if not escaped

yet, in hiding there, among leaves, among roots; cut off from dances of the country ground, from the stories and songs of the Green Spirit they used to sing, the grass-roots music they danced to in other times . . . .[60]

The contrast Rumaker makes between the exiled homosexual in what Carl Wittman called the 'refugee camps' of the cities and the gay man as part of a reclaimed natural world is a recurring theme in both his books about the gay ghetto, *A Day and a Night at the Baths* and its companion volume, *My First Satyrnalia*.[61]

Another gay man to offer a personal vision of the tubs was Dotson Rader, in his autobiographical novel *Gov't. Inspected Meat and Other Fun Summer Things*. The Everard again, which Rader calls the St James:

I found the place anti-sexual, overstated, ahuman, lacking any semblance of personal interrelationship, except on a highly contrived physical level. It made hustling seem warm and very human in contrast. It was not dirty sex as much as symbolic sex at the St James, the sex of promise and fantasy where the players moved in prescribed patterns as in a religious pageant. No one spoke, silent as hustlers, for speech, that carrier of reality, prevented the mind from play and loss. They were rigid because the poses were limited, the repertory of sexual gesture painfully bound to a kind of masturbatory theatre, a dream world where something lay precious and hidden in the movement, finally unpossessable, beyond reach, creating an image to take home and replay in the mind and to exhaust. The stance and the postures were inner-directed. They acted independently of the watchers, existing by themselves. And what I learned, it was essential for me to know and accept it if I was to grow up complete, was that the freedom lay elsewhere. It was not to be found in that unreal masque of the gay hunt. It was not in the streets. But it was elsewhere. No, not in the straight world, but somewhere farther, tougher, without ease. Somewhere inside.[62]

Gay activist Dennis Rubini's vision of the baths was very straightforward: he saw them as a prison. In an article published in 1976, he recounted a return trip to New York's Continental, 'first of the super-baths', now 'full of addicts, utterly filthy'. 'The Continental of today', Rubini wrote, was 'a bridge' between the outside world and 'stir' (jail). Any valuables not left at the desk would be stolen, and even the desk could only be trusted for amounts of less than a dollar. 'Whether it works or not, whenever you leave your room put all your goods in the locker so that it will appear, when a head pokes through the removable ceiling panel, as if no one has checked into the room.'

'The upper floors', Rubini advises, 'have fewer rats' but the 'regular inmates' (men who, when not incarcerated, live at the baths, turning them into a more exact replica of the cell blocks they already resembled) 'choose these floors so that struggles over property with the most desperate of the addicts will draw less attention'. The Continental 'houses many merely "situational" homosexuals who like the low prices and the location but get upset by the influx of weekender gays turning *their* joint into a "fuckin' fag factory".' They roam around the halls, darkly muttering about 'really fixing the fuckin' faggots tonight'.

Do not make trouble, Rubini warns, as you may be harmed or even killed. 'When some prescription drugs I had were ripped off, the security officer told me they would shortly be available from the nearest dealer.' The dancing, however, was 'well worth watching. Many of the dancers go for hours on end, taking short breaks only to shoot up a little skag and/or speed.'

The article ends with a wry recommendation to 'get dressed in any unstolen clothes (bringing along an old dress is a good precaution so you'll have something left) and make your way out. I had to grope my way since someone had climbed in during the night, been rebuffed, and retaliated by stealing my rose-tinted glasses. At the desk I received back the valuables I had entrusted to their tender mercies, as well as a validated card allowing recidivists a second term at half price.'[63]

In the euphoria of the gay movement after Stonewall, we wanted to break out of the confines of the ghetto, and we demanded to live openly in society, to be able to meet and love one another without subterfuge or shame, and to contribute to society on the same basis as the rest of humankind. But our needs were seen as the threats of a mythical Homosexual, who must be feared and opposed. As long as we allowed the myth of this predatory, self-destructive figure to be projected onto us, we remained its captives.

The bathhouses were constructed as secret monuments for the appeasement of mythical creatures. They were hidden because America did not care to watch the spectacle of its own children being herded into the sealed labyrinth, where a potent mix of drugs and disease was beginning to simmer in a concentration of negative energy with no permissible outlet.

Perhaps the most memorable of all the haunting images in *A Day and a Night at the Baths* comes at the very beginning. In setting out for the baths, Rumaker has taken the wrong train. As he hurries along West 33rd Street on his way to Fifth Avenue, he passes the Empire State Building. A man has jumped from the 85th floor, his plummetting body hitting a metal canopy with the force of a small explosion. 'As I turned away, heading down Fifth, my first impulse was to suppose, intimate with suicide among us, that the victim had perhaps been gay. And perhaps, too, tormented by traditional ignorance, that of hostility around him, and finally, his own, was driven to this high place and, in despair, perhaps with unutterable relief, flung himself down from . . . this aggressive memorial to patriarchal rigidities and cold cash.'[64]

Rumaker's account was written before the health crisis, but not before the mental patterns that underlay it. All three of our accounts offer essential inside information about a collective state of mind. Centuries of sexual repression and distortion are not quickly or simply overcome, though they can easily be repackaged and labelled Pleasure or Freedom. A society which had made hetero-sexuality into an absolute had provided no rules, no guidelines, no ways for men to relate affectionately and erotically with one another. As a result, many men had grown up so alienated from their own natures that they lacked the emotional capacity for gay relationships. Only an insistent sexual need persisted.

The physical arrangements of public buildings (such as bathhouses) are not accidental. As Michel Foucault wrote in his book on prisons, architecture 'is operative in the transformation of individuals'. With its claustrophobic grid of cubicles, the sealed, timeless labyrinth of the baths suggested the format of the maze – ancient symbol of the spiritual quest. At the center of the best-known of all labyrinths, at Knossos in Minoan Crete, lurked the Minotaur, a monster with a man's body and a bull's head, sought for ritual combat by questing youths *(see plate 4)*.

To enter a labyrinth is to undertake a symbolic journey into the underworld of the unconscious mind, where one will encounter ferocious versions of the self, which the Minotaur represents. The task is to free the human community by slaying the Minotaur, and, donning its flayed skin, transcend the self and escape the imprisoning labyrinth.[65] Theseus, in the legend, was able to find his way out of the maze only by following a thread given to him by Ariadne, who loved him.

The modern maze of the baths invited just such an exploration of pent-up subterranean energy forces. Water is the universal symbol of the unconscious, and the tubs offered a refreshing plunge into repressed emotions and a profound cathartic cleansing. But the dangers were great, and one could easily become lost. When stuck in the labyrinth, the best way to get out is to climb on top, like Daedalus, who flew away. Armed with perspective, escape is not difficult. But when the labyrinth is sealed, as in a carnival house of mirrors, or in the baths with their pulsing disco music and pervasive poppers odour, the only way out may be to retrace one's steps – not always easy, without the thread. Failing, one may find oneself, in time, becoming the Minotaur, taking his place, like Rumaker's young man, at the center of the maze and lying in wait for other youths whose flesh one is condemned to slay and devour. 'Really, what would a labyrinth be without a minotaur: a labyrinth without blood?'[66]

Rumaker's beginning *A Day and a Night at the Baths* with a suicide's jump from a gigantic American phallic symbol can be seen as a prophetic encoding of this theme: what happens when gay men attempt to reach the pinnacle of a society of 'patriarchal rigidities and cold cash'? Their sexuality is stripped of its warmth and meaning and sold back to its possessors in a form so toxic that they can barely breathe. At the baths, Rumaker found himself opening a lone, tiny window, sticking his head out and gasping for air.

As the Stonewall Experiment developed, other intuitive writers picked up the omens they found and translated them into remarkable poetic works, a few of which are examined in the next chapter. They were among the very few who sensed the debacle to come. Also at this time, the immediate post-Stonewall period, a number of works from the past began to float into the consciousness of both gay and straight audiences. Among them were two prophetic novels written just before the First World War by eminent, closeted, writers, which illuminated the possibilities and dangers of the paths now opening up before the fledgling gay community.

Plague and palladium

'Why in the world are they forever disinfecting the city of Venice?'
— Gustav Aschenbach, in *Death in Venice*

The first publication of E. M. Forster's long-suppressed gay novel *Maurice* and the release of the Lucino Visconti/Dirk Bogarde film of Thomas Mann's *Death in Venice* both occurred in 1971, at a crucial time for the direction of gay liberation. Both novel and film were very popular with gays and were widely reviewed in the newly emerging gay media; Forster's friend Benjamin Britten made Mann's novella into an opera.

Mann's theme in *Death in Venice* is the artist's potential for self-destruction. The artist in the novella, Aschenbach, is captivated and mesmerized by his growing fascination with a beautiful boy, Tadzio, while on a trip to Venice. His fixation on his idealized vision of Tadzio impels him to remain in the city even as it flounders in the grip of the plague (in this instance, cholera, a disease whose fatal convulsions mimic orgasm).

As Aschenbach's background and conventionality render him incapable of approaching Tadzio, or entering into any erotic relationship with a male, Tadzio remains a symbol of what might be or might have been. Aschenbach cannot tear himself away from Tadzio, from Venice, or from his own existential paralysis and impending death. Meditating on Greek culture, he compares Tadzio to various beautiful Greek youths – all of them fated to die young. Tadzio himself, Aschenbach feels, 'will not live to grow old'.

Towards the end of the story, Aschenbach has a terrifying dream, full of 'horned and hairy males', frenzied dancing, torches and pan-pipes. The 'steam of panting bodies' gives off a stench of 'wounds, uncleanness and disease'. The creatures 'laughed, they howled, they thrust their pointed staves into each others' flesh and licked the blood as it ran down'. Eventually, amid an orgy of flesh-eating and 'promiscuous embraces', he wakes up – and soon after, is killed by what has been closing in on him in spite of his strenuous efforts to ignore it. This plague is the emotional plague of his own inability to transmute idealism into true fulfillment. Aschenbach expires in a state of dementia, uttering words 'shaped in his disordered brain'.[67] Both he and Tadzio die of the plague, and their names can be added to the growing roster of fictional homosexual victims.

Some have read *Death in Venice* and seen Aschenbach's homosexuality as responsible for his death. But is sexuality the villain, or the myth of the homosexual, which was at its strongest on the eve of World War I when the story was written, and was still around in 1971 when the film was released?

In a few paragraphs in *Christopher and Gay*, Wallace Hamilton recounts going with a young friend to the newly-released movie of *Death in Venice* and musing about Thomas Mann, whose work he knew quite well. In the middle of this account of pre-AIDS gay New York, Wallace finds himself asking questions about the implications of *Death in Venice*, and of 'the culture that makes young gays want to die at thirty-five'.[68]

James Baldwin, in a book about the murder of children, observed that Aschenbach 'is centered on a self not so much diminished or irrecoverable or unknown as *static*: he will never sing, *The very day I thought I was lost, my dungeon shook – and my chains fell off!* And the horror of his unlived life and unloved love is conveyed by the fact that there is a plague raging in Venice, and every hour he spends there brings him closer to death. He does not, as you or I might do, pack his bags and pick up his bed, or his boy, and walk; no, he expires, elaborately, on the beach, supine victim, finally, of the icy workings of the chamber of commerce.'[69] The notion of the prim Aschenbach bursting into a negro spiritual may be unintentionally amusing, but Baldwin's insights into the nature of his fatal fascination are astute.

Suppressed during his lifetime, E. M. Forster's gay novel *Maurice* is a very different work from Mann's hermetic novella. Forster's inspiration for the story, which 'was to deal with homosexuality, would feature three main characters, and would have a happy ending' came to him suddenly and directly at the moment George Merrill put his hand on Forster's bottom during a visit by the young writer to Ted Carpenter's Millthorpe cottage in 1913. Forster recalled that at the moment George touched his backside, a strange sensation 'seemed to go straight through the small of my back into my ideas, without involving my thoughts'. Forster connected this with Carpenter's 'yogified mysticism' and recognized the meaning: 'that at that precise moment I had conceived'.[70]

The child of that conception, *Maurice*, could not be published in 1913 and Forster put it aside. Later in life, as an old man, he was uncertain about it. But though he was too timid to publish it during his lifetime, he carefully prepared it for posthumous publication. The novel lives up to its delightfully appropriate inspiration. Its hero, a young man of the upper middle classes, tries to come to terms with his sexual nature, endures a failed crush on a friend, a bout with a psychiatrist and thoughts of suicide (for he has been 'fed upon lies'), and eventually finds happiness with Alec, a young working-class man.

'He had brought out the man in Alec', Forster wrote, 'and now it was Alec's turn to bring out the hero in him. He knew what the call was, and what his answer must be. They must live outside class, without relations or money; they must work and stick to each other till death. But England belonged to them. That, besides companionship, was their reward. Her air and sky was theirs, not the timorous millions' who own stuffy little boxes, but never their own souls.' Eventually, the two lovers go to live together in the country, as Merrill and Carpenter did.[71]

Forster's brief vision of the remaining English Greenwood as a palladium, a safeguard, and the lovers' true legacy (emphasized by Alec's coming to Maurice through an open window) has been misunderstood and criticized by some commentators who see it as an unrealistic 'retreat' and a 'fanciful attempt to escape from the world'.[72] This reflects a fatalistic view of the homosexual as forever imprisoned in social constraints. But Forster, like Whitman, sees homosexual feelings as finding their free expression in the natural world. *Maurice* is Forster's version of that traditionally English vision, the Greenwood as Earthly Paradise, inhabited by a band of brothers, which also finds expression in Tolkien, in William Morris,[73] and in the legends of Robin Hood and his Merry Men. *Maurice*'s dream of gay drop-outs is the other side of poor Aschenbach's terrible nightmare of panic destruction and orgiastic cannibalism.

In Aschenbach's lonely death in the Plague City and Maurice and Alec's return to the Greenwood, two great writers from the past presented the gay men of the early 1970s with strong prophetic motifs and images representing positive and negative aspects of the emerging gay's encounter with his civilization.[74] *Maurice* is idealism realized, the return to the Greenwood symbolizing the gay man's final emergence from negation and self-hatred and his reclaiming of the natural world. *Death in Venice* is idealism frustrated: death by plague.

Any decision gay men would make between these two paths would not be a conscious one, but rather a further working out of unconsciously held, socially conditioned attitudes, now identified and pandered to by forces of organized crime and 'the icy workings of the chamber of commerce'. With the urge of gay radicalism to transform and heal North American society now stifled, the urban ghetto would be the crucible of whatever changes were to devolve on gay men in the immediate future.

The Stonewall Experiment began in the untutored hands of gay people who had had enough of being second-class citizens, partial people, never fully human. It was an experiment in reclaiming full humanity from the medical/governmental establishment. Within a few years, control of the experiment had fallen into other hands, and the initiators found themselves in the position of experimental animals. The new phase of the experiment involved the development of a commercial gay scene that could be test-marketed as a prototype of the urban lifestyle of the future.

Notes

1. The British Society for the Study of Sex-Psychology was founded in 1913, at the instigation of a number of (mainly homosexual) men of letters, inspired by Carpenter and the German homosexual emancipationist Magnus Hirschfeld.

2. Edward Carpenter, *The Intermediate Sex* (London: George Allen & Unwin, 1908), p. 116.

3. George L. Mosse, *Nationalism & Sexuality: Respectability and Abnormal Sexuality in Modern Europe* (New York: Howard Fertig, 1985), p. 149.

4. *Ibid.*, p. 135.

5. Thomas Mann, *Mario and the Magician*, transl. H. T. Lowe-Porter (London: Secker, 1930).

6. The chapter 'Eden's Folk' in James Webb's *The Occult Establishment* (La Salle, IL: Open Court, 1976) gives an account of parallel movements in Britain. For details of the early German homosexual emancipation movement, see Mosse, *Nationalism & Sexuality*; John Lauritsen and David Thorstad, *The Early Homosexual Rights Movement (1864–1935)* (New York: Times Change Press, 1965); and James D. Steakley, *The Homosexual Emancipation Movement in Germany* (New York: Arno Press, 1975).

7. For George's ideological influence and his opposition to the Nazis, see Eric Russell Bentley, *A Century of Hero Worship* (Philadelphia: J. B. Lippincott, 1944); and Ian Young, *Gay Resistance: Homosexuals in the Anti-Nazi Underground* (Toronto: Stubblejumper Press, 1986).

8. Mosse, *Nationalism & Sexuality*, p. 124.

9. See Volker G. Probst, *Arno Brecker: 60 Ans de Sculpture* (Paris: Jacques Damase Editeur, 1981), pp. 76–82.

10. Richard Plant, *The Pink Triangle: The Nazi War Against Homosexuals* (New York: Henry Holt & Co., 1986).

11. See Young, *Gay Resistance*.

12. Plant, *The Pink Triangle*, p. 187.

13. Len Richmond and Gary Noguera, eds., *The Gay Liberation Book* (San Francisco: Ramparts Press, 1973), pp. 42–9.

14. Don Jackson, 'Dachau for queers', in Richmond and Noguera, *Gay Liberation Book*, p. 46.

15. William S. Burroughs, *Naked Lunch* (New York: Grove Press, 1959), pp. 186–197. For a further discussion of *Naked Lunch*, see Chapter 6, pp. 224–5.

16. See Allan Berubé, *Coming Out under Fire: The History of Gay Men and Women in World War II* (New York: The Free Press, 1990). One herald of the American gay movement to come was the article, 'The homosexual in society' by the anarchist poet Robert Duncan,

published in Dwight Macdonald's magazine *Politics* (August 1944). Duncan brought the word 'gay' out of the closet, and used the terms 'family' and 'community' in a gay context, well ahead of his time. In the following issue of *Politics*, Parker Tyler provided another gay perspective on the issues Duncan had raised.

17. Walter L. Williams, *The Spirit and the Flash: Sexual Diversity in American Indian Culture* (Boston: Beacon Press, 1986), p. 202.
18. *Ibid.*, p. 203.
19. See Mark Thompson, 'Harry Hay: a voice from the past, a vision for the future', in his *Gay Spirit: Myth and Meaning* (New York: St Martin's Press, 1987), pp. 183–99.
20. Two of Heard's essays and an introduction to him and his ideas by Jim Kepner appear in Thompson, *Gay Spirit*, pp. 165–81.
21. Gerald Heard, *Training for the Life of the Spirit* (Blauvelt, NY: Steinerbooks, 1975), p. 67.
22. Jim Kepner, 'I should have been listening: a memory of Gerald Heard', in Thompson, *Gay Spirit*, p. 172.
23. *Ibid.*, p. 173.
24. Gerald Heard, 'A future for the isophyll', in Thompson, *Gay Spirit*, p. 177.
25. Gerald Heard, 'What is religion?', in Thompson, *Gay Spirit*, p. 181.
26. Thompson, *Gay Spirit*.
27. One participant, identified only as 'David', recalled: 'I had been to Judy's funeral that afternoon, and I went home to cry a little, and listen to some records. I was going to go out that night, meet some friends, hit the bars . . . Ron, a guy I knew, called and said that a lot of us were going to go down to the Stonewall, because a friend of ours was going to be in Judy drag. I thought that was a little tasteless, but I went and we stood around and talked about how awful it was. And then all of a sudden the cops burst in and first thing you know I'm screaming and kicking. Some cop starts pulling me towards a wagon, and I shout: "Take your hands off me".' Quoted in Byrne R. S. Fone, *Hidden Heritage: History and the Gay Imagination* (New York: Irvington, 1981), p. xvii.
28. Quote in Donn Teale, *The Gay Militants* (New York: Stein & Day, p. 25.
29. *Gay Post*, No. 6, February 1975.
30. *Ibid.*, p. 17.
31. From 'London' from *Songs of Innocence and Experience by William Blake, Tuned by Allen Ginsberg*, MGM Records, 1969.
32. *Ibid.*, p. 23.
33. Quoted in Teale, *Gay Militants*, p. 24.
34. James Baldwin, 'Everybody's protest novel', in *Notes of a Native Son* (Boston: The Beacon Press, 1955), pp. 20–1.

35. Flash Storm, 'Notes from aboveground,' *Gay Post*, No. 8, May–June 1973.
36. *Ain't It Da Truth!*, No. 11.
37. Wallace Hamilton, *Christopher and Gay: A Partisan's View of the Greenwich Village Homosexual Scene* (New York: Saturday Review Press, 1973), p. 96.
38. *Ibid.*, pp. 97–8.
39. Carl Wittman, *A Gay Manifesto*, reprinted in Karla Jay and Allen Young (eds), *Out of the Closet: Voices of Gay Liberation* (New York: Douglas Books, 1972), pp. 330–42.
40. Quoted in John Gruen, *Keith Haring: The Authorized Biography* (New York: Prentice-Hall, 1991), p. 35. I am also indebted to John Lauritsen's essay, 'Political-economic construction of gay male clone identity', *Journal of Homosexuality*, **24** (3–4), 1993. 'What was homogenizing the gay community', Lauritsen writes, 'was fragmenting the individual . . . Without learning the ABC's of making love [many gay men] became adepts at performing skin piercing, "tit jobs", rimming, enemas, "golden showers" and "scat", and other such acts which they had been taught by hard-core porn or S&M leather publications.' Lauritsen mentions the stencilled 'CLONES GO HOME' slogans which appeared at one point around the East Village. These, as it happens, were the work of Keith Haring.
41. *Ibid.*, p. 63.
42. Bob Mellors, 'Gay liberation', *LSE Magazine* (Summer 1990), p. 32.
43. Clara Voyant, 'N.G.T.F.: a profile in absurdity', *Gay Post*, No. 8 (May–June 1975).
44. Clara Voyant, 'N.Y.C. Gay Parade 1975: which direction is it going?', *Gay Post*, No. 8 (May–June 1975).
45. For several years, *Gay Post* continued to sponsor an alternative 'Gay Walk' on Stonewall Day, ending up with a celebration in Central Park, the largest open green space in Manhattan. The CSLD name was legally 'incorporated' by 'mobster bar baron' (*Gay Post*'s description) Ed Murphy, formerly manager at the Stonewall. His organization was granted a police permit.
46. 'Clara Voyant on the sodomites and the pigs', *Ain't It Da Truth!*, No. 11 (1975).
47. Peter Fisher, *The Gay Mystique* (New York: Stein & Day, 1972), p. 202.
48. *Ibid.*, p. 201.
49. See Daniel Curzon, *Something You Do in the Dark* (New York: Lancer Books, 1971).

50.   Aubrey Walter, ed., *Come Together – the Years of Gay Liberation 1970–73* (London: Gay Men's Press, 1980), p. 73.

51.   *Ibid.*, p. 87.

52.   Steve Dansky, 'GLF against the IRB', in Walter, *Come Together*, p. 72.

53.   Perry Brass, 'I have this vision of madness', in Ian Young, ed., *The Male Muse: A Gay Anthology* (Trumansburg, NY: Crossing Press, 1973), p. 17.

54.   Walter, *Come Together*, p. 13.

55.   Dennis Altman, 'Fear and loathing and hepatitis on the path of gay liberation', in Richmond and Noguera, *Gay Liberation Book*, p. 200.

56.   John Allan Lee, *Getting Sex: A New Approach: More Fun, Less Guilt* (Toronto: Musson, 1978).

57.   Walter, *Come Together*, p. 35.

58.   Michael Rumaker, *A Day and a Night at the Baths* (San Francisco: Grey Fox Press, 1979), p. 46.

59.   *Ibid.*, p. 25.

60.   *Ibid.*, p. 27.

61.   Michael Rumaker, *My First Satyrnalia* (New York: Grey Fox Press, 1981).

62.   Dotson Rader, *Gov't Inspected Meat and Other Fun Summer Things* (New York: Paperback Library, 1972), p. 165.

63.   Dennis Rubini, 'Continental Baths revisited', *Gay News* (Philadelphia), (September 1976), p. X5. It may be worth noting that this is the only article I have seen in a gay periodical from the pre-AIDS era that recommends the use of condoms.

64.   Rumaker, *A Day and a Night at the Baths*, p. 2.

65.   Many bath denizens, and other gay men, wore the skin of the sacrificed bull in the form of the totemic garb of the sacrificial Rebel – the black leather jacket. Significantly, one of the most powerful memoirs of the AIDS era, David Wojnarowicz's *Close to the Knives* (New York: Vintage, 1991), culminates with the author, now 'diagnosed', crammed into a stifling bull-ring to watch a particularly cruel bull-fight.

66.   The words are Denis Hollier's, from his study of a writer for whom the labyrinth was a central image: *Against Architecture: The Writings of Georges Bataille* (Cambridge, MA: The MIT Press, 1989), p. xi.

67.   Thomas Mann, *Death in Venice* (London: Penguin, 1972), p. 76.

68.   Hamilton, *Christopher and Gay*, pp. 187–8.

69.   James Baldwin, *The Evidence of Things Not Seen* (New York: Holt, Rinehart & Winston, 1985), p. 51.

70. P. N. Furbank, 'Introduction' to E. M. Forster, *Maurice* (London: Edward Arnold, 1971), p. v.
71. E. M. Forster, 'Terminal note' to *Maurice*, p. 223. In the novel's original – suppressed – epilogue, Maurice and Alec become woodcutters.
72. See, for example, Jeffrey Meyers, *Homosexuality and Literature 1890–1930* (London: The Athlone Press, 1977), p. 103.
73. Morris, like Blake, contrasted the Earthly Paradise with the country afflicted by plague.
74. *Maurice* would have to wait until 1987, though, to be filmed.

Chapter three

Canaries in the Mineshaft

Did the taboo against promiscuity have something to do with the danger of catching VD? But now VD is more easily cured than the flu . . . . Also, what difference whether you have the stigma of being a homosexual or the stigma of being a promiscuous homosexual? If you're going to be stigmatized, the least you can do is enjoy it.

— John Reid, *The Best Little Boy in the World*

WHEN Mark Freedman died of hepatitis while still in his twenties, gay men were shocked. In the early 1970s Freedman was a good-looking young psychologist, one of the first authors to write about gays as an openly gay professional, and his book *Homosexuality and Psychological Functioning* was one of the few pro-gay psychology books available.[1] With his death, the infant gay community was confronted for the first time with the idea that young gay men could be killed by a sexually transmitted disease. There was something of an air of mystery about Freedman's death, and the facts were never explained in any detail. Like the suicide of disillusioned gay activist Mike Silverstein at about the same time, this was felt to be a special case better left uninvestigated. These were forbidden areas, and no one was much inclined to explore them.

Perhaps there was a recognition that the 'lifestyle' implications of Freedman's death, and the rapidly increasing incidence of sexually transmitted disease in the ghetto, could not be investigated without opening up an enormous can of worms. In the midst of a political fight for basic rights and recognition against strong odds, concerns about health, ethics and spirituality seemed like secondary issues – unnecessary additional burdens that could only divert attention from more pressing matters. They could wait, it was felt, until another time.

When we began to come out of the closet *en masse* and attempted to participate in society openly, there was no sanctioned, relevant code of behavior for us to follow, break, adapt or develop. Having dared to cross the sexual rubicon, everything ahead was *terra incognita*, and maps were not only not provided but forbidden, ostensibly nonexistent.

The results were disastrous – especially in the area of sexual behavior. As the post-Stonewall decade progressed, gimcrack sexual ideologies sprang up like toadstools after a spring rain. On the one hand, much of the new gay political establishment adopted a defensive 'we're just like you' attitude to straights which simply perpetuated the myth of the homosexual by highlighting the 'one thing' said to constitute the only truly gay activity: having sex. In order that the claim appear true, everyone whose very existence proved it false was expected simply to disappear: *how* was never stipulated. The 'vanilla fascists' condemned all forms of gay behavior except the most tentative and least likely to offend. Nevertheless, in their out-of-office hours, many of them were to be found in quite unrespectable places hidden from the world outside the ghetto.

The extreme wing of this puritanical faction were the male effeminists, whose 'double-f' insignia inevitably conjured up the double-sig rune of Himmler's SS. The FF were true believers in a simplistically inverted sexual order, with women imperiously running the world and men doing the dishes. Erections were considered improper, and sexual acts which did not conform to stringent notions of reciprocal equality were strictly proscribed.

On the other side (and wielding control of much of the gay media) were the apostles of promiscuity and good fun, the 'party hearty' party. The Canadian gay magazine *The Body Politic* provided their slogan: 'Promiscuity knits together the social fabric of the gay male community.' Dangerous and abusive sexual activities went unquestioned, and anything less than indiscriminate anonymous coupling was characterized as a reactionary attempt to undermine sexual progress.[2]

Any middle ground between these vocal alternatives tended to meet with vehement denunciation from the Lifestyle and Effeminist parties and yawns all around from almost everyone else. Romance and commitment drew snickers. A great many of us, perhaps the majority, continued to believe in them, of course. But we were neither as vocal nor as knowledgeable as we might have been. At best, the community was groping, unaided, toward a moral order, its effort fatally undermined by the psychological and physical damage inflicted on us.

The countercultural revolt of the 1960s ended with the double debacle of the election of Richard Nixon in 1968 and the Manson Family murders in 1969. Charles Manson and his followers called themselves 'the Family' and their drug-fuelled parody only served to emphasize the decline of real family ties and the increasing alienation and atomization of Americans as 'the ME generation' came into its own. And who – among white males – was more alienated and atomized than the ghetto gay? Frequently cut off from his relations, without deep roots or even deep friendships, the work-hard, play-hard, relatively affluent urban gay man was a prototype of the neurotic yuppie to come. And he carried over from the pre-Stonewall era a number of traits, among them chronic depression, an accompanying propensity for alcoholism and drug dependence, and a fixation on youth that negated the possibility of old age while mythologizing suicide and premature death as acts of romantic rebellion.

A secular culture finds it difficult to accommodate the fact of death. No longer is it a transformation, an initiation, or a mystery. Death has become not only frightening but embarrassing. Death is in bad taste. When aging, dying and the spiritual growth symbolized by initiation have lost their meaning, the only goal left is that of an illusory, eternal youth, a kind of impossible dream of arrested development, a parody of the lifelong neoteny Heard so valued. And in no segment of the consumer society were these ideas clutched more tightly and more desperately than in the gay male subculture of the inner cities.

The commercial gay media and social scene of the 1970s and 1980s was a society of youth, with virtually no children or elders, and few women of any age. The ghetto was a country for young men. Life began in the late teens and ended somewhere in the late thirties or early forties. Between the coming out and the mysterious disappearance were twenty years of partying. 'Party hearty!' (or was it 'hardy'?) was a catchphrase of the time. Where did gay men go, after they reached a certain age? Like merchandise that had passed its 'best before' date, they simply disappeared. It is a telling comment on our continuing isolation that so many were able to disappear so mysteriously and so completely.

Breaking through the Stonewall left us with painful psychic wounds whose depths we could scarcely imagine. As one writer put it, 'After the confusion and repression of our teen years, many of us emerge into adult life sexually obsessed and emotionally broken.'[3]

Our isolation had begun to break down at Stonewall. There, for the first time, ordinary gays on the street protested spontaneously and *in public*. Our difficult journey towards becoming what Christopher Isherwood called 'a tribe', a people, had begun. But no people can cohere without social guidelines, and gays, aware of it or not, sought them desperately. When they came, they took the form of commercial messages, controlled for the most part by extensive criminal networks, promoting porn stars as role models, bathhouses as the chief recreation, and drugs to put the gay consumer in the right frame of mind.

America did not want to deal with the need for social evolution that emerging gays represented. Stonewall had shown that straightforward repression would no longer work. Small accommodations were made by the churches, the politicians and the medical establishment, but full acceptance was ruled out. Gay life remained an amoral, quasi-legal activity, and we were accordingly franchised out to organized crime. With our rituals dependent on the bar, the disco and the tubs, the Mafia became a kind of anonymous corporate sponsor of the gay lifestyle.

Frequent prescriptions of antibiotics helped to keep gay men sexually hyperactive, steady customers of doctors and gangsters alike. Gonorrhea and syphilis were said to have been conquered by the miracle of modern medicine; amoebic parasites were considered merely bothersome. Only hepatitis remained as an inhibiting factor, and even that was largely removed after the vaccine experiments of the late 1970s.

Newly liberated people tend to cling to their familiar, subservient mentality. Half-reluctant in their liberation, they find themselves dragged, or thrown, out of Egypt or Babylon and confronted during their years in the wilderness with the disturbing possibility of spiritual rebirth. The traumas inflicted on any people – whether slavery and the slave trade for American blacks or near-genocide for American Indians – are not negated with a snap of the fingers. Psychic wounds last for generations, and damaged spirits usually need a long convalescence.

As gay men, we had nothing with which to bind up our own psychic wounds but a myth in which premature death played a prominent role. Much of the frantic quality of many gay activities derived from the tensions generated by the lingering myth of the homosexual. Our greatest need was for rebirth – but how to achieve it?

By the mid-1970s, the Firehouse had been replaced as the centre of gay activities in New York by the Mineshaft, a warehouse in the meat-packing district that had been converted (by two ex-cops, it was said) into a sex club. In retrospect, the Mineshaft seems aptly named. The unsafe, unhealthy mineshafts of the Victorian era were often supplied with resident caged canaries as an early warning system. Toxic fumes or lack of oxygen would overcome the canaries first, giving the miners (if they were lucky) time to get out. In the Mineshaft of the Stonewall Experiment, gay men were the canaries. By the late 1980s, most of the Mineshaft's regulars were dead.

Under sentence of death

Certain sexual deviations are punishable by death.
— Anita Bryant

As the gay lifestyle accelerated after Stonewall, there was a parallel acceleration of the political forces ranged against gays. The times threw up an anti-gay 'crusade' whose figurehead was one Anita Bryant, a faded beauty queen and paid spokeswoman for the Florida citrus industry. An embarrassment to more worldly Americans, her sanctimonious vulgarity struck a responsive chord in the white hinterlands, and her name became a hated byword among

American gays. Her campaign, masterminded by her abusive husband and cloaked in the cynically canny slogan 'Save Our Children' began in 1977 with a successful attempt to eradicate the civil rights newly won by gays in Florida's Dade County. The Bryant campaign spread the image of gays and lesbians as child molesters – a projection onto a scapegoat group of the wholesale heterosexual child abuse just beginning to be identified in the American family. Bryant's popular book purported to deal with 'The Survival of Our Nation's Families and the Threat of Militant Homosexuality'. And she insisted that gays 'commit sexual suicide', a statement that one psychohistorian suggested was intended as a command.[4]

A subsequent series of 'Anita Bryant laws' began to dismantle gays' recently won civil rights across the country. A florid and power-hungry preacher, Rev Jerry Falwell was encouraged to form his Moral Majority, Incorporated which helped Ronald Reagan win the presidency in 1980, ousting the decent but beseiged Jimmy Carter whose 'born-again' rhetoric was turned against him. 'Direct mail' fundraising campaigns filled the coffers of right-wing groups picturing gays as a well-organized cabal of satanic degenerates intent on subverting America. Falwell's frequent preachings against gays promised that their 'vile and satanic system will one day be utterly annihilated and there will be a celebration in heaven'.[5]

Among the brains behind the homophobic campaign were such figures as the Rev Billy James Hargis, right-wing congressman Robert Baumann, fundraiser Spitz Channell and National Conservative Political Action Committee founder Terry Dolan, all closeted, self-hating homosexuals. Baumann and Hargis were forced out of the closet by sex scandals; Dolan was outed by writer Perry Deane Young in his book *God's Bullies*.[6]

Anita Bryant's cry was taken up by an opportunistic California State Senator, John Briggs, whose campaign to bar supporters to gay rights from teaching positions gained a great deal of support.[7] The United Federation of Teachers which should have defended the civil liberties of its members instead declared its opposition to gay rights, and as the hatred and vituperation increased, the level of violent attacks on gays and lesbians increased with it. A favorite target was the most prominent pro-gay Christian church, the Metropolitan Community Church, whose buildings suffered numerous firebombings.

This was the poisonous political atmosphere confronting gay men and lesbians in the post-Stonewall era. Anti-gay groups served as a malign superego for America, projecting confusion and hatred onto convenient scapegoats. One communication, quoted by Perry Deane Young, read, 'I know what you and I feel about these queers, these fairies. We wish we could get in our cars and run them down.' A number of Christian groups advocated capital punishment for homosexuals, and gay men were counselled to commit suicide rather than to go on living in sin.[8]

The campaign was reflected by the commercial gay media. A fundraising advertisement in the *Advocate* in 1975 began with the headline 'The only happy homosexual is a dead one', and spoke of 'a lifetime of suicide'.[9] A cartoon in the *Advocate* shows a man and a woman surrounded by cigarettes and liquor. She's saying to him, 'You're gay? Is that all? My God, I thought you were gonna tell me you were dying!'[10]

This build-up of death propaganda and the accompanying psychological pressure throughout the post-Stonewall decade was examined in a perceptive but little-read article by Casper G. Schmidt. Published in 1984 in the *Journal of Psychohistory*, the piece on group fantasy and the power of suggestion remained largely unknown to the gay community.[11]

Aware of the close connection between stress states and the impairment of cell-modulated immunity, Dr Schmidt located the beginnings of the downward spiral of health in urban gay men in the 'Shoot a Faggot for Christ' atmosphere that culminated in the assassination of Harvey Milk in 1978 (an event which Schmidt, curiously, does not mention). He refers to the right wing's 'sacrificial witch-hunt' against gays and the parallel campaign against drug addicts, which found both of these subgroups 'acting-out group-sanctioned and group-delegated roles, which acting-out takes place mostly outside of awareness'. The vehement attacks on gays 'resulted in an epidemic of depression based mostly on shame'. Schmidt connected these negative psychological states with conco-mitant cellular changes within the body, identifying the epidemic as 'a wished-for solution to pre-existing conflicts'.

Schmidt believed that such strong, shame-based reactions suggest a deep fear of abandonment, of death by emotional starvation. This would certainly reflect the situation of many gay people ostracized or neglected by their families. 'On a social level, within the group dynamics, this becomes the fear of exclusion from the life-blood of the group, and of ostracism which is the social death of the organism.'[12] 'It is my impression', Schmidt wrote, 'that many people who came out were ill-prepared for what was to follow once they were to meet prejudice face-to-face, since few had sufficiently worked through the issues of shame and guilt involved. More important, many people in mainstream America were just as ill-prepared for it, as became clear in retrospect . . . . In clinical experience, sudden freedom before a person has adequately been prepared is rarely tolerated well, since there is not always sufficient ego structure to cope with it.'[13]

It seems clear that among the results of the stress response cited by Schmidt was an increase in already existing feelings of guilt, loneliness, isolation, depression, powerlessness and anger. These are all emotions which are especially conducive to addictive patterns; through them, the promiscuous dependency on sex and drugs was reinforced, and the downward spiral of ill health accelerated, fuelled by pervasive suggestions of sacrificial death.

One widely-disseminated statement came from one of America's most prominent out-of-the-closet gays, Sgt Leonard Matlovich, a Vietnam combat veteran thrown out of the Air Force for being homosexual. In a 1977 cover story for *Time* magazine, Matlovich responded to the political campaign against gays; 'I fear repression', he said. 'Some gays are going to have to be prepared to make sacrifices – even die.'[14] A brave, conflicted and troubled man, Matlovich died of AIDS ten years later.

By the 1970s, America's projected fantasy of the myth of the homosexual had developed at least four major aspects. It was imagined that gays were (1) child molesters; (2) sinful outlaws; (3) sick; and (4) doomed to die. The 'child molester' charge, whatever political capital it may have had for the right wing, simply bounced off gays. Even among members and sympathizers of the minuscule North American Man/Boy Love Association, a fringe group with few real friends in the community, the majority were men whose tastes ran to boys in the mid-teenage range, not children. Gay men had no difficulty in seeing the child-molestation charge for what it was, a cynical political ploy to play on the fears and guilt of American parents. It made headway only among lesbian separatists, some of whom began to make common cause with censorious right-wing elements. But the attempt at scapegoating with this issue did not succeed on a large scale, because it had no basis of psychic truth. The accused couldn't be made to believe the accusations. Soon enough, the truth – that vast numbers of children, both girls and boys, were routinely molested while in the care of their families – was featured as news all over America. The projection onto the stigmatized group having failed, the dirty secret was soon out.

The myth of the doomed outlaw was not so easily overcome.

A career in suicide – part one: the phenomenology of risk

Caught in the fantasy that I was running free, I ran in chains.
— Rev Malcolm Boyd

The popular American myth of the doomed outlaw was eagerly internalized by gay men, as Casper Schmidt recognized. Another observer who recorded his perceptions on the matter was the poet George Whitmore. Living in New York City through the 1970s and 1980s, Whitmore observed that it had become un-fashionable and 'politically incorrect' to 'link "self-destructive" and "gay" in the same sentence'. Nevertheless, he admitted (even before the onset of AIDS), 'the bodies piled up around me. The roster of gay dead lengthened.'[15]

This fetish for the politically correct became something of a joke among committed gays through the late 1970s into the 1990s, in part because definitions of political correctness tended to blur and change in Orwellian fashion. Some of the contradictions were revealed by the shooting, in Greenwich Village, of the William Friedkin film *Cruising* in 1979. The *Cruising* controversy was a complex one, but at its center was a difference of opinion between on the one hand many gay leathermen and other habitués of the Village bars being filmed, and on the other an alliance of gays and lesbians who opposed co-operation with the makers of the film, seeing it as exploitative and likely to provoke anti-gay attacks.

The film, an interesting but confused portrayal of the 1970s gay lifestyle, focusing on leathermen and pickup bars, involved a running theme of murder and dismemberment, with Al Pacino as an undercover cop searching for a mysterious killer. The murders in the film were based on a then recent series of killings in the Village (including the one at the Anvil on Jamie's opening night). But *Cruising*'s main notoriety came from its offering the rest of America a peek into the refugee camp, and into a world that, without knowledge of depth or context, appeared bizarre and threatening.

The film's producers issued a cattle-call to local leathermen willing to play themselves as extras in the film, and many were happy to turn out and shake their money-makers for the cameras. Cattle-call notwithstanding, these were men who proclaimed themselves 'Proud to be Hot Sex Pigs!' and who saw no reason not to let the rest of the nation rubberneck over the door of the sty.

The diverse group opposing the film had more mixed motives. One of the leading shit-disturbers was the columnist Arthur Bell, who was widely suspected of acting out of jealousy because a big Hollywood production was being lavished on *Cruising* instead of his own gay murder book, *Kings Don't Mean a Thing*. Most of the protesters objected to the film's anticipated superficiality, stereotyping and exploitation of its subject. Beneath these qualms, however, lurked a largely unspoken fear: that the film might spotlight all too starkly aspects of urban gay life best left in the dark.

Most gay men joined neither group, lining up anonymously to pay for their tickets when the film appeared. Film critic Vito Russo made the point that 'middle class gays in America have sought to have it both ways. They do not want to see the sexual ghetto life . . . portrayed as the only side of the gay world, but at the same time they are unwilling to affiliate themselves as homosexuals in order to demonstrate the reality to the rest of America.'[16] This constituted a much more serious problem than either the straight world, or most gays, recognized.

Shame, ambivalence and simple prudence mingled behind the slogans of the protests, the simplest and most vocal of which was 'Stop *Cruising*', as an attempt was made to shut the movie down.

Gay businesses in the Village chose up sides as some expansively invited the film crews inside and others covered their street signs to prevent even outside shooting.

All over the Village, stencilled, spray-painted slogans began to appear:

STOP
CRUISING

Then the protesters recognized the double meaning of their message; the slogans seemed to caution as much against an activity as a film! Embarrassment all round. New stencils were quickly made up with the wording amended to:

STOP
THE MOVIE
CRUISING

A few years later, when AIDS hit and the bodies piled up in greater numbers than either *Cruising* or George Whitmore could have imagined, the faded remnants of the original 'Stop Cruising' stencils could occasionally be seen, spectral messages from the past, offering ambiguous advice to any still compulsively cruising sexual outlaws.

It was George Whitmore who linked the outlaw mindset to another pervasive American theme with which he was intimately familiar: loneliness. In a 1975 article entitled 'Living Alone', he wrote about 'an invisible piece of furniture in your apartment that you stumble over all the time – it's a mass of loneliness'. For many gay men, loneliness had become another addiction. George Whitmore again, in the same piece: 'Many of us who have put sex in its place are troubled by its frequent coincidence with love. Love,' he ventured, 'screws everything up.'[17]

He suggested that coming out means 'severing' yourself from your own past, becoming 'unmoored . . . floating', and in a chilling phrase, he warned that in the collective mind, the gay ghetto was nothing more than 'a leper colony'.[18] 'We were branded the enemy, exiled, ultimately invisible and isolated. Some of us are dead. That's the final kind of alone.' And in his conclusion, George counted himself among those who 'have found the means of being alone for the rest of our lives' – an honest observation that did not bode well.

Whitmore realized that 'Stonewall might have coincided with Judy's death, and the party line might have dictated that there were no more victims, but the phenomenon of gay self-destruction, of course, did not disappear.'[19] He recognized the depth of the psychological damage caused by millennia of repression, sex-negativism and self-hatred, and by deep wounds that in many cases would never really heal. For many, the closest door opened into a prison. In such dark places, 'leprosy' could only flourish, and there were many ways to commit suicide, with or without the help of doctors.

Whitmore saw what many less troubled observers preferred to ignore, and in another article, 'After a "career" in suicide: choosing to live', he provided some painful insights into the psychology of the lonely outlaw. In this piece, written in 1982, just as fear of the plague was beginning to impinge on the gay consciousness, Whitmore wrote about the three attempts at suicide he had made, the first when he was only seventeen. In one attempt, he overdosed on drugs prescribed to 'calm' him. Suicide was something, he said, that he applied himself to 'with dedication . . . . Like so many others, I was doing everything I could not to come to terms with an identity I'd been carefully taught to abhor.'[20]

He wrote wryly that when he travelled to New York City and came out, since he 'was no longer teetering on window ledges high above traffic, I didn't really appreciate the sophisticated means of suicide at my disposal. Now, when I do think of what I did to myself, the crap I poured into my system, the lost weekends, the risks I felt compelled to take – everything was considered "normal" in the process of coming out – it makes my hair stand on end. I can only conclude that accidentally I continued to live . . . . For I was judge, jury and executioner the likes of which the Moral Majority would fervently applaud.'

The piece continued with some more up-to-date experiences: 'It is 1981 and I am in the basement of the Mineshaft. Like most everyone else here, I have come to prove a point. The point is that we can do this without flinching. Oh, we might say we come here to have fun or let off steam, but there is an undercurrent here, a subtext. It is the element of risk. It is not just the risk of disease. It is that we have learned to witness certain acts with a jaded and sceptical eye . . . . It looks dangerous, but is it really? This is the phenomenology of risk, and we are expert at it.'

As Whitmore saw it, the Mineshaft and the other bathhouses and backroom bars 'joined nihilism to lust' in a kind of synthetic pornographic rebellion, in living color. (Quentin Crisp made the quip that 'pornography is the selling of sex without mentioning the price.'[21]) 'How long could you live', Whitmore asked, 'in the constant anxiety of placating a stern and unforgiving God knowing how warped, imperfect, how queer you were?' The Stonewall Experiment gave us the chance to find out, by inducing us to act out our rebelliousness – on the oppressor's terms.

'The Rebel', Whitmore wrote, 'is a consummate symbol of reaction, because that's all he does; his life revolves around rebellion, fury and denial.' Denial, denial, denial: trademark of the compulsive, addicted personality. The Rebel 'is a pyrrhic symbol of our revolt, an emblem of misdirected rage . . . . If society tells him the only way he can be gay is to crawl around on his hands and knees in a sewer five nights a week, the Rebel will oblige . . . . And having fervently embraced the role assigned to him – that of outcast and pariah – he must never relent, relax or weaken. He is, instead, driven to further extremities of alienation. Intimacy becomes impossible, even the one-night stand variety. The only actual relationship is a dim, ironic camaraderie with his fellows.'

Few in those days recognized as George did that 'this is how many gay men have misunderstood and internalized the message of gay liberation: sadly losing themselves in the process . . . . Almost all our common commercial institutions have been set up to promulgate a Rebel lifestyle. The most visible aspects of gay life are his, and the ones glorified by most of our magazines and even our ideologues.' George called this commercially promoted lifestyle a 'new kind of victimization, this unexamined life'.

The impulses that led young men to join in these darkly alluring activities had something in common with feelings that an older writer of the time recalled encountering in himself as a young man, decades earlier. 'It seemed to me', he wrote, 'that I had passed a threshold, and that in passing it, I was dimly dismissing something from where I had come: my land, my past, the traditions of my country. But these men fascinated me and I wanted to incorporate myself there. I perceived them as strong, generous and pitiless: beings without weakness who would never putrefy.' The words are those of the French author Christian de La Mazière, remembering his emotions when, thirty years earlier, he joined the Waffen SS.[22]

For both Whitmore and de La Mazière, the erotic image (whether of leathermen, biker, clone or SS man) invited and symbolized an aggression against society which drew on longstanding feelings of inferiority and victimization, and which was deeply conformist, destructive, and ultimately nihilistic. When such images of rebellion are seized upon, co-opted, packaged and sold, their meaning is necessarily transformed into that of group, rather than individual, phenomena. The manipulation of the iconography signifies the manipulation of the newly-defined group. When, in addition, powerful totems of masculinity are involved, all the dangers of the masculine dark side gather like a storm.

Both the pitiless Hitler Youth clones and the peaceful gay clones represented a resurgence of qualities long repressed in the Christian West – dionysian, homoerotic, pagan. In both instances, politico-economic forces determined that Homeros remain kept from his 'true light', and political manipulation ensured that the dark side of those qualities would predominate. Gay clones were a homosexual version of what masculinity had become, and was becoming, in the post-Nazi twentieth century. When it became clear that gays weren't going away, a commercialized, consumerist version of our sexuality was conceded to us, a sexuality all the more frantic for being emptied of deep emotion. This fuelled a machine without oil, which could only burn itself out until it seized up completely.

George Whitmore's observations were complemented by those of another perceptive insider, John Rechy. The hustler narrator of his novel *City of Night* is offered love, and rejects it as a myth 'which could lull you again falsely in order to seduce you – like that belief in God – into a trap – away from the only thing which made sense – rebellion – no matter how futilely rendered by the fact of decay, of death'.[23] Rechy's counterpointing of rebellion and decay is strikingly similar to de La Mazière's fantasy of the SS as offering young men salvation from 'putrefaction'.

In Rechy's books, gay sex constitutes an outlaw country, pitted against the everyday world. Promiscuous gays are revolutionary 'shock troops' and love is a slippery slope to a confrontation with the terrifying fact of one's true identity. Outlaws and shock troops are not known for their high rate of survival.

The years of the Stonewall Experiment were supposedly a time of liberation, yet with the brand of the outlaw still burned into faces and souls, there remained an ingrained need to gravitate to dark and dangerous places and faceless partners, as though still in an oppressive, lingering trance.

Whitmore remarked early in the 1980s that 'self-delusion makes it mandatory to rationalize' this behavior as merely a matter of taste. He saw it instead as having a 'great deal to do with how we perceive ourselves collectively and as individuals'. 'We are now', he wrote, 'a minority characterized more for our diseases and disabilities than for our achievements and aspirations; we are still handy victims, used to the role', unwilling to examine the lives we were living, or the substances we were taking.[24]

Addictive substances had a traditional role in disempowering fractious American minorities. The decimation and demoralization of the Indian was achieved in large part by liquor and disease, and for the American black, heroin and crack cocaine served as a powerful escape from intolerable conditions. Sales of both substances enriched white society while diluting the rage of subject populations. In the gay ghetto, you could 'choose your poison' from a considerable array.

The genie in the little brown bottle

Ahah! Heh heh heh heh heh heh heh heh! So! You won't take warning eh? All the worse for you. And now, my beauties – something with poison in it I think. With poison in it! But attractive to the eye!
— The Wicked Witch of the West, *The Wizard of Oz*

In 1902, Lionel Johnson, a homosexual poet with a reputation for alcoholism, decided to have just one more little drink, fell off his bar stool, cracked his head open and died at the age of thirty-five.

The debilitating effects of drug and alcohol poisoning have been a traditional hazard for our people, claiming many gay and lesbian lives – almost certainly more lives than AIDS. As I write this in the mid-1990s, the gay bar (often controlled by organized crime) is still the focal point of the gay community. It has been estimated that about 20 per cent of the gay population – both men and women – are afflicted by alcoholism.[25] And alcoholism injures every system of the body – including the immune system. By the 1970s, a variety of other substances had joined alcohol as 'recreational drugs' of choice in the inner city gay refugee camps. They were ubiquitous, and used with great avidity. Together with the antibiotics repeatedly prescribed for frequent venereal disease, they contributed to a potent chemical soup in the bodies of a large number of gay men for well over a decade.

Of all the drugs funnelled into the gay ghetto of the 1970s, the most noticeable, the most widely used and the most available (with the exception of alcohol and tobacco) were poppers. So called because they were first distributed in small containers that were 'popped' to release fumes, poppers usually came in little brown bottles with plastic, screw-on tops, selling for a few dollars each. Like tobacco and alcohol, they were quite legal, and needed no prescription.

When inhaled on the dance floor, poppers give a flushed, heady feeling, a kind of throbbing, warm 'rush' to complement the strobe lights and insistent beat. Inhaled during sex-play, they enhance sexual arousal and seem to prolong orgasm. They became a staple of ghetto life, promoted almost exclusively through the commercial gay magazines and gathering-places. They can be very addictive; as one investigator put it, 'the more you sniff poppers at any one time, the less effect they have on you.'[26] A lot of gay men came to depend on them so much they became unable to function sexually without them; even masturbation had to be accompanied by poppers.

In the gay ghetto of the 1970s, poppers were omnipresent. On any given night in the Anvil, a large percentage of the men on the dance floor would be taking frequent snorts from the little brown bottles being passed around. Some disco clubs would even add to the general euphoria by occasionally spraying the dance floor with poppers fumes. Michael Rumaker describes the bathhouses as 'permeated with that particularly inert, greasy odor of poppers. Wherever you went, the musky chemical smell of it was constantly in your nostrils.' When he stuck his head out of that little window, it was in order to breathe 'something other than the cold, kerosene smell of amyl'.[27]

My own most vivid memory of poppers in action is from Fire Island, sometime in the 1970s. I was visiting friends in the Pines and was spending a couple of hours at the disco one night. Inevitably there were one or two people I knew among the crowd. One of them was George Whitmore, whose observations from the floor of the Mineshaft we heard earlier. I had gotten to know George a little when I helped publish his book of poems, *Getting Gay in New York*. I liked him, but whenever I ran into him (usually at the newsstand on Sixth Avenue near Christopher Street) he struck me as a sad figure, solitary, unsmiling, rather downcast and always maintaining a perceptible distance between himself and everyone else. But on this occasion, George was dancing, and inhaling liberally from a poppers bottle in the pocket of his jeans. Somehow in the course of the evening, the bottle broke, spilling over George's thigh and burning into his flesh. I wondered what damage inhaling the stuff must do.

The original medicinal form of poppers was amyl nitrate, a vascular dilator prescribed for the occasional use of heart patients. A monopoly on the product was held by the giant British-based pharmaceutical company Burroughs Wellcome. When nitroglycerine tablets replaced amyl as the prescription of choice for angina during the 1960s, Burroughs Wellcome began to look around for other, more lucrative markets for the product. They found their test market in the jungle battlefields of Vietnam. During the height of the carnage in the 1960s, poppers were being shipped literally by the crateful to the boys in Nam – supposedly to counter the effects of gun fumes! *(see plate 5)*.

The average GI in that theatre of war was strung out on a variety of mood-enhancing substances including marijuana, opium, heroin and amphetamines. The military in those days had a casual attitude to drug use and quite a few back-line supply sergeants found they could use their Mafia contacts from civilian life to transport drugs from Southeast Asia to the US. From 1966 or 1967 until the end of American involvement in the war in the mid-1970s, drugs streamed into American cities from the war zone. The drug culture of the 1970s was fuelled by the Vietnam war, and when the war was lost, operations were transferred to Latin America, with cocaine and crack replacing heroin as the street drug of choice. For the boys in Nam, nitrite inhalents, legal and easy to carry, were a welcome addition to the chemical stew.[28]

In the wake of their popularity on the battlefields of democracy, the US Food and Drug Administration sanctioned over-the-counter sales, making poppers available to the American public. Profits soared, but after about a year, the first reports of peacetime casualties began to come in. Terrible skin burns, blackouts, breathing difficulties and blood anomalies caused amyl to be once again placed under government restriction.

Once the genie is released from the bottle, it is not so easy to put him back. The ban on amyl quickly became ineffective when a gay medical student in California, Clifford Hassing, made a slight change in its molecular structure and applied to patent *butyl* nitrite. When patent rights were denied, Hassing maintained it was because the Federal Government did not want to get involved in either banning or approving a drug that by then was being sold almost exclusively to homosexuals. 'They'll bury their heads in the sand', he said, 'as long as it's a homosexual issue.'[29]

It wasn't long before larger 'entrepreneurs' (nominally independent operatives controlled by big-time crime syndicates) elbowed their way into the now obviously lucrative poppers market, out-advertising and out-muscling Hassing's small company. And further chemical changes were made; both butyl and isobutyl nitrite are more toxic and even faster acting than the original amyl.

From this point, the story of poppers becomes a classic instance of free enterprise and government regulation coming to a mutually agreeable *modus vivendi*. The unwritten agreement seems to have been as follows: as long as the overall marketing campaign of poppers targetted only gay men, public distribution would be allowed. The cynical fiction which facilitated this arrangement was the claim that the product was a 'room odorizor' and that used as such it was not harmful! As the authors of the poppers exposé *Death Rush* commented, 'If a drug like butyl nitrite can be [legally] marketed as a "room odorizor", then anything could be sold as anything. Heroin could be sold as a mosquito-bite remedy . . . . Live hand grenades could be sold as paperweights.'[30]

But as one poppers manufacturer admitted, as long as the bottles were marked 'room odorizor' and sold only to gay men, 'nobody cared'. Poppers became a multi-million dollar business and most of the magazines aimed at gay men ran ads for them. The well known brands often took full-page color ads. A few of the more principled gay papers refused poppers ads. But for the more commercial gay media that increasingly had replaced the gay-run movement papers as sources of information for gay men, poppers manufacturers constituted the single largest source of income. For the ghetto gay, poppers became an accepted part of gay sex. There was even a gay comic strip called *Poppers*.

When reports on the results of medical research on poppers began to appear in scientific journals, a couple of gay activists, one on the West coast, one on the East, followed their curiosity and began to collect the evidence. Hank Wilson and John Lauritsen published their findings in their 1986 book *Death Rush: Poppers & AIDS*, which provides a compendium of evidence drawn from research studies on poppers' harmful effects and a look at the political campaign which was an essential part of the marketing strategy.[31] Apart from causing localized damage to the nasal membranes when inhaled, poppers have been linked to anemia, strokes, heart, lung and brain damage, arterial constriction, cardiovascular collapse and, most tellingly, the thymus atrophy and chronic depletion of the T-cell ratio associated with immune disfunction. Several studies of both mice and humans have connected the drug to AIDS, and specifically to the disfiguring skin lesions of Kaposi's sarcoma.

In the toxic playpen of the ghetto, poppers were everywhere, and only a few cautionary voices were raised. Articles on the possible dangers of nitrite inhalents appeared in *Christopher Street*[32] and a small magazine called *Coming Up!*[33] The financial magazine *Moneysworth* ran a brief interview with one researcher, Roger P. Maickel, who cited his finding that even small doses of nitrite inhalent tended to have the serious effect of de-oxygenating the blood. 'If you get enough of it in your body', he maintained, 'the chances of saving you are zero.' He warned (this was in January 1982) that if no action was taken, there would be 'a spate of deaths that could have been avoided'.[34] Oxygen deficiency was later found to contribute to T-lymphocyte irregularities and compromised immunity.[35]

In 1977, a complaint from a student in California resulted in an attempt to prosecute the makers of a brand of poppers known as Rush. The suit charged that the product could 'cause death when used as advertised'; evidence from emergency rooms, a gay doctor and the State's Drug Abuse Warning Network indicated various harmful effects. The manufacturer, the late W. Jay Freezer, 'the Pope of poppers', wrapped himself in the flag of private enterprise. When a temporary injunction was granted against Rush, Freezer simply changed the product name to Bolt and continued selling. The State gave up.

In 1978, Freezer commissioned several physicians (for a fee of $200,000 according to Lauritsen and Wilson) to issue a spurious 'research' report exonerating poppers from causing illness by the simple means of testing the drug as if 'used for odorizing purposes', in other words opened and left on a shelf to evaporate instead of being inhaled directly into the nostrils, the universal mode of use. Freezer was also able to corral a number of eminent medical men to deny poppers' harmful effects. On the basis of this disingenuous 'research' the State of California decided to continue to permit the sale of poppers without any regulation or control – as long as the words 'room odorizer' appeared in small print somewhere on the bottle!

A few years later, after the onset of AIDS, the 'room odorizor' ploy was worked again, this time before hearings in Wisconsin. On this occasion, the poppers industry's scientific 'experts' included the Establishment's favorite gay 'leader' Dr Bruce Voeller (of *Gay Post* notoriety). Voeller's most recent claim to fame at this time was his crediting himself with having coined the acronym AIDS to replace the politically incorrect GRID (Gay Related Immune Disorder). This time, the funky perfume argument failed and poppers were banned in the State of Wisconsin. According to the Committee to Monitor

Poppers, Voeller's 'expenses' on this junket were paid by Great Lakes Products, one of the largest of the poppers manufacturers.

Unfortunately, most of the gay men targeted by the poppers promotion campaign knew little or nothing of these battles. Dependent on poppers revenue, the commercial gay press for the most part kept quiet. One attempt to break the silence came from a public-spirited researcher, E. Sue Watson, who wrote in 1982 to the late Robert McQueen, editor of the *Advocate*, stating: 'Our studies show that amyl nitrite strongly suppresses the segment of the immune system (cellular immunity) which normally protects individuals against Kaposi's sarcoma, Pneumocystis pneumonia, herpes virus, Candida, amebiasis, and a variety of other opportunistic infections. The upshot of this research is that persons using nitrite inhalents may be at risk for development of AIDS . . . . Publication of this letter in the *Advocate* will serve to alert the community to the health risks of using amyl nitrite.'[36]

When McQueen did not reply to her letter, Dr Watson telephoned him. She was told, 'We're not interested.' Her letter never appeared. Soon afterwards, the *Advocate* began printing a series of ads for Great Lakes Products' brands of poppers. Obviously meant to counter rumours about the effects of the drug, the new ads bore the cynical banner headline 'Blueprint for Health' *(see plate 6)*. With the onset of AIDS, bathhouses were now being promoted as 'health clubs'. Columns by the paper's in-house health expert, Nathan Fain, touting poppers' harmlessness, were co-ordinated to appear in the same issues.[37]

A letter in the archives of the Committee to Monitor Poppers indicates a little more of the story. Written by the president of Great Lakes Products, it reads in part, 'As the largest advertiser in the Gay press we intend to use the extensive ad space we purchase each month as a vehicle for sending a message of good health and wellness through nutrition and exercise to the North American Gay communitites [*sic*].'

A study in the *American Journal of Psychiatry* estimates that by 1978, poppers industry profits amounted to $50 million a year, with about 100,000 bottles a week sold in a single city.[38] Hovering in the background of all this was a US Federal agency which plays a part in the story of AIDS as it did in the story of syphilis in a slightly earlier time, the Center for Disease Control. In spite of mounting evidence against poppers, and numerous entreaties both before and after the onset of the AIDS crisis, the CDC continually equivocated, stalled and stonewalled. Neither it nor its Canadian counterpart ever acted to warn the public about poppers or take them off the market. Where poppers were finally banned, it was state and provincial legislatures, responding to public pressure, that did the job, not the federal agencies responsible for public health and safety.

Legal loopholes and a massive advertising campaign made poppers so popular in the gay ghettos that one writer called the poppers bottle 'the holy vial' which when inhaled makes you 'roll into the sea'.[39] What were the messages of these persuasive ads?

Here is an issue of *Drummer*, 'America's Mag for the Macho Man', for 1981,[40] though it could be any one of a number of gay magazines for which poppers provided a major source of revenue. The front cover shows a good-looking young guy in an undershirt with his (obscured) cock in one hand and a can of beer in the other. The full-page color ad on the back cover provides our not-so-subliminal image. This ad is for a brand of poppers called Hardware which the secondary ad copy touts as 'The ultimate in purity . . . For power you can count on . . . Available at retail outlets worldwide.' There is a toll-free phone number for dealer enquiries and a customer order form. The full color air-brush painting is of an open bottle of the product surrounded by and seemingly giving rise to the distinctive, death-seeding mushroom cloud of an atomic (or hydrogen) bomb. In the head of this reddish-gold phallic cloud are two human, slightly blurred but apparently male, faces, their eyes closed, their noses appearing to melt or dissolve. 'Intensely Powerful' proclaims the prominent slogan *(see plate 7)*.

For the many gay male readers to which the ad, and hundreds of other poppers ads, were directed, the message's invitation to sex, potency and death was pretty clear. Just to impress the point, the atomic cloud also contains a second, subliminal image, rising vaporously out of the cloud-head and hovering between the melting faces: the head of a white bull, apparently snorting (for poppers, like coke, are 'snorted').

The subliminal image of the bull makes its appeal directly to the unconscious as one of the oldest and most universal symbols of earthy male potency and strength. It was a man with a bull's head who lurked at the center of the ancient labyrinth; and even earlier, the white bull was the traditional mount of Minu, the Egyptian ithyphallic god of sex and fecundity, who traditionally held his penis in his left hand – as does the young hunk on the other half of the wrap-around *Drummer* cover.[41]

Advertisements often depicted poppers as a speeding bullet or bomb, or with suggestive names like 'Satan's Scent': ads for this one, depicting a grimacing devil, offered a free Lambda pin – symbol of Gay Lib – with every purchase. An ad for a product called 'Cum' showed the poppers bottle itself as a dripping cock and balls. One widely used crystalline 'designer drug' was called Kryptonite, after the extraterrestrial rock that could weaken and destroy even Superman; a poppers manufacturer cashed in on Kryptonite's popularity by naming his brand Crypt Tonight.

In these promotions the mingled imagery of potency and death reflected the myth of the homosexual as a kind of sex machine, doomed by its own potency, much like the out-of-control robot called the Danish Vibrator in Leonard Cohen's novel *Beautiful Losers*, which eventually goes berserk and throws itself into the sea. For, as Cohen's compatriot, Marshall McLuhan, reminds us, ads 'are not meant for conscious consumption. They are intended as subliminal pills for the subconscious in order to exercise an hypnotic spell.'[42]

It was during the 1950s that McLuhan and others began their systematic studies of the psychology of advertising. One pioneer of market research, Pierre Martineau, saw that for maximum effect, cigarette ads should reflect 'the core meanings of smoking: masculinity, adulthood, vigor, and potency'. He cautioned that if these meanings were expressed too openly, consumers might reject them 'quite violently'. Indirect expression would be more effective.[43]

This approach was continued, and developed, in the poppers ads calculated to appeal to 1970s gay men, but while cigarette ads avoided any suggestion of harmful effects, some poppers ads used a hint of danger to spice up the appeal. The A-bomb ad uses death imagery at its most overt, combined with verbal and subliminal appeals to 'masculinity and potency'.

Poppers were among the most harmful of the various drugs and toxins systematically introduced into the gay ghettos. And in this pharmaceutical array, poppers stand out for three reasons. They were new, they were legal, and they were targeted almost exclusively at ghetto gays. It is because of poppers' legality that we have such a clear record of their promotion.

The legal, mass introduction of poppers into the gay community played a key role in determining the direction of the Stonewall Experiment. One aspect of that role was the influence poppers manufacturers were able to exert on the gay press. Before Stonewall, there had been few gay periodicals in America, generally produced on a shoe-string and with very small circulations, mostly among members of homophile organizations. The largest gay newspaper was the *Advocate*, which developed from a local Los Angeles newsletter into a national bi-weekly. After Stonewall, a flurry of new gay periodicals strung up, from radical Gay Lib papers to newly-visible glossy porno mags financed by organized crime. The *Advocate* was sold by its original owners to one David Goodstein, a millionaire gay entrepreneur with political ambitions in the newly tolerated gay mainstream.

Periodicals in America survive, for the most part, by selling advertising space. But even in the 1990s, very few large-scale, legitimate businesses would advertise in gay magazines. So the gay newspaper or magazine had to decide whether to try to survive more or less without advertising, or to seek and accept what advertising was available – and to conform to the needs and requirements of those advertisers. During the period from 1969 through the early 1980s, by far the largest single slice of gay advertising revenue came from poppers manufacturers, with much of the gay media heavily dependent on poppers revenue. Poppers manufacturers played a crucial part in determining which gay-oriented media would survive and which would not. And those that relied on poppers ads rarely criticized the source of their survival.

Both by their own pervasive presence, and by their mob-controlled suppliers' influence over gay men's major sources of information, nitrite inhalents helped mould the pattern of sexual and social relations of the post-Stonewall era. It would be foolish to expect criminal syndicates to have a tradition of community responsibility, and members of communities that are delivered into their hands may expect to be used and discarded as they are urged to use and discard one another. That is the nature of organized crime, which acts as a kind of rapacious parasite. The host society could eliminate the parasite, but chooses not to, imagining that its depradations will be limited to only one part of the body – perhaps a part which in ignorance is assumed to be useless. The result is corrosive, and lethal.

After poppers had been banned in my home province of Ontario, I was disturbed to see that the local bi-weekly gay magazine continued to advertise them for sale, imported from Quebec. In an unsuccessful attempt to persuade them to change their policy, I contacted one of the local AIDS action groups. Their spokesperson, a well-known Person With AIDS, told me bluntly that he would not help me as he was an enthusiastic user of poppers and believed they should be available to everyone. As this man was taking pentamidine treatments for his inflamed lungs, I suspect that, like so many gay men of our generation, he had become so addicted to poppers that even a potentially fatal illness could not deter him. He has since passed away, though his rubber gloves (for he was careful to practice only safe sex) are available for viewing at the Canadian Gay Archives in Toronto.

The allopathic model – drugs in the ghetto

But people dulled by pain can sing and dance till morning and find no pleasure in it.

— James Baldwin

> Bilbo screamed out loud, '*We are all drugged out of our tits!*'
> Fred thought: You name it, somebody's on it.
> MDA, MDM, THC, PCP, STP, DMT, LDK, WDW, Coke, Window Pane, Blotter, Orange Sunshine, Sweet Pea, Sky Blue, Christmas Tree, Mascaline, Dust, Benzedrene, Dexedrine, Dexamyl, Desoxyn, Strychnine, Ionamin, Ritalin, Desbutal, Opitol, Glue, Ethyl Chloride, Nitrous Oxide, Crystal Methedrine, Clogidal, Nasperan, Tytch, Nestex, Black

Beauty, Certyn, Preludin with B-12, Zayl . . . and the Downs,
keep it mellow, don't get too excited, Downs make us feel so
sexy!, Quaalude, Tuinal, Nembutal, Seconal, Amytal, Pheno-
barb, Elavil, Valium, Librium, Darvon, Mandrax, Opium,
Stidyl, Halidax, Calcifyn, Optimil, Drayl . . .

This list of popular recreational drugs is from Larry Kramer's
funny, bitter, heartbreaking *tour de force* through the gay ghetto of
New York in his 1978 satire *Faggots*.[44] Omissions (at that particular
party) include Ecstasy, several of the more sinister 'designer drugs'
and Warfarin, an anti-coagulent rat poison which occasionally got
sold as a stimulant called 'French blues'.[45]

The commercial gay scene was fuelled by drugs, both legal
and illegal. Their use served many purposes: suppressing anxieties
about sexuality and concealment, counteracting the continuing
sense of being devalued, enhancing identity, dulling pain and
providing escape. But another type of drug was just as ubiquitous in
the commercial ghetto, and just as essential for that ghetto's
continued functioning: antibiotics. From penicillin and tetracycline
(for countering gonnorrhea and syphilis) to flagyl and the various
heavy-duty killers (for handling amoebic and other parasitic infestations of the bowel) antibiotics kept the gay lifestyle afloat, and
kept gay men alive and ostensibly well until mid-1981.

An article in an issue of *Newsweek* magazine that year, just as
news of the illnesses that came to be grouped as AIDS was beginning
to break, drew attention to the 'unusual assortment of disorders'
that had arisen in the gay community. Among them: syphilis,
hepatitis, cytomegalovirus, amoebiasis (increased by 7,000 percent
since 1974), herpes and 'intestinal infections usually seen in the
tropics'. A New York internist is quoted as saying that 'the health
problems of homosexuals used to be no different from those of
heterosexuals. But in the last five or six years there's been a major
change.' The change, of course, was America's response to the
challenge of gay liberation: its promotion of the commercial gay
lifestyle. One physician with a largely gay practice mentioned that
'the large number of anonymous contacts in gay bathhouses
increases the risk'.[46]

Peter McGehee summed up the attitude of a generation of gay youth in his story 'Sex and love': 'I felt I'd actually arrived as I stood in the VD clinic taking my handful of penicillin. A real homosexual.'[47] Michael Callen recalled *Joy of Gay Sex* co-author Edmund White saying 'gay men should wear their sexually transmitted diseases like red badges of courage in a war against a sex-negative society', and he remembered nodding and saying to himself, 'Gee! Every time I get the clap I'm striking a blow for sexual liberation.'[48]

One former 'circuit queen' remembered: 'Life on N.Y.'s gay circuit meant three things: hard men, soft drinks, and drugs . . . Now, where did you go after you had spent the night on the dance floor of desperate optimism, waiting for the partner that failed to appear? Well, you could go home to a lonely apartment to take a Quaalude and some vitamins (ridiculous!) and sleep through the day, or you went to seek love at the baths. You might as well have panned the Hudson River for gold! . . . The circuit . . . didn't bring men together, the drugs only intensified our alienation. . . . We didn't learn to honor ourselves, our bodies, or our lovers.'[49]

Drugs and sexually transmitted diseases placed increasing stress on the health of gay men throughout the 1970s. And the system of allopathic medicine subscribed to by their doctors often attacked symptoms while neglecting underlying causes. Frequent bouts of sexually transmitted diseases were treated by progressively stronger doses of antibiotics. The weaker bacteria and parasites were wiped out; the stronger mutated, necessitating still stronger antibiotics. When combined with a generous selection of recreational drugs, the damage to the immune system was severe. Yet drugs were the fuel that kept the ghetto functioning, by keeping the consumers ambulatory and suppressing physical and mental symptoms.

This influx of chemical products into an emergent community recalled the social reaction to the rise of black militance a few years earlier. Brother Baldwin put it succinctly: 'Then, drugs were dumped into the ghetto, to take the young.'[50]

The 'hippie' movement was similarly countered. The Gathering of the Tribes, otherwise known as the Human Be-In, was held in San Francisco's Golden Gate Park on 19 January 1967. Thirty thousand young people assembled to hear The Grateful Dead, Jefferson Airplane, Jerry Rubin, Allen Ginsberg, Gary Snyder and Tim Leary in a promising coming together of the counterculture and the New Left. 'It was the last innocent, idealistic hippie event', wrote Ginsberg's biographer Barry Miles. 'That night the police swept down Haight Street; all soft-drug dealers were driven off the scene or arrested, and within weeks the area was flooded with amphetamine and heroin. The communal nature of soft drugs – pot and acid – as demonstrated by the cleaning up of the park, was destroyed and replaced by the amphetamine culture which would produce Charles Manson.'[51]

Now that it was gay men's turn to be emancipated, they suffered a similar fate, and many gay liberationists soon became frustrated, disappointed, or bitter at the outcome of their rebellion.[52] The important questions posed by Harry Hay years before still remained unanswered: Who are we? Where do we come from? What are we for?

Death rituals

The crisis consists precisely in the fact that the old is dying and the new cannot be born; in this interregnum a great variety of morbid symptoms appear.

— Antonio Gramsci

In an insightful study of drugs and initiation, the Italian psychologist Luigi Zoja discusses contemporary Western society's fear of death and its repression of the archetypes of death, 'the most extensive repressed area of our time'.[53] Zoja comments that 'when an archetype is repressed, it tends to resurface ever more irrationally . . . and eventually merges with other repressions – evil, destructiveness, and the archetype of the shadow.' He compares this process to the 'flaring out of control' of the witch-hunts as a consequence of Western culture's exaggerated denial of the feminine. In this ambivalent psychic tension about death, as in many other respects, the Stonewall Experiment signalled emerging psychosocial attitudes and problems.

Zoja emphasizes the powerful psychological need for initiation, especially among young males, making the point that when attempts at initiation are not fully conscious, and are unsanctioned and unprotected by society, the death element tends to become actuated, and death rituals begin to take shape.[54]

In the religious rites of consumerism, the initiatory process has been largely displaced, returning in negative form as addiction and drug abuse. Zoja writes that 'when the initiatory process is not satisfying and complete enough an experience, one can be tempted to persist in it with increasing fury. This insistence can at times lead to an intensification of the material process without necessarily augmenting the psychic one . . . A need which is not expressed symbolically always tends to become literalized.'[55] If a need for *symbolic* death and rebirth, for initiation, cannot be expressed, then the impulse to physical death, to suicide – by one means or another – comes to the fore.

Social critics such as Kenneth Burke and Thomas Szasz have contended that 'the sacrificial principle of victimage ("the scape-goat") is intrinsic to human congregation' and that in a scientific culture such as ours, sacrificial motives and rituals simply take on new forms.[56] In this scenario, drugs play a central role.

Dr Zoja's study, *Drugs, Addiction and Initiation: The Modern Search for Ritual* has special relevance here. Zoja deals with the relation between the pervasive abuse of drugs in Western society and the lack of any kind of socially sanctioned structures of initiation, especially for young men. Identifying the consumerist culture as the dominant religion of our time, he recognizes that the need for participation rituals is often assuaged – especially by alienated groups – by the consumerist rite of drugtaking, which offers both shared ritualistic experience and an escape from painful reality. As another commentator put it, 'the sharing of a common ceremonial . . . removes one of the curses of the modern world, the sense of belonging nowhere, of having no bonds or attachments, of being a bleak anonymity in a vast megalopolis.'[57]

An initiation is a symbolic death and rebirth – the death of the old status or personality and its rebirth in a transformed, reawakened state. When the pathways to self-discovery are blocked and the labyrinth sealed, with no apparent way out, rebirth – the coming together of living elements in a new creation – becomes impossible; only the death aspect of the experience remains. The

Minotaur devours the youthful sacrifices thrown to it. And 'it is in the world of drugs that the theme of death is continually activated . . . [A] link exists between turning to drugs and the unconscious theme of death-and-renewal.'[58]

Another researcher into homoerotic rituals, Robert H. Hopcke, also found structures parallelling those of well-known rites initiating males into the realm of archetypal masculinity. He discovered, however, that the final stage of initiation – incorporation back into the community with a new social status reflecting new understanding – was often poorly developed, compared to 'the creativity and profusion of the first two stages', separation and transition. Hopcke suggested the commodification of sexuality as one of the factors undermining ritual meaning and leading to 'ever-greater levels of stimulation or pain, with ever-increasing theatrics'.[59]

The deep need for the death of the old homosexual self and a rebirth into a new identity, was thwarted with the selling of urban refugee compounds as sex and drug theme parks. The resulting conditions produced addiction instead of benediction, and what Casper Schmidt described as 'a wave of shame-and guilt-induced depression' which was to have profound effects on the vital link between mind and body, the immune system.

One participant in some of the more extreme entertainments, the philosopher Michel Foucault, referred to them as 'suicide-orgies'.[60]

Dark circles, or, are you sick enough for hospital?

CAN YOU SPARE ANY CHANGE FOR A DYING QUEEN DAR-LING?
I MEAN I AM DYING
I KNOW YOU DON'T BELIEVE ME
BUT I KNOW WHAT I'M TALKING ABOUT.

— Jimmy Centola, 'Change for a Dying Queen' from
The Divas of Sheridan Square

The photo was taken the evening of 20 September 1980, the opening of New York's new gay disco, the Saint. 'The way we were', says the caption: 'The Saint's opening night crowd stretched around the block.' It is printed in an issue of the *Advocate* eight years later, in an article by Brandon Judell called 'The Saint says goodbye'.[61] The intervening years had taken a high toll of New York's gay disco set, the clientele of Studio 54, Flamingo and other clubs. The Saint's last night was a sad event.

In his article, Judell quotes an incident from Christopher Davis' novel *Valley of the Shadow*, in which the hero, a gay man with AIDS, remembers meeting 'a beautiful dark-haired boy with blue eyes and perfect teeth': 'We danced a while – he told me he was 19 – and then I offered him cocaine. We went to the balcony to do it, and after we each took some he offered me a bottle of poppers, which I accepted, and then when I was still feeling the rush from the poppers he knelt down and unzipped my pants, and for a few minutes it felt so good and I looked through the dimly lit dome at the flashing lights and heard the music and put my hands on the back of his head and began to move my hips and then suddenly, clearly, I thought, my God, I could be killing this young man, cutting off his life, destroying that beauty, and I pushed him away so hard he fell on his back, and before he could get up I ran down the tight-curving metal stairs, doing up my pants as I ran.'

The rest of the article and an accompanying interview with the Saint's creator, Bruce Mailman, deal with sex in the balconies, the club's notorious invitation to a public circumcision, rumours of even more bizarre sex ('The group of people who came here wanted that, it was what excited them') and an injunction not to blame the Saint or any other institution for AIDS, that it was 'just a barometer of what was happening in the community'. Even on the last night, 'two beauties' are chatting in the bathroom:

'Are you stoned yet?'

'No, I'm saving my drugs for later.'

But what catches the attention is the photograph accompanying the piece, the look of the gay men in the photograph, a disturbing look, brittle and gaunt. A friend, a gay activist from the old days, has written over the top of my copy: 'These are dying men – already in 1980.'

Ghetto gays of the time displayed certain tell-tale signs. Jack Fritscher, in his novel about the period, *Some Dance to Remember*, recalled that 'Dark circles under the eyes became a trademark of faces marked by drugs the way an even older generation of gays, who had grown up oppressed in the Fifties were marked in the face by the puffy, dead-give-away look of alcoholics.'[62]

Since I am taking you 'down there on a visit', via a brief bumpy tour of the gay scene of the late 1970s as its participants recorded it, we should rejoin for a while Pete Fisher and his lover Marc, whom we left in the last chapter pledging their vows on the steps of the Cathedral of St John the Divine. Eight years later, Fisher published his auto-biographical novel *Dreamlovers*, a painfully honest, idiosyncratic look at gay life and fantasy in the 1970s.[63] A lot had changed. By now the gay world 'was in flux. Gay people were questioning the nature of all their relationships.' The Gay Liberation movement, new in 1972, had suffered the twists and turns of a decade, and Fisher's novel was his personal witness to some of them.

By 1975, according to *Dreamlovers*, Fisher's lover was urging him to 'be free. Enjoy yourself as much as possible. Get into *pleasure*.' And pleasure for gay men was now the porn-and-poppers lifestyle. Fisher, whose two great joys in life are his writing and his lover, is confused, but not wanting to be possessive or rigid, he goes along. He and Marc soon find themselves in the dark orgy room of a bar with the not inappropriate name of Folsom Prison, where 'poppers perfumed the thick, murky air'.

By 1976, Fisher is writing in his diary, 'My fantasies are becoming realities . . . . My typewriter keeps breaking down. Obsessive depressions come on me in waves. All I can think about is what a failure I am . . . . Marc is my only reason for not killing myself . . . .' And Marc is urging him to go to the orgy bars alone. By 1977, seven years after their exchange of rings, Pete and Marc are staggering, drunk and drugged, through a frantic, confused tangle of emotions and crowding, ejaculating bodies.

> I came while they [Marc and another man] went at it, but my cry was a gasp of pain for being excluded, ignored, unwanted, unnoticed. It was a powerful orgasm, full of grief, and, when it was over, I knew I wouldn't come again that night. Now I wanted to attack Marc, punch him, hurt him
> . . .

On one level, I was in an icy rage, taken over by a raw hatred that stunned and shocked me. And yet I didn't feel the slightest bit threatened. My anger was under control. On another level, I felt that Marc was just playing and having a good time, big deal. I headed back to the bar, got another beer, and sat, almost catatonically, thinking.

Eventually, Pete finds Marc who is so stoned he has lost all track of time. 'As soon as we got outside, Marc began to throw up. I took care of him. He retched and retched. Just as he was finishing, I felt gorge rise within me, and I, too, puked. Afterwards, weak, drained, disgusted, I was glad that Nick was good enough to drive us home to Brooklyn.'[64]

At home, in a tranquilized, nightmarish sleep, Pete dreams of Marc fooling around at the edge of a roof, then falling off. He wakes up screaming. Things have reverted, apparently, to the instability, hurt and self-hatred Fisher had cast aside a few years before. Only now, drugs and a multiplicity of sex partners give an additional intensity to the fragmentation, anguish and loneliness. In an interview he gave several years after *Dreamlovers* was published, Fisher said, 'Nowadays I wonder if by participating in such frequent visits to the sex bars, I was acting out the verdict that society had delivered.'[65]

Dreamlovers, which was largely ignored by the gay press, is a poignant portrait of a people in transition – newly recognized, confused, still very off-balance, whose overpowering urge to celebrate is being thwarted and repressed. The novel's cover, by Dennis Forbes, shows two entwined figures, a speedometer,[66] and someone walking in what appears to be a shroud or winding sheet. AIDS is still in the future – but only just.

If Kramer and Fisher bore witness to the truth in their novels (and were chastised or ignored for it by many of their peers) some of the poets of the era looked even deeper, with black metaphors that seemed extreme or wilfully perverse at the time, but have proved uncannily prophetic of the darkness that was to come. George Whitmore's 'The Trucks' from his 1976 collection *Getting Gay in New York*[67] chronicles the eerily silent cruising scene in and around open trucks by the Hudson River:

The trucks held a cargo of men
like the Jews
who went quietly
(even smiling, nervous) . . .

. . . The trucks rest easy, mindless that I
am searching
for the Abadnego to fly
through the flames of the furnace with me

This parallel of the gay ghetto with the final ghetto of the
European Jews drew no public comment at the time, not from within
the ghetto, and certainly not from outside. A ghetto is a walled city;
in our case, the wall was an invisible one of discretion and silence, a
selective synaptic break in communications with the outside world
which left us both insulated and abandoned. The occasions when the
wall was breached – partially, temporarily, abruptly – stirred our
greatest anger: the film *Cruising*, the shots fired by a fanatical
Christian into the Ramrod, the Toronto bath raids. Perversely, they
proved how smothering the discretion had been – a silence, we
would come to realize, that equalled death.

That ferocious silence envelopes the central death-theme of
Kirby Congdon's book *Dream-Work*,[68] published in 1970, over a
decade before the onset of AIDS. It is a slim, taut collection of prose
poems about leather-clad young men taking part in orgies of mass
suicide which are 'quickly hushed up lest the contagion become
rampant':

Through the night the gun was passed from hand to hand . . .
like a barking demon . . . Some directed the gun on
themselves, devising new and original methods for its use.
Others passively allowed it to be used on them. A few
pleaded for it in desperate whispers as they ejaculated, saying
'Now! Now!' . . . our own survival, suicide or death was all
one to each member of the group, for each death was our
own death, as each survivor represented the survival of those
who were dead.[69]

All were young, some were handsome, but none died in athletic poses like graceful gladiators, but were often besmudged with dirt from the dust of poor soil in countries that did not even have beautiful landscapes. Or they dragged on, in awkward positions on creaky beds in ugly hospital wards, attended by the impersonal and sometimes cranky and always authoritative and militant nurses. Most died drearily from infections or organic malfunctions, and never for God, or a great moment in history . . . The morale of the country and the state had never been higher.[70]

Most American men, of course, even gay ones, did not, and do not, read poetry. With gays, magazines like *Folsom* were more popular. A 1981 issue of this oversized San Francisco glossy carried a photo-feature which in retrospect seems creepily foreboding. Entitled 'Are You Sick Enough for Hospital?' the text begins, 'About a hundred of the sickest men in San Francisco came to get cured at a joint *Folsom Magazine* and 'Handball Express' event. Volunteers from the Folsom community transformed the club into one of the most bizarre, erotic hospitals a patient could hope to find – move over Lourds [*sic*].' There followed a list of 'clinics open to the very sick' including a 'group clinic in deep Internal Therapy' and a 'Surgery Clinic' (*see plate 9*).

'While the Pharmacy dispensed plasma punch and serum suds', the article continued, 'most patients and doctors (because they, too, can be sick) brought their own prescriptions . . . . Needles played an important part in a number of clinics that evening. Among those open to the general public was Chief of Dermatology Clinic run by socialite Dr Payton who owns and operates [a local bar] in his spare time. Also in his spare time, he has developed a miraculous cure for the heartbreak of sexually transmitted herpes – until now untreatable . . . . This dermatologist has discovered that by using multicolored, sub-dermal injections he can cover the terrible eyesore. Most people in the non-medical community mistake the scar as a tattoo.'[71] The article concluded by announcing another party at a future date.

Another magazine of the time ran an account of a group of men 'gathered from all parts of the country' for a much-anticipated event called 'Inferno 9'. The article was a celebration of several men from the group nailing their cock-heads to a butcher block with stainless steel needles. This was accompanied by several graphic photos. The article concluded, 'Good News: John Preston was on hand to record the episode for posterity. Bad News: We had all had too much partying by that time and most of the photos did not turn out . . . . The beautiful sight of four sets of male genitalia nailed to one piece of wood exists only in the memory of those who saw it happen. But the photos here will give you an idea of what it looked like.'[72] A few off-center but suitably gruesome pictures were provided.

It would be wrong to conclude that gay men in America during the 1970s were flocking to events like these. Most did not live in the ghetto, were not party to the ghetto lifestyle, and would have been disturbed or horrified if they had known about such scenes. Even for most ghetto gays, such unusual get-togethers would have been frightening, too far beyond the pale. On the other hand, these events were hardly secret. They were publicized in magazines that were freely available; the gatherings were fairly widely advertised in the gay community. There were few, if any, protests. When, a couple of years into the AIDS epidemic, I lodged a protest of my own – against a 'demonstration' of 'blood sports' (entrance fee, $5) which included, among other things, shooting half-inch staples into a man's buttocks and 'hammering them home' with a paddle – I was dismissed as 'one of those mildly kinky numbers who crowd the bars and make things confusing for those of us who are serious'.[73]

For New York City, the Mineshaft was the symbolic epicenter of the plague. It was located in the middle of the meat-packing district. The gay men who spent the night there (or at the nearby Anvil) and left early in the morning, made their way home under corrugated iron abutments that sheltered the sidewalks, and past white-coated slaughterhouse workers hauling cold butchered animal carcasses on hooks. A photographer would have found it a compelling image: the men in black leather come from play, the men in white, splashed with blood, going about their work, each group carefully ignoring the other as they crossed paths at the intersection of the separate worlds of night and day, the invisible ghetto wall providing its deceptive two-way protection.

The theoretician of architecture and of the erotic, Georges Bataille, observed that 'the slaughterhouse relates to religion in the sense that temples of time past . . . had two purposes, serving simultaneously for prayers and for slaughter [of sacrificial animals] . . . Nowadays the slaughterhouse is cursed and quarantined like a boat with cholera aboard . . . The victims of this curse are neither the butchers nor the animals, but those fine folk who have reached a point of not being able to stand their own unseemliness, an unseemliness corresponding in fact to a pathological need for cleanliness.'[74]

Isolated and impregnable as the Bastille, the Mineshaft represented Ground Zero of this quarantined area which gay men, unseemly as meat, employed as their meatrack. The plague had not officially begun, but the quarantine was already in force. The Stonewall and the Mineshaft were never torn down; the Bastille was never stormed. The inhabitants perished. The revolution was over.

John Preston – the photographer at the impaling – sensed something ominous in the future. In 1981, he went to one of the periodic 'Black Parties' at the Mineshaft. 'Bus loads of hungry men descend on New York', he wrote, to enjoy this 'wallowing' experience. 'The fist fuckers, the piss drinkers, the cock suckers . . . the sadists, the pigs, all of them line up at the door and use the obligatory black masks to get ready to shed even one more layer of American respectability and approach one more step toward sexual fulfillment of their obsessive desires.'

This year's Black Party, he observed, was 'sleazier than ever. More cock, more piss, more flesh, more leather, more groans, more sex, more crisco, more men. As its reputation grows and its attendance continues to climb higher and higher, its life gets longer and longer, we all wonder: Where can this end?'[75]

Notes

1. Mark Freedman, *Homosexuality and Psychological Functioning* (Belmont, CA: Brooks/Cole, 1971).
2. Among the more dangerous New York activities: cruising the abandoned, collapsing piers and warehouses near West Street. Robbings, muggings and stabbings were an ever-present feature of these popular settings for anonymous sex. It was also easy to fall through rotting floors and break a limb, or to stumble into the fetid,

toxic waters of the Hudson. *Numbers* magazine once published a frank, cautionary 'cruiser's guide' to the piers (James Louis, 'Where angels tread', *Numbers*, February 1983, p. 5). David Wojnarowicz provided a pungent description of the scene ('The smell of shit and piss is overwhelming') in his *Close to the Knives: A Memoir of Disintegration* (New York: Vintage Press, 1991), pp. 17–19, 187.

3. Gregory Flood, *I'm Looking for Mr Right But I'll Settle for Mr Right Away: AIDS, True Love, the Perils of Safe Sex, and Other Spiritual Concerns of the Gay Male*, 2nd edn. (Atlanta: Brob House Books, 1987), p. 10.

4. Casper G. Schmidt, 'The group-fantasy origins of AIDS', *Journal of Psychohistory*, Summer 1984, p. 66. My thanks to John Lauristen for drawing this article to my attention.

5. Quoted in Schmidt, 'Group-Fantasy', p. 65.

6. Perry Deane Young, *God's Bullies: Native Reflections on Preachers and Politics* (New York: Holt, Rinehart & Winston, 1982).

7. The Briggs campaign provided a model for the cynical and demagogic LaRouche campaign to quarantine HIV 'carriers' in the same state a decade later. See Chapter 7.

8. Quoted in Schmidt, 'Group-Fantasy', p. 68.

9. *Ibid.*, p. 65.

10. *Advocate*, 24 December 1981.

11. Schmidt, 'Group-Fantasy'.

12. *Ibid.*, p. 53.

13. *Ibid.*, pp. 64–5.

14. *Time*, 20 June 1977, p. 59.

15. George Whitmore, 'After a "career" in suicide: choosing to live', *Advocate*, 3 March 1983, p. 25.

16. Vito Russo, *The Celluloid Closet: Homosexuality in the Movies*, rev. ed. (New York: Harper & Row, 1987), p. 189.

17. George Whitmore, 'Living alone', in Allen Young and Karla Jay, eds, *After You're Out: Personal Experiences of Gay Men and Lesbian Women* (New York: Link Books, 1975), pp. 52–61.

18. Like AIDS in the twentieth century, what was called leprosy in the ancient and medieval worlds was actually a number of different diseases, all of which stigmatized the sufferer as 'unclean'. George Whitmore was not the only gay writer to entertain visions of the homosexual as leper. Seymour Kleinberg recalled having made a connection between leprosy and the guilt he felt at his sexual encounters with men: 'This growing desire to touch them, to engage them, to *go to bed with them* frightened me: these men were sick; slowly, I was becoming leprous. . . . Could I live with sickness, with helplessness and unknown debilitations?' (*Alienated Affections: Being Gay in America* (New York: Warner Books, 1980), p. 20).

Rev Malcolm Boyd said that 'homosexuality for thousands of years has been the unnamable leprosy' (quoted in Leigh W. Rutledge, *Unnatural Quotations* (Boston: Alyson Publications, 1988), p. 25). Rev Ralph Weltge also wrote about society's view of the homosexual as 'a moral leper' (quoted in Barry Cunningham, *Gay Power: The Homosexual Revolt* (New York: Tower Publications, 1971), p. 139). In *An Alternative Approach to AIDS and Related Problems* (Mississauga, Ont.: Egret Publishing, 1992), Ching-Chee Chan, Ph.D., speculated about 'a modified version of Hansen's bacillus' (leprosy) as a possible cause of AIDS. James D'Eramo wrote about the use of the anti-leprosy drug Dapsone to alleviate KS, in 'A cure for Kaposi's?', *New York Native*, 9–24 April 1984.

19.   Whitmore, 'After a "career" in suicide', p. 25.

20.   *Ibid.*

21.   Quentin Crisp, *How to Go to the Movies* (New York: St Martin's Press, 1991), p. 119.

22.   Christian de La Mazière, *The Captive Dreamer* (New York: Saturday Review Press/E. P. Dutton, 1974), p. 31.

23.   John Rechy, *City of Night* (New York: Ballantine Books, 1973), p. 366.

24.   Whitmore, 'After a "career" in suicide', p. 53.

25.   See Dr Thomas O. Ziebold, 'Alcoholism and recovery: gays helping gays', *Christopher Street*, January 1979, pp. 36–44.

26.   David Reed, 'The multimillion-dollar mystery high', *Christopher Street*, February 1979, p. 26.

27.   Michael Rumaker, *A Day and a Night at the Baths* (San Francisco: Grey Fox Press, 1979), pp. 26–7.

28.   The history of poppers replicates that of benzedrine, which was regularly given to pilots and other combat personnel (on both sides) during World War II. Benzedrine inhalers remained legal into the 1950s, becoming popular with artists such as Lenny Bruce. Norman Mailer's novel *Why Are We in Vietnam?* (New York: G. P. Putnam's, 1967) examines the channelling of homoerotic tensions into the violent camaraderie of the Asian war.

29.   Reed, 'Multimillion-dollar mystery high', p. 22.

30.   John Lauritsen and Hank Wilson, *Death Rush: Poppers & AIDS* (New York: Pagan Press, 1986), p. 6.

31.   Among the studies cited by Lauritsen and Wilson are those of the Danish researchers Jorgensen and Lawesson which indicated that 'amyl nitrite may cause Kaposi's sarcoma in homosexual men' and Andrew Moss's comparison of sick and healthy HIV positive men in San Francisco, which concluded that use of nitrite inhalants is an important risk factor in the development of Kaposi's sarcoma: 'The

heavier the popper usage, the greater the risk.' I am indebted for much of my information to the Committee to Monitor Poppers and the authors of *Death Rush*.

32. Kenneth Mayer and James D'Eramo, 'Poppers: a storm warning', *Christopher Street*, No. 78, pp. 46–9.

33. Arthur Evans, 'Poppers: an ugly side of gay business', *Coming Up!*, November 1981.

34. Roger P. Maickel, interview in *Moneysworth*, January 1982.

35. See, for example, Sheldon Saul Hendler, MD, Ph.D., *The Oxygen Breakthrough: 30 Days to an Illness-Free Life – The Natural Program* (New York: William Morrow, 1989).

36. Lauritsen and Wilson, *Death Rush*, p. 49.

37. W. Jay Freezer, Robert McQueen and Nathan Fain died of AIDS.

38. Leonard T. Sigell, Frederic T. Kapp *et al.*, 'Popping and snorting volatile nitrites: a current fad for getting high', *American Journal of Psychiatry*, October 1978, pp. 1216–18.

39. Orlando Paris, 'Cruise of the gay witch' in *The Short Happy Sex Life of Stud Sorell and 69 Other Flights of Fancy* (San Diego: Greenleaf Classics, 1968), pp. 142–3.

40. *Drummer*, No. 45, 1981.

41. The symbol also has a negative side: the Hindu god Shiva (in his role as the Destroyer) travelled on a white bull; in this aspect he is often associated with drugs, self-starvation and self-mutilation. A number of gay men with AIDS (David Wojnarowicz, Michael Callen) recorded their dreams or visions of a dying bull.

42. Marshall McLuhan, *Understanding Media: The Extensions of Man* (New York: Mentor, 1964), pp. 22–3. Michael Ellner, president of the Health Education AIDS Liaison in New York City and a professional hypnotherapist, suggested that unrecognized hypnosis could be a risk factor in the development of AIDS. Though he was referring to the ubiquitous 'Living with HIV' announcements covertly promoting AZT to gay men during the epidemic, the same 'classic elements of hypnosis' were present in the frequently repeated poppers ads.

43. Quoted in David Halberstam, *The Fifties* (New York: Villard Books, 1993), p. 505.

44. Larry Kramer, *Faggots* (New York: Warner Books, 1979), p. 301. The novel's reception in the gay community is discussed in Chapter four.

45. See Stephen Wright, 'Full stop: the drug scene', *Follow-Up*, Vol. 2, No. 8, 1974.

46. Matt Clark and Mariana Gosnell, 'Diseases that plague gays', *Newsweek*, 21 December 1981.

47.   Peter McGehee, 'Sex and love' in Phil Willkie and Greg Baysans, *The Gay Nineties: An Anthology of Contemporary Gay Fiction* (Freedom, CA: Crossing Press, 1991), p. 67.

48.   Michael Callen, *Surviving AIDS* (New York: HarperCollins, 1990), p. 4.

49.   Yony, 'A foolish young circuit queen finds out what it means to be wise,' *PWA Coalition Newsline*, October 1987, pp. 29–30.

50.   James Baldwin, *The Evidence of Things Not Seen* (New York: Holt, Rinehart & Winston, 1985), p. 71.

51.   Barry Miles, *Ginsberg: A Biography* (New York: Simon & Schuster, 1989), p. 395.

52.   Among the disillusioned were some of the most prominent early gay liberationists, including Ralph Hall, Jim Fouratt, Arthur Evans, Perry Brass, Aubrey Walter, Bob Mellors, John Lauritsen, Ralph S. Schaffer and Mike Silverstein, as well as Mattachine leader Dick Leitsch.

53.   Luigi Zoja, *Drugs, Addiction and Initiation: The Modern Search for Ritual* (Boston: Sigo Press, 1989), p. 24.

54.   *Ibid.*, p. 44.

55.   *Ibid.*

56.   See Thomas Szasz, *Ceremonial Chemistry: The Ritual Persecution of Drugs, Addicts and Pushers*, rev. ed. (Holmes Beach, FL: Learning Publications, 1985), p. 29.

57.   Prof. Irwin Edman, quoted in Christopher Isherwood, 'Religion without prayers', in *Vedanta for Modern Man*, ed. Christopher Isherwood (New York: Collier Books, 1962), p. 45.

58.   Zoja, *Drugs*, p. 58.

59.   Robert H. Hopcke, 'S/M and the psychology of gay male initiation: an archetypal perspective', in Mark Thompson, ed., *Leatherfolk: Radical Sex, People, Politics and Practice* (Boston: Alyson Publications, 1991).

60.   James Miller, *The Passion of Michel Foucault* (New York: Anchor Books, 1993), p. 28.

61.   Brandon Judell, 'The Saint says goodbye', *Advocate*, 5 July 1988, pp. 40–1.

62.   Jack Fritscher, *Some Dance to Remember* (Stamford, CT: Knights Press, 1990), p. 297.

63.   Peter Fisher, *Dreamlovers* (New York: The Sea Horse Press, 1979).

64.   *Ibid.*, p. 65.

65.   Rich Grzesiak, 'Plunging into the dark with *Dreamlovers*' Pete Fisher', *Gay News* (Philadelphia), 31 March 1983, p. 33.

66.   Compare the scene in Kenneth Anger's classic gay film *Fireworks* where the hands of the sailors pull apart the flesh of the young man's chest to reveal a wildly oscillating speedometer.

67.   George Whitmore, *Getting Gay in New York* (New York: Free Milk Fund Press, 1976), no pagination.

68.   Kirby Congdon, *Dream-Work* (New York: Cycle Press, 1970).

69.   *Ibid.*, 'The Orgy', p. 39.

70.   *Ibid.*, 'The Battlefield', p. 56.

71.   *Folsom*, No. 3, 1981, p. 58.

72.   *DungeonMaster*, November 1980, p. 1.

73.   Ian Young, 'Touring New York during the AIDS crisis', *Gay News* (Philadelphia), – July 1983, p. 10; and David Lewis, 'G.M.S.M.A. clarification', *Gay News* (Philadelphia), 8 September 1983, p. 13.

74.   Quoted in Denis Hollier, *Against Architecture: The Writings of Georges Bataille* (Cambridge, MA: The MIT Press, 1989), pp. xii-xiii.

75.   John Preston, 'Black mask party at the Mineshaft', in *Drummer*, No. 27, 1982. In an article titled 'The Theater of Sexual Initiation', Preston revealed that, unknown to the patrons, some of the men at the Mineshaft were hired 'coaches, paid to show the novices the ropes, to let them see how . . . roles should be played'. John Preston, *My Life as a Pornographer & Other Indecent Acts* (New York: A Richard Kasak Book, 1993), p. 57. Samuel R. Delany wrote about the closing of the Mineshaft in the early 1980s: 'I just learned that the city finally closed the Mineshaft down: that a gay group . . . has been promoting what it calls 'safe sex' that entails wearing condoms, no exchange of body fluids, and more inventive ways of enjoying yourself with another man . . . They were doing live, active, hands-on sexual demonstrations . . . But all this got back to the city fathers, who were outraged . . . Newspapers that never had been concerned before . . . now became outraged that there were live sex demonstrations going on. To quell this moral outrage, they closed the bar down. Also the baths – where the demonstrators had also arrived with their exhibitions' (Samuel R. Delany, *The Mad Man* (New York: A Richard Kasak Book, 1994), pp. 179–80.

Chapter four

The Revolution Is Over

THE REVOLUTION'S A LOCKER ROOM JOKE
A PIPE DREAM OF HOPE GONE UP IN SMOKE
THE BLACK MAN FIZZLED
THE WOMEN DRIZZLED
THE DELICATE GAYS
UNHAPPILY
BROKE

THAT YELLOW BRICK ROAD LED US STRAIGHT TO HELL
WHERE ALL OUR BROTHERS AND SISTERS FELL
DON'T QUESTION
DON'T CRY
AND DON'T RING THE BELL
THE WIZARD'S A FAKE
DON'T BOTHER TO DWELL

WE HAVE BEEN PACKAGED AND NOW WE'LL BE SOLD
THE WORDS SOUND NEW BUT THE STORY'S OLD
A DAY IN THE SUN
A LIFE IN THE COLD
IT'S THE POOR MAN'S JOURNEY
FOR THE STRAIGHT MAN'S GOLD

— Jimmy Centola, 'The Revolution's Over' from *The Divas of
Sheridan Square*

IN its early years, the Gay Liberation movement was radical,
experimental, sometimes off-the-wall, occasionally dogmatic, but
lively, intelligent, strongly anti-capitalist (with anarchistic leanings)
and determined to construct alternatives to the oppression and self-
oppression of the past. Sometimes, past and future mind-sets rubbed
together, generating an odd sort of 'anything can happen' electricity,
as when (even before Stonewall) New York activist Randolfe Wicker
set up information tables (with hot coffee) in favorite gay cruising
spots – a tactic later adopted by London's Camden Gay Liberation
Front in its friendly night-time forays into Hampstead Heath.

Unhappily, the tactic was soon dropped – though the mixture of animated eagerness, friendly interest, studied coolness and outright hostility shown the GLFers made for an interesting night out. Early in the Stonewall Experiment, it became evident to many gay liberationists that their new revolutionary movement was threatened not only by political opposition from the straight world but also by deep psychic forces within gays themselves, the product of centuries of psychological warfare against us.

Historian and gay liberationist Arthur Evans, writing in the early days of the movement, made the point that 'All homosexuals (including those who appear to be doggedly apolitical) have experienced enormous personal rage at their own oppression. In the course of the years, for the sake of "adjustment" to heterosexual mores (passing as straight), this anger has been swallowed and pushed down into the inner soul. There it has festered, and, lacking any political outlet, has turned into guilt and self-hatred.' He urged gay spokespeople to 'speak with thunder' against 'the political powers that control the state'.[1] Speech alone, of course, even thundrous speech, could not exorcise this 'festering' in the soul. And many 'liberated' gay men never really spoke out, remaining psychically shrouded in the silence and secrecy they brought to the backrooms and blackrooms, the trucks and abandoned piers.

Another American writer/activist summed up the attitude of the cultural radicals in the early movement: 'What use, they argued, was the passage of legislation that would enable homosexuals to be openly gay without fear of losing their jobs, if there was no way to be gay outside of the tawdry bar scene? What must be developed in order for political gains to be meaningful was a new life style, an integral gay counterculture which could draw uptight gays out of their closets of secrecy and shame into a new expressive and creative way of life. What was needed, in effect, was the initiation of a grand social experiment, the creation of a new society within the old.'[2]

But like all the grand social experiments and new societies before it, Gay Liberation was necessarily a creature of its time and place. It stubbornly refused to remain pure, and quickly succumbed to deeply instilled guilt, shame and fear. These old enemies found numerous accomplices, each with its own vested interest in moulding the immediate future of gay men in America.

The early movement had made a bold attempt to build a gay infrastructure that was democratic, open, self-supporting, and without the ties to organized crime that had characterized gay meeting places in the past: as Arnie Kantrowitz put it, 'breaking the Mafia's stranglehold'.[3] The looting, and subsequent destruction, of the GAA Firehouse provided a vivid warning of the likely fate of those efforts. There was great disillusionment, and many simply dropped out of the movement – or committed suicide, like Ralph S. Schaffer and Mike Silverstein. The movement lost its sense of excitement and hope as its substance bled away.

As one of the founders of the London GLF, Aubrey Walter, wrote: 'We certainly didn't expect our aims to be achieved overnight. Quite the contrary. We saw gay liberation as a revolutionary movement, which challenged the existing society in a quite fundamental way, and expected we would meet with violent resistance from the state and other apparatuses of repression. Even such modest steps as holding gay dances, we anticipated, might lead to major clashes with the forces of law and order. We were surprised, looking back after a couple of years, that without any structural change in the sexist and capitalist society, this had managed to grant certain concessions that made life a lot more comfortable, at least for the minority of homosexuals who actually come out and live an openly gay lifestyle. . . . A great deal of the new infrastructure', he added, 'involved the encroachment of commercial interests.'[4]

Yet, looking back from the vantage point of the early 1980s, Walter argued that how little had fundamentally changed could be seen by recalling the final demand in the Manifesto of the British Gay Liberation Front: 'that gay people be free to hold hands and kiss in public, as are heterosexuals'. Writing in 1980, he felt 'we are actually less free to do this today than we were in the time of GLF, when we felt the support of a strong mass movement behind us, inspiring us with its warmth and solidarity. This shows all too clearly how we are forced to live on the margins of society. The ghetto has been gilded, but we should not deceive ourselves that this is liberation.' Only in the late 1980s with the emergence of Queer Nation (made up largely of young gays and lesbians coming out of AIDS activism) did the public kiss-in become (sporadically) part of the agenda again.

Walter cited 1973 as the end of the true Gay Liberation period, before 'the encroachment of commercial interests' had sufficiently co-opted the movement so that it no longer constituted a threat to the establishment. Independently, another gay liberationist active in those years, John Lauritsen, put 1974 as the date of the emergence of the gay clone lifestyle.[5]

Using different language, and from somewhat different points of view, both Walter and Lauritsen[6] connected the dissipation of gay radicalism with the incursion of commercialism, the overemphasis of hypermasculine images and behaviors and a concurrent devaluing of other important aspects of male gay experience. (Significantly, apart from the continuing bar culture and its attendant alcoholism, no similar, sex-and-drugs based 'lifestyle' emerged among lesbians. Some of their concerns were the same as gay men's, some diverged; their overall agenda, however, was quite different.[7])

In 1974, as it was becoming obvious that the original impetus toward gay liberation had more or less come to a halt, Patricia Nell Warren published her gay bestseller *The Front Runner*.[8] The story of a young Olympic athlete coached by his older lover, this was one of the last of the old-fashioned 'tragic ending' gay novels, and one of the first of the more political, gay-positive novels to come. It was also a prophetic allegory.

In the novel's climactic scene, Billy Sive is the 'front runner' of the race (a subliminal pun, as he is portrayed as front runner of the human race as well). He is assassinated from the bleachers, shot in the head just as the political front runner Harvey Milk would be four years later. In a controversial ending, he lives on thanks to a son conceived posthumously via artificial insemination. Billy's son, 'unafraid, dignified', resembles his father, and even shares the same astrological sign. His mother is a lesbian.

The Front Runner appeared at the crucial turning point of the Stonewall experiment. Billy's clone-like son was born just as the phenomenon of the urban gay 'clone' appeared on the scene. The very concept of the clone – a campy repudiation of heterosexual reproduction – signalled an ironic acceptance of the world as industrial assembly line, mass-producing a product half human, half manufactured. A stylized gay version of the ideal of consumerist man, it incorporated both futuristic assumptions and a complex, covert nostalgia.

William Burroughs' novel *The Wild Boys* was popular in this period, with its sexy young insurrectionists replicating themselves viruslike, through a gelatinous, ecstatic process strangely reminiscent of Milton's angels. Andy Warhol, with his art 'factory', emerged as the representative artist of the time. When he survived an assassination attempt, he assumed the role of a contemporary Sebastian, the bullets that tore through his body serving as a modern transformation of the arrows that pierced the saint's vital organs but miraculously spared him.

The West Coast or Castro Street version of the clone was eloquently described by Edmund White: 'a strongly marked mouth and swimming, soulful eyes (the effect of the mustache): a V- shaped torso by metonymy from the open V of the half-buttoned shirt above the sweaty chest; rounded buttocks squeezed in jeans, swelling out from the clinched-in waist, further emphasized by the charged erotic insignia of colored handkerchiefs and keys; a crotch instantly accessible through the buttons (bottom one already undone) and enlarged by being pressed, along with the scrotum, to one side; legs moulded in perfect, powerful detail; the feet simplified, brutalized and magnified by the boots'.[9]

This look, something of a cross between a lumberjack and a chorus boy from *Oklahoma!*, was to become (a few years before White described it in 1980) a sort of international gay clone uniform. Writing at the end of the 1970s, in his aptly titled *Alienated Affections: Being Gay In America*, Seymour Kleinberg described the preferred look as elegant, expensive, and butch: 'Hardness is in. But talk to these men, sleep with them, befriend them, and the problems are the old, familiar ones: misery when in love, loneliness when one is not, frustration and ambitiousness at work, and a monumental self-centredness that exacerbates the rest. These', he observed, 'have been the archetypes of unhappiness in homosexual America for as long as I can remember.'[10] His comments recall George Whitmore's meditations on ever-present loneliness.

In a reflective paper on gay male identities written in 1987, John Lauritsen makes the point that this lifestyle was not constructed in the interests of gay men, but rather constituted a 'subculture largely evolved according to the profit-logic of an expanding sex industry'.[11]

By the mid-1970s, most of the more radical aims of the Gay Liberation movement – as outlined in the Carl Wittman and London GLF manifestos – had been shelved or swamped. The tremendous energy of the early movement was being successfully diverted into the gay lifestyle, with a 'Mafia musak' sound track and 'civil rights' (*possibly* . . . if you're good) as the icing on the cake.

The shift in attitude was reflected even in publications free of criminal control, such as Canada's *Body Politic*, a leading gay newsmagazine with an international readership. In a piece by a leading member of the paper's editorial collective, it was asserted that cruising in the 'traditional hunting grounds' (bars, baths, parks) for 'frequent and prolonged periods' is 'precisely the circumstance which makes political organization a possibility for gay men . . . Bars and baths are to the gay movement what factories are to the labour movement.'[12] Again, the parallel with industrial production: did anyone imagine the sweat-shop floor a pleasant place to be? 'Commercial establishments', the piece maintained, constituted 'the fountainhead of the gay movement.'

This was the article that coined the much-quoted phrase, 'Promiscuity knits together the social fabric of the gay male community.' In contrast to the freedom and solidarity awarded by promiscuity, 'the imposition of marriage-like coupling inevitably goes hand-in-hand with the abolition of that community'.[13] Here, promiscuity is seen as essential to gay survival, and 'marriage-like coupling' as both imposed and threatening; no other options are considered.

In the same issue, another writer expressed similar sentiments: 'We are all, like it or not, animals of the ghetto . . . The ghetto preserves and protects gays and their subculture . . . Long live the ghetto and the ghetto attitude.'[14]

Some liberationists were divided in their own minds about the new direction the community was following. The heavy politicos who hectored (and alienated) newcomers at a gay meeting with some dogmatic schema of politically correct sexuality would later be spotted anonymously prowling around the piers or politely ignoring one another at the baths. Others proved largely immune to the blandishments of the lifestyle, but took a libertarian position, considering it a matter of personal preference.

As the movement foundered, familiar patterns of thought and behavior quickly reasserted themselves, employing bits of left-over liberationist rhetoric as useful camouflage. Some of the psychic adjustments gay men were making in this pivotal period were tellingly reflected in the work of a writer whose observations of the alienated, lonely American are some of the most searing and bitter in literature: John Rechy.

The sexual outlaw, or what's a nice boy like you doing in a place like this?

'It may be that, among all the numbers of people, you've been looking for the number,' Emory suggests.

'But the number is death!' Sebastian surprised everyone by saying – though he smiled and said it lightly.

—John Rechy, *Numbers*

John Rechy's 1967 novel *Numbers* is a relentless chronicle of what by the 1980s was beginning to be described as sexual addiction.[14] The book's tragic hero, Johnny Rio, is also the hero of Rechy's controversial first novel, *City of Night*, published four years earlier. In *Numbers*, we are told that Johnny, in a moment suggestive of *Dorian Gray*, has caught a glimpse in a mirror of a 'depraved distortion' of himself, and as a result, has tried to break his obsessive need for the promiscuous sexual encounters which, hit-and-miss fashion, serve both to shore up and to devastate his fragile ego. But his attempt to break with his compulsive pattern has failed, and he returns to his old hustling territory of Griffith Park in the 'foggy city of dead angels' to see how many scores he can make in an apparently arbitrary period of time: ten days. His goal is thirty – a printer's term for The End.

The world of *Numbers*, which is the world of Griffith Park as experienced through the desperate, obsessive-compulsive ego of Johnny Rio, is one of self-regarding lovelessness wrapped like a cloak around a crucial, central paradox: it is precisely Johnny's fearful *refusal* to face the fact of his attraction to men that propels him into an increasingly futile, and increasingly death-oriented quest. And *Numbers* is peppered with references to death: 'Death, which he avoids thinking of, seems determined to permeate his awareness; it does so like a knife in his flesh.'[16] Even the birds in the park seem suicidal, inviting annihilation by getting in the way of Johnny's cruising car! And Johnny's ultimately 'aimless' accumulation of human numbers 'strikes his consciousness like a sniper's bullet'.[17]

In a moving section of the novel, Johnny briefly leaves the park to visit some friends. As a result, he meets another young gay man who offers the possibility of an affectionate, erotic relationship. Johnny's inability to enter 'that further country', to face that tantalizing, terrifying possibility – which is to say, himself – propels him, inevitably, back into the 'game which can't be won'.

Another of Rechy's novels, *Rushes*, a grim work published at the height of the merrymaking in 1979, is a keenly unsparing look at the regular patrons of a gay cruise bar. The stifling, agonized atmosphere seems an extension of Johnny Rio's mental state in *Numbers*. But with *Rushes*, an entire network of men is caught in a fevered nightmare of judging, rejection, and endless repetition, made even more claustrophobic by the dark, indoor setting. 'It is as if all have been trapped in a dream of squalor.'[18]

It is a dream, though, which seems more and more to end at age thirty-five, for Rechy comments on the disappearance of older men from the gay scene that they 'are not welcome here nor in many of the other bars, orgy rooms, baths; increasingly, posted notices bar the entrance to "over 35s" – or those who look over 35. Even when there are no restrictive signs, such men may be banned from entering the "private clubs" because they are not "properly dressed" or because of a Fire Department ordinance limiting the number of clients; yet others pass by.'[19] Such restrictions (unusual in more *laissez-faire* centers like New York, but increasingly common on the West coast) fed into the myth that gay life was for youth only, that 'nobody loves you when you're old and gay' – 'old' being over thirty-five. After that, one was presumably expected to vanish discreetly – as indeed many did, one way or another.

The increasing popularity of the clone look also drew comment from Rechy: 'The former "sissies"', he writes, 'have developed a rough, bruised beauty, as clearly homosexual as drag; contrived, studied. Unreal. Increasingly alike . . . . There is a new conformity, a marked sameness among the men of this sexual army – not only in the "uniform", the cut of the hair, the stance – not even in the strange laughter in common, no, it is in a look not yet quite etched into the faces – a new look of defiance and disdain, but aimed at their own; of hurt defiance, terrified disdain. With it there seems to be a vulnerable meanness that charges the sexual arena with tensile hostility. In groups men remark brutally, coarsely – like buyers at an auction – about others walking by alone, coarsely if approvingly, brutally if not. Yet in a second an unhealed scar is brushed among them, and angered pain bleeds out.' Elsewhere, he writes of the 'brutal code' and 'scent of sexual blood'.[20]

We have seen this 'dream of squalor' before, in George Whitmore's dispatches from the floor of the Mineshaft. Significantly, Whitmore cited the common romantic justification for 'crawling around on hands and knees in a sewer five nights a week': one of the most pervasive and glamorous of myths, and one adopted with a vengeance in America – the myth of the rebel, the outlaw. It was that myth, Whitmore believed, that was being used to induce us 'to act out our rebellion – on the oppressor's terms'. And of course, in the myth, the rebel – whether James Dean or Monty Clift, Fred Halsted or Christopher Rage – usually dies young.

Rechy's 1977 book *The Sexual Outlaw*,[21] a mixture of fictional, autobiographical and 'documentary' passages, employs many of the same venues and descriptive elements as the novels, but this time with the author's political commentary interwoven with the narrative. Now, the promiscuous gay man, the 'rough trade' (or pseudo-rough trade) hustler, the furtive cruiser, are endowed with an elevated status as sexual rebels, political outlaws, and ideological heroes.

Interviewed by a gay magazine while work on *The Sexual Outlaw* was still in progress, Rechy asserted his belief that promiscuity was 'one of the few political actions that gays are taking . . . . For me', he said, 'the promiscuous homosexuals are the heroic homosexuals.'[22] His characterization of promiscuity as a heroic way of 'taking the revolution to the streets' was a popular one among ghettoized gay men of the 1970s. The acts in question may indeed have been taken to the streets, but the streets were otherwise deserted; the revolutionaries remained quite invisible to all but themselves and the occasional contingent of undercover police. Thus one could enjoy the same furtive and anonymous pleasures as in the old, unliberated days – the difference being that now, one was a sexual hero, a rebel, a storm trooper in the front lines of the 'sexual army'. The activities – and many of their psychic and physical consequences – remained the same. Gay Liberation had tried, in its first few revolutionary years, to initiate a different course – and failed. All that was left was the rhetoric, an intellectual satisfaction, paper-thin.

Rechy himself revealed in the same interview, 'Sometimes I come home after a night of hustling and then moving to dark cruising alleys, I come home and literally think of nothing but suicide. Other times, when I'm caught in it, I think: "Jesus, God this is the most exciting thing in the world".'[23]

The sexual goings-on in these books constitute an 'arena' in which the action appeared to one commentator as appropriately 'gladiatorial'.[24] The relegation of sex to 'the safety-valve of outlaw country', remarked Stephen Adams, in an essay on Rechy's work, 'is a dubious model of revolutionary freedom . . . Rechy is committed to the maintenance of an underground, demanding only "better conditions for the workers", not the overthrow of the system.'[25]

But if Rechy's reasoning is sometimes questionable, he is nevertheless an invaluably honest witness. And perhaps the time for the 'overthrow of the system' had simply come and gone. After the riots, the Mafia's Stonewall Inn was left standing. It was our own Firehouse that was torched.

Faggots

[Americans] have needs which, for them, are literally inexpressible. They don't dare look into the mirror. And that is why they need faggots. They've created faggots in order to act out a sexual fantasy on the body of another man and not take any responsibility for it.

— James Baldwin

The year 1978 brought events that were profoundly to affect the incipient gay community and change, irreversibly, both its idealized picture of itself and its hopes for its political future. The most shattering of all, the assassination, in November, of the most able and charismatic political leader to emerge from that community, is considered later in this chapter. The tragedy had been preceded earlier in the year by a scandal following the publication of a book one critic called 'a novel without precedent'.[26] Among gays themselves, it proved to be the most controversial gay novel ever written, Larry Kramer's *Faggots*.

The central story of *Faggots* is the story of Fred Lemish, a movie writer of thirty-nine – Jack Benny's age, the last age at which one can still, barely, get away with claiming youth. It recounts Fred's quest for love – if possible in the form of the heart of the feckless Dinky Adams. He must find love, he feels, before he is forty, and as the novel begins, he has only four days to go. As with *Numbers*, then, there is a kind of countdown, a kind of desperation. But Fred Lemish's desperation, unlike Johnny Rio's, is as much for his fellows as for himself, and both he and the fellows are vividly, wickedly, drawn.

As in earlier gay novels (*The Heart in Exile*, *The Charioteer*, *City of Night*) the story entails guiding the reader through the gay milieu. Unlike its predecessors, *Faggots* avoids any suggestion of the rubbernecking tour; it is experienced totally from inside the gay world. No potted summary could do justice to the intricacy of the plot, which seems to unfold artlessly while the high and low humor of the various scenes is holding center stage. The satire comes across as a combination of Dickens, Waugh, and the Wyndham Lewis of *The Apes of God* – though with a necessary, if surprising, sexual frankness.

The cast of characters – Boo Boo Bronstein, Randy Dildough, Leather Louie, The Winston Man, Ike Bulb, Dr Irving Slough, Lance Heather, Yootha Truth, Patty, Maxine and Laverne, Blaze Sorority (columnist for the *The Avocado*), their itinerant, ubiquitous drug dealer The Gnome, and the rest – are not simply a gallery of grotesques, but, as in the book's literary successor, Tom Wolfe's *The Bonfire of the Vanities*, real people distorted by the demands of their environment, which they seem powerless to change, or leave. Below the surface satire, there is a moral dimension, an angry plea for dignity and love. Beneath that, like a number of small depth charges, are planted a variety of intriguing references, some of them biblical.

Faggots is Kramer's warning to gay men that 'We're fucking ourselves to death!' The book's penultimate scene involves Boo Boo Bronstein's attempt to bury himself alive in a shallow grave in Fire Island's outdoor meatrack ('the convergence of all ill auguries') while a bevy of leather queens in Nazi regalia wander around the site in search of fun. This is the outcome of Boo Boo's crackpot scheme to extract a million dollars from his elderly Jewish father. The scene is cruelly hilarious, with the mock-Nazis taking the unfolding father-and-son drama as part of the weekend's scripted entertainment, and the baffled Abe Bronstein whispering, 'We are perhaps in some concentration camp?'

These weird goings-on alongside a symbolic grave are the vehicle for the working out of love, and avowals of love, between father and son, which psychically involve all the men on the island, and their relations with one another. Dropped into Kramer's text at this point are several references to John Steinbeck's *East of Eden*, and to the Elia Kazan/James Dean film of parts of that novel. The themes of exile, of father–son love as a necessity for manhood, and of the death of youth, all resonate from Steinbeck's story and Dean's film, with the biblical tale of Abel's death at the hands of his brother Cain forming a barely noticeable, but nevertheless key, subtext.

When Fred Lemish, at the end of the novel, walks out of the Grove, successful in his quest, and finally able to feel love for his imperfect fellows, the grove he leaves is also the original Grove, the Garden of Innocence; and his dotty, determined walk toward the sunrise contains a fragment of the same sadness and promise as the first Fall.

In interviews shortly after the publication of *Faggots*, Kramer, echoing the recently slain Harvey Milk, spoke of the pressing necessity for the whole of the gay community to make itself visible, and to provide role models for young gays 'outside of the ghetto, outside of the Mineshaft'. He expressed his anger and frustration that certain aspects of the commercial gay lifestyle had become 'legitimized' within the ghetto where 'it's OK to take a lot of drugs and you're square if you don't, it's OK to go to the Mineshaft every weekend and you're square if you don't – it prevents people from examining why they're doing these things'.[27] And he lamented that most gays seemed unconcerned with 'our contribution to society'.

The immediate reaction to *Faggots* among American gays was like nothing any gay novel had ever stirred up before. Its author wrote tellingly about it a decade later.[28] He pointed out that his book – and the main question it posed: Why did there seem to be so little love in the gay ghetto? – struck a responsive chord among many gay men. The book became a best seller, and certainly not from the purchases of curious straights alone. Kramer received a great number of letters about the book, not one of them negative, according to his own account; no angry or 'hate' letters. The European gay press was for the most part approving, and often insightful. Yet the reaction from the North American gay press and from the gay political movement, such as it had become, was one of hostility and anger. *Cruising* was nothing compared to this!

Philip Derbyshire, a Marxist critic writing in England's *Gay Left*, remarked that *Faggots* owed its importance to, among other things, its radical depiction of a setting 'in which gay men are plural, engaged with each other, creating, choosing, changing partners, are *social*.'[29] Those who were savaging the book might do better, Derbyshire suggested, to consider how its text illuminated the very material conditions that made it possible.

Hugo Marsan, in the Paris magazine *Le Gai Pied*, was bitterly eloquent in defense of the book: 'What can become of passion when the beloved wallows in the same pleasure-spots, when each dim corner of the baths reveals him given up to anonymous caresses, when hour after hour his aura fades because the same carnal evidences cause him to grow pale? This is the heart of the narrative, the de-mythification of physical love.' *Faggots*, Marsan wrote, 'mocks the alibi of "forbidden sex" . . . We cannot deny that it lays bare the reality of a universe temporarily without tenderness. This novel has the merit of shifting its scrutiny, and its analysis from within is a revolution.'[30]

In America, Kramer was resented. New York's Gay Activist Alliance (by now a diminished, rather impotent version of its former self) solemnly added his name to its 'enemies list', which seemed to be made up in equal parts of broken-down Republican politicians and gay writers: Andrew Holleran was on it, and John Rechy, and Quentin Crisp – Crisp because, he said, he 'insisted on taking the blame for something on which judgement was no longer passed'.

In the gay press, reviews of *Faggots* was scathing. Even the usually unflinching George Whitmore was shaken. In the pages of the *Body Politic*, he called for a boycott! Warning his readers that *Faggots* was 'sleazy . . . an offensive and anti-gay tract' with 'something fundamentally and profoundly wrong with it', he admitted to wishing the book's distribution possibilities were 'nil'. He recommended another gay novel of the season instead, Paul Monette's *Taking Care of Mrs Carroll*, describing it as 'an entertaining book all of us gay lib types can really relax with'.[31]

Faced with such responses from the organs of Gay Lib, Kramer concluded that he must have 'touched some essential painful truth that some do not want to look at, and methinks those who protest protest too much'. Perhaps naively, he had not imagined his satirical story would elicit controversy, and was 'completely unprepared for its hostile reception in certain political quarters'. He was, he wrote, 'wounded and frightened' by the uproar: 'I found myself actually shunned by friends. My best friend stopped speaking to me, even to this day. People would cross the street to avoid me. . . . On a visit to Fire Island Pines . . . the setting of my novel's concluding section, it was made pointedly clear to me that I was no longer welcome.'[32] As a result, he went into something of a retreat for three years, until the appearance of AIDS made new demands on his energies and his eloquence.

A workshop

The awareness of another which is the basis of love is a development of the biological capacity to receive information from the environment. The spontaneity and initiative which are utilized by personal power are derived from the biological capacity to control the environment.

— Paul Rosenfels

No one reading *Rushes* or *Faggots* could doubt that American gay life had developed in a drastically different direction from the future envisioned either by the homophile movement of the 1950s and 1960s or by the Gay Liberation movement of the early

1970s. Nevertheless, the Stonewall Experiment was not without important successes that counterpoised the rise of the urban gay lifestyle.

The struggle for gay civil rights had been a frustrating, 'two steps forward, one step back' affair. The inclusion of gays and lesbians in the municipal civil rights ordinances of several US cities began to be revoked in the wake of Anita Bryant's success in Dade County. In Canada, 1978 saw the first of a series of police raids on the offices of the gay newsmagazine the *Body Politic*, initiating a debilitating sequence of drawn-out legal battles. Britain's *Gay News* was similarly harrassed, charged not with obscenity like the *Body Politic*, but with blasphemy, for a poem by James Kirkup about the Crucifixion. The legal changes brought about in Britain by the implementation of the Wolfenden Report were harshly contained during the Thatcher era.

Nevertheless, the legal situation in much of the English-speaking world by the end of the 1970s was much improved from what it had been only ten or fifteen years before. The success was due in large measure to the varied efforts of branches of the gay movement, from the Albany Trust to the GLF. Gays – at least in many jurisdictions – no longer lived under the threat of legal penalties simply for congregating, or engaging in private, consensual sex. Apart from the obvious benefits, this eliminated at least some of the ever-present threat of blackmail, and, perhaps most important of all, began to remove some of the heavy psychological stigmata.

Barriers to professional status and employment were also eroding. In some states, homosexuals had been forbidden to hold a driver's license or work as, for example, a barber. For a time, these popular phobias subsided, until AIDS triggered a resurgence. As more gays came out into the open, acceptance increased. Nevertheless, avowed gays constituted only a small minority of the total homosexual population. Even relatively open gay men continued to lead, to some extent, double lives, insulating their ghetto activities from their jobs and families. Even partial exposure of darker aspects of the double life could cause near panic, as the *Cruising* controversy showed.

In the sphere of civil rights, things were moving slowly from the vantage point of the troops on the ground; from a historical point of view, progress had been rapid. The benefits of that progress, however, fell largely on white, middle-class, urban gay men. (Lesbians were aided more by the women's movement, in which they were prominent, though usually closeted, and which worried about whether to accept them.)

Largely left behind were the poor, the old (and even the not-so-old), blacks, Hispanics, native people, prisoners, those remaining outside the urban centers, the high proportion of suicidal gay and lesbian teenagers, and the untold thousands of runaways and throwaways hustling and trying to survive on city streets all over America. The crucial issue of endemic anti-gay violence tacitly endorsed by important segments of the political and religious establishment was given some attention, but not addressed as a top priority.

But slowly and quietly proliferating since the late 1960s was a network of gay and lesbian organizations, social clubs, religious affiliations (from Catholic to pagan), political action committees and special interest groups. By the 1990s there were groups for gay stamp collectors and lesbian daughters of Holocaust survivors. Though two or three lobbies claimed national status, the groupings were for the most part independent of one another, or, as in the case of many religious groups, allied in loose federations. A *de facto* anarchism prevailed.[33]

By the end of the 1970s, there were as many as a hundred such associations in the New York City area alone. It was this development (the beginnings of a true, rather than simply rhetorical, 'gay community') that was to prove invaluable when the AIDS epidemic struck, by giving a face and a voice to gay people, blocking what otherwise would have been the inevitable next step, quarantine – and preventing a far greater disaster. It may be instructive to look briefly at one of these small independent groups and see what it was up to while *Faggots* and *Rushes* were being written.

Opened in March 1973, the Ninth Street Center operated out of a small basement headquarters in Manhattan's Lower East Side where it provided its gay male constituency with various regularly scheduled events: open talk groups, acting and drawing classes, buffet suppers, game nights and private counselling. The Center's literature described it as 'designed for those who want their homosexuality to help them lead more fulfilling lives . . . . We believe in the creative individual who is attempting to expand the dimensions of his world, and want the Center to become a workshop of human resources.' Privately funded by gay members and supporters, the Center made an effort to 'provide a setting where gay people can learn about themselves and develop their relationships with others'. New projects were solicited, especially if they were 'unconventional and probing'.

The Ninth Street Center was founded by students of gay psychotherapist Paul Rosenfels, an original and independent figure on the New York scene. A physician and former Assistant Professor of Psychiatry at the University of Chicago, Rosenfels (in his fifties at the time of Stonewall) had also been chief of psychiatry in a California prison and a therapist in private practice. He had become increasingly disillusioned with classical psychiatry and had eventually moved to the East Village, where he began advertising his services in the local underground papers and counselling residents at low rates, with the first session free. Early in the 1970s he came out as gay, and his practice started to focus largely on gay men. A recovering alcoholic, he was particularly eager to help his clients overcome the need for drugs by exploring emotional growth.

Rosenfels' writings on the nature of love, the construction of sexuality and the interaction of history and psychology are complex, challenging and often profound. His writing style, unfortunately, is dense, philosophical, and relentlessly theoretical; ideas are never illustrated by examples, anecdotes or case studies. One reader described his books as 'all meat and no gravy' – or was it 'all steak and no sizzle'? This, as much as his originality, led to his being virtually ignored by the gay, popular and professional press. Nevertheless, through his books and through the Ninth Street Center, he developed a loyal following.

Another reason for Rosenfels' unpopularity was his unfashionable view of the nature and meaning of male/male relationships. Stressing the importance of mated behavior in gay men, the interaction of love and power, and the working polarity of dominant and submissive (or 'masculine' and 'feminine') aspects, Rosenfels emphasized the need to maintain the original inner spark that leads one to gayness in the first place: the spiritual drive to individuality, creativity and same-sex bonding.

In his major work on homosexuality, published in 1971, he wrote: 'In a homosexual romance love and power are released to find their own destiny. Men face the fact that love is an entity which is not automatically brought into being because socially supported eroticism exists, but must be built in a workmanlike fashion out of true devotion to an idealized object. In a similar way, the personal power capacities must discover the nature of human resources. Such growth experiences increase personal honesty and courage to a degree which threatens the stability of social beliefs and institutions.'[34]

Rosenfels worried about the compulsive promiscuity he was seeing in his young gay friends and clients. Like Gerald Heard twenty years earlier, he connected promiscuous patterns to a more general emotional constriction in society, and saw a rediscovery of personal creativity as the key to the way out: 'The homosexual must deal with the high level of promiscuity which any release of eroticism in a sexually dishonest society brings. The promiscuity of the homosexual is his heritage of the society's failure to face this problem, and insofar as he is capable of developing toward a level of human involvement which goes beyond promiscuity, he attains the creative expression of an inner identity for which his sexual honesty and flexibility have laid the groundwork.'[35]

'If freedom takes its entire being from an absence of restraint', Rosenfels wrote, 'restless wandering replaces the freedom to choose commitments, and the individual finds that he is running loose in a desert.'[36] The metaphor is reminiscent of Rev Malcolm Boyd's allusion to 'running in chains'. Compulsive promiscuity and sexual repression are revealed not as opposites, but as two aspects (or consequences) of the same crisis, a crisis of fear, with both social and personal dimensions – what Wilhelm Reich called 'the emotional plague'.

In the ghetto, gay men were learning all too well the lesson that *Faggots* dramatized: 'Love is an entity which is not automatically brought into being because socially supported eroticism exists.' The resulting frustration, as well as the growth of an incipient gay community fuelled a resurgence of political determination.

That frustration and determination, from both the inter-twined branches of gay society – the commercial gay male lifestyle, and the developing lesbian/gay social network – were tapped by a canny, popular, prophetic, and genuinely representative gay leader who emerged in 1970s San Francisco: the owner of a small camera store, a Jewish socialist named Harvey Milk.

Coup de grâce

If a bullet should enter my brain, let that bullet destroy every closet door.
— Harvey Milk

'The story of Harvey Milk is, to a large extent, the story of the gay movement in San Francisco, and, ultimately, the nation', wrote Milk's biographer, Randy Shilts.[37] If so, his assassination on 27 November 1978 was the *coup de grâce* of that movement in its post-Stonewall phase. The network of gay and lesbian organizations continued, grew, and survived into the AIDS era as an invaluable legacy of Gay Lib. But if, by the mid-1970s, the Gay Liberation movement proper had been co-opted, its lingering spirit died with the man who had worked to revive it. It existed as a rather embarrassing ghost for three years, and then was swept away by the health concerns of the 1980s.

Harvey Milk was elected as a Supervisor (alderman) in the city of San Francisco in 1977, on a platform stressing neighborhood power, alliances among previously disenfranchised minorities, and inventive ideas for maintaining a liveable city. His district included the gay ghetto. Some of his thoughts were summed up in a pair of speeches he delivered shortly after his election:

> I understand very well that my election was not alone a question of my gayness, but a question of what I represent. In a very real sense, Harvey Milk represented the spirit of the neighborhoods of San Francisco . . . . The American Dream starts with the neighborhoods. If we wish to rebuild our cities, we must first rebuild our neighborhoods. And to do that, we must understand that the quality of life is more important than the standard of living. To sit on the front

steps – whether it's a veranda in a small town or a concrete stoop in a big city – and talk to our neighborhoods is infinitely more important than to huddle on the living-room lounger and watch a make-believe world in not-quite living color.[38]

He spoke of a disturbing decline in the quality of life, 'the touch, the warmth, the meaning' of life, as technology advanced. The present leadership of the city, he said, 'seems to have taken the money route: bigness and wealth'. And he proposed as an alternative 'the route that has little room for political pay-offs, deals', and 'where the people are more important than highways'.

San Francisco can start right now to become number one. We can set examples so that others will follow. We can start overnight. We don't have to wait for budgets to be passed, surveys to be made, political wheelings and dealings . . . for it takes no money . . . it takes no compromising to give the people their rights . . . it takes no money to respect the individual. It takes no political deal to give people freedom. It takes no survey to remove repression.[39]

In spite of – and probably because of – its reputation as a 'gay Mecca', San Francisco in the 1970s had been responsible for what one reporter characterized as a 'gusher of violence' against gays – beatings, muggings, murders, rapes, bombings and arson – against which the city's police force provided little or no protection.[40] A strong element in the force had been gunning for the liberal mayor, George Moscone, since his election, and he had received a number of death threats. One former official described the police as having a 'perverted poisonous anger and a paranoia that gives them a sense of themselves as above the law'. The city's broad-minded sheriff, Richard Hongisto, carried a gun because, according to his former deputy, he was concerned that 'someone in the police department or sheriff's department would try to kill him'.[41] He kept a sealed letter in his desk, to be opened in the event of his 'sudden death'.

Milk had campaigned hard, and successfully, to have city supervisors elected directly from neighborhoods, rather than by the city at large. This meant that the largely gay area of the city would be able to elect its own representative. It was also a severe blow to the big business interests that backed one of Milk's rivals, conservative ex-policeman Dan White. Another Milk opponent was Rick Stokes, owner of the Ritch Street Baths, who was supported by David Goodstein's *Advocate*. Milk defeated Stokes in the race for supervisor from the gay district.

Harvey Milk liked to speculate about alternative futures for America, and was always urging gay people to come out of their closets. He also liked to ask gays, 'Why are we here? Why are gay people here? And what's happening?'[42] Harry Hay's questions of thirty years before were popping up again, and Milk's suggestion that gay people could help show the way to a more fulfilling future echoed earlier gay evolutionary philosophers Ted Carpenter and Gerald Heard. Milk's brief tenure of civic office infused a welcome wave of optimism into a gay community frustrated and discouraged by the right-wing backlash of the 1970s. Milk was dogged and shrewd, and funny in a way that was occasionally reminiscent of Lenny Bruce. And he was enormously threatening.

He was shot in the head, just as he had predicted. His political ally, Mayor George Moscone, was killed by the same 'lone assassin', Milk's political rival, Dan White. The literature that had gotten White elected had characterized his opposition as 'splinter groups of radicals, social deviates and incorrigibles'. 'You must realize', he had written to his constituents, 'there are thousands upon thousands of frustrated angry people such as yourselves waiting to unleash a fury that can and will eradicate the malignancies which blight our beautiful city.'[43]

George Moscone's election as mayor had been assured with the assistance of busloads of members of the People's Temple, a local religious cult led by Rev Jim Jones, a one-time vendor of discarded research monkeys. Jones, who had apparently abandoned his previous right-wing views, had been a missionary in Brazil where he maintained close ties to the CIA through his friend Dan Mitrione and the CIA-financed International Police Academy, which was instructing various repressive governments in counter-insurgency and torture techniques.[44]

When accusations of massive voter fraud necessitated an investigation, San Francisco District Attorney Joe Freitas (a close friend of Rev Jones) appointed lawyer Tom Stoen to do the job. Stoen was Jones' legal adviser. Soon afterwards, any evidence of vote-tampering was eliminated when the voting rosters were destroyed.[45] It was alleged that in return for some well-organized help on polling day, Moscone ignored a little habit Jones had of surreptitiously shipping weapons out of the country.

Jones later became internationally notorious for the so-called 'White Night' holocaust. After he had moved the People's Temple to a remote part of Guyana, he and hundreds of members of his cult died shortly before the Milk/Moscone assassinations, in what was said to be a mass suicidal imbibing of a local version of Kool-Aid, laced with cyanide. San Franciscans were still reeling from the Jonestown revelations when the Dan White double assassination dealt them another blow.

The full story of Jonestown has never been fully documented. Many of the corpses displayed none of the hallmarks of cyanide poisoning. The leading Guyanese pathologist at the scene reported fresh needle marks at the back of the left shoulder-blades of 80 to 90 per cent of the victims.[46] In addition, huge quantities of mind-altering drugs were found stored at the site. Congressman Leo Ryan, who was assassinated while on a fact-finding mission to Jonestown, had been a leading critic of the CIA and the co-sponsor of a bill limiting CIA activity. The bill died with him.

These and other aspects of the tangled background to the holocaust night in the Guyanese jungle suggest that Jonestown may have been part of the evolving series of CIA experiments in mind-control which began with the Montreal-based Project MK-Ultra.[47] One local journalist, musing on police involvement in the lead-up to the City Hall killings, remarked that the incident was 'so much like Jonestown . . . . They were both cult murders . . . . In San Francisco, it was a cop cult.'[48]

The sequence of local events leading up to the double murder is detailed in Randy Shilts' *The Mayor of Castro Street*. A few factors invite comment. Harvey Milk's financial backers were thousands of people from the community, many of them giving no more than a few dollars or a few cents. Dan White's financial backers were large, powerful real estate interests promoting downtown development with, in Shilts' words, 'all the trappings of old-fashioned political corruption'.[49] These 'entrepreneurs' had not only given White political support but had financed a small business for him, a hot potato stand, which he and his wife operated with indifferent success. Political payoffs to White for services rendered were suspected and, according to Shilts, the ex-politician was under FBI investigation at the time of the assassination.

Before the killings, Dan White had suddenly and unexpectedly resigned his office, and in doing so had surrendered a council seat crucial to his business backers' attempts to block the civic reforms championed by Moscone and Milk. Suddenly, ten days after his resignation, White changed his mind and asked the Mayor to reinstate him. At first, Moscone agreed. When Milk and others pointed out that this might not help his re-election bid, he decided to appoint a substitute instead, as was his prerogative under the city's constitution. White made a phone call, picked up a gun and headed for City Hall.

What accounted for White's apparent change of mind? He was burdened with financial and marital problems, and apparently 'relieved and cheerful' to be rid of his supervisor job (which he had come to regard as tiresome). Why did he react so angrily to the failure of his bid for reinstatement?

Just before White's flip-flop, he conferred with two groups of important backers: the Police Officers' Association and the city's Board of Realtors. According to Shilts' account, it was his meeting with them that led him to reverse his decision to resign. As White's council seat held the key to whether neighborhood or 'real estate' interests would dominate the city's future development, his backers, to whom he owed so much, could not have been pleased with his sudden, unexpected resignation and its potential to undo all their plans.[50]

We do not know what pressures might have been placed on White to regain his seat on the council, whether he was given an ultimatum of some sort, or whether he simply realized (perhaps, in his naiveté and arrogance, for the first time) that such decisions were

Plate 1
Gay Sebastian – Eddy Marsh, patron of the arts and Churchill's private secretary (*c*.1912).

Plate 2
Commemorative plaque at the Stonewall Inn (1978).

Plate 3 Ain't It Da Truth! cover (1977).

Plate 4
Man, Minotaur and fist –
advertisement in *Drummer*
(*c.* 1980).
Note: The SandMUtopia
Supply Co. is no longer
in existence.

Plate 5 Poppers were popular with American troops in Vietnam.
This advertisement appeared in gay magazines in the 1970s.

ISSUE 390   MARCH 20, 1984

THE CLASSIFIEDS

A PULLOUT SUPPLEMENT TO THE ADVOCATE

BLUEPRINT FOR
HEALTH

7

IT'S A GREAT FEELING!

A great deal of positive response has been initiated through our 'Blue Print for Health' series, and we are pleased to find that so many individuals share our interest in increasing the quality of life. We have received inquiries from all over the U.S., Canada and Europe; not only from individuals, but from Congressmen, publishers, AIDS organizations, and many medical and allied health personnel.

To those who have taken time to respond and to the doctors, researchers, authors and investigators who gave their time and expertise to this project, we extend our sincere and heartfelt thanks. You have solidified our belief in this worthwhile undertaking and contributed extensively to its success, which is indeed a great feeling that we wish to share.

This is the last in a series presented by Great Lakes Products on AIDS awareness. Reprints and research documentation are available by writing: BLUEPRINT FOR HEALTH, P.O. Box 44336, Indianapolis, IN 46204. Please include a self-addressed, stamped ($1.00) 10" x 13" size envelope.

Joseph F. Miller
President
Great Lakes Products, Inc.

The Worlds Most Refined
Nitrite-Based Scents

The Effects of Nitrite/Nitrates are
Currently Under Medical Investigation

Plate 6   Poppers as a 'blueprint for health' (*The Advocate*, 1984).

Plate 7 (left)
Poppers as an atomic cloud, with melting faces and the head of a white bull (*Drummer*, 1981).

Plate 8 (right)
ACT UP poster imitating the familiar red-and-white Coca-Cola logo (1990). Reservations about AZT appear in small print.

Plate 9 (below)
'Are you sick enough for hospital?' Fantasy photo-feature from *Folsom* (1981) just prior to the advent of GRID.

Enjoy

AZT

The U.S. government has spent one billion dollars over the past 10 years to research new AIDS drugs. The result: 1 drug- AZT. It makes half the people who try it sick and for the other half it stops working after a year. Is AZT the last best hope for people with AIDS or is it a short-cut to the killing Burroughs Wellcome is making in the AIDS marketplace? Scores of drugs languish in government pipelines while fortunes are made on this monopoly.

IS THIS HEALTH CARE OR WEALTH CARE?

STORM THE N.I.H. MAY 21. INFO 212-989-1114

Are You Sick Enough For

HOSPITAL

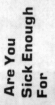

About a hundred of the sickest men of San Francisco came to get cured at a joint **Folsom Magazine** and **Handball Express** event. Volunteers from the Folsom community transformed the club into one of the most bizarre, erotic hospitals a patient could hope to find—move over Lizards.

While the Pharmacy dispensed Piña Coladas and Suds as a preventive medicine, most patients and doctors (because they, too, can be sick) brought their own prescriptions to finding health and happiness.

The clinics open to the very sick included:

Deep Internal Therapy: This was a group clinic run by Dr. Painless (see his *Pig Personal*). Heart massage and aortic palpations were done through the latest technique of trans-anal insertion. For those of you who are not familiar with this recently discovered method, it involves dilating the sphincter and other do-da's to the level of the descending colon. This is by insertion of a series of increasingly larger latex instruments (usually balloon shaped on the end of a handle). When the patient can comfortably handle an instrument the size of a wrist, the attending physician inserts instead his

hand and forearm in order to palpate and massage the afflicted areas. The Chief of Staff was very pleased to see the number of interns willing to play the part of the patient in order that their fellow students could learn how to perform this new Deep Internal Therapy.

Needles played an important part in a number of the clinics that evening. Among those open to the general public was **Chief of Dermatology Clinic** run by socialite Dr. Payton, who owns and operates **The Cave** bar in his spare time. Also in his spare time, he has developed a miraculous cure for the heartbreak of sexually transmitted herpes—until now untreatable. Unlike acupuncture which relies on needle depth and position, this dermatologist has discovered that by using multi-colored, sub-dermal injections he can cover the terrible eye-sore. Most people in the non-medical community mistake the scar as a tattoo.

The Surgery Clinic was maintained by Dr. Peter, this issue's cover man. See his interview on *Piercing* in the **ABC's**.

Another party, **Hospital 2**, is planned for Sept. 5th, the Saturday of Labor Day weekend.

Plate 10
'How to clone a fist'
– advertisement
in *One* magazine (1965).

Plate 11
Prophetic gay New Year's greeting
for 1981
(*Zipper*, 1980).

no longer his to make, and that he had painted himself into a very tight corner. Unfortunately, after White's indictment for murder, corruption charges against him were not pursued, and whatever pertinent information may be in his FBI dossier has been marked for internal discussion only.[51]

On the night of the slayings, thousands of San Franciscans poured into the streets in a huge candlelight vigil. After lying in state at City Hall, Harvey was cremated. At his own request, his ashes were mixed with the contents of two packets of grape Kool-Aid, placed in a box wrapped in *Doonesbury* and *Peanuts* comic strips and scattered on the Pacific Ocean. They made a pretty patch of lavender as they mingled with the crosscurrents of San Francisco Bay.

Dan White's trial was a farce. White was presented to the jury as an upstanding citizen. The prosecution seemed timid and inept. According to an article in the *Nation* after White's release, the Assistant District Attorney in charge of the case was subjected to intimidating remarks by a group of police 'drinking buddies'. A phone call White admitted to having made immediately before the killings was never investigated. The foreman of the jury was an executive of a company which had contributed to White's campaign fund.[52] And so on.

During the trial, a number of people commented on White's friendliness with his guards, and on the prosecution's obvious reluctance to probe motives or upset the police. Jim Denman, a former county court official, remarked, 'The more I observed what went on at the jail, the more I began to stop seeing what Dan White did as the act of an individual and began to see it as a political act in a political movement.'[53]

Laughing and joking with his police friends in the cells, Dan White took the tactic of assuming a zombie-like pose in the courtroom, his lawyer claiming that (although he had carried the murder weapon – and extra bullets – to City Hall and entered surreptitiously by a side window) he had nevertheless been suddenly and unexpectedly overcome with an irrational urge to kill, perhaps as a result of having eaten too many Twinkies. This cynically ingenious defense recapitulated an earlier explanation for the JFK assassination suggested by a photo of Lee Harvey Oswald with a bottle of Coke in his hand – and conflated it with the word 'twinkie' as a slang expression for homosexual. It became notorious as the so-called 'Twinkie Defense', and lawyers all over America began to research the eating habits of their homicidal clients.

White's defense attornies told the jury that people from White's 'fine background' (married, white, cop, owns own business) just didn't kill people in cold blood. They were careful to exclude gays from the jury, fearing that 'a gay might believe that the slaying of Milk . . . was a political assassination committed to block gay power', and this of course would have been delusionary and 'contrary to the facts'.[54] The all-straight jury convicted White only of two counts of manslaughter; he would be free in about five years. 'What does this mean?' a reporter asked Milk's colleague, Cleve Jones. 'It means that in America, it's all right to kill faggots.'[55]

When the gays of San Francisco marched again that night, the mood was very different. They shouted 'Out of the bars and into the streets!', 'Dan White was a cop!', 'Avenge Harvey Milk!' and 'All-straight jury, No surprise, Dan White lives and Harvey dies!'[56] As the anger rose, the march turned into a second Stonewall. A block-long line of police cars was set on fire; the police retaliated and many gays were injured, some by cops with concealed badges. A new slogan was coined that night: 'We all live in San Francisco!'

One gay man told a reporter, 'Dan White getting off is one of a million things that happen in our lives; the beatings, the murders, the people driven to suicide by the hostility of straights.' Another man setting fire to police cars shouted, 'Tell people we ate too many Twinkies!'[57]

Shortly before the trial and the 'White Night Riots' that followed, the poet David Emerson Smith and a group of friends published an anthology of poems in memory of Harvey.[58] The final poem, whose lines provided the book's title, was by a writer using the pen-name The Fag Nun Assunta Femia. The poem's title refers to the virginal Greek nature goddess Artemis. Identified with the new moon rising from her purifying bath, she also displays a contrary aspect: wild, death-dealing and dangerous, especially to men. The poem is addressed to Dan White:

155: *The Revolution Is Over*

From Artemis an Oracle

white
dan white
it's been driving
me mad
to tell you this:

for the murder of one
italian middle class
allegedly heterosexual
liberal mayor

and for the murder of one
petit bourgeois
jewish faggot

i promise you this

if you plead insanity
if you plead insanity

i promise you this

if you get off because
of insanity

i promise you this:

you will go stark
            raving
            mad.

Dan White was released from prison after five years. The satirist Paul Krassner remarked that this was two years less than the regulation shelf-life of the Twinkies in his kitchen cupboard, and wondered if he finished his snack when he got home. Shortly afterwards, White climbed into his car, turned on the ignition, and poisoned himself with exhaust fumes. Like Jim Jones, White recalls the figure of Kurtz in Coppola's film *Apocalypse Now*: a useful fanatic, manipulable, unstable – and expendable. By the time of his presumed suicide, gay America had other deaths on its mind.

Spiral path – or dead end

Come Out, Come Out, Wherever You Are . . . *Follow the Yellow Brick Road!*
— The Munchkins

As anyone familiar with Munchkinland in *The Wizard of Oz* knows, the Yellow Brick Road begins with a spiral path. But comments on Dorothy's journey to Oz will have to wait for a later chapter. For now, our look at the pre-AIDS era of gay history must end with a few words on a book that appeared just as the health crisis was about to cast a harsh light on some elements of our journey, and to bring questions of survival and mortality to the forefront of the gay consciousness: David Fernbach's *The Spiral Path: A Gay Contribution to Human Survival.*[59]

Radical feminist, heretical communist and former editor of the writings of Marx, David Fernbach had met his lover, GLF co-founder Aubrey Walter, while they were both students at the London School of Economics in the late 1960s. In 1980, together with their friend, Richard Dipple, they founded Gay Men's Press (which published *The Spiral Path* and Walter's anthology of early Gay Lib material *Come Together*).

The Spiral Path is an unabashedly philosophical (though very readable) book, which sets out to ask some searching and pertinent questions about gay people and the gay movement in a global context. 'What has gay liberation to do with environmental pollution?' was one of those questions. Another was: 'In what particular way can gay people help to bring the present crisis of humanity to an outcome of survival and higher evolution?'

On his way to answering these and other questions, Fernbach had necessarily to deal with the Stonewall Experiment, the gay lifestyle that had arisen in North American cities during the 1970s, and which, in a smaller, less intense fashion, was making itself felt in Britain. As an undogmatic, but committed gay socialist, he did not care for much of what he saw. 'In a notable display of false consciousness', he wrote, 'it has become popular in the gay community, especially in the United States, to define our marginalized existence as a "lifestyle", implying that it is essentially freely chosen rather than an adaptation to oppression.'[60]

He pointed out that

> in the gay subculture of today it can be very difficult to establish any lasting relationships, based on a love fed by the sublimation of sexuality into affection for which our species has a peculiar disposition.
>
> Without this sublimation, our sexuality simply follows the ever-changing flux of desire, seizing on partial objects, surface appearances, rather than being used to form genuine interpersonal bonds. This has actually been glorified by certain theorists of sexual promiscuity . . . . The experience of the gay subculture, however, is that this is a destructive dead end. The drive behind so much gay promiscuity is not that this is more satisfying than the cultivation of 'deep meaningful relationships' (not that these cannot also leave a certain room for casual, purely recreational sex as well). It is rather as a resigned second-best, if not actually a desperate quest for a 'Mr Right' who, almost by definition, will not be found by this route . . . . [It] is unquestionably a symptom of some very deep malaise that gay men so often find it hard to form ties of solidarity, and live so individualistic an existence.[61]

Fernbach's study explored questions of androgyny (Carpenter's 'intermediate types'), and he speculated that part of the unconscious mechanism behind the superficiality of many urban gay relationships was the negative value placed on the androgynous Self – and the androgynous Other. By confining his sexual contacts to the superficial, even anonymous, level, the gay man need never deal with anything but the image, recoiling before the person behind the image can be revealed. 'This is particularly the case when consummation takes place in bars, saunas, toilets, parks, disused warehouses, etc. – often without a word being spoken. A minute's conversation or a glance around his apartment would immediately belie the butch image, but it need never come to that.'[62] In buying into the sexually polarized society's denigration of the Intersex, the Androgyne, the Uranian, the Isophyl, the contemporary gay man was denying his nature, impoverishing his emotional life, and driving himself to despair, even to death.

The gay movement may have been inevitable, as the birth of a baby may be inevitable, but, Fernbach added, 'its birth alive and well is certainly not so'.[63] In spite of the advances made, he asserted, many gays continued to be 'lost souls, deprived of a place or even a definition in society', with despair as 'the secret inwardness of our outward revels', and suicidal impulses just beneath the surface.[64]

Emphasizing the role of gays and lesbians in breaking down the polarized and ossified 'gender system', Fernbach set out his belief that gay patterns, patterns between people viewing each other as equals, would provide guides for living to a new future majority whose freer sexuality would subsume heterosexual, gay, lesbian and bisexual alike. He echoed Whitman, Carpenter and Heard in his assertion that there are good evolutionary reasons for gay people's continued existence in this world, and that the gay spirit may pioneer the creation of new kinds of relationships to help heal a badly damaged planet.

Fernbach urged a re-examination of Utopian communism, the libertarian tradition of Carpenter, Wilde and William Morris, which he regretted had dwindled almost to nothing in public consciousness, as well as being 'virtually banished' from the nominal Communist movement, where it had been replaced with an ideology as rapacious as the capitalism it claimed to oppose.

One of Fernbach's key insights in *The Spiral Path* was the realization that in many ways 'the gay subculture of today simply shares the problems of our society as a whole, often in the most glaring degree'.[65] Even as he wrote, those problems had already begun to manifest themselves in the form of various 'twentieth century illnesses' that were most pronounced among gay men.

It is significant that *The Spiral Path* was dedicated to the loving and compassionate Buddhist goddess/saint Quan Yin, who 'in the very process of attaining Buddhahood . . . "hearing the cries of the world", turns back and vows to renounce her own divinity until, with her aid, all the suffering of the world is extinguished, and all beings have attained the same highest level of spiritual existence'.[66] Fernbach expresses his belief that the coming of Quan Yin into society on any large scale would necessarily entail 'a process of

... reasserting the maternal culture, not as something ascribed solely to women, but as a quality that men must equally display'.[67]

Fernbach suggested this as a process desperately needed, not only by a society dangerously overbalanced with 'masculine' qualities, but also by all the clones and numbers, the sex consumers and uniformed rebels who had assembled in the ghetto, and in their innocence, had been sold a concoction that turned out to be tainted.

Fernbach's prophecy was accurate. Quan Yin would appear, in what many might have thought an unlikely place. It would take a few years, any many human tragedies, before the manifestation.

A bloodbath

Well remember everything is illusion. But illusions try to make themselves as real as possible, naturally, in order to gain currency.
— William S. Burroughs

In the spring of 1980, Jamie and I left New York on a crowded, bring-your-own-sandwiches Wardair charter from Kennedy Airport to London, England, where I had family and friends. I found work in an art college on Charing Cross Road while Jamie convalesced from life in the ghetto. We moved into the top floor of a gay house across the street from the drab George Orwell comprehensive school in unfashionable Finsbury Park. Our live-in landlord was a friendly, shrewd Australian with a shady past.

Jamie planted a herb garden, set up a miniature stone circle, and got his first taste of the world outside the planet of Manhattan and its satellites as we made our journeys to Stonehenge, Castlerigg, Long Meg and her Daughters, and the New Forest, with its Rufus Stone marking the site of the mysterious death of the last pagan king of England. I was glad to be home, and to feel – as much for Jamie as for myself – that a thickening psychic tie had been cut, relieved that we had escaped over the ghetto wall.

One night in the old house on Turle Road, I woke up for some reason, and wandered down to the ground-floor kitchen and the bathroom which led off it. The lights were out; I was the only one awake. I went, for some reason, into the bathroom. When I turned on the light, the old porcelain, claw-foot bath was covered in blood.

Blood ran down its white sides in rivulets, as though poured from a container or a freshly slaughtered and freely bleeding corpse.

Strangely, there was not a drop of blood anywhere else – not on the floor, the rug, the towels, the toilet. Only in the bath. The house was quiet, and there was no other sign of disturbance. I opened the back door, listened and looked out. The neighborhood seemed quite normal. The chickens were asleep in their coop (I had thought of them first, and second, a rather wild gay skinhead on the second floor). A dog barked with no particular conviction from the next street, then stopped. I was alone in a silent house with a lot of blood.[68]

The next morning, neither Jamie nor our landlord could explain what I had seen. Nothing in the house or the people in it seemed changed. To this day, I have come to no conclusion about the nature of whatever it was I saw, whether natural or supernatural. I know only that one night in the summer of 1980, I saw a vivid, puzzling vision of a bloodbath.

Jamie and I returned, briefly, to Manhattan later that sizzling summer, before moving on to Toronto. Neither of us was to take up permanent residence in New York again. If I had stayed, I might well have been in the Ramrod on the night of 19 November 1980, when a thirty-eight-year-old ex-transit police officer fired at least 77 shots from an Uzi machine gun into and around the front windows of the bar, killing two gay men, George Wenz and Vernon Koenig, and wounding several others in the bar and on the sidewalk outside. People said it was a miracle the list of victims wasn't longer.

The killer, a fanatical Christian, said he was 'enraged' to have to watch 'all those faggots on the street'. He told police he had driven by the site many times, with others: his wife and daughters, he claimed in court, routinely establishing for the jury the cozy image of a family man.

John Preston, in a report titled 'The white candles come to New York', wrote that 'telephones rang all over Manhattan as friends and lovers called one another and sighed and cried with relief to hear the voice on the other end of the wire. "Thank God it wasn't you".'[69] He added that 'everyone knew that he had been at least symbolically shot [that] night'. The following night, two thousand men marched to protest the killings in a candlelight vigil singing 'We

Shall Overcome'. It was a smaller, but eerily similar version of the events in San Francisco after the murder of Harvey Milk.

Preston wrote that the shooting and mourning 'have produced a cohesive sense to gay New York that never existed before. The personal identification of every man I know who lives and socializes in Greenwich Village now includes the knowledge that the gun could be aimed at him.' He ended his piece by predicting the killings would politicize and radicalize the gay community. 'And we will be ready to carry new white candles if we must.'

There would be many thousands of new white candles carried in memorial processions in the future. The vigils held for Harvey Milk, George Wenz and Vernon Koenig were the first of many to come.

Notes

1. Arthur Evans, quoted in Toby Marotta, *The Politics of Homosexuality* (Boston: Houghton Mifflin, 1981), p. 209.
2. Pete Fisher, 'Reflection on reflections', unpublished paper (1971) quoted in Marotta, *Politics of Homosexuality*, p. 191. Chapter 7 of Marotta's book describes the wrangling within the Gay Liberation movement between neo-Marxist politicals and cultural radicals.
3. Arnie Kantrowitz, *Under the Rainbow: Growing Up Gay* (New York: Pocket Books, 1977), p. 150.
4. This and subsequent remarks by Aubrey Walter are from the Introduction to his *Come Together – The Years of Gay Liberation 1970–1973* (London: Gay Men's Press, 1980). This essay remains one of the most thoughtful considerations of the fate of the Gay Liberation movement in the 1970s.
5. John Lauritsen, 'Political-economic construction of gay male clone identity', *Journal of Homosexuality*, 24 (3–4), 1993, p. 221.
6. And others: see, for example, Gregg Blatchford, 'Male dominance and the gay world', in Kenneth Plummer, ed., *The Making of the Modern Homosexual* (New Jersey: Barnes & Noble, 1981). Blatchford refers to gay men being in a situation in which 'the sub-culture itself, through its own actions, cannot alleviate the conditions that led to these problems'.
7. Lesbian novelist Rita Mae Brown's account of her surreptitious visit to a gay baths was good-humoured and largely sympathetic. Nevertheless, she felt the atmosphere to be 'hungry, frightened and slightly savage', with the immediate aims masking deeper needs for simple human contact and love. 'Queen for a day: a stranger in

Paradise', in Karla Jay and Allen Young, eds., *Lavender Culture* (New York: Jove Books, 1979), p. 69.

8.   Patricia Nell Warren, *The Front Runner* (New York: Morrow, 1974).

9.   Edmund White, *States of Desire: Travels in Gay America* (New York: Dutton, 1980), p. 45.

10.   Seymour Kleinberg, *Alienated Affections: Being Gay in America* (New York: Warner Books, 1982), pp. 194–5.

11.   Lauritsen, 'Political-economic construction', p. 5.

12.   Ken Popert, 'Public sexuality and social space', *Body Politic*, July–August, 1982, p. 29.

13.   *Ibid.*, p. 30.

14.   Steven G. P. Blanchard, letter, *Body Politic*, July–August, 1982, p. 4. The phrase 'preserves and protects' echoes 'To Serve and Protect', the slogan of the police force in Toronto, where *The Body Politic* was published.

15.   John Rechy, *Numbers* (New York: Evergreen Black Cat Editions, 1968).

16.   *Ibid.*, p. 11.

17.   *Ibid.*, p. 190.

18.   John Rechy, *Rushes* (New York: Grove Press, 1979), p. 81.

19.   *Ibid.*, p. 57.

20.   *Ibid.*, p. 19. Rechy's apt metaphor is another in a considerable catalogue of references to blemishes, unhealed scars, leprosy and bleeding wounds, scattered through gay writing in the years immediately prior to the outbreak of AIDS. Gay journalist Arthur Bell wrote in *Dancing the Gay Lib Blues* (1971), 'Internal tumors are realized as social cancers.'

21.   John Rechy, *The Sexual Outlaw* (New York: Dell, 1977).

22.   Reprinted in Winston Leyland, ed., *Gay Sunshine Interviews, Vol. I* (San Francisco: Gay Sunshine Press, 1978), p. 263.

23.   *Ibid.*, p. 262.

24.   Stephen Adams, *The Homosexual as Hero in Contemporary Fiction* (London: Vision Press, 1980), p. 97.

25.   *Ibid.*, pp. 97–8.

26.   Seymour Krim, quoted on the cover of the paperback edition of Larry Kramer, *Faggots* (New York: Warner Books, 1978).

27.   Tim Dlugos, 'Larry Kramer', *Christopher Street*, February 1979, p. 59.

28.   In Larry Kramer, *Reports from the Holocaust: The Making of an AIDS Activist* (New York: St Martin's Press, 1989), pp. 5–7, 16–22.

29.   Philip Derbyshire, *Gay Left 9*, quoted in Kramer, *Reports from The Holocaust*, p. 18.

30.   Hugo Marsan, *Le Gai Pied*, September 1981, quoted in Kramer, *Reports from the Holocaust*, pp. 18–19.

31.   George Whitmore, 'Beer, baloney and champagne', *Body Politic*, September 1978, p. 13.

32.   Kramer, *Reports from the Holocaust*, pp. 6–7.

33.   Avowed anarchists had their own groups, such as the Mackay Society, and the New York Gay Anarchists, at whose forum (co-sponsored by the Libertarian Book Club) I first presented and discussed some of the ideas in this book.

34.   Paul Rosenfels, MD, *Homosexuality: The Psychology of the Creative Process* (Roslyn Heights, NY: Libra Publishers, 1971), p. 28.

35.   *Ibid.*, p. 140.

36.   *Ibid.*, p. 17.

37.   Randy Shilts, *The Mayor of Castro Street: The Life and Times of Harvey Milk* (New York: St Martin's Press, 1982), p. xiii. Much of my information on Harvey Milk and Dan White has been provided by Shilts's biography and the works by Warren Hinckle, Paul Krassner and Thomas Szasz cited below.

38.   Harvey Milk, 'A city of neighborhoods', in Shilts, *Mayor of Castro Street*, p. 353.

39.   Harvey Milk, 'A populist looks at the city', in Shilts, *Mayor of Castro Street*, p. 349.

40.   Warren Hinckle, *Gayslayer! The Story of How Dan White Killed Harvey Milk and George Moscone and Got Away with Murder* (Virginia City, NV: Silver Dollar, 1985).

41.   Jim Denman, quoted in Hinckle, *Gayslayer!*, pp. 26–7.

42.   Harvey Milk, 'The hope speech,' in Shilts, *Mayor of Castro Street*, p. 360.

43.   Quoted in Shilts, *Mayor of Castro Street*, p. 162.

44.   Mitrione's execution by Uruguayan guerillas was the subject of Costa Gavras's film *State of Siege*. See John Judge, *The Black Hole of Guiana: The Untold Story of the Jonestown Massacre* (Santa Barbara, CA: Prevailing Winds Research, n.d.).

45.   See Paul Krassner, 'The Twinkie murders: The Milk–Moscone case revisited', *Nation*, 14 January 1984.

46.   'Coroner says 700 who died in cult were slain', *Miami Herald*, 17 December 1978; and Judge, *Black Hole*, p. 2.

47.   See the report of the Senate Subcommittee on Constitutional Rights, *Individual Rights and the Federal Role in Behavior Modification* (Washington, DC: Government Printing Office, 1974); and John Judge, *Black Hole*. After the massacre, Jonestown was repopulated with Hmong tribespeople from Laos. Many of the Hmong grew opium for the CIA during the Vietnam war, and were paid in

weapons, with which they were expected to fight the communists. After the US withdrawal, they became refugees.

48. Randy Alfred, quoted in Hinckle, *Gayslayer!*, p. 27.
49. Shilts, *Mayor of Castro Street*, p. 200.
50. One of White's chief campaign contributors, and the financial backer of his business, was developer Warren Simmons (who was later convicted of making illegal political contributions under false names to White and others). Diane Feinstein, who became mayor after White killed Moscone, had originally put White in touch with Simmons.
51. Shilts, *Mayor of Castro Street*, p. 200.
52. Krassner, 'Twinkie murders'.
53. Jim Denman, quoted in Hinckle, *Gayslayer!*, p. 27.
54. Stephen Scherr, quoted in Thomas Szasz, 'How Dan White got away with murder', in *The Therapeutic State: Psychiatry in the Mirror of Current Events* (Buffalo: Prometheus Books, 1984), p. 142.
55. Shilts, *Mayor of Castro Street*, p. 325.
56. *Ibid.*, pp. 327–8.
57. Quoted in Hinckle, *Gayslayer!*, p. 15.
58. David Emerson Smith *et al.*, *I Promise You This* (San Francisco, CA: 1979). The book bore the inscription 'This collection of poems is in part a response to the homophobic murder of Harvey Milk and George Moscone (a passionate homophile).' Various rumors about Moscone's sexuality had circulated around San Francisco for years.
59. David Fernbach, *The Spiral Path: A Gay Contribution to Human Survival* (London: Gay Men's Press, 1981).
60. *Ibid.*, p. 103.
61. *Ibid.*, p. 104.
62. *Ibid.*, p. 102.
63. *Ibid.*, p. 114.
64. *Ibid.*, p. 206.
65. *Ibid.*, p. 104.
66. *Ibid.*, p. 13. Fernbach is quoting from Rudolph Baro, *The Alternative in Eastern Europe* (London: New Left Books, 1978), p. 364.
67. *Ibid.*, p. 182.
68. I wrote about this incident in my book *Sex Magick* (Toronto: Stubblejumper Press, 1986), pp. 68–71.
69. John Preston, 'The white candles come to New York', *Alternate*, December 1980.

Chapter five

News for the 4th of July

Human beings who become conscious of their sexual needs because of changing mores, but who simultaneously lack the ways and means of naturally discharging their sexual energy and experiencing full gratification, are necessarily torn apart.

— Wilhelm Reich, *The Cancer Biopathy*

IT was the muggy Friday of the 1981 Fourth of July holiday weekend, and as the little groups of gay men escaped muggy New York for the breezes of Fire Island, an inside page of the *Times* tucked in their shoulder-bags carried the headline: 'Rare cancer seen in 41 homosexuals'. Reports of Kaposi's sarcoma, pneumocystis pneumonia and other unusual illnesses afflicting a sector of the gay male population had first been reported by the gay newspaper *New York Native*. The Centers for Disease Control, which presided over one segment of the complex of overlapping medico-governmental jurisdictional zones, had dismissed the accounts as unfounded rumors, mere gay gossip.[1] Now America's 'newspaper of record' had made it official. If the post-Stonewall era died with Harvey Milk, its official memorial came that day. The Stonewall Experiment had entered a new phase; though the disease syndrome had not yet acquired its name, the age of AIDS had arrived.

'A few friends had died mysteriously. Several others were sick with unrecognized symptoms', wrote one gay man. 'I'd had many of the sexually-transmitted diseases that the article said I shared with these forty-one homosexuals . . . I was scared.'[2] The catastrophe had been creeping up for some time. In the AIDS era, the young gay men who in their adult lives had never known a time without AIDS, imagined that the epidemic had suddenly struck out of nowhere; until then, they believed, urban gay men had been paragons of health. 'Previously healthy' and 'apparently healthy' were phrases one came across repeatedly in the media. Mark Freedman's death, among others, and the sex- and drug-related health problems of many of the 'refugees from America' told another tale. Years before AIDS, the health crisis of gay men could be seen daily in the lengthening lines at the VD clinics, the same men returning again and again.

For years, the renowned homeopathic physician George Vithoulkas had been warning that inordinate amounts of medically administered antibiotics, hormones and vaccinations would result, inevitably, in seriously weakened immune systems and hard-to-diagnose illnesses for a large portion of the population.[3] Urban gay men had been among the most eager consumers of these medical products and services, and of illicit pharmaceuticals as well. Now, Vithoulkas' prediction had begun to come true – with white, gay, middle-class men as its first socially visible victims.

Those first AIDS patients (before the acronym had been coined) died with terrible swiftness, just as the first victims of syphilis had done when that disease surfaced in Europe a few centuries earlier. In a medical rush to judgement, AIDS quickly came to be regarded as a necessarily fatal syndrome. Doctors, for professional as well as humanitarian reasons, did not like to lose patients, particularly not patients as young as these, and if they died, surely it could only be because death was inevitable. Nothing could be done; AIDS was '100% fatal'. And so it would be, in the popular mythology and in the press, well into the course of the epidemic, though there were men walking around and talking and boiling up their odoriferous Chinese soups and attending their visualization seminars, having survived AIDS for over a decade.

But on that first July 4th weekend, the gay men who boarded the Sayville ferry to the Pines or Cherry Grove would discover (if they read far enough into their newspaper) two pertinent facts that, in the face of all the claims and predictions, would continue to characterize the epidemic for years into the future: that young gay men were dying, and that doctors were puzzled.

Question period: gay men on the GRID

Self-criticism was not the strong point of a community that was only beginning to define itself affirmatively after centuries of repression.
— Randy Shilts

From the beginning, AIDS was presented by the medical establishment and the press as something mysterious, baffling. It involved, apparently, the most dreaded of the twentieth century diseases, cancer, which had apparently won the 'war' declared on it by the White House, though no one liked to admit it. And not just any old cancers, but 'rare cancers', 'gay cancers' and 'rare pneumonias'. This frequent description conjured up fabled beasts, almost unknown, and even defying identification.

The facts were somewhat different. The array of illnesses presented by those forty-one gay men, and by the many gay men to follow, may have been rare, but they were not new. They could be divided into two sorts. Those initially diagnosed had, for the most part, been seen before under certain special circumstances: both Kaposi's sarcoma and pneumocystis pneumonia had been noted in patients whose immune systems had been damaged by syphilis or suppressed by pharmaceuticals, in some instances to prevent the rejection of transplanted organs. Those which at first presented even more of a puzzle also turned out to be not new, but new to the species. Gay men were coming down with sheep diseases, bird diseases and swine fevers, illnesses of livestock to which humankind had previously been immune. The situation was thought to be without precedent. And yet, to those who remembered, it was reminiscent of the late 1960s and the hippies of Haight-Ashbury. Tom Wolfe recalled that at the Free Clinic there, doctors had been treating diseases that had 'disappeared so long ago they had never even picked up Latin names, diseases such as the mange, the grunge, the itch, the twitch, the thrush, the scroff, the rot'.[4] Except that the hippies rarely died of their thrush or their rot; the gay men were dying in increasing numbers.

It was apparent that the integrity of the human organism was breaking down. The immune system (only recently given much scientific attention and still only vaguely understood) had, somehow, been undermined, leaving the individual unprotected. The biophysical boundaries between the individual and the environment were dissolving. Gay men developed sores which would not heal, disorientation, chronic dehydrating diarrhea, and a wasting away of the muscles and flesh.

The new element here was not the diseases themselves but the syndrome of their constellation in a single patient, American, white, middle-class and ostensibly in previous good health. The doctors, emphasizing what, to them, was their patients' most striking characteristic, coined the term Gay-Related Immur.e Deficiency, GRID. The acronym brought to mind those gridiron torture devices employed to sear the flesh of legendary saints or heretics under interrogation, as well as those meticulous systems of cross-hatching that aid the artist or mapmaker to render an accurate representation of nature. But GRID did not last long. It was soon replaced by the equally curious but more politically correct AIDS, a term the scientist and poppers apologist Bruce Voeller claimed to have personally coined.

The first three years of the epidemic, from 1981 to 1984, though frightening, offered something of a window of opportunity, a question period, in which a certain amount of speculation occurred as to the nature of the syndrome, and the approaches that might be taken to remedy it. The authorities in those years did very little to respond to the deepening medical emergency.[5] Only when AIDS was represented as a threat not only to gays or drug addicts or Haitians, or even hemophiliacs, but to that inclusive, faceless entity 'the general public' did official America begin to move. In one reporter's revealing words, 'So long as AIDS could be thought of as "the gay disease", as the ultimate wage of sinners, we could think ourselves better. But now AIDS attacks those we love.'[6]

While many died needlessly, the medical establishment's admitted bafflement permitted a certain amount of healthy speculation. That situation was to change abruptly in the year 1984, as the next chapter will explore. In the meantime, the question period was beginning to generate some thoughts about health, illness, and the ramifications of the various practices gay men had been engaging in.

In the years before AIDS, gay men had been among urban America's most avid consumers of health services and products. Gyms and health clubs proliferated; the easing of prejudice and restrictions against gay physicians led to doctors whose practices consisted almost solely of gay men; labs that did nothing but test stool samples for parasites found their businesses thriving; the VD clinics were always full. Yet the vast majority of urban gay men knew little about medicine, nutrition or health, choosing to rely for the most part on their physicians for information and treatment. Many later regretted their ignorance, and their trust.

Chuck Grochmal, a Toronto man with AIDS who wrote a regular column for a gay paper until his death in 1990 wrote, 'I wish I had learned about AIDS sooner than I did. My doctor was gay. He treated me for syphilis, gonorrhea, hepatitis and so on. I thought I was in good hands. I figured that, if I had anything medical to worry about, he would tell me. The consequences of my (and a large number of others') sexual lifestyles were never presented to us so there was never anything to decide for ourselves. Can any doctor look at my medical history and fail to notice that I needed a warning?'[7]

The problem was not that the doctors, many of them gay, did not care about their gay patients. These were the first generation of relatively open gay physicians, and out of self-protection, few of them, as they made their way through medical school and internship, had dared to deviate from the narrow injunctions of orthodox medicine. They tended, as a group, to be scarcely less conservative than their colleagues in a very conservative (and homophobic) profession. And standard medicine in America had become largely a matter of drug therapy. The doctors' offices and clinics of the ghetto were the points of consumer contact for the huge pharmaceutical companies whose glossy literature kept physicians abreast of the tempting perks available to prescribers.[8]

When AIDS came, these doctors knew little more than their patients. Some of them became patients themselves. But few of them took advantage of the three-year question period to begin to learn from other medical traditions that could provide clues to what was happening. Among physicians and laypeople alike though, a clear division of opinion began to appear: between those who felt that a single new infectious agent was causing the new constellation of illnesses, and those who suspected there were multiple causes.

Inevitably, the focus of attention fell on recreational drugs and promiscuity, the be-all and end-all of gay life for so many in the post-Stonewall period. High on the list of possible culprits were the ubiquitous poppers. Reacting to surfacing fears, Great Lakes Products, one of the biggest of the poppers manufacturers, launched the cynical Blueprint for Health advertising campaign, which featured a line of vacuous reassurance: 'We are pleased to find that so many individuals share our interest in increasing the quality of life', and so on.[9] Another suspect, among both gays and their physicians, was the popular 'sexual sport' known as fisting.

MAFIA

Handball will not destroy your body. There are many beautiful muscular men who handball. Maintain your exercise regime and you will stay as beautiful and attractive as ever.

— R. A. Fournier, *The Intelligent Man's Guide to Handball*

The novel *Faggots* begins with a quotation from Evelyn Waugh: 'the ancients located the deeper emotions in the bowels.'[10] Along with unprecedented promiscuity and drug use, a characteristic activity of ghetto gays from the mid-1970s on was the practice known as fist-fucking, fisting or handballing: erotic, manual manipulation of the inside of a partner's rectum and lower intestine. It came about when it did because the proliferation of (largely Mafia-controlled) sex shops and mail-order houses advertising in the gay press made large rubber and plastic dildos widely available. It was a simple step from dildos the size of a forearm to the forearm itself. Not that all ghetto gay men, or even a majority, indulged in fisting. Like drag or certain sorts of S/M, it was a decidedly minority activity that was nonetheless considered a distinctively gay marker. Fisting was *the* 'new' sexual act of the 1970s. Unfortunately, forearmed was not forewarned.

Early gay liberation badges had shown a raised fist accompanied by such slogans as Gay Power! or Gay Is Good. Now, the emblem of a fist, worn on the back or sleeve of a jacket, was more likely to indicate an interest in brachiopractic eroticism. Fist patches were dispensed by the various fisting clubs including the FFA (Fist

Fuckers of America), TAIL (Total Ass Involvement League) and MAFIA (Mid-America Fists In Action).

Surveys of the habits of AIDS patients (in the early days when such surveys were still being conducted to any degree) revealed that, along with drug-taking and promiscuity, the practice of fisting was especially popular. Did fisting – somehow – cause AIDS? Though this was only one of many queries posed about the causes of AIDS during the three-year question period, it was naturally pondered with special apprehension by members of the sub-tribe of devoted fisters.

The phenomenon of fisting, and the beliefs surrounding it during the health crisis, throw light on a number of gay activities, attitudes and concerns that were by no means confined to fisting alone. We can obtain a good view (as it were) of fisting from two separate pre-AIDS sources from the Gay Archive: a pseudonymous Canadian journalist signing himself 'Angus MacKenzie', and New York gay activist Seymour Kleinberg.

Angus MacKenzie's piece, written for the *Body Politic* in 1982, recounts a rubbernecking tour of a ghetto fisting party. Postponing his plans to pick up some cocaine that evening, MacKenzie found himself side-tracked into tagging along with a friend, whom he describes as 'a fister's fister'. MacKenzie was observant enough to note his host's drug intake: muscle relaxer, uppers, downers. The distinctive fisting etiquette is explored: 'In establishing an encounter, one may ask, "Are you wide or deep?" "Wide" can mean two fists; "deep" can mean up to the elbow.' In one man's view, 'it makes no difference what a fist partner looks like or whether he has a sparkling personality. We are interested in each other's asses and hands. That's all.'

The usual horror stories (of the sort gay men were beginning to call 'war stories') are exchanged: two men who had 'died last year of injuries from careless, or maybe vicious, fisting'. MacKenzie describes the comfortable set-up of the fisting loft, and the thoughtful precautions taken (washing hands between encounters, for example). Liquor is not allowed, but Coca-Cola is: 'It's thought to give the drug combination the right hit.'[11]

Seymour Kleinberg, in his 1980 book *Alienated Affections*,[12] provides a perceptive view of the whole fisting fraternity which sprang up in the 1970s, its dedicated, hard-core members, its many fringe participants, and the social and pharmaceutical rituals that characterized it.

We are told that many participants in a fisting session will not eat for two days beforehand, so as to keep the colon free from interference with the sport at hand. 'I never cook now. I've forgotten how', says one member of the gay fisting couple who spoke with Kleinberg, an old friend. 'Besides, we don't eat on weekends, what with all the douching and the drugs; it's best to keep your stomach a little empty . . . . On a full stomach you'd throw up.' Ordinarily, of course, such fasting would entail hunger pangs. But as these are not part of the desired sensations, pharmaceutical appetite-suppressants are routinely used. The couple's dieting, we are told, 'keeps their weight down', and indeed, many gay men achieved a rail-thin appearance. Though Kleinberg does not mention it, various types of 'diet pills' were easily available on the street or from physicians known to dispense them with no questions asked.

'Douching', Kleinberg remarks, 'is the main topic of conversation among fisters. It takes two or three hours to ensure that the body is as empty as one could hope. Between sessions of douching, they begin their drugs.' As more and more downers are ingested, the body becomes more and more relaxed and 'the food in their systems descends lower into the intestines. Before a fisting party or orgy, they check each other out. Sometimes, Pete gets so excited during the hygiene inspection that he has an orgasm.'

As the narrative continues, the requisite substances are itemized in detail. 'John likes a tab of mescaline and five milligrams of Valium to begin the night with: they can keep him hard for hours. During the orgy he will take some MDA, a form of speed, of course grass and poppers, and, if he is particularly heedless, a toke of Angel Dust. Both take Mydol, sold over the counter to relieve menstrual pain, which they say prevents intestinal cramps.' And so on.

'It is a rare day', apparently, without some sort of sexual session. 'The orgies are reserved for the weekends: large ones twice a month, otherwise a party of six men or so: "Six is a nice combo; everybody can make it with each other".' The drugs, as well as augmenting or suppressing sensation, allow greater activity for longer periods, with more partners. And the fisters become more knowledgeable about how much they can 'tolerate'.

Finally, 'like other promiscuous gay men, they accept with resignation venereal disease as a hazard, particularly amoebiasis, which they come down with at least annually'. Though the douching masks the symptoms, they remain 'carriers', presumably until a medical checkup provides a diagnosis. One man remarks, 'I'm glad when I get it; I need the break.'

These practices were quite typical. A survey of 102 fisters published in 1981 indicated that 99 per cent of those polled 'always', 'almost always' or (20 per cent) 'sometimes' used drugs as part of their fisting scenes.[13] The types of drugs used included poppers, speed, marijuana, alcohol, cocaine, LSD and quaaludes. One fisting aficionado (significantly, a professional medical writer specializing in 'the pharmacokinetics of new prescription drugs') warned against the use of drugs during fisting, describing it as 'unnecessary and contradictory to the purpose of the act'. He acknowledged, however, that many men did resort to using drugs, including pain-killers and deep muscle relaxants.[14]

If fisters were over-represented among men who developed AIDS, it might well have had something to do with the massive drug intake which they shared with many other ghetto gay men, at a time when taking half a dozen drugs during a night at the disco was a common practice. The resulting disturbance to the system was augmented by frequent bouts of immunosuppressive amoebic parasites and other sexually transmitted diseases, and by repeated doses of penicillin, tetracycline and powerful anti-parasitic drugs such as flagyl, administered to keep symptoms in check.

Flagyl became the most common anti-parasitic treatment of the 1970s and early 1980s, a drug strong enough to act against a debilitating health problem that reached epidemic proportions a few years before AIDS came on the scene. Many gay men, like Kleinberg's couple, were being repeatedly dosed with flagyl by their doctors; some even built up a resistance to it and had to be switched to even stronger drugs. Others were routinely given flagyl when gentler treatments might have worked as well or better.

In at least one urban center with a large gay population, the overprescription of flagyl by a public clinic led to a malpractice suit.

The Committee for Representative Media launched a suit against the drug's manufacturers, the University of California Medical Clinics and the San Francisco Department of Public Health. The suit charged that not only was flagyl 'dangerous and needlessly expensive', but also a sexual and emotional depressant – a 'side-effect' that was well-known among flagyl users, who often counteracted it by heavier use of recreational drugs in order to 'stay hard for hours'. The Public Health Department's logic in favoring flagyl over other treatments and recommendations was based, said the suit, on 'the punitive merit of treatment' and the belief that 'pain and anguish will curtail sexual expression' – as well as on the extremely generous profits accruing to the manufacturer, up to ten times the cost of other treatments. The Committee also pointed out the frequency of false diagnoses due to professional ignorance.[15]

A possible additional health factor in fisting might have been the use of a pound or more of lubrication for each engagement (according to the 102-man Lowry/Williams study; five pounds according to the *Advocate*'s advice columnist).[16] Animal research has suggested – unhappily for the animals – that the hydrogenated fats contained in anal lubricants may cause immune suppression. There are indications that hydrogenated and polyunsaturated fats may inhibit the body's production of prostaglandin E1, a substance which helps regulate T-cell production.[17] Absorption of large amounts of such substances directly through the mucous membrane of the bowel could not have contributed to overall health.

And most fisters, like Kleinberg's couple, also engaged in other sexual activities; many frequented the baths, trucks, piers and backrooms, presumably no less promiscuously than other patrons. The fisting lifestyle, facilitated by medicinal and recreational drugs, entailed a massive assault, not only on the delicate membranes of the rectal mucosa but also on the immune system.

No conspiracy or collusion between the suppliers of these drugs was ever necessary. It was sufficient that an unacknowledged community of interest was established and maintained. The Mafia and the pharmaceutical companies made a great deal of money, the doctors maintained their practices, and the gays enjoyed their liberation. But in this test-tube model of consumerism, only the consumers reaped another, less satisfactory reward as widespread immunopsychological depression and malnutrition reinforced one another in a downward spiral of ill-health.

Those who noticed the statistical correlation between fisting and severe immune suppression, but who knew little or nothing about the fisting phenomenon, could only speculate in ignorance. After a single retrovirus was declared to be the cause of AIDS, they concluded that through fisting, viral particles must escape through minute cuts in the skin of the hand, enter the bloodstream of the passive partner through the rectal walls, and so trigger AIDS by some unknown mechanism. Parasitic infestation, sexually transmitted diseases, drugs and the reasons for drugs were seldom considered. Professional focus on the sexual orientation of AIDS patients amounted to what one gay writer characterized as nothing less than an 'obsession'.[18] These patterns of thinking will be examined in the next chapter. For the moment, we must consider the reasons for the rise of the fisting fad in the first place.

A research survey conducted in San Francisco in the late 1970s suggests widespread instance of a particular pattern of muscular rigidity related to psychological stress (what Wilhelm Reich called 'character armor') among all sections of the American population. This survey, and the therapeutic work that followed it, were conducted by Dr Jack Morin, who discussed it in his book *Anal Pleasure & Health*.[19] Morin found himself dealing with numerous instances of general anal spasm and tension, and he discovered that in many people, this general, chronic anal tension was present all or most of the time, with particularly stressful situations making it worse. 'A person with this pattern has tense anal muscles at work, at play, even at rest, whether or not his/her anus is being touched', Morin wrote.[20] Given American culture's nervous rectophobia – with 'asshole' and 'bum' as common terms of all-purpose abuse – it was not surprising that many Americans became permanently tight-assed.

For gay men, fisting represented a drastic attempt to loosen up this tight-assed armor and to break through the deep-seated taboo against anality into feelings of trust and bliss. Though involving slow and careful manipulation of the rectal canal by a gently inserted hand, the accompanying mental fixation (as indicated by the preferred name) was on the clenched fist, the symbol of masculine aggression.

Being fisted, like being fucked, symbolizes trust. But gay men in America had been conditioned *not* to trust other men – as a matter of survival. Drugs provided a quick way to attack this emotional stalemate: muscle relaxants to break through the rigid character armor, recreational drugs to achieve the necessary emotional state, anal anaesthetics to mask the pain of entry, antibiotics to alleviate resultant infections.[21]

The sensation of being fisted has often been compared to that of giving birth (though not, as far as I am aware, by women who have experienced both). The posture is identical, the man lying on his back with his legs raised – but in a womb-like pelvic sling made of animal skin. The preliminary of filling the belly with water creates a feeling similar to that of pregnancy. Even the chemical changes in the body have been compared to those occurring during labor.[22] In the era of the neo-masculine clone, fisting, like drag, was a way of reaffirming the feminine.

Intense rituals can be occasions of catharsis, initiation and bonding, healthy tests and trials of humanity and manhood. But in the fisting lifestyle, as with the mock hospital shenanigans, 'blood sports', impalings and dangerous cruising excursions, ghettoized gays had begun to develop a sequence of repetitive death rituals.

Whatever their scientific merit, questions about a possible connection between fisting and AIDS reflected in part our ambivalence and unease about the rituals we had been developing, and our growing realization that we would have to invent new ones – quickly.

How to have sex in an epidemic

AIDS/KS outbreaks could prove to be a dramatic opportunity for the gay community to make a leap in consciousness, both individually and collectively.
— Purusha Larkin

In the early 1980s, gay men became very frightened. Tests such as those conducted by Dr Michael Lange on gay subjects drawn

from Columbia University showed a widespread pattern of dangerous immune deficiencies: four-fifths of those tested had a serious
depletion of the critical T-helper lymphocyte levels. Randy Shilts
paraphrased Lange's fears: 'They may not be showing overt signs of
gay cancer yet, Lange figured, but substantial numbers of gay men
clearly have something wrong with their immune systems, and there
is a disaster of great proportions lurking ahead.' He tried to alert his
colleagues. He was told, 'This is nothing. It will disappear.' He was
warned his interest in the gay disease was jeopardizing his career.[23]

Meanwhile, Larry Kramer's pleas for a little financial
assistance from the Gay Liaison office of 'Faggot Congressman
Krotch' (now Mayor of New York) were being ignored. The various
levels of government, it was obvious, were not interested in paying
much attention to a disease that was perceived to strike unpopular
minority groups. Gay men would have to rely on themselves.

Larry Kramer had been instrumental in founding an organization aptly named Gay Men's Health Crisis, a self-help group for
New York gays with, or concerned about, AIDS. The story of this
organization has been told in *And the Band Played On* and in
Kramer's own *Reports from the Holocaust*. Suffice it to say that the
irascible Kramer fell out with his colleagues. Among other points of
contention, Kramer felt it would help if the head of the Gay men's
Health Crisis were openly gay! Paul Popham was not only in the
closet, but had prided himself on never having been involved in 'gay
politics'.[24]

This peculiar state of affairs was not atypical of the group of
AIDS activists the 1980s would produce. Just as many of the gay
liberationists of the 1970s had little contact with or knowledge of
the homophile movement of the 1950s and 1960s, so the activists
galvanized by the health crisis were drawn, with some exceptions
like Marty Robinson (a former GAA activist), not from the scattered
ranks of political gays, but from those gay men whose friendship
groups were hardest hit by AIDS. These included closeted clerks and
executives, bath boys and disco bunnies, who suddenly found
themselves transformed by adversity into fighters and care-givers.
AIDS may have frightened many to stay in their closets, but many
more came out fighting. Unfortunately, the fighters were too often

unarmed; their intellectual and political weapons had to be acquired on the job, grave mistakes were made, and time was short.

One of the most important efforts of the early AIDS activists was the publication of a little booklet entitled *How to Have Sex in an Epidemic: One Approach*.[25] Written by Richard Berkowitz and Michael Callen, with help from Dr Joseph Sonnabend, who provided a foreword, *How to Have Sex* is important firstly because as the earliest AIDS-era sex guide it had a profound influence on the 'safer sex' approach of the 1980s and 1990s, and secondly because it provides an instance of the thoughts and advice gay men were sharing with one another in the pre-HIV period between July 1981 and April 1984, when a *fiat* of the Reagan administration put an end to the question period.

In time, 'safe sex' and 'safer sex' were to become popular catch-phrases of the AIDS era. But the campaign for safer sex did not originate with physicians or health bureaucrats, but with ghetto gays themselves. Michael Callen, co-author of *How to Have Sex* was later to take stock of his own history: 'I calculated that since becoming sexually active in 1973, I had racked up more than three thousand different sex partners in bathhouses, back rooms, meat racks, and tearooms. As a consequence, I had also had the following sexually transmitted diseases, many more than once: hepatitis A, hepatitis B, hepatitis non-A/non-B, herpes simplex types I and II, venereal warts, amoebiasis, including giardia lamblia and entamoeba histolytica, shigella flexneri and salmonella, syphilis, gonorrhea, nonspecific urethritis, chlamydia, cytomegalovirus (CMV), and Epstein-Barr virus (EBV) mononucleosis, and eventually cryptosporidiosis and, therefore, AIDS.'[26] He was diagnosed with AIDS at the age of twenty-seven. His co-author, Richard Berkowitz, was also an 'AIDS victim' (the term 'person with AIDS', indicating a rejection of the victim psychology, had not yet been invented).

The third member of the triumvirate, Dr Joseph Sonnabend, was an African born researcher and infectious disease specialist with a general practice in Manhattan where he became one of the first physicians to encounter cases of AIDS in gay men. His background was unique. A member of the Royal College of Physicians, he had served as a doctor in the London slums and on pilgrim ships making the journey from Indonesia to Mecca, where he first encountered most of the illnesses he later treated in his gay AIDS patients. Sonnabend was also an experienced cancer researcher, having worked as assistant to the discoverer of interferon, Dr Aleck Isaacs.[27]

These three men put together the forty-page booklet that was to begin a process of change in the sexual habits of gay men in America. Until then, the usual AIDS advice to gay men, even from sympathetic physicians like Dr Alvin Friedman-Kien, had been: 'Stop having sex!'[28]

Callen, Berkowitz and Sonnabend wanted to address a community of highly sexually active men with advice on prudence and self-preservation. They provided a run-down of sexually transmitted diseases endemic among gays and summarized both the 'single factor' and 'multiple factor' theories of the cause of AIDS. Joe Sonnabend tended to favor a multicausal explanation, with repeated exposures to herpetic cytomegalovirus (CMV) being of crucial importance.[29] The ethics and responsibility of sex and the possible risks of various activities are discussed, and places of multiple, anonymous sexual contact are cautioned against as particularly likely to breed disease. Using 'rubbers' (condoms) is urged on gay men, and instructions are provided on how to use them. As Callen wrote later, 'with the frenzy of recently reformed whores singing gospel, we were *testifying* about the urgent need to "avoid the exchange of potentially infectious bodily fluids".'[30] The booklet concluded with two frank sections on love and liberation.

The first of these, titled simply 'Love', read in part: 'It came as quite a shock to us to find that we had written almost 40 pages on sex without mentioning the word "love" once. Truly, we have been revealed as products of the Seventies.' The authors referred to the unfortunate and unforseen side-effects of the concept of 'recreational sex' and the separation of sex from love and affection. 'Without affection, it is less likely that you will care as much if you give your partners disease.' They asked, 'did gay male culture of the Seventies encourage us to substitute the *fantasy* of the man we were holding for his reality?'

Callen and Berkowitz alluded to the socialization of all American men, gay men included, to *compete*. 'The challenge facing gay men in America is to figure out how to love someone you've been trained to "destroy". The goal of gay liberation', they suggested, 'must be to find ways in which love becomes possible despite continuing and often overwhelming pressure to compete and adopt adversary relationships with other men.' And they wondered: 'Is it possible that all this great sex we've been having for the last decade has siphoned off our collective anger which might otherwise have been translated into social and political action?'

'The commercialization of urban gay male culture today', they wrote, 'offers us places to go and get sick and places to go and get treated . . . . Sex and "promiscuity" have become the dogma of gay male liberation . . . . But has it become any easier to love each other? Men *loving* men was the basis of gay male liberation, but we have now created "cultural institutions" in which love or even affection can be totally avoided . . . . Maybe affection', they suggested, 'is our best protection.'

The booklet's last brief section, 'Closing Thoughts', said plainly what was now becoming apparent to all: 'The party that was the Seventies is over.' But 'what's over isn't sex – just sex without responsibility'.

How to Have Sex made a heartfelt, eloquent plea. Written and published by two PWA's and a compassionate physician, it was one of the first important gay statements of the age of AIDS. Viewed in retrospect, it seems to take up where Carl Wittman's *Refugees from Amerika* left off. Now the refugees Wittman wrote about were beginning to disappear into the biological concentration camp of AIDS.[31]

'Don't say conspiracy!'

Conspiracy: A striking concurrence of tendencies, circumstances or phenomena as though in planned accord.
— Webster's New International Dictionary of the English Language

While participating in a panel discussion in Toronto in 1990, Dr Joe Sonnabend was asked the reason for the stringent limits on public discussion of the health crisis among gays and intravenous drug users. Why, a member of the audience wondered, were so few dissenting views on the cause and nature of AIDS made available to the public? The good doctor quickly reassured his audience that there was 'no conspiracy or any such thing. There's just an informal . . . This was in 1984. There was a desperate need to produce an answer. The motive was political . . . Certainly no conspiracy or any such thing.' With these words, he became the first (and last!) speaker of the day to mention the C-word.

By then the gay community's initial reaction to AIDS had passed rapidly through a number of overlapping phases: disbelief, denial, confusion, fear, and along with fear, puzzlement and suspicion. An article on the epidemic in *Life* magazine prominently featured a large color photograph of a man with AIDS. Gaunt, wheelchair-bound, isolated, wrapped in a flimsy hospital gown and speckled with skin lesions, he was looking into the camera lens with an expression not only of sadness, but of intense bewilderment and a kind of sustained terror. The photographer had revealed in its most painfully concentrated form the fear pervading the gay community and giving rise to all sorts of speculation.

During the three-year period in the early 1980s when speculation about the causes and nature of AIDS was still acceptable, the gay political establishment that had grown up during the 1970s wasted much of its time trying to minimize the impact of the new epidemic, partly to 'keep the lid on' and prevent panic, partly because a cherished way of life was perceived to be threatened.

The *Body Politic* ran an article by microbiologist Bill Lewis titled 'The real gay epidemic: panic and paranoia'.[32] Lewis maintained that 'certain viruses probably cause a small number of human cancers. These include KS' (Kaposi's sarcoma, the crypto-cancer that was one of the chief symptoms of AIDS). Lewis' contention was a reference to the viral cancer hypothesis that had been the basis of the Nixon administration's highly publicized War on Cancer. This much-publicized, well-financed program had produced a number of tangential successes, including the genetic mapping of retroviruses by Dr Peter Duesberg. But it did not confirm the anticipated causal link between retroviruses and cancer that formed the central hypothesis of the program. Viruses, and retroviruses, were certainly found in some cancer patients. But they were found in many healthy controls as well, and eventually, in spite of a massive investment of money and hopes, the theory had to be set aside.

Yet the notion of a virus-cancer link, still flickering like a mirage, here cropped up in an article whose thrust was to play down the seriousness of AIDS, which was depicted as a danger more to gay lifestyle than to gay life. The 'panic and paranoia' Lewis warned against referred not only to a growing fear of 'gay cancer', but also to ideas that were beginning to dart about beneath the surface, including suspicions of a possible medical and/or governmental conspiracy, perhaps involving the CIA. As the Canadian writer Timothy Findley put it, 'I'm paranoid enough to still hold a little thing in the back of my mind, to think someone has done this to us.'[33]

Such 'conspiracy theories' emerged from time to time, and rapidly sank from view again, as elusive and fascinating as the Loch Ness Monster. When they were alluded to in print, it was usually briefly and with derision; when in conversation, with nervous laughter. For the most part, they remained unspoken. Still, there they were, lurking darkly beneath the surface of official, and unofficial, AIDS discourse. Sometimes, they were mere speculation. When specifics were offered, they were occasionally intriguing, but more often inconsistent, far-fetched, or highly inventive (Lieutenant Colonel Thomas Bearden's theories of AIDS being caused by Soviet electromagnetic beams and spread by Asian Tiger mosquitos never caught on.)[34] More significant than the usually murky details of these suspicions was the clear premise underlying them: that in some way not yet known, government and medical authorities acting in concert were behind the AIDS epidemic.

Suspicion of governmental, particularly CIA, involvement in the creation of AIDS was a pervasive subtext during the plague years, and even an unspoken suggestion of conspiracy could cause a good deal of nervousness and embarrassment; it certainly made Dr Sonnabend jumpy. The widespread belief in an AIDS conspiracy among American blacks was even alluded to on one network news segment. Black scholars and activists were shown (but not heard) apparently regaling public meetings with 'conspiracy theories', but the viewers never did find out what the conspiracy theories were! Apparently, as American blacks began to realize that a high disproportion of people with AIDS were black, they also began to speculate on the reasons.

What was the basis of these suspicions? The government had conducted unethical medical experiments on blacks before. Like the ghastly medical experiments of the Third Reich, these had relied heavily on the participation of reputable physicians and medical researchers.[35] Since World War II, the CIA had initiated a variety of experiments on unsuspecting subjects. These involved mental reprogramming techniques and chemical and biological warfare experiments. At one point, an aerosol spray had been developed that would induce pneumonia in any unfortunate asthma sufferer who used it. There were experiments involving the spraying of various concoctions into crowded subway stations. These were the modest beginnings from which later large-scale biowarfare projects grew.

One of the most ambitious was Operation M-K-Ultra, based at McGill University in Montreal and headed by Dr Donald Ewen Cameron, veteran lobotomist and 'the most powerful single figure in North American psychiatry – if not in the Western world'.[36] M-K-Ultra involved a series of CIA-financed mind control experiments performed on patients referred to Dr Cameron for treatment and counselling. Their 'treatments' included physical restraints, enforced sleep or sleep deprivation, massive quantities of drugs (including LSD, Thorazine and barbiturates), frequent electro-convulsive shock, bright lights and continual interrogations. They were experiments in brainwashing and torture.

Cameron's own innovation was the repeated playing of tape loops with doctored versions of a subject's own personal revelations during psychotherapy sessions. (Women, out of their minds on LSD, were subjected to endless tapes of their own voices saying 'I am a bad mother.') 'Uncooperative' subjects were denied food, or paralyzed with injections of curare. As Cameron's victims often lost track of time and space, and even of personal identity, his staff called their torture chamber 'the zombie room'. Cameron's paymaster was CIA head Allen Dulles, but the 'driving force' behind M-K-Ultra was said to be his deputy, Richard Helms, who was also to organize assassination plots against Fidel Castro.[37]

Aspects of M-K-Ultra were incorporated into other CIA attempts at individual and group mind control. The National Institutes of Health in Maryland continued Cameron's brain-frying experiments, using apes instead of Canadians. In their laboratories, monkeys, driven insane by enforced isolation and bombarded by radio and radar waves, were decapitated and their heads transplanted onto one another's bodies: 'Operation Resurrection'.[38]

In another series of experiments, sick children were subjected to massive, lethal doses of radiation, with the results passed on to the National Aeronautics and Space Administration, which was curious about the effects of radiation in space.

The notorious Tuskegee Experiment which lasted for over forty years, well into the 1970s, was conducted on black men in rural Georgia under the auspices of the Centers for Disease Control. Its aim was to discover the effects of untreated syphilis in the human male. To this end, several hundred men with syphilis were monitored for decades but neither told of their condition nor treated for it.[39]

The Tuskegee Experiment involved the deaths of many of its subjects from syphilis or syphilis-related conditions. Some of their wives and children (and presumably other, untraced sexual partners as well) were affected; there were a disproportionate number of stillbirths among the wives. At least one government official admitted that the program had been 'a literal death sentence for some of those people', and an attorney who acted in a suit against the government called the experiment 'a program of controlled genocide'.[40]

The cruel, racist nature of the Tuskegee Experiment has tended to obscure its purpose: providing the federal government with information on the consequences of untreated syphilis in men. As it happens, the Georgia study was only one of many contributing to the reservoir of information on syphilis that was accumulating from the 1930s through the 1960s. This was the time when penicillin and other 'wonder drugs' were supposed to be eradicating syphilis for good. As it happened, increased promiscuity (especially among gay men), inadequate tests and insufficient treatment standards were complicating the problem. Wide administration of antibiotics was tending to suppress the usual initial symptoms, and a new crop of syphilis-related diseases was beginning to surface. By 1970, a report in the journal *California Medicine* warned that widespread misuse of antibiotics was driving syphilis underground, creating an 'ominous prospect of a widespread resurgence of the disease in its tertiary form'.[41] A possible link between hidden syphilis and AIDS was one course of investigation urged on researchers by AIDS dissidents in the 1980s and 1990s.[42]

According to one dissident, 'the scientific literature from the 1940's and 1950's appears full of references to . . . deaths from interstitial pneumonias, cancers such as basal and squamous cell epithelioma, Kaposi's sarcoma, lymphomas, mycobacterial infections such as extra-pulmonary tuberculosis, cytomegalovirus and herpes zoster infections, toxoplasmosis, and dementia. These deaths occurred among populations known to be suffering from untreated or inadequately treated chronic syphilis.'[43] In the 1980s and 1990s, all these illnesses would come to be counted as standard AIDS symptoms. The branch of government assigned to oversee the AIDS epidemic, the Centers of Disease Control, based in Atlanta, Georgia, was the same division of the US Public Health Service that for several decades had been quietly administering the Tuskegee Experiment. One attorney, meditating on the ignorance and trust of the Tuskegee participants (many of whom died never realizing what had happened to them), commented, 'The sad thing is that it could happen all over again.'[44]

Those who suspected it *might* have happened again, with AIDS, were usually dismissed as conspiracy theorists – as potent a political stigmatization as 'Communist' had once been. The phrase could be employed to intimidate people from any attempt at analysis. AIDS brought a reign of terror, and at such times, people resist analysis and cling to certainties, however dubious.

But some gay men wondered about another government program, one that had been aggressively promoted in the gay ghettos six years after the Tuskegee disclosures.

Dr Szmuness's casebook

In the mid-seventies, hepatitis B became the 'gay' sexually-transmitted disease which most intrigued the government scientists. Newly 'liberated' homosexuals were anxious to cooperate with the government in matters of 'gay' health.

— Dr Alan Cantwell, Jr

The same month Harvey Milk was assassinated, the US Federal government recognized the existence of gay men and 'the gay lifestyle' for the first time. It introduced a newly developed vaccine against hepatitis B into a group of gay New Yorkers.

By the late 1970s, with syphilis no longer considered a serious threat, hepatitis B and amoebic parasites had become the most worrisome sexually transmitted diseases of urban gay men. And hepatitis could be lethal. At that point, some thousands of gay men were encouraged to become human test subjects for the manufacture and distribution of a new vaccine that it was hoped would prevent hepatitis B – a mixture prepared from the blood of gay men carrying the hepatitis B virus. The mastermind behind this study was Dr Wolf Szmuness, a Soviet-trained researcher with a unique background. Before we glance at Dr Szmuness, we should take a brief look at the trials themselves, and the questions they raised.

The hepatitis study was funded by grants from a number of government agencies, including the Centers for Disease Control which had managed to weather criticism of its Tuskegee experiment. After screening blood from about ten thousand gay male volunteers, 1,083 were selected to participate in the next phase of the study, supervised by the New York City Blood Center, where Dr Szmuness was chief of epidemiology. Those selected had a number of characteristics in common: they were all gay or bisexual; they were all under forty, with an average age of twenty-nine; they were healthy, though some had contracted venereal disease in the past; and they were not monogamous.

Why was this particular group selected with such great care? This stage of the experiment was to be 'double-blinded', (half the men being given the vaccine and the rest a placebo) and the results – who got hepatitis and who did not – duly recorded. But for the experiment to be effective, the test subjects had to be at high risk of contracting hepatitis B. At first, Dr Szmuness had considered finding his subjects among drug addicts, Alaskan natives, or patients and staff from dialysis centers.[45] Eventually, non-monogamous gay men were chosen 'in order to avoid serious legal and logistical problems'.[46]

Additional trials in the series conducted on thousands of gay men in Los Angeles, San Francisco, Chicago, Denver and St Louis, were supervised by Dr Donald Francis of the Centers for Disease Control. Dr Francis, and his former boss, Dr Max Essex, had both been involved in the unsuccessful virus/cancer program. Later, they would both graduate to leading positions in the AIDS establishment.

Once the vaccine was approved, it was urged on groups of health professionals traditionally at risk for hepatitis B. Whatever their reasons, the health workers were not enthusiastic. Only a third of the US Veterans' Administration employees agreed to be vaccinated, and out of twelve hundred selected University of Illinois health workers, only 237 rolled up their sleeves. The vaccine may have been effective, but clearly the public relations campaign was not.

At this point, the gay community got back into the act. As gay men had donated much of the blood to make the vaccine, had provided the original test group, and were no less at risk than health workers, gay spokespeople made the point that it was unfair not to give us access. The government mounted an unusually swift response, and the unused stocks of vaccine were aggressively promoted through advertising campaigns in the gay press. Thousands of gay men lined up at clinics for anti-hepatitis shots.

In 1981, AIDS broke out in just the subset of the gay population – young, urban, non-monogamous – that had been involved in the hepatitis B experiments. A few inquiring minds began to wonder about the possibility of a connection between the programs of Drs Szmuness and Francis and the AIDS epidemic.[47] The involvement of the Merck drug company in the manufacture of the vaccine caused a certain amount of apprehension, because of Merck's extensive background in biowarfare technology.

Understandably, once HIV was pronounced the official 'cause' of AIDS, the immediate reaction was to wonder whether the blood from sick gay men that went into the vaccine might have contained HIV. Apparently, 6.6 per cent of the original test group already had HIV antibodies in their blood.[48] Others, of course, contracted it as time (and their sexual activities) went on. Though the makers of the vaccine were cautious in stating that it had been 'manufactured utilizing several processes believed to inactivate all known groups of viruses', no one ever produced evidence that any of the hepatitis vaccine contained HIV. But other questions also began to be raised.

Homeopaths and holistic physicians had long been arguing that the wholesale vaccination of entire populations was (along with the overuse of antibiotics, hormones, pesticides and other manufactured substances) an ill-considered practice that would lead not only to a few immediate and obvious bad reactions, but also to a broad spectrum of contamination and generally weakened health over the long term. There have been numerous reports implicating vaccinations in immune dysfunctions.[49] It seems that the vaccination of a group of men known to be at risk for a variety of venereal diseases, many of whom also habitually took a variety of drugs, offered particular dangers. How many gay recipients of vaccine, believing themselves now to be out of danger of contracting hepatitis B, became – in the absence of proper counselling – more promiscuous than they would otherwise have been, and increased their chances of serious illness?

In addition, much of the statistical information on AIDS and HIV available to the public was extrapolated not from the population at large, but from studies of men who had donated blood samples to the hepatitis B experiments. These gay men came to be known as the 'hepatitis B cohort', and it was the fate of this group – particularly the San Francisco hepatitis B cohort – that scientists used as a model for the projected future of all HIV positives. As Dr Alan Cantwell wrote, 'the gay "hepatitis cohorts" that formed under the auspices of the government eventually became the epidemiological "model" for AIDS in America'.[50]

The prime mover behind the assembling of young, urban gay men for vaccine experiments was Dr Wolf Szmuness. A Polish Jew held in a Siberian prison camp after World War II and trained in the Soviet Union, Szmuness had held a number of minor positions in Polish regional health departments. During a stay in a health center, he shared a room with the priest who was to become the first Polish pope. They were to remain friends and carry on a correspondence for years. There are conflicting stories on just why and how Szmuness was allowed to leave Poland – with his wife and family – and come to America. At any rate, he ended up at the New York Blood Center the year of the Stonewall riots. According to a brief biography written by a colleague, he began as a lab technician and 'in what must be record time, he was leap-frogged to full Professorship at the Columbia School of Public Health'.[51]

In 1975, he returned briefly to the Soviet Union, apparently under the special protection of the US State Department. Perhaps not since Lee Harvey Oswald had a civilian travelled so freely between America and the Eastern Block! Certainly he appears to have been in unusually good odour with both the American and Soviet medical and governmental establishments. By the late 1970s, he was 'phenomenally successful' in his career as an expert on hepatitis, epidemiology and transfusion medicine. He also maintained close ties with certain African countries such as Senegal, which obliged him by providing blood specimens from its armed forces. In 1978, he was entrusted with overseeing the most extensive Federal program ever to involve out-of-the-closet gay men.

Whatever the motives of Dr Szmuness, the Federal Government, or the Centers for Disease Control, the hepatitis B experiments of the late 1970s raise a number of unanswered questions. Chief among them is whether it is possible that this widely-advertised program could have played some part, direct or indirect, in weakening the immune systems of the men who took part in it, and of their many sexual partners.

These were among the doubts beginning to be raised during the question period between the initial reports of AIDS in 1981 and the Reagan administration's announcement three years later that the cause of AIDS had been discovered and that a vaccine was a mere two years away.

Notes

1. Randy Shilts, *And the Band Played On* (New York: St Martin's Press, 1987), p. 67.

2. Larry Kramer, *Reports from the Holocaust: The Making of an AIDS Activist* (New York: St Martin's Press, 1989), p. 9.

3. See George Vithoulkas, *The Science of Homeopathy* (New York: Grove Press, 1980), pp. 52, 80–82, 86, 111–17, etc.

4. Tom Wolfe, 'Brave new world bites the dust', *Globe & Mail*, 14 January 1988, p. A7.

5. See Shilts, *And the Band Played On*.

6. Lawrence Wade, *Washington Times*, 19 November 1986.

7. Chuck Grochmal, 'Deadly decisions', *Xtra!*, 14 July 1989, p. 22.

8. Pharmaceutical companies routinely offer incentives to doctors to prescribe suggested amounts of particular drugs over a given period. Among the prizes in the prescribing game: paid vacations and computers on long-term loan – to allow removal if prescription quotas are not met.

9. See, for example, *Advocate*, 20 March 1984, Classifieds p. 1.

10. Larry Kramer, *Faggots* (New York: Warner Books, 1978), p. 11.

11. 'Angus MacKenzie', 'Lust with a very proper stranger', *Body Politic*, April 1982.

12. Seymour Kleinberg, *Alienated Affections: Being Gay in America* (New York: Warner Books, 1980), pp. 236–47.

13. T. P. Lowry and G. R. Williams, 'Brachiopractic eroticism', *British Journal of Sexual Medicine*, January 1981, p. 32.

14. R. A. Fournier, *The Intelligent Man's Guide to Handball (The Sexual Sport)* (New York: R. A. Fournier, 1983), p. 42.

15. 'Amebiasis treatment protested: lawsuit against university medical clinic', *Alternate*, January 1981, p. 5.

16. Pat Califia, *The Advocate Adviser* (Boston: Alyson Publications, 1991), p. 185.

17. See J. Mertin *et al.*, 'Nutrition and immunity: the immunoregulatory effect of n-6 essential fatty acids is mediated through prostaglandin E', *International Archives of Allergy and Applied Immunology*, No. 77, 1985, pp. 390–5; and Michael L. Culbert, D.Sc., *AIDS: Hope, Hoax and Hoopla* (Chula Vista, CA: The Bradford Foundation, 1989), pp. 147–50.

18. Shilts, *And the Band Played On*, p. 172.

19. Jack Morin, Ph.D., *Anal Pleasure & Health: A Guide for Men and Women* (Burlingame, CA: Down There Press, 1981), pp. 207–36.

20. *Ibid.*, p. 213.

21. For an attempt at a more holistic approach to fisting, see Purusha Larkin, *The Divine Androgyne According to Purusha* (San Diego: Sanctuary Publications, 1981), pp. 103–15.

22. See, for example, Geoff Mains, *Urban Aboriginals: A Celebration of Leathersex* (San Francisco: Gay Sunshine Press, 1984), p. 133.

23. Shilts, *And the Band Played On*, p. 124. Later researchers found

that the immunosuppression and multiple infections found in many urban gay men *preceded* HIV infection, 'setting the stage for AIDS'. See Robert Root-Bernstein, *Rethinking AIDS: The Tragic Cost of Premature Consensus* (New York: The Free Press, 1993).

24. *Ibid.*, p. 91.

25. Richard Berkowitz and Michael Callen, *How to Have Sex in an Epidemic: One Approach* (New York: News from the Front Publications, 1983).

26. Michael Callen, *Surviving AIDS* (New York: HarperCollins Publishers, 1990), pp. 5–6. In spite of his crowded medical history, Callen became well-known as a long-term AIDS survivor.

27. See Barry Adkins, 'Looking at AIDS in totality: a conversation with Joseph Sonnabend', *New York Native*, 7–13 October 1985.

28. Shilts, *And the Band Played On*, p. 84.

29. See Joseph Sonnabend, 'The etiology of AIDS', *AIDS Research*, 1 (1), 1983; Joseph Sonnabend and Serge Sadoun, 'The acquired immunodeficiency syndrome: a discussion of etiological hypotheses', *AIDS Research*, 1 (2), 1984; Joseph Sonnabend *et al.*, 'A multifactorial model for the development of AIDS in homosexual men' *Annals of the American Academy of Sciences*, No. 437, 1985; Richard Berkowitz, 'Joseph Sonnabend', *Christopher Street*, No. 68, 1982, p. 20.

30. Michael Callen, *Surviving AIDS*, p. 7. Later, as this cautionary approach became popularized, it deteriorated into a belief that latex condoms, rubber gloves and dental dams alone would, if universally employed, restore health to the community. Where medicine had failed, plastics technology would succeed.

31. Two pre-AIDS novels had predicted the decimation of the gay community through political repression: Paul O. Welles' *Project Lambda* (Port Washington, NY: Ashley Books, 1978); and Alabama Birdstone's *Queer Free* (New York: Calamus Books, 1981).

32. Bill Lewis, 'The real gay epidemic: panic and paranoia', *Body Politic*, November 1982.

33. Timothy Findley, quoted in Nik Sheehan, 'Poetic pessimist', *Xtra!*, 23 November 1990, p. 19.

34. Thomas E. Bearden, *AIDS Biological Warfare* (Greenville, TX: Tesla Book Co., 1988).

35. As about 45 per cent of German physicians were members of the Nazi party, there was presumably a large pool to draw from.

36. Gordon Thomas, *Journey into Madness: Medical Torture and the Mind Controllers* (London: Corgi Books, 1989), p. 367. I am indebted to this study for much of my information on Project M-K-Ultra.

37. *Ibid.*, p. 133.
38. *Ibid.*, pp. 380–1.
39. James H. Jones, *Bad Blood: The Tuskegee Syphilis Experiment* (New York: The Free Press, 1981).
40. *Ibid.*, p. 207.
41. See Armand J. Pereyra, MD and Richard L. Voller, MD, 'A graphic guide for clinical management of latent syphilis', *California Medicine*, May 1970.
42. See Harris J. Coulter, *AIDS and Syphilis: The Hidden Link* (Berkeley, CA: North Atlantic Books, 1987); Stephen S. Caiazza, MD, *AIDS: One Doctor's Personal Struggle* (Highland Park, NJ: 1990); and Robert Ben Mitchell, *Syphilis as AIDS* (Austin, TX: Banned Books, 1990). Syphilis among PWAs was playing the role of the dog that didn't bark: a population with high levels of all other sexually transmitted diseases registered curiously low levels of syphilis, leading to questions about the accuracy of syphilis testing and the effects of undetected and undertreated syphilitic infection.
43. John Scythes, quoted in Colman Jones, *AIDS and Syphilis: What Is the Connection? Has the Great Masquerader Made a Deadly Comeback?* (Toronto: privately printed, 1991), p. 22.
44. Billy Carter, quoted in Jones, *Bad Blood*, p. 219.
45. According to Dr Alan Cantwell, *AIDS and the Doctors of Death: An Inquiry into the Origin of the AIDS Epidemic* (Los Angeles: Aries Rising Press, 1988), p. 75.
46. *Ibid.*, p. 104.
47. Among them, physician Dr Alan Cantwell and medical journalist Jon Rappoport, author of *AIDS Inc. Scandal of the Century* (San Bruno, CA: Human Energy Press, 1988).
48. Cantwell, *Doctors of Death*, p. 93.
49. See for example Sir Graham Wilson, *The Hazards of Immunization* (New York: Oxford University Press, 1967).
50. Cantwell, *Doctors of Death*, p. 330.
51. Aaron Kellner, 'Reflections on Wolf Szmuness', *Proceedings in Clinical and Biologic Research*, **182**, 1985, p. 3. Quoted in Cantwell, *Doctors of Death*, pp. 102–5.

Chapter six

The Myth of the Lone Assassin

The one-shot theory of history is dead. Singular causality and singular perspective are as dead in truth-telling as in science, where the stress is now on the confluence of forces, on synchronicity and simultaneity.

— Oliver Stone

AMERICAN public life in the 1980s was carried out in the shadow of events that had marred the previous two decades: the assassination of one president in circumstances questioned by a majority of Americans, and the resignation of another after his cover-up of clandestine activities.

The post-war period in America had seen an enormous increase in the control of American institutions by organized crime, and by the 1980s, there was speculation that both the beloved Kennedy and the disgraced Nixon had relied on criminal associates.[1] In addition, the Mafia was widely suspected of having organized the JFK assassination – a possibility that independent investigators pursued, but officialdom seemed reluctant to explore.

Anyone who suggested even the existence of an organized crime syndicate to the perennial director of the FBI, J. Edgar Hoover, could expect a rude dismissal. 'Baloney!' was the word he usually used. Internal FBI reports on organized crime were routinely quashed and agents who probed the Mob too zealously would find their investigations blocked and their careers stalled. During the Eisenhower administration, pressure from Hoover resulted in the disbanding of a Federal Task Force on Organized Crime and the shelving of its recommendations.

Hoover, who headed the nation's central law-enforcement body for half a century until his death under mysterious circumstances in 1972, much preferred compiling files on dissidents to chasing mafiosi. A lifelong bachelor, he was as hostile to gays as his closeted friend and confidant Roy Cohn and *his* closeted friend and confidant Frances Cardinal Spellman, the most powerful churchman in America. Hoover and his close companion of many years (and Number Two man at the Bureau) Clyde Tolson routinely spent their annual vacations at Mob-owned resorts, and their regular bets at Mob-controlled race-tracks paid off with unusual frequency.

Johnny and Clyde's evenings at home – among the antiques, nude male statuary and (in the rec room) pinups of Marilyn Monroe – were often enlivened by tape-recordings of the sexual activities of prominent citizens, including Marilyn herself, and Hoover's particular *bête noire*, Rev Martin Luther King, Jr. It was the FBI's vast cache of incriminating information, and Hoover's willingness to use it, that ensured the Director's tenure of office through the administrations of nine presidents.[2]

Hoover's connections with organized crime have never been fully explored, but some intriguing bits of information have come to light, including his frequent journeys to New York to meet with Mafia boss Frank Costello. Costello was a pivotal figure in the criminal underworld; he had been Al Capone's lieutenant and the senior partner in the lucrative bootlegging business of Joseph P. Kennedy, politically ambitious father – and bankroller – of the famous dynasty.

John F. Kennedy achieved his rise to power with the assistance of criminal elements. Pushed by his power-hungry gangster father into the world of Hoover, the CIA and the Mob, Kennedy as President began to realize that he was foundering out of his depth. When he failed to recapture Cuba for American criminal interests, the Mob considered itself betrayed – the more so as the President's brother and Attorney General, Bobby, was pursuing a relentless vendetta against union leader Jimmy Hoffa and his Mafia colleagues. But Bobby just could not stop. He had, as his aides usually phrased it, 'a hard-on for Jimmy', and the hard-on just would not go away until Jimmy was destroyed.

The rule of the Kennedy brothers ended in November 1963 when the presidential motorcade driving through Dallas came under fire and the President was killed, Mob-style, with two or more bullets to the head. When Malcolm X heard the news, he made the caustic comment that Kennedy 'never foresaw that the chickens would come home to roost so soon'.

The shooting of the nation's most glamorous leader was an event of such enormity that it was usually viewed, in the decades following, as a singular event. Yet it was one of a series of assassinations and attempted assassinations that began with Medgar Evers in the summer of 1963, and continued with George Lincoln Rockwell, Malcolm X, Martin Luther King, Jr., Althea King, Andy Warhol, Bobby Kennedy, Allard Lowenstein, Marilyn Monroe, George Wallace, Jimmy Hoffa, John Lennon, Leo Ryan, Huey Newton and Harvey Milk.

Many of these attacks involved elements that official investigations left unexplained, including the possible involvement of criminal and/or governmental organizations. But these suspicions – and the considerable literature they generated – met with deep denial and resistance on the part of those in power. Even into the 1990s, official America retained a defensive attachment to the idea that assassinations in America were necessarily carried out by lone, deranged madmen, acting independently of any outside institutions or forces. As late as 1993, President Clinton held a press conference to assure a skeptical citizenry that Lee Harvey Oswald alone killed JFK!

Whatever the facts of any particular case, this reflexive attitude seemed deeply ingrained in the collective psyche of the establishment. The idea that traumatic public events could be attributed to single, readily identifiable causes – the 'lone assassin' theory – was favored by those who had reason to fear what might crawl out if too many rocks were overturned.

America is a country of powerful national myths. But in the late twentieth century, a growing number of those myths, the myth of Camelot among them, seemed to rely on the myth of the lone assassin as insurance of their continued survival.

The election to the Presidency of Ronald Reagan at the end of the 1970s involved an anxious public need to shore up a number of

American myths that were perceived as endangered, myths involving national strength, wisdom, progress, invulnerability and scientific superiority. When his assumption of office coincided with the advent of a strange new kind of epidemic, for which medicine could offer neither remedy nor explanation, the stage was set for another version of the myth of the lone assassin, this time with a science fiction twist befitting the Star Wars President.[3]

The myth mutated into its viral form in that much-awaited year, 1984.

1984

Your worst enemy, he reflected, was your own nervous system.
— George Orwell, *1984*

In the early years of the epidemic, the government virtually ignored the growing holocaust of urban gay men. Federal authorities were only spurred to action when AIDS was suspected of spreading from the original 'Four H' groups – homosexuals, heroin addicts, hemophiliacs and Haitians – to white, heterosexual, red-blooded, non-mainlining Americans. By 1984, three years into the epidemic, the medical/industrial establishment had managed to come up with nothing useful and AIDS was beginning to make them look bad. When they moved to position themselves in a better light, they did so in a way that would become almost routine in the years to come. Some AIDS activists would describe it as 'science by press release'.

The theoretical model of scientific disclosure and debate goes something like this: a hypothesis is formed; funding is obtained; research is undertaken; experimental results and conclusions are reviewed by peers and published in a professional journal; debate is entered into as others attempt to duplicate the results; a provisional conclusion is arrived at. In the real world, things are a little different, with the 'funding is obtained' clause tending to elbow the others out of the way.

The AIDS years were also a time when questions began to be raised about the part played by big business in determining what constitutes American science and American medicine. The medical/

industrial establishment began to attract a few annoying gadflies.[4] A disturbing amount of scientific duplicity and chicanery was being unearthed, and some of the scandals brewing over apparently fraudulent published work involved researchers almost as eminent as the by now forgotten Dr Ewen Cameron.

The official hypothesis on the cause of AIDS was not advanced through the usual scholarly channels, but rather by government *fiat*. The result was an incipient international scandal that had to be stifled at the highest levels. For the moment, though, the news looked good.

On 23 April 1984, President Reagan's Secretary of Health and Human Services, Margaret Heckler, held a press conference in a small auditorium jammed with scientists and reporters. Mrs Heckler's previous moment in the news had been her successful blocking of an attempt to overturn the anti-homosexual laws in the District of Columbia. She stood at the lectern and made her announcement: 'Today we add another miracle to the long honor roll of American medicine and science.' American scientists had discovered the virus that caused AIDS, she said, and a vaccine would be available within two years.

Only the more knowledgeable among the journalists present remembered that an English researcher, Dr Abraham Karpas, and a French team, led by Dr Luc Montagnier, had separately isolated novel viruses from the blood of AIDS patients – and that Dr Montagnier had been waiting for a US patent on the appropriate blood tests for some time. No one remarked on the egregious religious terminology. Reagan himself had apparently been incapable of even uttering the word 'AIDS'. But now his administration had spoken, through the medium of the intrusive oracle, Heckler: HIV was a miracle!

Guest star on the Margaret Heckler show was a scientist from the National Cancer Institute, one Dr Robert Gallo. This first appearance of Dr Gallo in the national spotlight was described by David Black, author of *The Plague Years*: 'He approached the podium like the only kid in the school assembly to have won a National Merit Scholarship. He was fastidiously dressed. None of Sonnabend's ratty sweaters and baggy slacks for him. He wore aviator glasses – a Hollywood touch – and his hair was rumpled, but just enough to make it look as if he had recently emerged from handling a crisis. His manner seemed to me condescending, as though he were the Keeper of Secrets obliged to deal with a world of lesser mortals.'[5]

It was this press conference, confused as it was (at one point Secretary Heckler introduced a researcher who was not there) that would determine, more than any other single event, the view of AIDS that would continue to be tenaciously maintained by the mass media and the public.

AIDS was caused by a virus. That was the gist of the announcement made that day in 1984. From then on, AIDS the complex syndrome began to be concealed by AIDS the simple acronym. The official decision that Gallo's retrovirus was the single necessary and sufficient cause of AIDS would replace discussion about other possible causes with what medical journalist Jad Adams called HIV fundamentalism, a doctrine quickly adopted *en bloc* by the government, the medical/industrial complex and the press.

The myth of the lone assassin had arisen in reaction to a series of disturbing political killings, serving as a distraction and an anodyne. The single-shot approach (whether by rogue gunman or rogue virus) had the power of a reassuring simplicity. In the case of AIDS, the multiple victims, overwhelmingly members of outcast social minorities, were still struggling for their lives, and the putative assassin remained very much alive. The result was a profound ambivalence about how HIV could be presented to the public so as to encourage sexual caution and inhibition, yet forestall outright panic. Myths, however, have their own lives, which mere government proclamations may be powerless to stop.

The putative assassin would take on several changes of name and nature: (at first HTLV-III was said to be a leukemia virus, then a lymphotropic virus; eventually, as part of a complicated international compromise, it became Human Immunodeficiency Virus, HIV (or HIV-I, with HIV-II, -III and so on waiting in the wings). Like the Oswald clones that seemed to be popping up everywhere in Dallas and New Orleans prior to the JFK shooting, the putative AIDS virus had one face, and many.

HIV as it was presented to the public via physicians, government spokespersons, the media and the burgeoning AIDS bureaucracy was an invisible killer that could strike 'anyone', lying dormant in a 'latency period' for years, or decades, before the inevitably fatal strike.

Diagrammatic representations of HIV in the popular media were oddly varied. *Time* depicted an octopus-like creature, 'magnified 135,000 times' and supposedly photographed in the act of destroying human T-cells. (Scientists later admitted it did no such thing.) *Scientific American* represented it as the kind of old-fashioned, spherical deep-sea mine with protruding knobs known as a depth-charge. Gay men and others who tested positive for antibodies to 'the deadly virus' were now said to be 'walking time-bombs' – a metaphor appropriate to the military model of disease that had developed from nineteenth-century germ theory.

The time-bomb image is a technological equivalent of the voodoo death curse. It conveys, to those who believe it, a simple, frightening idea. Many gay men now began a definitive reorientation of their psychophysical functioning – away from any expectation of a normal lifespan, and toward belief in early, imminent death.

Germs, gays and guerillas

Perhaps the greatest advance is that AIDS has had a chastening effect on us scientists. We aren't saying any more that we've conquered all the infectious diseases in the world.

— Dr Jay Levy

The debate over the causes of AIDS has its beginnings in conflicting theories on the nature and origins of illness that arose in the nineteenth century at the same time as the myth of the homosexual was being medically constructed.[6]

The first of these competing theories was contagionism: the belief that 'certain microscopic entities – whose appearance in space and time correlates well with other physical manifestations of illness – are causative of illness'. The theory that illnesses were primarily due to contagion, being passed from person to person by microscopic organisms, was consistent with a worldview that regarded humanity as existing in a state of perpetual warfare; the natural world was the enemy, replete with hostile creatures to be subdued.

Understandably, this conception found its greatest popularity among military physicians. But its most eminent champion was the renowned Louis Pasteur, whose germ theory provided it with a working model.

The weakness of the contagionist approach was that very little was known about the immune system, and no explanation could be provided as to why some individuals exposed to a particular germ fell ill and others did not. Even Pasteur worried about this, and in 1882, he revised his theory, now considering germs a secondary rather than primary cause of disease. (The rumour that he renounced the germ theory entirely on his death bed has persisted to the present day.) But, Pasteur notwithstanding, the original, cruder, theory was eagerly seized on by the emerging medical establishment and became a fixed belief in the collective consciousness of the culture.

The germ theory blamed disease on microbes, rather than on the toxins, traumas and unhealthy living conditions that provided microbes with fertile ground. The preeminence of the microbial 'single cause' paradigm was secured in 1910 with the influential Flexner Report on Medical Education in the United States and Canada. This was sponsored by the Carnegie and Rockefeller Foundations, whose corporate financiers favored single causes as they threw responsibility for illness onto individual patients.

Opposing the contagionists were the environmentalists, who stressed social causes of disease such as poverty, poor food and sanitation, unhealthy working conditions and the stresses of industrialism. They observed, for example, that during the Great Plague of London in 1665, most of the people who moved away from the sewage and squalor of the city proper to the edge of Hampstead Heath survived. The area, which became known as the Vale of Health, still exists as a small residential community in the heart of modern London.

Environmentalists tended to interpret the relationship between mankind and nature as symbiotic and interdependent rather than mutually hostile. 'Social medicine' was advocated by political liberals and radicals who believed the social reforms they championed would increase public health. They believed factors such as diet and mode of life contributed to the level of resistance to disease. Germs could only breed where conditions allowed. Environmentalists tended to ignore such phenomena as the mass destruction of the North American Indians by European diseases (though even under such traumatic conditions, there were survivors).

These two models of health and disease had parallels in other nineteenth-century controversies. Charles Darwin's theory of evolutionary struggle and Peter Kropotkin's observations of social co-operation in nature were both studied for their political ramifications.

One prominent opponent of contagionism was the French physician Antoine Bechamp. Bechamp's scepticism about the germ theory was radical. He speculated that germs might not necessarily enter the body from outside but could develop from the body's decaying cells, as part of a natural life cycle. These 'germs' might well play an important role in handling the effects of 'serums, drugs and other toxic materials'.[7]

The Canadian holistic healer Ellen Lipsius points out that 'after 1848 when a series of working class rebellions [was] crushed, the influence of social medicine began to wane and contagionists . . . slowly gained the upper hand' as diseases like tuberculosis, cholera and dysentry lost their potency. Yet the decline in death rates, Lipsius argues, was due mostly to the impact of social medicine and improvements in sanitation and general living conditions.[8] Nevertheless, contagionism came to dominate the teaching hospitals, at the expense of preventive medicine.

A contemporary example of the opposing explanations offered by the infection/invasion model and the toxic environment model is provided by the increasing incidence of sea animals washed ashore dying, their bodies infested with viruses and parasites. The waters these animals inhabit have been severely polluted with various kinds of toxic waste. Are the animals being killed by viruses? Or by the poisons human civilization has introduced into their habitat? One such instance, of clams in polluted beds, allegedly infected with a viral disease similar to AIDS, caused a fisheries director to confess, 'I don't believe we know what action to take . . . . We don't even understand how it goes from one clam to the next.'[9] Unprotected anal intercourse?

With the advent of an arsenal of drug weapons as defense against the relentless armies of microbial invaders, the germ theory seemed a doubly sound investment. World War II inaugurated an age of 'miracle drugs' such as broad-spectrum antibiotics, giving the contagionist theory a further boost. Yet, in time, the allegedly defeated diseases (such as syphilis) returned, sometimes with complications. Drug-resistant strains of pathogens caused new problems. At the same time, the incidence of degenerative ailments such as cancer and heart disease skyrocketed, parallelling increases in stress and environmental contamination. Contagionism, though a sure money-maker, was proving less and less able to cope with modern health problems.

In the face of strong opposition from orthodox medicine, environmentalism began gradually to resurface. Bechamp's ideas enjoyed something of a resurgence with researchers of the so-called 'pleomorphic school'. From observations made through a process known as dark field contrast microscopy, micro-organisms inside the body were observed to change their forms in response to a range of environmental influences.

When bacteria were discovered, they were blamed for all human ills and a campaign of general extermination was mounted. Later, we began to realize that our lives depended on symbiosis with bacteria. When intestinal flora were eliminated by antibiotics, for example, less benign parasites were able to proliferate, causing serious bowel infestations, including the so-called 'gay bowel syndrome'.

The advent of AIDS brought the old contagionist/environmentalist debate into new focus. As the Vietnam war went horribly wrong and the Cold War waned, the 'war against the viruses' appropriated the old military terminology and 'nuke the gooks' approach. Television newsbroadcasts of CDC officers briefing the public about AIDS showed them wearing the khaki, shoulderstraps and braid of military officers. One commentator even referred to AIDS as a 'viral Pearl Harbor'.[10]

Illustrations and computer graphics in the mass media often depicted the supposedly relentless and invincible advance of HIV by thick arrows suggesting infantry pincer movements or lightning attacks, and drawings resembling battle maps of military campaigns. Such pictorial representations, appealing directly to the unconscious and the nervous system, were at least as effective as the printed word in creating reactions of terror and despondency in those who believed they were, or might be, HIV positive.

A variation on the insurgency model was offered by a poster produced by the Canadian Public Health Association and the Canadian federal government's Department of Health and Welfare. 'Join the Attack on AIDS!' it screams, in blood-red letters in a style imitative of spray-painting by inner city gangs. HIV was viewed as a variety of guerilla insurgent, a new kind of dangerous subversive which could – somehow – be blown off the face of the earth by a sufficient blast of Agent Orange-style chemical warfare – or a fist in the face to 'carriers'.

The *blitzkrieg* model of anti-viral warfare was being advanced by powerful multinational drug companies just as a reassessment of the results of toxic technology was beginning to spread. The first photographs of the earth spinning in space, taken from a satellite in 1968, had provided a powerful icon of a beautiful, unified, vulnerable planet. We wanted to make peace with the earth, and new, holistic terms were being proposed.

While they were seldom referred to overtly, these two views of health and disease were to dominate the controversies surrounding AIDS, surfacing repeatedly in the terminology that was automatically and unconsciously employed. The model of counter-insurgency warfare triggered emotions rooted in the recent, lost Vietnam conflict. The model of coexistence, paralleling the end of the Cold War, found its most compelling symbol in the popular image of the turning sphere of blue and white, traditional colors of the Divine Mother.

As both models, the environmentalist as well as the contagionist, tended to downplay the crucial role of the mind in the creation of health and illness, plenty of room was left for a third tradition, whose analysis overlapped somewhat with the environmental approach. The spiritual factor, stressed in the past by such mavericks as the eminent British bacteriologist Dr Edward Bach, originator of the Bach Flower Remedies, was to surface again in the

AIDS crisis through the new science of psychoneuroimmunology, and through the work of Louise Hay, Dr Bernie Siegel and others.

A quotation from Dr Walter Barton, MD, provides an intriguing footnote to these crosscurrents: 'In modern microbiology', he wrote, 'the older idea of infectious disease as a "fight" against foreign "invasion" has to a great extent been superceded by the concept of man and his bacteria and viruses as habitually living together in various states of symbiosis or germ-host relationships involving infection, with or without apparent disease. Accompanying this has been a strong revival of the multiple-cause theory of disease at the expense of the one-germ-one-disease viewpoint.'

Barton's remarks were quoted in a book published in the mid-1960s. Already, the balance of opinion was beginning to shift as the old controversy flared up again. The relevance of the debate twenty years later over the causes of AIDS is obvious. What is surprising is the book itself: not a medical text but R. O. D. Benson's *In Defense of Homosexuality; A Rational Evaluation of Social Prejudice.*[11] Writing a few years prior to Stonewall, Benson used Dr Barton's quote to help explain a conservative medical establishment's belief that homosexuality was a sickness, with a single cause – and so, by implication, a single cure.

Seen in retrospect, this allusion to the nature of virus–host relationships in a quarter-century old text by a gay apologist suggests future events casting shadows before them.

The immortal Henrietta Lacks

A 'HeLa' is a scientific claim that sucks people into a line of work for a while, a line that is later refuted or shown to be a waste of time. It's a type of error in science that occurs fairly often.

— Virologist Wade Parks

Richard Nixon wanted to be remembered. As it happened, events took some unexpected turns. But one of the things he wanted to be remembered for was winning the War on Cancer, and his spectacularly endowed National Cancer Institute (Robert Gallo's stomping ground since 1965) was Battle HQ.

Nixon's researchers hoped to prove that human cancers were caused by viruses rather than by environmental conditions such as radioactivity, pollution, smoking, stress, toxic food and ozone depletion. By early 1970s, cancer virus researchers had blighted or terminated the lives of countless rats, monkeys, dogs and other creatures, but, in spite of a sixty million dollar a year piggy bank, had so far come up with nothing.

The competition was fierce. Michael Gold, who wrote the definitive book on the key Henrietta Lacks case, set out the stakes: 'To find the virus that causes human cancer would open the way to a vaccine . . . . Cancer would be on its way to extinction, and a Nobel Prize would be the least an appreciative world would do for the scientist who made it possible. The high-pressure race had already led to several premature claims of victory . . . . One of the most recent "winners" of the Human Cancer Virus Sweepstakes even received official congratulations from Richard Nixon after the good news was leaked to the press.'[12]

But the alleged agent turned out to be a stray mouse virus in the wrong place, and 'the rat race was on again'. This business of 'contamination' (usually by monkey viruses and other animal pathogens) kept cropping up again and again to bedevil the cancer research race, whose challenge was soon taken up by other countries, from Britain to Soviet Russia. It was to surface again, in spades, in the years that followed.

Cancer laboratories in different countries were in the habit of using air freight and dry ice to swap cell lines with one another and keep each other abreast of their researches. All over the world, scientists were studying what they took to be distinct forms of cancer as they manifested themselves in a wide variety of human cells: liver, blood, bone marrow and what have you. A tremendous amount of brain-power, resources and tax revenues went into the study of these diverse cell cultures and their interreactions with viruses and other pathogens.

Along the way a number of curious facts popped up. One of them was the apparently spontaneous transformation in the lab of benign cells into rapidly replicating malignant cells. Another was that certain identical traits kept cropping up in supposedly diverse cancer cells – in Michael Gold's phrase, like 'winning lemons in a casino full of rigged slot machines'. Armed with all this new information, the research, and the funding, continued apace.

Then the bombshell landed – but didn't go off. Two independent-minded investigators, Stan Gartler and Walter Nelson-Rees, working separately, made the same astonishing discovery. They found that most of the allegedly varied human cell lines that viral researchers had been so carefully studying over the years (liver cells from Russians, lung cells from California migrant workers, squamous cells from African villagers) were not at all what they were supposed to be. Instead they were all derivations from a particularly hardy line of malignant cells originally taken from the body of one Henrietta Lacks, a young black woman who had died at Johns Hopkins Medical Center in 1951 of an unusually aggressive form of cervical cancer.

The cancerous cells taken from Henrietta Lacks's body had continued to proliferate after her death. Named the HeLa line, they proved exceptionally hardy specimens, and were soon endearing themselves to researchers frustrated with the difficulties of getting tissues cultures to yield a cell line that would last long enough *in vitro* for them to study. The result was that, as Michael Gold put it, 'a number of laboratories set up full-scale production and began passing around HeLa cultures the way McDonalds shovels out its burgers and fries'.[13] Chief among them was the National Cancer Institute (NCI), which distributed Ms Lacks's cells – wrongly identified – all over the world. HeLa was even carried aboard the Discoverer XVII satellite. As scientific tinkering continued, new strains and subfamilies of HeLa began to develop, giving rise to new and exciting fields of study and funding, and further complicating the mix-up. HeLa solved many problems for cancer virus researchers around the world – or so it seemed.

The revelation that most of the cancer studies of the past fifteen years had in fact been studies of the apparently immortal remains of Ms Lacks was a profound embarrassment to the wealthy and powerful cancer establishment. As one researcher admitted privately years later, 'Naturally, at the time, I was very defensive because I saw fifteen years work go down the drain.'[14] The defensiveness was widespread, and efforts were made to silence the whistle-blowers. It took about eight years for the HeLa fiasco to be publicly exposed, during which time HeLa strains continued to be misidentified, and time, talent and money were wasted on useless research. During those eight years, the incidence of cancer deaths in the United States climbed off the charts.

One of the whistle-blowers, Walter Nelson-Rees, mulled over how such a monumental gaffe and cover-up could have occurred. The sheer sloppiness of so much laboratory procedure was one reason, he concluded. Apparently, research's purportedly meticulous standards existed largely in the realm of public relations. Another reason was 'more lasting and insidious'. This, he said, had to do with 'frailties of the human ego' on the part of ambitious researchers, particularly when combined with 'exigencies of profit margins' and 'the threat of cuts of support in contractual arrangements'. This airing of science's dirty laundry was not well received. 'The bureaucrats of the National Cancer Institute never tried to survey the wreckage', Michael Gold wrote. 'Very few of HeLa's victims . . . would ever detail how much time, effort and money they had wasted, or how many colleagues they had led astray.'[15]

Henrietta Lacks deserves to be allotted as significant a place in the psychohistory of gay men as Judy Garland. Because the HeLa scandal illustrates the mentality prevailing in the medical science establishment that would mould research and public opinion during the gay health crisis. What that establishment chose to learn from the HeLa case was how to cover up mistakes, and how to silence whistle-blowers. The real lesson of Henrietta Lacks was not learned, and those who do not learn from history tend to repeat it.

The HeLa fiasco *was* repeated – more than once. In separate incidents, two leading virologists, Doctors Gallo and Essex, both misidentified animal viruses as human. But these were mere warm up acts for the gala AIDS circus to come, which involved a misjudgement at least as severe as the HeLa error, followed by a more effective smothering of criticism. At the center of the new fiasco (involving the alleged key to the AIDS puzzle) was the National Cancer Institute, and its chief researcher, Margaret Heckler's white-haired boy, Dr Robert Gallo. It was under Gallo's direction that the cancer virus establishment transformed itself into the AIDS virus establishment.

First came God, then came Gallo

Nixon did exactly the right thing. It's unfortunate that he got caught.
— Dr Robert Gallo

In 1974, Richard Nixon resigned from the White House in disgrace. His Vice-President and Attorney-General had preceded him, under indictment for serious criminal offenses. Two more years saw the fall of what remained of the Republican regime, now figure-headed by Tricky Dick's successor and pardoner, Gerald Ford. As it happened, the new President, Jimmy Carter, had long been con-cerned with the effects of the environment on health. His appointee as the new Director of the National Cancer Institute was a non-virologist whose special interest was the health hazards of atomic radiation. It was a clear message that the cancer virus program may have seen its most lucrative days. And in fact, the NCI's budget was indeed cut. The old battle between contagionists and environmenta-lists surfaced again; viral research, it seemed, would now be gradually superseded by environmental research – at least, as long as Jimmy Carter remained in office.

For the first time in years, funding for the cancer virus establishment was diminishing. The looming image of thousands of unemployed retrovirologists lining up for unemployment insurance began to cause panic. But the Carter administration turned out to be a brief interregnum. Under Ronald Reagan and George Bush, the cancer virus establishment quickly transformed itself into the AIDS establishment.

There was another, less public, aspect to cancer virus research. According to biowarfare investigator Richard Hatch, the National Cancer Institute's cancer virus program 'funded and supervised some of the same scientists, universities, and contracting corporations – ostensibly for cancer research – which had con-ducted biological warfare research' in the 1950s and 1960s.[16]

At least two former biowarfare facilities, in Fort Detrick, Maryland, and Oakland, California, became cancer virus program centers, continuing their investigations into the possibilities of viral biowarfare using cancer research as a respectable cover. The Fort

Detrick facility in particular was responsible for 'the large scale production of . . . suspected oncogenic (cancer-causing) viruses'.[17] These experiments, involving thousands of animals, were linked with US Navy research into the possibilities of bubonic plague warfare, Rift Valley fever and meningitis. According to Hatch, the National Cancer Institute also contracted Charles Pfitzer & Co. to supply animal cancer viruses adapted to grow in human cell lines. Many of these turned out to be more bits of Henrietta Lacks.

From 1962 through the late 1970s, NCI contracted with a company called Bionetics Research Laboratories (later Litton-Bionetics) to implement virus inoculation experiments involving thousands of monkeys. Bionetics also worked on biowarfare projects for the US Army, which had its own research facilities, insulated from the orthodoxies of the civilian establishment. (This independence showed up some years later when the Army's Dr Shyh Ching Lo broke with HIV Fundamentalism and suggested that mycoplasmas might play a role in AIDS.) The experiments were crude, to say the least. They involved injecting the captive monkeys with everything from human cancer tissues to rare viruses and even sheep's blood, in an effort to find a transmissible cancer.[18] Many of the unfortunate monkeys eventually developed immunosuppression and died. Robert Gallo was one of the 'project officers' supervising this monkey holocaust.

A key aim of the biowarfare program was outlined in military testimony provided to the House Committee on Appropriations in 1969: 'Within the next five years', it was estimated, 'it would probably be possible to make a new infective micro-organism which could differ in certain respects from any known disease-causing organisms. Most important of these is that it might be refractory to the immunological and therapeutic processes upon which we depend to maintain our relative freedom from infectious disease.'[19]

Scientists at NCI and in other countries began blending genetic material from viruses that caused disease in different species. Only after tissue from African Green monkeys went astray from a European vivisection lab causing the deaths of several people, did it occur to scientists that continuing with this kind of research might be dangerous.

When an epidemic of immune suppression broke out in urban America, one of the key symptoms was the hyperplasia known as Kaposi's sarcoma. Because its most visible sufferers were gay men, it was quickly assumed to be infectious and sexually transmitted – a conclusion that had never been made about KS in the past. When Robert Gallo himself blamed the outbreak on a supposedly 'new' virus, those who knew something of the background of cancer virus programs naturally suspected that perhaps yet another experiment had gotten out of hand.

Paradoxically, the AIDS establishment's insistence on a single virus as the cause of the epidemic not only diverted attention from other toxins and pathogens, but also fuelled speculation about the possible laboratory origins of the alleged culprit. To the suspicious, the central role played by Robert Gallo suggested a hidden link to biowarfare. Gallo's revamping of the old cancer virus arguments to explain AIDS prompted them to wonder: was Gallo an agent who had come to believe his own cover?

As the National Institutes of Health has been described by past employees as 'a den of thieves',[20] the first of what was to become a series of scandalous revelations did not come as a total surprise. Gallo's 'AIDS virus' was revealed to be the clone of a retrovirus previously discovered by Dr Luc Montagnier's team at the Pasteur Institute. This French retrovirus, like the HeLa line, had grown well *in vitro*, and samples the French team had trustingly sent to America later popped up in Gallo's own research. Margaret Heckler's 'miracle of American science' was the result of either another serious mixup or a deliberate fraud.

The French 'LAV' retrovirus had been given little attention in the American media, and Montagnier's application to the US Patent Office for the potentially lucrative rights to a blood test for it had been stalled somewhere in the bureaucratic machinery. Until the Pasteur Institute's discovery, Gallo's research had concentrated on HTLV-I, a virus associated with leukemia. As leukemia involves a proliferation of T-cells – just the opposite of AIDS – this speculation not surprisingly came to nothing. Then, while Montagnier's claim was on hold, Gallo shifted the focus of his research. His new investigations, using the viral isolate obtained from Montagnier, proceeded apace, resulting not in the scientific debate that might have been expected, but in the Reagan Administration's official announcement.

Robert Gallo filed for a patent on the blood test kit for 'his' virus that very day. The patent was quickly awarded, and Montagnier was livid. An international scandal was only avoided by delicate political negotiations at the highest governmental level. By the terms of the resulting accord, Montagnier and Gallo were to share the credit as 'co-discoverers' of the retrovirus, now renamed HIV; royalties from the blood tests soon to be aggressively promoted to gay men and inhabitants of the Third World would be evenly divided. The accord, it was hoped, would prevent a scandal that would dwarf even the Henrietta Lacks affair. Thus were the cracks papered over, but the seepage of Gallo's reputation could not be stopped.

Variously described as arrogant, charming, egomaniacal, belligerent, unscrupulous, charismatic and relentlessly competitive, Robert Gallo, in his still potent ability to manipulate the press, seemed as symbolic of the medical-industrial complex he represented as Dr Ewen Cameron had been in the 1950s. One colleague, Dr Flossie Wong-Staal, baldly stated what seemed to be the required politically correct attitude of the establishment: 'First came God, then came Gallo.'[21]

Then, in November 1989, the *Chicago Tribune* published a book-length supplement by reporter John Crewdson, which revealed many of the scientific shenanigans surrounding HIV, from incompetence to outright fraud.[22] Gallo, according to Crewdson, had made something of a habit of appropriating credit from colleagues, tampering with records to boost his own reputation, threatening to 'destroy' co-workers and refusing to share samples of 'his' retrovirus without guarantees that it would not be investigated too closely. Crewdson's report on these scandals was thorough and detailed, with one important omission: the key question of whether HIV actually did cause AIDS.

The press played a key role in the psychodrama enacted in the minds of gay men during the AIDS years. With only two important but (in terms of public exposure) minor exceptions – the gay *New York Native* and the rock periodical *SPIN* – the North American press acted as a conduit for an official AIDS doctrine that was simple enough for a headline, a ten-second newsbite, or a quick quote from a designated expert. HIV is 'the fatal virus that causes AIDS'. Other, related assertions – that AIDS came originally from Africa courtesy of a lost tribe and a green monkey, that one contact with HIV is sufficient to cause AIDS, that HIV's presence in the blood is revealed by an antibody test, or that AZT (or some similar cytocidal drug) would 'extend life' – were all dependent upon the myth of the lone assassin.

Not that controversy about AIDS was muted. This, after all, was America, not Soviet Russia. On the contrary, debate raged, but within boundaries clearly defined and very seldom transgressed. The loud but circumscribed arguments favored by the American media were reflected in books like *AIDS: Opposing Viewpoints*.[23] This annotated anthology of arguments reprinted from the daily and periodical press juxtaposes pronouncements about civil liberties, sexual morality and proposed legislation, with liberal and conservative views exquisitely 'balanced' and equally strident. The crucial questions of the cause and appropriate treatment of AIDS are off-limits. No AIDS dissidents, no AIDS activists, no holistic practitioners, are included. The 'opposing viewpoints' constitute a shouting match over irreconcilable dichotomies like 'Are civil rights as important as public health?' This exercise in conceptual obedience is topped off by a cover drawing of the Grim Reaper.

Eventually, Luc Montagnier began to move away from the made-in-America AIDS orthodoxy. In an interview with *Omni* magazine, when Montagnier was asked if he was permitted to talk about the details of the accord that had succeeded, for a time, in cementing an international united front on HIV, he answered: 'It's not exactly a gag order, although it's stated in the agreement that no one will reopen the scientific argument.'[24]

By then, however, the scientific argument had already been reopened as neatly as a can of worms can be, by a party at least as eminent as Gallo and Montagnier, a fellow researcher who, almost alone among his fellows, was unintimidated by the governmental gag order: the University of California at Berkeley's Professor Peter Duesberg.

The little dog who won't let go

Indeed, some 50 to 100 latent retroviruses have been found to reside in the DNA of all humans, passed along to each successive generation for as long as human beings have existed.

— Peter Duesberg and Bryan J. Ellison, *Is the AIDS Virus a Science Fiction?*

During the 1960s, the university town of Berkeley, California had given birth to the Free Speech Movement. As a traditional center of dissident activity, it was an appropriate location for biologist Peter Duesberg to mount his attack on scientific orthodoxy.

Dr Duesberg had rained on the parade before. Like Gallo and many other top AIDS researchers, he had a background in cancer research. But Duesberg had been able to demonstrate that certain cherished and much-heralded conclusions about cellular oncogenes and cancer were incorrect. Nobel Prizes are not awarded for commenting on the Emperor's nakedness, and Duesberg's whistle-blowing made him somewhat unpopular, though not nearly as unpopular as he would become.

Retroviruses were Duesberg's speciality. It was he who developed the genetic map of the retrovirus in the first place. And when his old colleagues on the East Coast began to be awash in AIDS funding after Secretary Heckler's HIV pronouncement, Duesberg saw no reason why Berkeley should be left out. He began studying the published literature, and it was the poor quality of the literature that first triggered his skepticism. He concluded that a simple retorvirus did not possess the devious, lethal characteristics necessary to a lone assassin.

Duesberg published two detailed, meticulous, scientific papers on AIDS, cancer and retroviruses in 1987 and 1989.[25] These papers supported what Joseph Sonnabend and many holistic health practitioners had thought: that a single retrovirus could not cause AIDS. At the heart of Duesberg's argument are a number of observations about the HIV hypothesis, and the nature of viral and retroviral infection. He pointed out that 'HIV is latent and inactive, not only in the 1–2 million Americans who test positive for [antibodies] but also in the 10,000 who annually develop AIDS'. He drew attention to the very small percentage of lymphocytes and T-cells affected, to the difficulty of finding evidence of the virus itself in

PWAs, and to the inscrutable contradictions of the claimed 'latency period' of several years, when anti-viral immunity is induced within a few weeks. Any sickness caused by HIV, Duesberg contended, would have to be caused *before*, not after, the onset of immunity as indicated by the appearance of antibodies.

'It seems clear', he wrote, 'that the virus-AIDS hypothesis fails to make a case for sufficiency. It offers no explanation for why less than 1% of antibody-positive persons develop AIDS and why the mean latency between infection and disease is five years . . . . Since the transmission of AIDS depends on frequent contacts involving the exchange of *cells*, the case for a viral cause remains open.'[26]

In his 1990 article, 'Is the AIDS virus a science fiction?' Duesberg and his collaborator Bryan J. Ellison, considered the long, and increasingly elastic, 'latency period' between HIV infection and illness, noting that when 'diseases are said to occur only years after infection by a virus, it can be difficult to be sure that other risk factors have not instead caused the disease. Second, because HIV is conspicuously absent from lesions, scientists had to hypothesize that the virus caused disease by indirect means in the body, in spite of a troubling lack of evidence for such notions. Inventions such as these can be used to blame virtually any microbe for any disease.'[27]

Duesberg's comprehensive, point-by-point arguments against the prevailing view of the cause of AIDS were not met with rebuttals in kind, but rather with a wall of silence, breached only by occasional *ad hominem* attacks. When pressed about Duesberg's dissent, Robert Gallo replied, 'Believe me, it's going to have zero impact. No one believes Peter, except a few people that don't matter. That's the simple fact. Why would anyone go to Duesberg? He is hanging around with some unusual people isn't he, rather than his own peers. Strange. Very strange. He comes to meetings with guys [in] leather jackets.'[28]

Yet in spite of the attempt, by both official scientists and the media, to bury Duesberg's opinions, both he and the questions he raised persisted: Gallo, his genuine annoyance showing through the veneer of condescension, took to referring to him as 'the little dog who won't let go'.

What baffled many of Duesberg's colleagues was not so much his skepticism (many of them had their own quiet doubts) but rather why one of the leading scientists in his field, secure in his position and reputation, should stick his neck out to pioneer a dissenting opinion in the face of an officially endorsed and almost unanimous consensus. One colleague mused, 'He makes a lot of sense, but the one thing I always wonder is, "Why did Duesberg do it?" . . . He was so secure in his position as a scientist, he could have lived, and lived well, happily ever after. Why would he want to jump in the fire like this?'[29] Gallo and the other retrovirologists who had jumped on the HIV bandwagon had become millionaires through royalties on patented blood tests and shares in pharmaceutical companies. Duesberg lived on his professor's salary – and suffered a severe cutback of his research funds for not falling into line.

Over the next few years, a few eminent scientists – among them Harry Rubin, the 'dean of retrovirology', and Nobel Prizewinners Walter Gilbert and Kary Mullis – came out in support of Duesberg. None of them was from the AIDS Establishment. 'I am often asked', Duesberg wrote, 'why it is just myself, Harry Rubin, Joseph Sonnabend and a handful of others who question the virus-AIDS hypothesis. Why doesn't a young, ambitious scientist make a name for himself by questioning it? The answer lies in the strong conformist pressure on scientists, particularly young, untenured scientists, in the age of biotechnology. Their conceptual obedience to the establishment is maintained by controlled access to research grants, journals and positions, and rewarded by conference engagements, personal prizes, consultantships, stocks and co-ownership in companies. A dissenter would have to be truly independent and prepared for a variety of sanctions.'[30]

Early in 1992, the Centers for Disease Control announced that, once again, the criteria for a diagnosis of AIDS had changed. Diseases had been added and subtracted before, with Duesberg quipping that 'they have moved the goalposts again!' Now, the two chief AIDS illnesses, Kaposi's sarcoma and pneumocystis carinii pneumonia, were no longer deemed necessary for a condition of AIDS to exist. Instead, a complicated system of nine different types of AIDS was drawn up. Even the CDC's spokesperson, Dr Ruth Berkleman, admitted that 'such a broad expansion of the AIDS case definition will make interpretation of trends in incidence and characteristics of cases more difficult'.[31] It would also have the effect of expanding the figures to more closely fit the CDC's projections.

These developments followed the Sixth International AIDS Conference in San Francisco in 1990. There, Dr Luc Montagnier, whose Pasteur Institute team had discovered HIV in the first place, announced that he had revised his opinion on HIV. He no longer believed that HIV alone could cause AIDS, and was investigating mycoplasmas with Shyh Ching Lo. When Dr Lo himself was asked, 'Do you think it's conceivable that HIV alone could cause AIDS?' he replied, 'That's a very political question'.[32]

Unlike Gallo, who had long denied the possibility of 'cofactors' to 'his' virus, Montagnier compared the action of HIV to that of 'a lion hunting a troop of gazelles. It will bring down only the weakest among them . . . with immune systems [weaker] than the others'. The immune systems of homosexuals are already depressed. The virus searches for favorable terrain in which to establish itself. It created an epidemic in territory already prepared by the cofactors that homosexuality generates. Not only the establishment of the virus but also its transmission is aided by these cofactors.'[33] This constituted a giant step away from Gallo's lone assassin theory, and it made the American AIDS establishment very unhappy with Dr Montagnier. When American researchers at the conference began to give him the cold shoulder, he headed back to Europe.

Another break with orthodoxy came when the researches of Dr Alvin Friedman-Kien led him to report early in 1990 that HIV was unlikely to be a cause of Kaposi's sarcoma, considered one of the main indicators of AIDS in gay men.[34] By this time, links between KS and poppers were becoming more evident. Friedman-Kien's conclusion was reinforced by the findings of HIV skeptic Dr Robert Root-Bernstein, who conducted a survey of KS as far back as the first paper published on the subject by Dr Moritz Kaposi in 1872. He found reports of hundreds of KS patients whose condition fitted the CDC definition for AIDS – many of them teenagers and young men.[35] HIV, it seemed, had been around for a long time – predating by decades the grim monkeying around of cancer virus researchers.

Piece by piece, the stone wall of AIDS orthodoxy was crumbling. But the ruins were heavily defended. Over a decade into the epidemic, the public was still being told by newspapers and television, and by all but a tiny handful of physicians, that a positive result from an HIV antibody test showed present and lifelong 'infection' by the virus; that the virus was certain or very likely to lead to AIDS; and that AIDS was universally fatal. None of these assertions had been proven. Yet the psychological effect of believing them could be catastrophic. And as heavily funded advertising promoted mass antibody testing, more and more people became 'HIV positives'. In the post-1984 world, a growing number of people considered their allotted blood 'status' as the key to both their identity and their fate.

The myth of the homosexual had long conditioned gay men to expect an early death. Now that myth was reinforced with the perfect techno-metaphor: 'You're a walking time-bomb – and the fuse is short.'

A growing movement of AIDS dissidents (composed of gay activists, skeptical scientists, holistic healers and others) arose during the 1980s. Their ideas were seldom reported in the mass media. A clue to why important AIDS controversies went unreported can be found in a copy of the 'backgrounder' on AIDS issued by the *Globe and Mail* ('Canada's National Newspaper').[36] There are similar internal information sheets for the use of editors and journalists on daily papers all over North America. After warning its employees against the dangers of 'over-reaction', 'under-reaction', 'scare tactics' and 'complacency', the *Globe* goes on to lay out the AIDS facts to which its staffers must adhere. They are: 'YES, IT'S FATAL' (the capitals are theirs); it 'probably evolved' through African Green monkeys, and it is caused by HIV which 'destroys' the T-cells (this was in 1987, just as the T-cell zap theory was about to be quietly jettisoned). The inevitable Two Sides of the 'mass-testing issue' are set forth in point form. There is not even a hint of scientific debate on the cause or causes of the epidemic.

The key section is the final one, 'Contacts', directing staffers to further information. The first six recommended contacts are government agencies. The remaining three (for the real eager beavers) are the Red Cross, the chairman of a medical advisory

committee and the head of a health subcommittee of the National
Action Committee on the Status of Women, a quasi-governmental
organization only tangentially concerned with AIDS. No AIDS
organization (not even the most orthodox), no gay group, and
certainly no dissident scientist or researcher is even mentioned.

'Medical journalists', said one AIDS dissident, 'seem to think
the public are best served by giving them unadulterated information
that comes direct from the government. It's something no other
journalist does.'[37]

As a result, thousands of HIV-positive gay men were told by
their daily papers and their doctors that they should prepare for
AIDS, and death. Some began taking the toxic medicines urged on
them to 'extend life'. Others, like the novelist Marco Vassi, who
deliberately contracted pneumonia, simply committed suicide –
singly or in couples.

Harvard professor Walter Gilbert eloquently summed up
press attitudes in his comments for the independent British television
production 'The AIDS Catch':

> The general public accepts what the media tells them, and the
> media and the scientific community – parts of it – have blown
> up the virus as the cause of AIDS because it is more
> convenient to have a neat explanation than to be in the
> situation which we often are in science, at which the
> questions still face us and our knowledge proceeds gradually
> to overcome them . . . .
>
> The community as a whole doesn't listen patiently to
> critics who adopt alternative viewpoints, although the great
> lesson of history is that knowledge develops through the
> conflict of viewpoints – that if you have simply a consensus
> view it generally stultifies; it fails to see the problem of that
> consensus. And it depends on the existence of critics to break
> up that iceberg and permit knowledge to develop. This is one
> of the underpinnings of democratic theory, it's one of the
> basic reasons we believe in notions of free speech, and it's one
> of the great forces in terms of intellectual development.[38]

The problems of consensus were further heightened in 1994 when newspapers began reporting that HIV directly causes cancer.[39] For a decade, they had contended that cells infected with HIV die off quickly. Now we were being told that cells infected with HIV replicate out of control! Such was the mental climate of the times that many people believed both these contradictory stories from the official explanation for AIDS. George Orwell had coined a term for this phenomenon of government: doublethink.

HIV fundamentalism benefited a bloated medical establishment that was politically powerful, scientifically shaky and ethically corrupt, deeply compromised by its links to the pharmaceutical giants and clandestine operations of mass murder, and surviving by political power and intimidation. The American medical/industrial complex had all the arrogance and desperation of a totalitarian government at the end of its run.

As with all such establishments, its continued existence was bound up with a number of half-believed but oddly potent myths. For the discredited biowarfare and cancer researchers who had found a new lease on life as the gay health crisis deepened, the standard-bearer of their new doctrine was the same little creature whose stray parts had caused some of them a few troubling thoughts several years before: the African Green Monkey.

Affair with a green monkey

I am talking about millions of men who have been skilfully injected with fear, inferiority complexes, trepidation, servility, despair, abasement.

— Aimé Césaire, *Discourse on Colonialism*

In 1959, in a book called *A Touch of Strange*, Theodore Sturgeon published a suggestive short story called 'Affair with a Green Monkey'. In this story, a straight couple rescues a young man from an apparent gay-bashing. It is explained that the man was attacked because he is 'a green monkey – painted green so the other monkeys will attack it . . . because it's different. Not dangerous, just different.'[40] At the end of the story, the young gay man mysteriously disappears, and there is a suggestion of supernatural, or extraterrestrial, origins. One of his rescuers, whose name is Alma (Latin for kind), begins to look at her kind but somewhat limited heterosexual lover with a more skeptical eye. As a result of the couple's 'affair' with this stranger, and the changes he brings to them, the green monkeys are able to establish a 'beachhead' in contemporary society.

Related with Sturgeon's usual perceptive irony, the story is a parable of intolerance inflicted on a sexual scapegoat, for which the words 'green monkey' stand as a code phrase. In the AIDS years, the world heard a great deal about Green monkeys – specifically the African Green monkey, a near-mythical creature found in jungles and laboratories, and fingered by Western scientists as a conduit for the viral killer.

Historically, venereal diseases have been assumed to originate in foreign parts, where people are dirty and their folkways repellent. The doctrine of racism, evolved to excuse imperialism and the slave trade, associated black people with dirt, disease and a supposedly animal-like sexual promiscuity. As one pair of commentators observed (from an African vantage point), 'When a new and deadly sexually transmitted disease . . . emerged . . . it was almost inevitable that black people would be associated with its origin and transmission.'[41]

The myth of the Green monkey, as it evolved in the 1980s, went something like this: the virus that causes AIDS is an old disease of Africa. Once restricted to a lost tribe concealed in the hinterland of the Dark Continent, the virus broke out in recent years by way of the Green monkey. As the Green monkeys did not have the virus, it must have mutated on its way. There were several versions of what happened next. Dr Gallo thought that black slaves – and/or monkeys – might have started the ball rolling by taking the first human retrovirus to Japan with them in the seventeenth century.[42] Others suggested that African monkeys, kept as pets in Haitian male brothels, might have put the bite on the paying customers from America, and spread the virus that way.

Two British 'AIDS experts' put forward another possibility, that a hunting or cooking accident might have brought people into contact with infected Green monkey blood, or that dead monkeys might have been used as dolls by African children.[43] Others stretched the racist fantasies further, darkly suggesting jungle monkey-fucking by depraved black women (or black sodomites) as the root of the plague; this was a great favorite of fundamentalist churchmen from the Southern states. The idea that lust between woman and ape might threaten the American Empire is, after all, the theme of one our most memorable cinematic icons: the black-and-white image of King Kong scaling the Empire State Building with Fay Wray writhing masochistically in his giant rubber hand.

These group fantasies of bestiality harked back to nineteenth century occultist and pseudo-scientific ideas that became popular with the Nazis, notions of human interbreeding with beasts bringing about racial degeneracy through dark pollutions of the blood. Randy Shilts' Patient Zero, a promiscuous and much-travelled airline steward of vampiric disposition and pointedly un-American background, seemed the ideal conduit to bring the killer virus out of the steaming monkey-jungles of the Dark Continent and into the heartland of White America.

As old nightmares circulated in new, scientific guise in the Western media, African scholars seethed with anger and frustration. A Zimbabwean living in England, Richard Chirimuuta, together with his Australian wife Rosalind, wrote a lucid exposé, *AIDS, Africa and Racism*, which was published by a small press in Britain. The Chirimuutas challenged the doctrine of a continent approaching annihilation by clinical AIDS, pointing out that many common African diseases were now frequently diagnosed, sometimes retrospectively, as AIDS, and that unreliable tests conducted on ancient blood samples were being trotted out as proving official African origin theories.

Though HIV was apparently widespread among some African groups, only a very small number contracted the diseases which were linked to AIDS in Westerners. Squalid conditions and the promiscuous use of Western pharmaceuticals (many of them black-market, outdated, contaminated or misprescribed) may have contributed to much of the purported AIDS epidemic in Africa. But these were touchy subjects, and far from the orthodoxies of HIV and African genesis.

The Chirimuutas summed up as follows: 'Because scientists found it so difficult to imagine that white people could infect Africans with AIDS and not the reverse, such a possibility has never been seriously investigated.' The African genesis and Green monkey myths 'fitted in very nicely with the belief that Africans were both evolutionarily and physically closer to monkeys than to people elsewhere'.[44]

An intriguing alternative to the Green monkey myth was raised by the science editor for *The Times* of London, Pearce Wright. In a front page story in May 1987, Wright discussed evidence for the possibility that the World Health Organization's smallpox vaccination campaign in several African states, Brazil and Haiti had caused the high incidence of illness (now labelled AIDS) occurring in the very same areas.[45] Were there contaminants in the vaccines? Did the extensive reuse of needles contribute? Or did the serum itself further weaken the immune systems of a population already in less than optimal health?

The Times article was not reprinted in America, and the possibility of a connection between AIDS and inoculations – whether for smallpox or hepatitis B – was seldom aired. In time, a number of investigators began to re-examine the accepted AIDS statistics for Africa, and to question whether there was really an AIDS epidemic there at all.[46]

HIV fundamentalism, originating in a scientific hypothesis, had become a popular folk belief highly resistant to analytical challenge. The health crisis had generated its own version of the myth of the lone assassin: the myth of the killer virus.

The myth of the killer virus

They call HIV the AIDS virus, and it's this generation's symbol of terror. It has come to rule us, our lives, our relationships, our sexuality. A microscopic dictator. We have erected buildings, organizations, conferences, and global programs in an attempt to placate it. It is a demon, and we worship it with our terror.

— Celia Farber

Just as the development of the microscope in the nineteenth century led to the idea that bacteria must be responsible for our ills, so in the era of electron microscopes and computers, the viral metaphor became a dominant thought-form, eventually being used to explain everything from the power of advertising to foreign computer tampering. *Time* magazine provided a classic conflation of racism and viral paranoia in a 1988 story on computer viruses which singled out for particular loathing something it called 'the Pakistani virus', a vile annoyance allegedly concocted by a small, cut-rate foreign store in order to 'punish' Yankee tourists.[47]

The origins of the electron microscope go back to the experiments of the eccentric Croatian-born genius Nikola Tesla. Tesla was a leading pioneer of electrical technology (he demonstrated wireless telegraphy five years before Marconi) who drafted plans for an inexpensive system of wireless electrical transmission that would draw on the earth's natural electrical field. After Tesla's death, his American papers were impounded by the FBI and his European papers fell into the hands of the SS, leaving Himmler and Hoover each with half the treasure map.

One aspect of Tesla's research that especially interested the Nazis was his purported perfection of a death ray which would beam concentrated particles at enemy aircraft and incinerate them. German scientists carried out a great deal of experimentation with high-voltage X-rays and tried to develop a device that would destroy matter through intersecting infra-red beams. Though they were never able to manufacture a death ray in time to turn the tide of war, one offshoot of their efforts was the electron microscope, developed in response to Hitler's banal remark that 'if we had more powerful microscopes, we would discover new worlds'.[48]

Once the electron microscope facilitated the discovery of viruses – identified as an intermediate stage between living and inanimate matter, using the cells of living organisms to replicate – the new knowledge led inevitably to a virus-like proliferation of the viral model and viral theories of disease. Older thought-forms of Western civilization – particularly the racial and sexual myths and fears which Nazism grew from and manipulated – bonded to these viral models, which then proceeded to further infect the body politic.

The technology to detect viruses was widely believed to have come along 'just in time' to allow identification of new, virus-caused diseases. Our materialistic philosophy calls this a coincidence. One philosopher of history, writing in the late 1940s, offered a different view: 'To a 21st century history-writer', he suggested, 'the most important thing about the cells, ether-waves, and cosmic rays of our time will be that we believed in them. All of these notions, which the age considers *facts*, will vanish into the one fact for the 21st century that once upon a time this was a world-picture of a certain kind of Culture-man. So do we look upon the nature-theories of Aristarchus and Democritus in the Classical Culture.'[49]

The most vivid examples of the virus as mental construct recur in the works of William S. Burroughs, whose darkly kaleidoscopic work *Naked Lunch* we first looked into in Chapter 2. Written at about the same time as Sturgeon's 'Affair with a Green Monkey', Burroughs' prophetic novel imagined a viral venereal disease 'indigenous to Ethiopia . . . "Not for nothing are we known as feelthy Ethiopians," sneers an Ethiopian mercenary as he sodomizes Pharaoh, venomous as the King's cobra.' Burroughs' viral epidemic has its origins in Addis Ababa, but these being modern times, soon spreads to New Orleans and Seattle. It shows 'a distinct predilection for Negroes, is in fact the whitehaired boy of white supremacists'. It languishes in the guts of jungle mosquitoes and 'the saliva of a dying jackal slobbering silver under the desert moon. And after an initial lesion at the point of infection the disease passes to the lymph glands of the groin . . . Elephantiasis of the genitals is a frequent complication . . . "Treatment is symptomatic" – which means there is none.'[50]

Here Burroughs presented, as early as the 1950s, an astonishingly accurate version of the group fantasy of AIDS as it would develop in white heterosexual America over two decades later. A fatal, incurable venereal disease originating in Africa, with 'a predilection for Negroes', involving animals and mosquitoes and migrating to America: all these are actual or putative characteristics of AIDS. Even the 'elephantiasis of the genitals' is experienced by some AIDS patients. Substitute Sturgeon's green monkey for Burroughs' jackal and the scenario is almost exact.

Another passage in *Naked Lunch* tells of a man being 'taken over' by his anus, which learns to speak and grows teeth that bite through his clothing, finally covering him with a viscous growth.[51] This and other Burroughs creations (such as the sexually predatory creature known as the Mugwump, whose eyes are blank as glory holes) suggest a kind of sexual cannibalization of the autonomous self brought about by various versions of a 'homosexual virus', i.e. the myth of the homosexual in contemporary viral form.

Phobias about the anus and anal eroticism have always fuelled anti-gay sentiment. Even homosexual apologists like Carpenter felt the need to minimize the incidence of anal sex among Uranians. D. H. Lawrence, who was influenced by Carpenter but could never quite accept homosexuality, was fascinated by heterosexual buggery. Burroughs provided visceral imagery for such deep-seated fears. When AIDS erupted, many found it satisfying to blame anal eroticism for both gay and African versions of the syndrome, seeing it as a dangerous, alien practice originating with homosexuals and blacks. The extended equation was: Africa = dangerous animals = blacks = dirt = anal sex = death.

Twenty years before AIDS, Burroughs' hyper-sensitive antennae had detected crucial ideas and group fantasies in the American race-mind, born of the same sexual and racial fears that gave rise to the Ku Kluxism, homophobia and lynchings that provide black humor throughout Burroughs' work. When it was first published, *Naked Lunch* was banned in the United States. A quarter of a century later, sections of it could be read as a fairly detailed guide to some of the chief fears and fantasies of the age.

In the years following its publication, Burroughs developed his concept of the virus as a pertinent metaphor of the workings of contemporary society and culture. He also kept alert to the proliferating signs of decay on the underside of the governmental/medical/industrial superstructure. In the late 1970s, he zeroed in specifically on American medical politics in his film outline, *Blade Runner*.[52]

Published in 1979, two years before the first recognized AIDS cases, Burroughs' scenario is set in an unspecified time in the near future. A conspiracy by government, the medical establishment and the drug companies has undermined public health, and large sections of the population have no access to effective treatment. The repression of experimental and holistic medicine has continued. As a result, a clandestine system of illegal holistic and do-it-yourself treatments has been cobbled together, a self-financed underground running medicines and surgical equipment out of abandoned buildings and subway tunnels. The hero of the story is Billy, a gay man who is a 'blade runner', a courier of medical contraband. His attempts to spread the word about a new medicine are hampered by the atmosphere of distrust and paranoia generated by the official Health Control as well as by an illness he has contracted – pneumonia.

Little more than three years later, gay men in Burroughs' own neighborhood, Manhattan's Lower East Side, would be joining regular early morning lineups to receive smuggled, illegal Mexican AIDS drugs handed out by clergy and volunteer workers. Groups of enlistees in government medicine 'trials' would be taking their drugs to underground labs for analysis, dividing up what they liked among themselves and throwing away the rest. Medical bureaucrats then solemnly recorded and publicized the invalid results. Community research initiatives and drug buyers' clubs sprang up, and recipes for home-made versions of banned, Israeli-made egg-lipids were treated as valuable *samizdat* documents, photocopied and passed on hand to hand.

One 1980s memoir described the scene as follows: 'People with AIDS across the country are turning themselves into human test tubes. Some of them are compiling so much information that they can call government agencies and pass themselves off as research scientists and suddenly have access to all the information that's been withheld and then they turn their tenement kitchens into laboratories, mixing up chemicals and passing them out freely to friends and strangers to help prolong lives.'[53]

In such a setting, gullibility and skepticism intermingled as the AMA warned of rampant quackery, the Centers for Disease Control fiddled with fatality projections and the dying were inundated with emergency press releases. The gay press began to feature articles with titles like 'Home remedies for the Holocaust' and 'Dallas gays set up guerilla AIDS clinic'. And gay men with pneumonia had become commonplace.

Here is William Burroughs, two years before AIDS, on the crisis to come: 'The FDA and the AMA and the big drug companies are like an octopus on the citizen . . . Is this freedom? Is this what America stands for? . . . So America goes underground. They all make their own medicines in garages, basements, and lofts, and provide their own service. The population, drenched with increasingly effective antibiotics, had lost all material resistance and became as vulnerable to the infections as the Indians and South Sea Islanders on first contact with the Whites . . . The miracles of modern medicine, by interfering with natural immunity, in the long run give rise to more illnesses than they prevent.'[54]

Blade Runner predicts 'not just an increase in cancer but . . . a breakdown in the immunity system'. It asks, 'Why does a cancer or any virus take a certain length of time to develop? Immunity. Remove the immunity factor, and virus processes can be accelerated.' As a some-time addict, Burroughs had long seen addictive behavior as a human manifestation of the viral metaphor. In the gay ghettos, increased addictive-compulsive behaviors facilitated the removal of the immunity factor, viruses proliferated, and Burroughs' fictional prophecies began to come true. HIV fundamentalism determined which treatments would be allowed and funded and which neglected and driven underground.

The idea of a killer virus had originated in America's biowarfare labs, whose Green monkeys and megadeath predictions surfaced as popular scientific bogeys in the AIDS era. It gave rise to *Naked Lunch*-style incidents like the one in Cincinnati in 1991 when a gay PWA who was beaten up by four policemen was charged with four counts of attempted murder for bleeding on his attackers. When he finally recovered from the assault and could leave his hospital bed, he was fitted with an electronic monitoring device to track his whereabouts.[55]

As America witnessed the attrition of gay men, blacks, Hispanics and IV drug users, the epidemic seemed more and more like a paranoid's nightmare. Wrote Burroughs: 'A paranoid is someone who has all the facts.'

Notes

1. David E. Scheim, *Contract on America: The Mafia Murder of John F. Kennedy* (New York: Zebra Books, 1988).
2. For Hoover's political and private life, see Curt Gentry, *J. Edgar Hoover: The Man and the Secrets* (New York: Plume, 1991); and Anthony Summers, *Official and Confidential: The Secret Life of J. Edgar Hoover* (New York: G. P. Putnam's Sons, 1993).

3. For science fiction precursors of AIDS, see Michael Crichton, *The Andromeda Strain* (New York: Alfred A. Knopf, 1969); Thomas Scortia and Frank Robinson, *The Nightmare Factor* (Garden City, NY: Doubleday, 1978); and William S. Burroughs' *Naked Lunch* and *Blade Runner*, discussed in other sections. Frank Robinson was a speechwriter for Harvey Milk.

4. See, for example, Ivan Illich, *Medical Nemesis: The Expropriation of Health* (London: Calder and Boyars, 1975); R. S. Mendelsohn, *Confessions of a Medical Heretic* (Chicago: Contemporary Books, 1979); and the works of Thomas Szasz.

5. Quoted in Jad Adams, *AIDS: The HIV Myth* (New York: St Martin's Press, 1989), p. 56.

6. See Bruce Livesay and Ellen Lipsius, 'AIDS: modern medicine's Achilles heel', *Canadian Dimensions*, October 1989, p. 27.

7. Ellen Lipsius and Derek Mackie, 'AIDS: the medical dilemma and solutions', *Canadian Tribune*, 11 July 1988, p. 5.

8. Livesay and Lipsius, 'AIDS: . . . Achilles heel', p. 28.

9. 'Clams dying of "AIDS" ', *Toronto Sun*, 19 September 1987, p. 31.

10. Max Klinghoffer, 'AIDS: a viral Pearl Harbor', *Journal of Civil Defense*, April 1987. (Earlier, Henry Kissinger had envisioned Chile's independence from the US as a virus that would 'infect' the whole region, and even spread to Europe!)

11. R. O. D. Benson, *In Defense of Homosexuality: A Rational Evaluation of Social Prejudice* (New York: Julian Press, 1965), pp. 63–4.

12. Michael Gold, *A Conspiracy of Cells: One Woman's Immortal Legacy and the Medical Scandal It Caused* (Albany: State University of New York Press, 1986), p. 4. Much of my information on Henrietta Lacks and the cell culture fiasco is drawn from this study.

13. *Ibid.*, p. 24.

14. Cyril Stulberg, quoted in Gold, *A Conspiracy*, p. 36.

15. Gold, *A Conspiracy*, pp. 74–6, 87.

16. Richard Hatch, 'Cancer warfare', *CovertAction Information Bulletin*, Winter 1991, p. 14.

17. National Cancer Institute, *Special Virus Cancer Project Progress Report* (US Department of Health, Education and Welfare, Public Health Service, 1972), p. 33.

18. Hatch, 'Cancer warfare', p. 17.

19. Quoted in Robert Harris and Jeremy Paxman, *A Higher Form of Killing: The Secret Story of Gas and Germ Warfare* (New York: Hill & Wang, 1983).

20. Seth Roberts, 'Lab rat', *Spy*, July 1990, p. 72.

21. Quoted in Roberts, 'Lab rat', p. 72.

22. John Crewdson, 'The great AIDS quest', *Chicago Tribune*, 19 November 1989.

23. Lyn Hall and Thomas Modl, eds., *AIDS: Opposing Viewpoints* (St Paul, MN: Greenhaven Press, 1988).

24. Luc Montagnier, interview in *Omni*, December 1988.

25. Peter H. Duesberg, 'Retroviruses as carcinogens and pathogens: expectations and reality', *Cancer Research*, March 1987; and 'Human immunodeficiency virus and acquired immunodeficiency syndrome: correlation but not causation', *Proceedings of the National Academy of Sciences*, February 1989.

26. Peter Duesberg, 'A challenge to the AIDS establishment', *Bio/ Technology*, November 1987.

27. Peter Duesberg and Bryan J. Ellison, 'Is the AIDS virus a science fiction?' *Policy Review*, Summer 1990.

28. Anthony Liversidge, 'AIDS: words from the front', *SPIN*, March 1989, p. 55.

29. Celia Farber, 'AIDS: words from the front', *SPIN*, April 1990, p. 114.

30. Peter Duesberg, Introduction to Adams, *AIDS: The HIV Myth*, p. x.

31. Quoted in *Positively Aware*, September 1991, p. 4.

32. Quoted in Anthony Liversidge and Celia Farber, 'AIDS: words from the front', *SPIN*, September 1990, p. 71.

33. Montagnier, *Omni* interview.

34. Alvin Friedman-Kien *et al.*, 'Kaposi's sarcoma in HIV-negative homosexual men', *The Lancet*, 335 (8682), 20 January 1990, p. 168.

35. Robert S. Root-Bernstein, 'Do we know the cause(s) of AIDS?' *Perspectives in Biology and Medicine*, Summer 1990. See also Robert S. Root-Bernstein, *Rethinking AIDS: The Tragic Cost of Premature Consensus* (New York: The Free Press, 1993). The incidence of KS prior to 1981 was probably the tip of the iceberg. Robert Crimp wrote, 'What is now called AIDS was first *seen* in middle-class gay men in America, in part because of our access to medical care. Retrospectively, however, it appears that IV drug users – whether gay or straight – were dying of AIDS in New York City throughout the 1970s and early 1980s, but a class-based and racist health care system failed to notice': Robert Crimp, ed., *AIDS: Cultural Analysis, Cultural Activism* (Cambridge, MA: MIT Press, 1987), p. 249.

36. *Backgrounder for Editors and Writers of the Globe and Mail*, (Toronto, n.d.).

37. *The AIDS Catch*, Meditel Productions video, UK, 1990.

38. *Ibid.*

39. 'AIDS virus causes cancer, research shows', *Globe and Mail*, 8 April 1994.

40. Theodore Sturgeon, 'Affair with a green monkey', *A Touch of Strange* (New York: Berkeley-Medallion, 1965), pp. 71–2.

41. Richard and Rosalind Chirimuuta, *AIDS, Africa and Racism* (London: Free Association Books, 1989), p. 1.

42. Robert Gallo, 'The first human retrovirus', *Scientific American*, December 1986; Drew Hopkins, 'AIDS in Africa: is it a myth?' *Cityweek*, 10 October 1988, p. 16.

43. S. J. Green and D. Miller, quoted in John Lauritsen, 'The racism connection', *New York Native*, 2 May 1988, p. 29.

44. Chirimuuta, *AIDS, Africa*, pp. 134–5.

45. Pearce Wright, 'Smallpox vaccine "triggered AIDS virus" ', *The Times*, 11 May 1987, p. 1.

46. See Joan Shenton, 'AIDS and Africa', *Rethinking AIDS*, May 1993; and Anver Versi, 'AIDS: the epidemic that never was', *New Africa*, December 1993, p. 8.

47. Philip Elmer-De Witt, 'Invasion of the data snatchers', *Time*, 26 September 1988, p. 50.

48. Nigel Pennick, *Hitler's Secret Sciences* (Sudbury, Suffolk: Neville Spearman, 1981), p. 69.

49. Ulick Varange (Frances Parker Yockey), *Imperium: The Philosophy of History and Politics* (Sausalito, CA: Noontide Press, 1962), p. 27.

50. William S. Burroughs, *Naked Lunch* (New York: Grove Press, 1959), pp. 41–3.

51. *Ibid.*, pp. 132–3.

52. William S. Burroughs, *Blade Runner: A Movie* (Berkeley, CA: Blue Wind, 1979). This scenario, based on a novel by Alan E. Nourse, has no relation to the Ridley Scott movie with the same title.

53. David Wojnarowicz, *Close to the Knives: A Memoir of Disintegration* (New York: Vintage, 1991), p. 107.

54. Burroughs, *Blade Runner*, no pagination.

55. Rachel Lurie, 'PWA charged with murder attempt for bleeding', *Advocate*, 19 November 1991, p. 53.

Chapter seven

The AIDS Concentration Camp

The ghetto has become . . . a sort of Nietszchean experimental
laboratory which only supermen can survive.
— A resident of the Lodz Ghetto, *c.* 1943

SOME time during the 1970s, the Pink Triangle replaced the
Lambda as the most recognizable gay sign. The original pink
triangles had been sewn onto the uniforms of homosexual men in
Nazi concentration camps. They reappeared as powerful, ambiguous signs pinned, like arrow wounds, to the breasts of clones.

A black-and-white postcard from the late 1980s shows a
pink triangle and a photo of traumatized, uniformed inmates behind
barbed wire. The caption reads: 'QUARANTINE is a nice way to say
. . . CONCENTRATION CAMP.' In 1986, gays in California had fought
hard to defeat a ballot proposition to quarantine all PWAs. This was
the brainchild of Lyndon LaRouche, a well-funded crypto-Nazi, and
William Dannemeyer, a Republican congressman representing Dis-
neyland. Veteran LaRouche watcher Dennis King wrote of the
campaign: 'LaRouche scored a major ideological breakthrough for
neo-Nazism in America. He took a previously taboo idea – enforced
isolation for the Scapegoat – and elevated it into a topic of legitimate
discourse. He did this by reframing the discourse in pseudo-medical
terms and targeting a minority less well organized than the Jews.'[1]

The California quarantine proposal was not unique: rum-
blings from the Right included William F. Buckley's call for all HIV
positives to be tattooed – intravenous drug users on the forearm,
homosexuals on the buttocks. In Toronto a city councillor

advocated mandatory uniforms for all PWAs. Already, reports from abroad were ominous. Sweden was preparing to ship certain of its HIV positives to off-shore islands; Bavaria threatened detention in 'special houses'; Cuba was using incarcerated PWAs for medical experiments, and in Christian missions in India, HIV-positive residents were chained to their Bibles. Only the vigilance and educational work of a network of gay and lesbian organizations made similar moves in North America seem more trouble than they were worth.

Yet it was significant that fear of possible political quarantine affected primarily those who did not (yet) have AIDS. The saying that the generals are always ready to fight the previous war was true of our own leadership. While they scanned a political Maginot Line for indications of incipient barbed wire and guard dogs, such crude arrangements had already been replaced by high-tech weapons designed for the new, psychobiological battlefields. Once more, those fortunate enough to remain outside could fairly easily ignore the smoke, the chimneys and the smell; they only had to hold their noses and look the other way. But those with AIDS did not waste their time fearing concentration camps. For them, AIDS *was* the concentration camp.

It began with the disappearances. One black minister wrote: 'Walking through the African American and Caribbean communities of New York, I didn't see people I used to see, and nobody seems to want to discuss where they have gone.'[2] Cultural historian Michael Bronski observed that the same was true of the gay ghetto: 'Because the gay male community is large and loosely knit – made up of groups of friends as well as large socializing networks or bars and baths – a great many people know one another casually or just by sight. It has become commonplace . . . to presume that a bar regular may be dying or dead if he is absent for a while . . . . Sometimes life feels like living under a fascist regime: People just disappear without a word.'[3] The novelist Andrew Holleran summed it up in two words: 'The Fear'. Urban America was not El Salvador or rural Guatemala, but an advanced, scientific nation. The death squads were not on the street but in the blood.

A gay artist's memoir provides a strikingly vivid sketch of the psychic conditions of the period: 'I felt I was in the midst of wartime and the fucking explosions and heat were getting closer and closer; in fact I could see the bodies flying through the air just mere inches away and every fucking minute of every fucking day I felt like I could do nothing more than wait for that moment where I'd hear the whistling sound and feel the presence of the bomb tracking me. I was diagnosed not long after that.'[4]

The crisis seemed to permeate all of life. One gay man living in Los Angeles, considering how supplements and T-counts tended to take over every conversation, felt that 'AIDS seems to be the only topic there is. I have the feeling now, that we're like in the Warsaw ghetto, in a kitchen where we're all sharing as much information as quickly as we can. We want to know how far away are the Nazis, how many blocks are still standing, and if anybody has weapons to fight back with. Like I imagine those kitchens were at the time; there's a great deal of gallows humor going on.'[5]

Comparisons of the AIDS crisis to war and the Nazi holocaust arose spontaneously – and were just as often dismissed with the nervous embarrassment that can arise when something one would rather not think about suddenly impinges on the consciousness. But the parallels were too acute to be ignored: the fear; the deaths, both sudden and lingering; the occasions of grief so repeated and relentless that we all became numbed out of simple self-protection; the alternations of intense comradeship and equally intense isolation; the illness and exhaustion; the sense of futility and injustice; and, tantalizingly, the categories of victim, collaborator, survivor – at times discrete, at other times blurred and obscure.

So intense was the psychological pressure that some men expressed relief when their 'diagnosis' ended the protracted agony of expectation. And it was usually referred to as simply 'diagnosis', as in 'Is there life after diagnosis?' The psychology is startlingly similar to that recounted by survivors of the Stalin purges when millions of Soviet citizens kept a suitcase permanently packed, and held their breath every time a car drew up. When arrest finally came, terrible as it was, it felt as though a weight had been lifted from their shoulders. Shostakovich's remark about that period could be echoed by many in the AIDS era: 'I was remembering my friends and all I saw was corpses, mountains of corpses.'

The most apparent point of similarity was between the physical appearance of concentration camp inmates and of many

AIDS patients. Nicholas Nixon's black-and-white photographs of AIDS patients were among the most widely displayed images of the epidemic. They show emaciated and exhausted men (and a few women), their skin marked by lesions, their hair dry and sparse, some isolated, some accompanied by supportive friends, lovers or family; dressed in pyjamas, barely able to stand, gaunt, fearful, and brave – or apathetic.

Nixon's images elicited angry criticism from many of the new crop of AIDS activists, who viewed his work as politically suspicious. PWAs should be shown, they felt, only as 'empowered', angry groups of arm-linked street demonstrators suggestive of the invincible, muscled workers in 1930s socialist realist tableaux. The need to fight back against the pervasive official subtext of despair and inevitable early death became confused with simple denial: PWAs who looked like AIDS patients were a reminder of continuing defeat, an embarrassment.

Another, more polemical, work of the time, by Canadian artist Bruce Eves, suggests even more forcefully the conflation of identity between PWA and concentration camp inmate. 'Burn the Quilt' is a collage showing three emaciated men wearing striped pyjamas. It is impossible to tell which are death camp prisoners, which AIDS patients.[6]

'The Quilt' was the central artefact of the Names Project, the brainchild of former Harvey Milk aide Cleve Jones: an enormous comforter which could cover a vast ground area with panels bearing names and symbols of the AIDS dead. The first memorial created by the immediate survivors, it was publicly displayed in the nation's capital, where it was ignored by Presidents Reagan and Bush.

Psychohistorian Casper Schmidt compared the Quilt to the Aztec institution of the *tzompantli*, the pyramid of human skulls which the gods would look down on to decide when enough victims had been sacrificed.[7]

While the Quilt was impressive and moving, much of the literature of official, government-funded AIDS organizations featured smiling groups of people, often meticulously multi-racial, accompanied by injunctions to use condoms for sex, and to enter the official programs of 'early intervention' with the approved drugs. The first issue of *ACTlife*, the official publication of the AIDS

Committee of Toronto, was one example among many. The eight-page newsletter contains no less than thirty photographs of smiling people and blandly assures its readers that coping with the dying 'can help us feel good about ourselves'.[8]

The course of AIDS could be protracted or stunningly swift, but was always frightening and devastating, taking a toll on both mind and body. Mental symptoms were often bizarre: one prominent scholar lost his ability to walk forwards – but not backwards; another man wanted to eat nothing but chocolate. Some of the terms that came into popular use to describe the course of the illness are revealing. The early stages, with relatively mild effects, came to be called with a macabre irony, 'the honeymoon period'. Denied the right to a honeymoon with one another, we were readily granted one with a disease. Following this came the nauseating 'rollercoaster ride' as the interaction of symptoms and medicinal side-effects led to erratic ups and downs. A campy form of black humor was much in evidence: the outrageous young queen sunning himself in the outdoor restaurant at Fire Island Pines, ostentatiously swallowing his pills while grinning ghoulishly at gawking middle-aged straights on nearby yachts; the PWA who started a magazine called *Diseased Pariah News*. These ideas fed the resurgence of vampire fiction and vampire lore that took place in the 1980s and 1990s.

Adding to the atmosphere of fear, desperation and campy courage were the questions surrounding the medicine most frequently recommended and prescribed to PWAs, and, increasingly, to HIV positives and healthy members of 'risk groups', the Burroughs-Wellcome product known variously as Retrovir, zidovudine and AZT. It became the official AIDS drug, a desperate remedy that came to be widely regarded as either a placebo or a poison.

The golden standard

It is a characteristic feature of the history of healing that people often prefer a cure that kills to no cure at all.
— Thomas Szasz, *The Therapeutic State*

By 1987, Ralph Hall had left New York for Hollywood, Florida, where he furnished his wardrobe and apartment from 'the local KKK thrift shop' and published a characteristically irreverent newsletter for PWAs called *Tacky Times*. He had moved to the sunny South after his own AIDS diagnosis in the early 1980s. His doctors had, in his words, 'set the death clock' by giving him eighteen months to live, but three years later, Ralph, never a clock-watcher, was still alive, thanks, he said, to herbal medicine, a positive attitude, and the friends who had been 'coming out of the woodwork' since he got sick. He was living alone and feeling that 'for the first time in my life I control my own world'.

Early in 1988 he became very sick and began having blood transfusions. He had been persuaded to take AZT, but had stopped taking it by the time he wrote to me in February of that year. 'It was killing me. I'm now trying to save myself', he told me, 'but it may be too late, the damage has been done. I'm so anemic, and my bone marrow depleted I don't know what to do.' He was planning the new issue of *Tacky Times*, and invited me to contribute. He phoned me after he left the hospital, and told me that, though he had survived AIDS for years, he doubted he could now recover from the AZT. Soon afterwards, I learned he had died.

I remembered the talks we'd had as we sat outside Ty's, or rode the subway uptown – about the baths, or anarchism, or monogamy, or the betrayal of the movement by the 'gaycrats' (who always elicited funny remarks from Ralph, and bitter monologues from his lover Flash). I pondered his remarks on AZT, and began to read all I could about it.

As it happened, another old friend from Gay Lib's early days, movement activist and historian John Lauritsen, was already investigating the drug most physicians were prescribing to PWAs and HIV positives. Trained in statistical analysis, John was a survey research analyst by profession, and when he began to analyze the available data on AZT, he was appalled.

AZT is a DNA chain terminator. Originally designed to kill lymphocytes (which proliferate in cases of leukemia) its use in cancer treatment was rejected as ineffectual and highly toxic. In 1987, it was approved as a treatment for those testing positive for antibodies to HIV. The rationale behind AZT was rather crude: as HIV was thought to cause AIDS, AZT would (as part of its nonspecific termination of DNA synthesis) prevent HIV from replicating in the body. The thinking was similar to US Army tactics in Vietnam: as the guerillas took refuge among the civilian villagers (and were, in fact, indistinguishable from them) the indiscriminate destruction of Vietnamese and the defoliation of their habitat with poisons would, it was reasoned, necessarily, eliminate the guerillas. As it happened, this approach worked no better against AIDS than it had against the Viet Cong.

John Lauritsen's detailed reports on the campaign to have thousands of gay men, prisoners, pregnant black women and IV drug users take AZT appeared as a series of investigative articles in the *New York Native*.[9] He concluded that AZT was a toxic drug with no scientifically proven benefits. The core of his argument was formed from his analysis of the published reports of the Food and Drug Administration trials that preceded the marketing of the drug, and from 500 pages of related, censored, material obtained by the group Project Inform under the Freedom of Information Act.

Lauritsen discovered that the supposed double-blind, placebo-controlled studies had been unblinded early in the proceedings as PWAs detected differences in the taste of their pills, had them analyzed, and generously shared the AZT among themselves so that everyone would get at least some of the new 'wonder drug'. Further analysis of the tests revealed sloppy, poorly controlled and even fraudulent procedures. Some of the official accounts bordered on the farcical, with projected probabilities reported as if factual. In at least one testing center, recipients of AZT and of the placebo may even have been switched. All the official AZT studies were prematurely concluded, and what happened to the participants after the studies was never published. No valid conclusions could have been derived from such chaotic and duplicitous proceedings.

Peter Duesberg, who provided an introduction to a collection of Lauritsen's AZT pieces, *Poison By Prescription*, wrote that AZT might conceivably provide 'short-term benefits against AIDS to a person with acute microbial infections like tuberculosis, pneumonia, candidiasis or herpes, since these diseases are called AIDS if HIV antibody is present, by killing these microbes together with host cells. However, such infections could be controlled much better with confirmed, specific therapeutics than with the randomly toxic AZT.'[10]

Dr Robert Hoffman, Professor of Cancer Biology at the University of California at San Diego, noted that those cells that AZT does not kill, it may cause to become cancerous, and that, even with monitoring, the drug's toxicity can easily reach the point of no return.[11]

The editor of *BioTechnology* magazine, Harvey Bialy, noted that AZT kills T-4 cells, the white blood cells vital to the immune system which gradually diminish in those with AIDS, and that 'the most common and severe side effect of the drug is bone marrow toxicity. That is why they need blood transfusions.' He agreed with Duesberg that 'there is no good evidence that HIV activity replicates in a person with AIDS'. AZT, he said, mostly killed healthy cells. 'I can't see how this drug could be doing anything but making people very sick.'[12] Dr Charles A. Thomas, Jr, in an interview with journalist Tony Brown, made the most telling observation of all: 'AZT kills the very immune system cells that HIV is imagined to kill – but doesn't.'[13]

Another commentator who examined the data described the trials as 'perhaps the sloppiest and most poorly controlled trials ever to serve as the basis for an FDA drug licensing approval . . . . Despite this, and a frightening record of toxicity, the FDA approved AZT in record time.'[14]

Those familiar with the history of the FDA knew of its inadequacies and its long history of collusion with industry, of which the poppers affair, which had also involved Burroughs-Wellcome, was only one instance. As the FDA had no testing facilities of its own, it relied for its information on the developers of drugs and medical procedures; the result was a long series of medical disasters.

How this time-honored system worked in the case of AZT was illuminated by reporter Celia Farber in a piece in *SPIN* magazine. Farber revealed that even one of the FDA's own directors had warned that to approve AZT would represent 'a significant and potentially dangerous departure from our normal toxicology requirements'.[15] Panel chairman Dr Itzak Brook believed 'the drug could actually be detrimental'.[16] In the end, these cautious voices were overridden when Burroughs-Wellcome reassured the FDA that AZT would be released only 'as a stopgap measure for very sick patients' (in other words, to those who would soon die). Uneasily, and with Dr Brook dissenting, AZT was approved.

Burroughs-Wellcome did not keep its promise. Within a few months, the company was aggressively urging physicians to prescribe its product even to asymptomatic gay men, in spite of side-effects so toxic that many patients required blood transfusions to tolerate its effects. 'The worst-case scenario had come true.'[17] As the only Federally approved antiviral AIDS drug and at about $10,000 a year per prescription, it pushed the price of Burroughs-Wellcome shares through the roof.

In 1992, Wellcome Trust, Burroughs-Wellcome's parent company, completed the biggest private stock sale in history, despite a global recession. A Wellcome representative expressed satisfaction that the profits would reinforce the Trust's ties with universities and medical schools: 'We fund the individuals, the teams, their equipment and sometimes the buildings. We're going to do much more of that through these additional funds.'[18]

In the United States, a nation with no national health insurance, the high cost of AZT produced yet another devastating side-effect: poverty. But the insurance industry came up with an ingenious solution. Gay magazines began to run full-page advertisements from companies proposing to buy the life insurance policies of PWAs (leaving their heirs with nothing) in return for an allowance of '55% to 80%' of the stated value – a tempting offer to those burdened with skyrocketing medical bills. One company offered a special free bonus for holders of the juiciest policies, $100,000 and up: a lifetime supply of AZT! In Canada, AZT was dispensed free of charge to PWAs; those who preferred holistic treatments had to pay for them out of their own pockets.

The scandals surrounding AZT did not prevent its being promiscuously prescribed as an 'antiviral' to thousands of gay men in the 1980s and 1990s. The experiences of my own gay friends are typical. Danny, who had never been tested for HIV antibodies, went to his doctor for a bruise on his leg. It was suggested he take AZT. Robert (also untested) developed a rash which later turned out to be eczema. AZT was also recommended to him. Aaron (HIV antibody positive) was hospitalized with an enlarged heart, swollen limbs and an array of other problems, many of which were probably drug-related and which did not include any of the major AIDS symptoms. His doctor could not understand why he refused to take AZT which was, the doctor kept repeating, 'the golden standard' of health care for HIV positive men.

Another gay man wrote: 'When a doctor suggested that I use AZT, I asked him, "Do you feel it is good?" Answer: "I have nothing else to give you." '[19] This prescriptive pattern led Peter Duesberg to speculate that as AZT could cause the symptoms it was supposed to alleviate, a new wave of iatrogenic AIDS cases might well break out among its users. AZT was mimicking AIDS as mercury and arsenic treatments had mimicked syphilis, and as radiation cured, and then caused, cancer.

AZT's persistence as the golden standard of AIDS drugs derived not from its efficacy (which seemed to show up only on tests conducted by its manufacturers) but from a massive and sophisticated advertising campaign.[20] Every issue of the *Advocate* contained full-page ads paid for jointly by Burroughs-Wellcome and an array of medical and AIDS organizations. Headed 'Living With HIV', the ads appropriated the language of PWA support groups ('I found hope'; 'I'm back in control') to promote 'early medical intervention'. AZT was the invisible product in these vague notices, which played on gay men's deep feelings of anger and victimization.

Mainstream journalists rarely questioned the AIDS establishment's claims for AZT. One of the few who did, Elinor Burkett of the *Miami Herald*, saw her work greeted with 'almost hysterical' reactions from physicians and patients alike. 'The . . . scientific community feels that it shouldn't have to answer to the rest of us', she wrote. 'So the notion that a non-scientist would go in and question the research that they used, the accuracy of their data and the truth of their interpretation provoked a tremendous controversy throughout the research establishment.'[21] Such behavior is typical of a religious hierarchy that has become entrenched and defensive.

While the mainstream, government-funded AIDS organizations went along with the Burroughs-Wellcome line, activist groups like ACT UP were thrown into confusion. At first, they focused their anger on the high price of AZT, reacting with hostility when critics drew attention to its high toxicity and possible carcinogenic qualities. Then, as members of the group began to experience AZT-related health problems and stopped taking their prescriptions, group attitudes became more ambivalent. As Gene Fedorko of the alternative AIDS group HEAL put it, 'there was a panic, and then there was this realization that the drugs that they were begging the government to get into their bodies were very ineffective, if not toxic'.[22] Demonstrators began carrying placards denouncing AZT as 'the great pacifier'.

This was the point at which AIDS activists began to paste colorful posters all over New York, containing the following text in small print: 'The US government has spent 1 billion dollars over the past 10 years to research new AIDS drugs. The result: 1 drug – AZT. It makes half the people who try it sick and for the other half it stops working after a year. Is AZT the last, best hope for people with AIDS, or is it a short-cut to the killing Burroughs Wellcome is making in the AIDS marketplace? Scores of AIDS drugs languish in government pipelines, while fortunes are made on this monopoly' *(see plate 8)*.

Attitudes were clearly beginning to change, but the poster's principal message confirmed a lingering unconscious resistance to the disheartening new information on AZT. The slogan 'Enjoy AZT' leapt out at the viewer in large, white letters on a red background, drawn to resemble the Coca-Cola logo. This command, rendered in the familiar script of the product most identified with the saccharine satisfactions of American consumerism, drew attention to itself in bold red and white from every lampost. As in the old days of heavy fisting, Coke was once more 'giving the drug combination the right hit'. Passing viewers could not help absorbing the blatant commercial; most did not bother to stop and scrutinize the fine print.

The Coke-script image came to be more associated with AZT than its makers' official logo, stamped on each blue and white capsule, so tiny only the keenest eyesight could readily discern what it was: the silhouette of a unicorn. Traditional Christian mythology associates the unicorn with virginity and chastity; its horn was considered a purifier and an antidote against poison. The unicorn imprinted on the capsules had no depth or life, but was curiously flat, like a cardboard cutout.

The array of chemicals gay men were pumping into their bodies in the AIDS era perpetuated the wholesale drugging that occurred in the preceding post-Stonewall years. The drugs were different, but the mentality remained much the same. Sal Licata observed that 'in the old days people would talk about quaaludes, cocaine and Ecstasy. Today, they talk about AZT, AL-721, and doctor's appointments.'[23] The blunt demand 'Drugs Into Bodies!' became a familiar AIDS activist slogan, and if the available drugs were too expensive, or too deadly, then it was assumed other drugs from the same system would surely provide the elusive cure.

Side-effects from the array of medications, anti-depressants and sleeping pills frequently prescribed for AIDS-related conditions included: peripheral neuropathy, psychosis, Alzheimer's-type dementia, memory loss, low white blood cell count, myopathy, pancreatitis, convulsions, myalgia, fatigue, weight loss, hepatoxicity and liver failure, acute meningo-encephalitis, anorexia, pneumonitis, thrombocytopenia and leukopenia (due to cytotoxic effects on the bone-marrow reserve), red or purple skin rashes, phlebitis, retinitis, anemia, myelosuppression, paralytic ileus, bronchospasms, diarrhea – and Kaposi's sarcoma (from steroid therapies). Most of these symptoms, listed in the standard reference books, were also counted as symptoms of AIDS.[24]

One counsellor wrote that 'the medicine cabinets of many people with AIDS are filled with assortments of mood-altering, psychoactive drugs. "Scripts" are written by doctors willy-nilly, without considering the results, without a plan for detoxification, without offering alternative, non-pharmaceutical methods for relieving pain and anxiety.'[25]

An addictive behavior specialist complained, 'Some physicians don't give a damn, and they'll let their AIDS clients have anything they want. They'll give them all the psychoactive medication that they possibly can handle. First, they're so busy that they don't know what the hell's happening. County [Hospital], I think, has seven hundred cases; you don't see the same doctor twice; the guy doesn't have time to read your whole chart. If you come to the clinic, he is just trying to keep you alive, so you end up with four or five medications and a drug problem. Nobody's monitoring what you're getting. Or . . . you get the physician who figures, Well, they're dying, what the hell, we'll give them whatever they want.'[26]

Routine prescription of strong drugs was especially dangerous for the addicts and former addicts who made up a disproportionately high percentage of gay PWAs. Ron Vachon, Director of New York City's Office of Gay and Lesbian Health Concerns remarked, 'This is just anecdotal evidence, but because of my job and because I'm gay, I've been in touch with a lot of people with AIDS, and I have this guesstimate in my head that at least 90 to 95% of these people have abused drugs and have abused alcohol.'[27] A community worker at Project Connect at the Gay and Lesbian Community Services Center in the same city said she was beginning to see addiction and AIDS as the same epidemic.[28]

Yet some physicians actually discouraged their HIV positive patients from trying to overcome alcoholism or drug dependency, regarding addiction as a useful 'coping mechanism' and maintaining that stopping would be too stressful. Others saw substance abuse programs as threatening the doctor-patient relationship.[29]

The judicious use of certain drugs – like Bactrim (Septra) to prevent pneumocystis carinii pneumonia – proved of great help. But the heavy reliance on drug-based solutions, to the exclusion of other approaches, continued the wholesale drugging pattern common to many gays in the past. 'I think', said one gay man, 'that my alcoholism, and whatever drugs I did, were about self-loathing; it was a slow form of suicide. And I think that there's a direct correlation with AIDS.'[30]

The case of David Parkin provides a cameo portrait of one gay man caught up in the AIDS system. Parkin was a robust, ostensibly healthy man living with his male lover in the middle-sized city of Windsor, across the border from Detroit. Having lost a number of friends to AIDS, when he came down with a cough and a bit of nausea, he confided his concerns to his physician, and told him he was gay. The doctor arranged for Parkin to take the 'AIDS test'.

When Parkin's test results were interpreted as positive, he began a nightmarish journey. He was given a prescription for AZT and a bewildering array of other drugs so extensive he had to carry them around with him in a shoulder-bag. One of the city's large hospitals diagnosed him as having Kaposi's sarcoma for which he was subjected to radiation sessions. In a few months, Parkin had lost sixty pounds. His joints ached and his muscles were wasting away.

His cough was worse and he had constant nausea and frequent vomiting. He realized he was a very sick man, and he prepared to die.

He ended up at Sunnybrook Hospital in Toronto. There, someone gave him another HIV antibody test. When it came up negative, Parkin decided to discontinue the AZT, the radiation and the pills. And he got better. He regained his lost weight and returned to his home and job in restored health. The KS was rediagnosed as psoriasis; the cough and nausea were assumed to have been the flu.

Parkin stayed healthy and HIV negative. But he remained worried about his health because, as he put it in an interview on Canadian television, 'no one knows the long-term effects of these drugs on a healthy person'. Or, it might be said, on a sick one. Parkin's case was unusual only because of the reversal (or misinterpretation) of his HIV status. But medical blunders involving PWAs were anything but rare.

Once David Parkin entered the AIDS system, his health went into a precipitous decline. He was lucky: his diagnosis was reversed and his medication discontinued. For many thousands of gay men, there was no such reversal. Like Parkin, they did as they were told, attributed their failing health to AIDS, and made out their wills. Unlike Parkin, they did not survive.

Among them was George Whitmore, whose ongoing story also reveals some typical patterns of thought.

A career in suicide – part two: the spell of a machine

My life ran on four-hour shifts. I was participating in my own genocide, addicted not only to the structure and control of the drug, but to the Russian Roulette of the 'randomized dose' . . . I was under the spell of a machine.

— Steve Rose

When we left George Whitmore, he had positioned himself at the center of 'the Rebel lifestyle', which he had begun to identify as 'a new kind of vitimization', and was comparing the popular tricking trucks to the cattle cars used as transport to the concentration camps. His dual role as participant and observer reflected his continuing struggle with his own suicidal impulses.

After the complex of gay diseases had been given the designation of 'AIDS' and attributed to a fatal virus, Whitmore quickly suspected he was one of the 'carriers' and began writing about the effects of the epidemic. 'AIDS', he wrote, 'had turned me and others like me into walking time bombs.'[31]

In a quasi-autobiographical novel published in 1980, *The Confessions of Danny Slocum or Gay Life in the Big City*, Whitmore had described his leading character as clinging to old habits to protect himself from the human contact he feared 'like the plague'. He felt enormously vulnerable, he wrote, 'like the boy in the glass bubble, the one who was born without defenses against ordinary germs'.[32] A year before the onset of AIDS, this was an extraordinary metaphor: human intimacy as a plague, which only the numb armour of repetitive experience could ward off. A year later, the imagined plague had mutated, and become real, with the apparent protector revealed as the chief accomplice.

Early in 1986, George discovered a small, strawberry-colored spot on his calf. It was diagnosed as Kaposi's sarcoma, a prime indicator of AIDS, and George, at the urging of his doctors, began taking AZT.

If the physical action of AZT were not terrifying enough, the method of administration was downright hair-raising – particularly in the light of the self-destructive tendencies George had cannily pinpointed in himself and many other gay men. People, both sick and healthy, who had been persuaded by their doctors to take AZT, were told to carry with them twenty-four hours a day a smooth, slick, plastic box in a tasteful shade of off-white. On the box were two small square black buttons marked STOP and START, and two small triangles, one pointing up, the other pointing down. This contraption, known as a Micronta Drug Timer, was equipped with a beeper that sounded every four hours, night and day, ensuring that the carrier never enjoyed a good night's sleep.

George's description of the beeper box's effect ran as follows: 'The beeper has a loud and insistent tone, like the shrill pips you hear when a truck is backing up on the street. Ask anyone who carries one – these devices insidiously change your life. You're always on the alert, anticipating that chirp, scheming to turn off in time before it can detonate [*sic*]. It's relentless.' George now carried a Micronta

Timer with him at all times.[33] It had become his most constant companion.

Systematically interrupted sleep is one of the most effective devices of mind control. In the words of one student of these matters, it 'induces in the captive a curious state of unreality in which he is easily influenced and directed by any stable, consistent rules . . . . Sexual asceticism is almost invariably imposed and as the captive progresses, actual forms of physical punishment, sometimes, self-inflicted, may be added.'[34]

The beeper box interrupted not only essential sleep but also the all-important dream cycle, as essential to the health of the unconscious mind as the bone marrow is to the health of the body. By following the instructions of the medical establishment, gay men were literally destroying their ability to dream.

'Having written about the devastating effects of AIDS on others, the author now describes the impact of the disease upon himself', was how the cut-line read on George's cover story in the *New York Times Magazine*. Readers were allowed a peek through an open, fire-engine red metal door, into a laboratory where George sat with a white-coated research assistant, dourly watching a large machine that monitored the level of AZT in the bloodstream.

'I have no doubt', George wrote, with bleak optimism, 'that, administered in combination with drugs that boosts the immune system, antiviral drugs like AZT will eventually prolong the lives of countless people like me.' And there the story was left, even when the AZT soon made George so sick he decided to abandon it. Neither he nor the *Times* ever wrote about these debilitating effects. George died shortly afterwards, his endorsement of AZT never rescinded, and the last chapter of his struggle untold. Even to the last, the two aspects of George's being – clear-seeing survivor and driven suicide – remained locked in polarized antagonism, conflicting archetypes of gay consciousness as seemingly inseparable as Holmes and Moriarty, hurtling together over the Reichenbach Falls.

After I wrote about George in the pages of the *New York Native*,[35] the paper printed a response from Steve Rose of the AIDS Watchdog Group in Boston. Rose spoke eloquently for those who had once been 'AZT Zombies . . . under the spell of a machine so omnipotent – and so insidious – that I even welcomed its presence

. . . . Nobody volunteers for an unsure, unsafe existence at the hands of the research establishment during an epidemic; the predicament is forced upon us by our fear, and by a system that preys upon it brilliantly.'[36]

'Gay men in growing numbers', Rose wrote, 'are being reduced – through subtle and not-so-subtle forms of infantilizing dehumanizing mind games – to a pool of useful laboratory animals, and many are amazingly docile . . . . Gay men are being told not to bite the hand that feeds them – even though many suspect that they are being fed poison . . . . Like the drugged wenches in *The Stepford Wives*, we have slaves among us, deprived of sleep, existing for some distant bureaucracy, many not aware that they have, in the eyes of the researchers and doctors, waived their human and civil rights.'

Referring to the highly addictive sedatives and 'Star Trek antidepressants' he was routinely prescribed, Rose described an inhumane research structure that was 'a labyrinth of bad ethics and bad science'. Rose felt that one reason the self-destructive tendencies programmed into gay men could be so keenly identified and played upon by 'our many oppressors' was because 'many of them are closeted homosexual and bisexual men who are "working within the system," posing as the doctors who are "helping us".'

'Marcus Welby *is* a Nazi', Rose warned. 'I firmly believe that I am alive today because I had the presence of mind to get out of the AZT nightmare before it killed not only my body, but my spirit . . . . The guerilla warfare taking place in the trenches of the AIDS crisis includes a frightening component of psychiatric terrorism.' He ended with a note of hope, but warned against the 'familiar signposts' that led to dead ends.

Cliff Goodman, a member of a group helping people get off AZT by going cold turkey like recovering heroin addicts, told an interviewer, 'I've seen them waste and their hair fall out, and their muscles shrivel . . . and I've seen many males become impotent, so there's no way I'm going to take something like that. I think it's almost like a punishment.'

Another young black man in the same group who had taken AZT and then stopped, recalled that, as well as dizziness and nausea, 'I had fingernails that were so black it looked like I had nail polish on . . . . Nothing tasted right. And the main thing: it affected you so you couldn't listen to people because you don't want to hear them because you're hurting so bad. And it left me impotent. It destroyed my hopes for living, you know.'[37]

A decade earlier, young, idealistic gay liberationists, having thrown all the tales of injustice collecting into the trash, would never have believed that in just a few years, they would be waiting, even as they slept, for a shrill sound from a little plastic box to signal the swallowing of a few capsules of slow-acting poison – voluntarily, 'without flinching'.

In 1988, at an International Gay Health Conference and AIDS Forum, a small group of anti-AZT activists set up a stand serving purple Kool-Aid to delegates. As one activist wrote, 'The Jonestown metaphor was clear to a few, but infuriated many . . . . But what amazed us was the number of people who drank the sickish purple liquid without even seeing the protest placards or asking what it was.'[38]

Nevertheless, AZT's manufacturers went a little too far. Even those well enough to continue taking the drug balked at the Every Four Hours rule, turned their screeching timers off at night, and even began to scale down the dose – and then scale it down again. 'I cheat', one friend confessed to me. 'I'm not actually taking as much as they think I am.' Perhaps for some, the very act of taking medicine was the most necessary factor. Burroughs-Wellcome hurried to announce its discovery that half doses were 'just as effective' – and promptly recommended them to twice as many people, stabilizing the value of their shares. The unpopular Every Four Hours rule was also jettisoned. And when AZT and a rival company's similar drug, ddI, began to vie with each other for profits, it was announced that the two drugs taken together were especially effective.

While some gay men took these proclamations as gospel, scanning newspapers and company press releases for the latest official information, others were skeptical. And some began to see them as part of a psychodrama, a hi-tech psychobiological war-game of mind-control and mass delusion, with ostracized 'risk groups' as the battlefield. A few, like Steve Rose and John Lauritsen, began to regard what was happening as a form of genocide.

Pointing the bone

There is nothing like the threat of death to get the glands under control.
— Gary Bauer, White House Advisor

A gay man writing in 1986 described his visit to a clinic for HIV antibody testing:

> I went to San Francisco to take the AIDS [*sic*] antibody test. The hospital setting was almost guaranteed to produce negative energies. I did my best to bathe the waiting room in healing golden light, but I found my efforts constantly thwarted. I became exhausted just waiting.
>
> The group taking the test was ushered into a room where we watched a video which is used by an AIDS organization. In the video they show a cartoon of someone being invaded by the unconquerable AIDS virus (depicted as nasty triangles). I was horrified! They didn't seem to understand that they were projecting the same fatalistic image the world presents about AIDS, and that, since the imagistic level of the brain lies deeper than the discursive, they were affecting people at a subconscious level.[39]

Time magazine's graphics went further, showing the 'invading AIDS virus' as an army of *pink* triangles.[40] A Toronto radio station even broadcast what it described as a 'transcription into music' of the structure of HIV. Apparently, the virus, when rendered by a sepulchral organ, sounds remarkably like the creepy parts of a horror-movie soundtrack!

Psychiatric nurses, composers, graphic artists and disc jockeys were not trying to undermine gay men's will to live. The one who points the bone to issue the death sentence does not see himself as a murderer, but as a messenger, a professional, a teller of truth. This is a subtlety of little relevance to the one hexed. If he believes the prophecy, the 'death clock' within him begins to tick.

After Dr Luc Montagnier broke with HIV fundamentalism, he began addressing conferences of AIDS dissidents with an important message: 'AIDS', he told them, 'does not inevitably lead to death, especially if you suppress the co-factors that support the disease. It's very important to tell this to people who are infected. Psychological factors are critical in supporting immune function. If you suppress the psychological support by telling someone they are condemned to die, your words alone will have condemned them.'[41]

The procedure known as 'pointing the bone' derives its name from studies of aboriginal shamans who are said to issue death hexes by means of a pointed bone. But it is by no means exclusive to them; any powerful priesthood, including the scientific, may 'point the bone' effectively at those who believe in its powers.

The sequence of events surrounding this pointing of bones was elucidated by Sanford I. Cohen, in an article titled 'Voodoo death, the stress response, and AIDS'. 'So-called voodoo or hex death', he wrote, 'is a classic example of a biophysical interaction. It is a dramatic demise that occurs when a person feels cursed by another believed powerful enough to kill or . . . to create a feeling of hopelessness. The victim has to feel that the hex works and that he cannot control it. The role of the community and family is crucial. If a hexed person resists his fate, the community, including the family, withdraws support. The hexed feels cast out, isolated, alone. He sees death as the only escape from an intolerable loneliness. Only when he accepts the inevitability of death does the community return and act in various ritual ways suggesting death positively.'[42]

It was a frequently repeated remark of PWAs that their new-found 'status' (the term is significant) 'showed them how much they were loved'. Some observed that dying gays received far more support and acceptance than living ones ever had. The isolation, loneliness and fear caused by the ironically named 'positive diagnosis' contrasted with the institutionalized comforts offered by hospices for those who were actually dying. Even Princess Diana visited AIDS hospices – an honour no organization for healthy gays ever received!

Long-term AIDS sufferers such as Michael Callen met with a different reaction when they offered their own continuing survival as an encouragement to others. They were sometimes spat upon and denounced. One resident of Casey House, Toronto's best-known AIDS hospice, imprudently uttered the taboo phrase 'when I get out of here' to one of his nurses. She was shocked, and quickly reminded him, 'You're never going to get out of here.' He promptly left Casey House, and resumed his studies at the university.

Bone-pointing is by no means a crude skill: it is almost infinitely adaptable. And the late 1980s and early 1990s began to see the promotion of changes in attitude to AIDS among women, and particularly among lesbians – changes resulting in part from a type of bone-pointing carried out with the special psychic needs of women in mind. A typical 1991 magazine headline announced, 'AIDS does not discriminate against women' – a slogan taken up with gusto by some political lesbians. With the exception of the heavy drug users among them, lesbians were the group least subject to AIDS. Against this background of relative health, a campaign was developed promoting the idea that as 'the virus does not discriminate', therefore lesbians must necessarily, *logically*, have as much AIDS as anybody else! If statistics suggested otherwise, then 'lesbian AIDS', presumed to be spread through cunnilingus without benefit of plastic dental dams, had to be both endemic and under-reported. It was the kind of abstract logic beloved of ideologues.

Women were told that AIDS (whose list of symptoms had always been rather elastic) displayed in women a range of symptoms entirely different from those of either Africans or gay men. Such increasingly common female complaints as pelvic inflammatory disorder were – whenever the talismanic HIV antibodies could be detected or assumed – to be reclassified as AIDS, with their sufferers eligible to enter the ever-expanding AIDS system.

Just as PWAs had rejected the full-dose AZT sleep-buster program, so they also felt it important to stress that they were 'living with AIDS' rather than necessarily dying from it. But now, ACT UP San Francisco turned the tables by distributing a poster with the slogan 'Women are not living with AIDS, they are dying from AIDS'. With the development of the 'AIDS does not discriminate' campaign, the spectacle arose of lesbians virtually *demanding* to be AIDS patients, almost as though it were a civil right accruing to them as one of the perquisites of full sexual equality.

Already, AZT was being given to pregnant black women –
free to those in prison or on welfare – supposedly to prevent their
giving birth to HIV-infected babies, a procedure that drew criticism
even from within the establishment. Dr Carol Levine, executive
director of the New York City Commission on AIDS, warned that
'people ought to be very clear about what they are doing here',
remarking that the experimental administration of a toxic drug to
fetuses and newborns 'who may be healthy' was 'unprecedented'.[43]

When a lifestyle was sold to gay men, the advertising and
packaging offered what gay men felt they had been most denied and
were desperate to experience: sexual interaction and pleasure. That
approach would not work with lesbians, whose psychology was
quite different. Lesbian sex had never been outlawed. What lesbians
perceived themselves as lacking was *equality* with men, because of
systematic discrimination. 'AIDS does not discriminate' was a
powerful slogan, employing the spectre of discrimination to induce
women – especially 'women-identified women' – to enter the AIDS
system.

These approaches did not arise from the plots of machiavel-
lian conspirators hunched grimly around a table. They grew from
the organic logic of HIV fundamentalism, and from the group
mind's idea of lesbians and gay men as sick and morally stigmatized.
The lesbian tennis champion Martina Navratilova made the perceptive remark that had it been she, rather than the supposedly
heterosexual Magic Johnson, who had picked up the HIV virus from
several hundred sex contacts, the public reaction would have been
considerably less positive. Everyone knew she was right.

Lesbians, it was widely felt, *should* be getting AIDS. And so,
to them, a different bone was thrown, with a different set of death
runes scratched on it. As the definition of 'AIDS' was periodically
expanded, minimizing the statistical gap between official projections
and actual cases, the bone was pointed at more and more people. By
the 1990s, increasing numbers of both gay men *and* lesbians were
being given death sentences by their doctors. AZT was discredited –
even *Time* magazine ran an exposé – but still being prescribed.
Therapies that cleansed the body, stimulated the immune system,
and strengthened natural energies remained underfunded and
politically marginalized.

A *maze of questions*

It's a rat-race out there – and the rats are winning!
— Paul Lynde

As long as the HIV doctrine retained its political clout, few were willing to risk challenging it. But some scientists – those who harbored doubts but did not want to see their funding cut as Peter Duesberg's had been – after bowing respectfully in the direction of HIV fundamentalism, went on to suggest possible 'co-factors'.

Then in 1991, two separate sets of experiments with laboratory animals brought many of the orthodox assumptions about viruses and antibodies into serious question. A pair of researchers, writing in the journal *Science*, suggested that when their captive white mice produced two immune responses at the same time – to HIV and to foreign lymphocytes in blood or sperm – the responses tended to become directed against one another, leading to a collapse of the immune system. From this basis, they went on to discuss 'a possible role for allogenic stimuli in the pathogenesis of AIDS'.[44]

Perhaps the most intriguing part of their experiments was the discovery that mice exposed to lymphocytes from another mouse strain began to make antibodies to parts of HIV *without ever having been exposed to it*. At about the same time, a second research team's separate experiment with monkeys also prompted the conclusion that the presence of virus might not be the sole determinant of the production of antibodies.[45]

These experimental results were reminiscent of Bechamp's contention, over a hundred years earlier, that pathogens might be generated from within the body, as stages in the natural metamorphosis of living and semi-living entities as they respond to changing conditions in the bodies of their hosts. A more specific version of this theory had been put forward by the Canadian microscope pioneer and cancer researcher Gaston Naessens in the 1970s. The old contagionism/environmentalism argument had returned in new form.

Was it possible for HIV antibodies to appear in response to environmental stresses *other than HIV itself*? If mice could produce antibodies to bits of a human retrovirus that they had never encountered, was it possible that *humans* could produce antibodies to the complete retrovirus that *they* had never encountered? The possibility posed a dramatic challenge to orthodoxy. If antibodies could be generated *without* virus, clearly everything would have to be rethought.

None of the commentators on the monkey and mice experiments made a connection with a set of equally intriguing findings publicized some years before by the Cambridge biologist Dr Rupert Sheldrake. Dr Sheldrake's main area of study was the science of morphogenesis, i.e. how living things come to assume their particular forms. This line of enquiry tied in with Bechamps' and Naessens' speculations on the life-cycles of microscopic entities. During his investigations into the synchronous changes occurring in crystalline forms around the world, Sheldrake became interested in the surprising results of a series of experiments conducted with rats and mazes: the so-called Labyrinth Experiments.[46]

These experiments were carried out from 1920 through the 1960s, by William McDougal of Harvard, F. A. R. Crew of Edinburgh University and W. E. Agar in Melbourne. The experiments began in an attempt to resolve the old Lamarckian chestnut: can acquired characteristics be inherited? To find out, scientists coached cohorts of thousands of rats on three continents to negotiate labyrinths faster than their untrained fellows. The offspring of these rats, and *their* offspring, for many generations, were then sent through identical labyrinths. All the scientific teams found that, indeed, new, untrained, generations of rats *did* make it through the maze more quickly, and after twenty generations, were learning as much as ten times more quickly!

But any conclusion that this undoubtedly acquired characteristic (maze negotiation ability) might have been genetically inherited was exploded when Crew decided to use rats that were the same breed as McDonald's, but completely unrelated. The unrelated rats' rate of learning began where McDonald's had left off! A whole subsequent generation of rats, *even those unrelated to the maze students*, knew – somehow – how to find their way out! They had picked up a characteristic acquired by a previous generation – but not, apparently, by genetic inheritance or physical contact.

Sheldrake posited an inspired theory of 'morphogenic fields' to explain an array of occurrences, from synchronous precipitation of crystals to apparently spontaneous learning by rats: a theory that proved so unsettling that the editors of the prestigious journal *Nature* wanted to throw his book on the bonfire!

Whatever the validity of the morphogenic theory, it could at least provide an explanation for synchronous crystal changes, maze-hopping rats, and the development of virus-free antibodies in lab animals. Were the animals beginning to develop antibodies in synchronicity with their generational fellows in other labs who *had* contacted the virus? This suggested the possibility that a similar phenomenon might be arising in humans.

Mice in laboratories live under conditions of considerable stress. They would much rather be frolicking in fields or under floorboards. It was a frequent observation among AIDS workers that very often their clients had lived highly stressed lives, and had seroconverted to HIV positive status in the wake of some traumatic event or series of events. Was the continuing high rate of seroconversion among gay men a kind of sympathetic phenomenon, a group response to the traumas of the health crisis? Could it be that gay men, like lab mice, were experiencing *en masse* a psychically generated development of protective antibodies to what a growing minority of scientists felt was a relatively harmless retrovirus, similar to thousands of others that had lived in harmony with mankind for millennia? The labyrinth experiments suggested that prevailing views of human/viral interaction might be woefully simplistic – a view that was shared by a slowly increasing number of AIDS dissidents.

One of the earliest dissidents was physician and psychohistorian Casper Schmidt, who had long believed that factors other than HIV played crucial roles in the declining health of gay men. Schmidt had studied the body chemistry of long-term stress, and concluded that many gay men tended to react to socially induced guilt, shame and anger by repressing their feelings into the body. This somatization caused profound biophysical changes, one of the most important being the continuous simulation of the 'fight or flight' syndrome.[47]

The 'fight or flight' syndrome occurs at times of increased stress on the human psyche, and is accompanied by temporary immune suppression and raised levels of adrenalin, endorphins and cortisol. Ordinarily, this syndrome occurs only occasionally, in instances of immediate danger. But gay men in the late twentieth century had to cope with intensely confusing cross-signalling: ubiquitous commercialized inducements to drug-induced promiscuity, screened against a background of moralistic guilt and shame messages. In addition, a great deal of their sexual activity took place in dangerous places – parks, piers, trucks. Biochemical changes associated with the syndrome became a condition of life.

According to Schmidt, unconscious fears and 'poisons' in the group psychology of ghetto gays created powerful psychological stressors, including repetitive negative behaviors of group members toward each other. These, in turn, affected the neuro-immuno-endocrine homeostasis of each member of the group, depressing the immune system through the mediation of cellular messengers (cytokines), peptides and protohormones.

Schmidt suggested that the attenuated 'fight or flight' syndrome that resulted would trigger a sequence of chemical changes in the body, including the overproduction of cortisol and antibodies and the depletion of T-lymphocytes. Given the level of sexual activity, this reduction in cellular immunity would manifest first in an increase of STDs and amoebic parasites, and later in continuing T-cell apoptosis and eventual immune collapse.

Whether this collapse is considered to have been 'caused' by pathogens, drugs, or emotional stress depends on one's point of view. Schmidt felt that all these factors played a part, with psychological factors initiating the process.

These various researches on the fringes (or the cutting edge) of science drew little attention. But they did offer a small window or two, opening onto other views.

You and the night are gone, but the malady lingers on

The black wind sock of death undulates over the land, feeling, smelling for the crime of separate life, movers of the fear-frozen flesh shivering under a vast probability curve . . . Population blocks disappear in a checker game of genocide . . . Any number can play . . .
— William S. Burroughs, *Naked Lunch*

The protracted health crisis had a numbing, paralyzing effect on gay leadership, aspirations and institutions. For all the grieving that had occurred, a great deal was still being held back out of sheer self-protection. People assumed that if a cure was found, there would be a tremendous celebration; but it seemed more likely there would be great relief – and then a tremendous release of all that pent-up grief, and anger.

Those who were now beginning to regard themselves as survivors were affected in some odd ways, which our psychohistory must record. What happened to our leaders, and our institutions, during the plague years?

In a 1990 column, Larry Kramer drew attention to the many gay leaders and institutions who simply sold out. He singled out one California businessman named Rick Stokes. Stokes was the bathhouse owner the *Advocate* had supported in opposition to Harvey Milk back in the 1970s. In the AIDS era, he popped up as a 'health advocate', a paid consultant to a company called Lyphomed, which Kramer described as 'greedy profiteering manufacturers of aerosolized pentamidine, which is available for $30 in England but costs $200 here'.[48] Kramer attacked Stokes and the other gay 'leaders' who defended the right of pharmaceutical companies to charge whatever they want, 'in effect bleeding to death their own dying brothers and sisters'.

Whether set up to organize, lobby, help the sick or bury the dead, AIDS organizations were started and initially staffed by gay men, with some help from sympathetic women. But as fear spread that AIDS might affect 'the general population', the government got into the act and AIDS organizations quickly became bureaucratized, evolving into million-dollar agencies with staffs paid – and policies determined – by government funds. Old-line gay activists were fired and rumors of large-scale embezzlement were common.

AIDS organizations began to 'sanitize' and 'de-gay' their agenda. The rhetoric of nondiscrimination was often used to justify their distancing themselves politically from the communities who founded them. AIDS activists were less than enthusiastic about the spectacle of the 1987 National March on Washington for Lesbian and Gay Rights, worrying that it might compromise federal AIDS funding; and they tried hard to quash a public same-sex wedding being staged as part of a demand for spousal rights.

When the Boston AIDS Action Committee held a dance during Lesbian and Gay Pride Week, they called it a 'Pride Dance': not 'Gay' please, AIDS is for everyone! The New York Gay Men's Health Crisis became simply 'GMHC' – with the 'H' underlined.[49] By the 1990s, though gay and lesbian social organizations continued to proliferate, the gay political movement seemed virtually defunct, reflecting the psychological trauma of the AIDS years.

One gay psychotherapist expressed his profound unease about the mental state of those gay men who did *not* have AIDS, those commonly called 'the worried well'. 'In my opinion', wrote Walt Odets, 'there is now a psychological *epidemic* among HIV survivors, and it is one that, were it not for the stupefying impact of the [AIDS] epidemic itself, would have anyone concerned with the gay community and its future in a panic all by itself'.[50] Dr Odets identified shame and guilt – as well as 'the continuing seroconversion among gay men' – as major problems. He referred to one New York study suggesting that 'fully 39% of HIV asymptomatic, presumably healthy gay men meet the American Psychiatric Association's diagnostic criteria for clinical mood- or anxiety-related disorders'.

Odets also found traditional male sexual dysfunctions becoming widespread, though little discussed, among gay men. Sexual disinterest or aversion, impotence, inhibited orgasm, and hypochondria, were becoming common as a result of 'phobic anxiety'. And, while AIDS itself had become a respectable multi-million dollar industry, the psychological and social problems churned up in its wake were being neglected.

One gay man's personal meditation on this state of affairs caused a stir on both coasts: Darrel Yates Rist's 'AIDS as apocalypse: the deadly costs of an obsession'.[51] Rist began by contrasting San Francisco's gay Castro district, 'The Promised Land', with that city's less publicized Mission and Tenderloin areas where homeless PWAs and teenage runaways hustled for meals and drugs.

'Shouldn't we start worrying again', Rist wondered out loud to some dinner companions, 'about all those issues we've forgotten in the epidemic?' He wondered what we were giving the next generation of gays to live for. But as his friends tucked into their pork roast, they seemed hypnotized by what they presumed were their own impending deaths. Rist suggested that much of the future devastation of AIDS would be among indigent blacks and Latinos, not the white gay men who held prominent positions in the AIDS establishment. And neither gays nor blacks nor Latinos controlled the AIDS agenda. The government, the medical/industrial complex and the press controlled the agenda, and the allocation of funds.

Rist's piece was one expression of a widespread frustration at the paralyzing fear AIDS had brought to the gay community. He pointed out that 'only a minority of homosexuals' and almost no lesbians have been or will ever be stricken with AIDS, yet the shock of the epidemic itself and the apocalyptic predictions of government scientists seemed to have unsettled the gay community's reason. There have always been gay men', he wrote, 'who've wanted more than sex and obsequious privacy, whose cause has been politically radical and impolite. They've been largely shouted down by the politics of this epidemic.'

Rist's controversial article contains a paradox. 'It is the nature of the servile', he wrote, 'to deny all responsibility for their plight.' Unless we reclaim our self-worth, the genocide of silence would continue, he warned, even after AIDS had gone. Yet at the same time, he saw 'our own shame, a morbid failure of self-respect and sane, self-righteous anger' as terribly destructive to our lives. 'If we care about nothing but AIDS now, it is because identifying with sexually transmitted death plays to some dark belief that we deserve it.'

'In these last eight years', he said, he had watched 'men dearest to me sicken black-magically and die.' The AIDS war was being waged in large measure by a kind of magic: by information control and the manipulation of signals and symbols.[52]

Dr Odets noticed something else about many of his gay clients that disturbed him. 'For those gay men on the fringes of a rejecting heterosexual society', he wrote, 'the acceptance gained by having AIDS can feel irresistible. Many are finding it easier to be threatened by AIDS, to die of AIDS, or to be guilty for not dying of it, than it has ever been to *be gay*.' He identified an 'unconscious desire to *not survive*' and an 'unconscious belief that one *will not survive*' – a belief encouraged by messages from physicians, the press, and other authority figures.

The United States in the 1990s was experiencing a crisis in its health care system. The nation still had no comprehensive medical insurance plan, and many PWAs could not afford the treatments they wanted. The businesses that offered to buy PWAs' life insurance policies for a lump sum understandably found many customers. As legislature and courts debated the issue of spousal benefits for gays and lesbians, desperate PWAs were being urged to disinherit their loved ones.

Another twist was added to public perceptions of AIDS in 1990, when a Florida student named Kimberly Bergalis – white, female, heterosexual – claimed she had contracted AIDS after a routine visit to her dentist, Dr David Acer, a gay man. The accusation tapped into the powerful popular stereotype of the sadistic dentist. Fear of dangerous barbers and dentists goes back as far as Delilah, reappearing in popular entertainments like *Sweeney Todd* and *The Little Shop of Horrors*. According to Ms Bergalis, Dr Acer had carried on rather like Laurence Olivier in *Marathon Man*, who kept hissing '*Is* it safe?' as he tormented poor, immobilized Dustin Hoffman.

In order to accommodate Ms Bergalis and her conservative political sponsors, HIV fundamentalists resorted to fine points of statistical science. Yes, they conceded, AIDS *could* be acquired in the dentist's chair, and the chances were precisely one in 2,631,579 – which by coincidence was the exact number of angels able to dance on the head of a dirty needle. The announcements were music to the ears of right-wing, gay-hating Senator Jesse Helms, and when Ms Bergalis made a tearful, carefully scripted, nationally televised plea from her wheel-chair ('I didn't do anything wrong!) the US Senate passed a bill threatening HIV positive medical workers with dismissal, fines and imprisonment.

Ms Bergalis became an AIDS poster girl for the rabid Right. Her expenses were paid by the same Congressman Dannemeyer who had sponsored the LaRouche quarantine referendum. The press reported her allegations as fact; the *Advocate* even ran a diagram of a dental drill, showing the 'danger areas'! Only Steve Sternberg of the Cox News Service did some homework and reported that although Bergalis swore she had never had sexual intercourse, a subpoenaed physical examination revealed she had a venereal disease.[53] This tended to undermine her credibility.

Gay physicians and health workers had collaborated *en masse* with the AIDS establishment, bone-pointing, handing out death sentences, dismissing alternative therapies and prescribing wholesale amounts of AZT at retail prices. Now, with the Bergalis case a big media event, their HIV fundamentalism turned around and bit them. Suddenly, *they* were in danger of losing their licences, and even of going to jail. They were speechless.

As they dithered and consulted their attorneys, their role in the conferring of blood status was slipping from them. The Becton Dickinson company of Sparks, Maryland announced it had developed a home HIV testing kit that would indicate the presence of HIV antibodies in five minutes – by the appearance of a pink triangle.[54]

The cohort factor

Men, it has been well said, think in herds. It will be seen that they go mad in herds, while they only recover their senses slowly, and one by one.

— Charles Mackay, *Extraordinary Popular Delusions and the Madness of Crowds*

In America, what was called AIDS confined itself almost entirely to a few distinct social groups. It found its epicenter in the gay men who made up the hepatitis B cohort. For all the jaundiced observations of *Faggots* and *Rushes*, these were men who felt an enormous empathy and solidarity with one another. Like war, AIDS provided what novelist Peter McGehee described as 'the camaraderie of the front lines'.

Scientific literature's frequent use of the word 'cohort' to describe this group of promiscuous, urban gay men is not without its psychohistorical significance. The word was adopted not from any general American usage, but from the language of sociology. Karl Mannheim's well-known essay of 1927, 'The sociological problem of generations'[55] explored the concept of shared psychological and historical events shaping members of the same generation, and consequently their group influence on history. From this, other sociological demographers evolved the concept of the 'cohort' as a group (usually born at or around the same time) sharing 'a significant psychological experience'. Psychohistorian Peter Loewenberg emphasizes that a cohort 'may include people of all ages, even those *in utero* . . . who were influenced by a single traumatic event'.[56]

Deriving from the name of a division of the Roman army, the term has most usually been applied to groups of young men, notably the Hitler Youth and SS generations in Germany. As Loewenberg points out, the SS and Hitler Youth cohort consisted of young men whose childhood and adolescence were traumatized by World War I and the subsequent national collapse, and who were left with no father figures deemed worthy of love or respect. Strong idealism and a need for close male bonding led to the vast growth of the *wandervogel* organizations of young seekers after health and companionship that overlapped considerably with the emerging homosexual emancipation movement.

This cohort's lack of psychological integration (which Loewenberg relates to shattering physical and emotional deprivations in childhood and adolescence) left the movement ripe for a Nazi takeover that uncovered and exploited repressed feelings of impotence, shame, rage and hatred.

The parallel with the hepatitis B cohort in the America of the 1970s and 1980s is striking. Many of the young gay men of the Stonewall decade also felt misunderstood, shunned, abandoned and betrayed by their fathers and their fathers' society. Like de La Mazière and his fellow Nazi recruits, they felt adrift, isolated and frustrated in their need for community and self-assertion.

In both the *wandervogel* and the Gay Liberation movements, destructive, and self-destructive, urges were being channelled: martialled and let loose on society in the first instance, confined and sealed off in the second. Both groups of young men were drawn into 'the madness of crowds', running amok in seemingly anarchic but actually carefully channelled ways. 'Such outbursts', Gerald Heard had maintained, 'always come after a period when spontaneity has become completely inhibited, when all delight in Dionysian expression has been driven down . . . and the patient has for some time seemed almost a sleepwalker.'[57] Though the nature of the madness was radically different, co-optation by Nazism and by consumer capitalism both involved a tormented and imprisoned Homeros enslaved by experimental social agendas. Though one youth cohort was led to take on the role of murderers, the other of victims, they represent two faces of the same phenomenon: the corruption and betrayal of youth.

Stuart Marshall's comments on the Nazis' attempt to regulate desire throughout the whole population are illuminating: 'The Nazis were very modern in one sense. This is where the contemporary gay movement and the AIDS activist movement can find their analogies between contemporary and Nazi society.' Marshall refers to a Nazi-era academic study of the supposed spread of homosexuality among the Hitler Youth. 'This study was worked out in great detail and was given an aura of scientificity, with diagrams and flow charts that visualized a theory of homosexual desire rather like the transmission of a disease. When people see these diagrams today, they immediately notice their similarity to the early "contact tracing" diagrams purporting to describe the transmission of HIV among gay men in Los Angeles.'[58] George Whitmore's seemingly hyperbolic comparison of the orgy trucks with Nazi cattle-cars also intuited a connection.

In his book *AIDS: The Deadly Seed*, Klaus Dumke raises the question of an apparent psychic link between AIDS and the Nazi period.[59] Though he makes little effort to explore the connection, the unusual intensity of what he calls the demonic forces involved in both Nazism and AIDS, has tended to set others – Stuart Marshall, Larry Kramer and David Wojnarowicz among them – thinking in the same direction.

The lack of psychological integration which Loewenberg identified in the Nazi Youth cohort was also observed by the Dutch physician Arie Bos as characteristic of many PWAs. In a 1989 study, Bos points out that AIDS especially affects 'those cells which are particularly related to the "I"' (such as the blood) and 'the boundary regions between the inner and the outer world . . . the skin, the lungs, the digestive tract'.[60] He remarks on AIDS' 'dissociation of the members of the human being because the "I" is no longer able to carry out its tasks of integration . . . . AIDS', he writes, 'is an attack upon the ability of the "I" to carry out both its structural and vitalising tasks.'

This concept of self-identity and self-definition, of 'vital structure' – 'Who am I?' and 'Who are we?' – has always been central to the dilemma of gay people in a society which does not recognize our existence as meaningful or valid. These questions of identity, origin and purpose, articulated by gay thinkers like Carpenter, Heard, Hay and Fernbach, have come upon us at intervals in our history like waves, or tides, receding for a time, only to return with greater force and urgency, decades later.

If we date the beginning of what we think of as our century at about 1910 (the end of Victorianism's nostalgic and deceptively reassuring Edwardian coda) we can see our time as being bracketed by the phenomena of World War I and the AIDS epidemic – both typically 'modern' events involving the gruesome deaths of large numbers of young men.

Intellectual, artistic and erotic life in the years leading up to World War I was lived in the shadow of the Oscar Wilde debacle. Wilde had seen clearly both the historic significance of his sacrifice, as the latest in a long series of 'monstrous martyrdoms', and the parallel between his own fate and that of St Sebastian, whose name he took in exile. The persecution of Wilde served to frighten and mute intellectual and sexual heretics for decades. Only Carpenter, apparently protected by a strong Guardian Angel, carried on the battle for 'the intermediate sex'.

As the Edwardian period ended, a new generation arose, less intimidated, and with an adventurous idealism infused by Homeros. This new spirit was to have proclaimed itself in the First International Congress for Sexual Research, which Hirschfeld, Carpenter and Havelock Ellis had planned to take place in Berlin in 1914. When the Great War broke out, the congress had to be cancelled.

A generation of young men saw many of their friends and lovers slaughtered in the war, and significantly, many of the bards and elegiasts of that war were men with a strong homoerotic component: T. E. Lawrence, Wilfred Owen, Rupert Brooke, Siegfried Sassoon, Harold Munro, Herbert Read, and their precursor A. E. Housman, the author of *A Shropshire Lad*.

The Great War and its aftermath gave rise to an upsurge of homoerotic idealism and bonding among the young soldiers and survivors.[61] But the sunny optimism of the *wandervogel* and kindred movements such as Britain's Kibbo Kift concealed a dark side, which Nazism moulded into a militaristic cult with the spectacle of youthful death at its center.

In his biography of Hitler, Joachim Fest describes how the dictator's directorial talents were always galvanized by funereal events:

> Life seemed to paralyze his inspiration . . . . On the other hand his pessimistic temperament tirelessly won new lighting effects from the ceremony of death. The carefully developed artistic demogoguery had real high points, when he strode down the broad avenue between hundreds of thousands to honor the dead . . . with gloomy music in the background.
>
> He also had a distinct preference for nocturnal backdrops. Torches, pyres, or flaming wheels were continually being kindled. Though such rituals were supposed to be highly positive and inspirational, in fact they struck another note, stirring apocalyptic associations and awakening a fear of universal conflagration or doom, including each individual's own.[62]

This pervasive atmosphere of darkness and death-obsession, illuminated by omens of apocalypse, provided a sinister psychic underpinning for the uneasy male bonding so crucial to the Nazi enterprise.

After the Third Reich's defeat, the gay movement regenerated, sprouting from the fertile soil of wartime comradeship, with the newly demobbed GI Joe its Johnny Appleseed. As the movement grew, it began to appeal to the young, and to become more political – and more threatening to the establishment. For the second time in this century, the social upheaval brought about by war generated a movement for homosexual emancipation.

When youthful idealism was once again co-opted, it was not by old-fashioned nationalism but by a new kind of heroic hedonism. The contemporary weapon of advertising (whose dangers Carpenter and Heard had been among the first to identify) selected the cohort of young refugees from America as a 'target' group, and sold them a destructive, immunosuppressive lifestyle.

Every advance gay men have made in forging a group identity, and in pioneering male affection in the larger society, has been countered, and driven back – by the imprisonment and judicial murder of Wilde, by the devastation of the Great War, by the concentration camps, by AIDS. Three times in this century, emerging Homeros has been enlisted, co-opted and corrupted – each time with the same result: the mass destruction of youth in an atmosphere of fear and doom. Each period of our emergence as a people has been pioneered by a youthful cohort of gay men, sharing an intense emotional bond, whose advance to maturity and community has been halted by catastrophe.

The dark side of Homeros is Death: a fact borne out by gay art and history from *The Epic of Gilgamesh* to *Scorpio Rising*. Homeros' dark side always comes to the fore when his true nature is repressed, when his sexual or spiritual aspect, or both, are denied and condemned to imprisonment in the unconscious.

The 'significant psychological experience' which the gay cohorts of the 1970s and 1980s shared was their status as outsiders, rebels, 'refugees from America', their participation in the myth of the homosexual, and consequently their selection as appropriate subjects for social experimentation. The unforseen consequences that followed were neither intentional nor accidental, but arose from the psychohistory of those who initiated the experiment, and those who reacted to it.

Manifestations of Quan Yin on the Yellow Brick Road

The principal cause of disease which all premodern medicine shares (whether Eastern or Western) is that it is the result of a community's failure to live according to the whole truth about the purpose of human life on earth . . . . There are certain diseases which are understood in terms of the whole community's failure to attend to the higher level in its ways and actions.

— Joseph Needleman, *Consciousness and Tradition*

As I was about to begin writing this section about Quan Yin, I attended a talk by four 'long-term survivors', sponsored by the AIDS Committee of Toronto. All four were gay men in their thirties who had lived for up to ten years with HIV and various serious immune disturbances.

The men spoke frankly of their own backgrounds. Three of the four described themselves as recovering from addictions and sexual compulsions. One of them had been told by medical experts several years earlier that he had no more than a year to live. Another had a physician who told him nothing could be done to help him. Each of these men had put together his own protocol, composed variously of naturopathic, Chinese and homeopathic therapies, careful nutrition, supplements, exercise, meditation and visualizations. None of them was taking AZT or any of the similar cytocidal medicines. They emphasized the values of openmindedness, caution, listening and sharing. They acknowledged the benefits of having a good 'HIV primary care physician' whom they used mostly for arranging bloodwork and other tests, and supporting them in their battles with specialists. They spoke of the close connections between the immune system and mental patterns. All of them were involved in some form of AIDS activism, healing circles or meditation groups. One spoke of using mantras to calm the mind.

As *Blade Runner* had predicted, underground medicine was coming into its own. In the 1980s and 1990s, the ongoing destruction and pollution of the planet's atmosphere, soil, water, forests and wildlife finally began to draw widespread public attention. As chronic fatigue syndrome, cancers, heart disease, chronic asthma and serious allergies proliferated, and the cost of orthodox medicine skyrocketed, the toxic effects of our technology began to be recognized. Orthodox medicine was in crisis, and AIDS caused many more to abandon it for more preventive methods, or to modify and supplement it with alternatives. Women and gay men made up a large proportion of those dissatisfied with standard medical treatments and approaches.

Many gay men with immune problems stopped listening passively to their physicians and started to take charge of their own healing, using professionals as counsellors and partners, rather than as sacred authority figures. In New York, the Dalai Lama's physicians counselled PWAs using traditional Tibetan medicine in a program funded by the AIDS Treatment Project, founded by poet John Giorno and his old friend William S. Burroughs. There was a groundswell of interest in homeopathy, a gentle, meticulous system of medicine that thrived in Britain through Royal protection, but had been politically squeezed out in North America.

These alternatives presented serious problems. Insurance seldom paid for alternative treatments, and there was almost no money for research. Often, holistic medicine was turned to as a last resort, when damage was too far gone to be repaired. And there were many legal obstacles placed in the way. Physicians in some jurisdictions lobbied to pass laws that only they could legally administer acupuncture (which very few of them knew how to do), with the result that PWAs had to give up their acupuncture treatments, or travel out of state.

Government agents often intimidated merchants selling holistic medicine. Obscure patent laws were invoked, and some herbs were banned outright. In Tacoma, Washington, armed agents of the Food and Drug Administration, dressed in bullet-proof vests, burst into an alternative clinic using unauthorized treatments. In Texas, health inspectors raided health food stores across the state, removing hundreds of products including Vitamin C, aloe vera and herbal teas.[63] But, in spite of these difficulties, people found ways of making their own health care choices.

The alternative medical disciplines shared a holistic view of health and illness that was also being rediscovered by open-minded physicians like cancer surgeon Dr Bernie Siegel, author of the best-selling *Love, Medicine and Miracles*, and by pioneers of the 'new' science of psychoneuroimmunology. The mechanistic model of illness with its fragmentation of the person, simplistic germ theories and battleground metaphors, was being challenged from several quarters. Advanced science was coming to the same conclusions as holistic and spiritual healing disciplines: mind and body, individual and environment, were once more being acknowledged as a complete system, and immune dysfunction was being seen as a syndrome with multiple causes. AIDS was the crisis point that marked the turning of the tide against scientific orthodoxy and the medical priesthood.

In the 1930s, Gerald Heard had written of the increase in diseases which 'are in ever greater number of cases traced back to ... an outlook on life which puts an intolerable strain on the individual'. He saw the 'iron outer world' of Calvinism, mechanism and medical orthodoxy as 'to an indefinite degree our construction. Therefore, if we change ourselves, changing our power of apprehension, we change the universe confronting us.'[64]

In the early 1980s, a minister in California began applying similar metaphysical ideas to the complex of problems involved in AIDS. In August 1983 (a time when no one was offering much hope for people with AIDS and the medical profession was predicting everyone with the disease would be dead in a year) Louise L. Hay made an audio tape, *AIDS: A Positive Approach*. Word of her ideas spread quickly, and in January 1985, she and six PWAs met in her living room to have dinner, share ideas, and discuss the beginning of a support group. In a few years, similar groups were being held all over America.

A practitioner of the spiritual philosophy called Science of Mind, and the author of a popular book called *You Can Heal Your Life*, Louise Hay spoke from her own life experience: 'With my background of being raped at five and having been a battered child, it was no wonder I manifested cancer in the vaginal area' – cancer that had gone into remission after intensive nutritional and mental therapies.

On her AIDS group, she wrote:

> We decided to take a positive approach. We gathered every bit of positive information we could and shared it. If one person was feeling better, we asked what he was doing, and

everyone tried it. Eating habits were improved as we learned about nutrition. We did a lot of releasing of resentment and much forgiveness work . . . . We did meditation and visualization. And above all, we worked on learning to love ourselves.

In a few months, there were eighty-five people hanging out of the windows and standing at the door and spilling into the dining room. We moved to larger quarters, and the next week there were 150 people at the meeting . . . . By the spring of 1988, there were over six-hundred people at each meeting. Not everyone has AIDS. There are friends and lovers and 'the worried well'. There are women and even children. We have nurses, hospice workers, alternate therapy people, ministers, and doctors . . .

Fear was the biggest issue that each member was dealing with . . . . Self-esteem, self-worth. Anger and resentment. All sorts of guilts. The usual parental problems, plus how to tell parents they had AIDS or even that they were gay. We discussed sex and safe sex. How to forgive. How to feel good about themselves when they believed they were under a death sentence . . . [65]

In her work with gay men, Louise Hay discovered deep reserves of induced self-hatred and self-disgust, of destructive ways of thinking, such as the belief that gay men, when they get older, will be useless and unwanted. 'It is almost better to destroy themselves first – and many have created a destructive lifestyle. Some of the concepts and attitudes that are so a part of the gay lifestyle – the meat rack, the constant judging, the refusal to get close to another, etc. – are monstrous. And AIDS is a monstrous disease.'[66]

James Baldwin once wrote that people are more afraid of love than they are of death. For many, Louise Hay's beliefs (love is the most powerful immune stimulant; our thoughts are creative; what we believe about life and ourselves becomes the truth for us) seemed shocking and threatening. And, like other AIDS dissidents, she attracted a great deal of hostility. One prominent critic was the novelist Paul Monette, who chronicled his lover's death from AIDS in his books *Love Alone* and *Borrowed Time*. To Monette, Louise seemed 'a pernicious, disgusting . . . creature'.[67] Another commentator described her as a 'marketer of "feel good" therapies and fatuous homilies', contrasting this with what he felt was Monette's more realistic view of the world as 'a sewer of darkness'.[68]

Much of the hostility directed toward Louise Hay came because she was a woman (and therefore not a traditional authority figure) and because her ideas challenged a victim psychology common to gay men. One HIV-positive man told an acquaintance of mine that were he offered a cure, he wasn't sure he would take it! He had been so conditioned to see himself as a victim that any other way of thinking alarmed and frightened him.

Louise Hay told people, 'If you have AIDS or AIDS-related disease, don't just make it your goal to get back to where you were before you got ill. That was not a well place to be, or you would never have been able to get this disease . . . . Body, mind, and spirit must go together. If they were to find the wonder drug to knock out the AIDS virus tomorrow, would you really be healed and made whole? Or would you just accept the cure for your body and immediately go on with your old mental and physical lifestyle, only to create something else to put in its place?'[69]

Old thought patterns still pervasive in the gay world were illustrated by the contents of a single issue of the *Advocate*, published in the late 1980s. It contained such headlines as 'Will protests and bloc votes make pols [politicians] the slaves of New York gays?', 'Gay rights gone too far', 'The danger zone' (a piece on gay intimacy) and even 'Is gay sex repugnant?'

In *The Spiral Path*, David Fernbach had recognized that in subscribing to such negative fixations, 'the gay subculture of today . . . shares the problems of our society as a whole, often in the most glaring degree'. He saw a need to re-establish a balance of masculine and feminine qualities in society. Just as the health crisis of gay men was about to surface in the form of AIDS, Fernbach predicted the coming of Quan Yin as a symbol of that balance.

As gay men began turning to holistic healing in the 1980s, an alternative medical center sprang up – on San Francisco's Market Street – that was to become internationally known for its holistic AIDS treatments, traditional Chinese medicine, nutritional therapies, herbalism, meditation, bodywork, counselling and support groups. Its founders called it the Quan Yin Acupuncture and Herb Center. It survived the earthquake of 1990 to become an established institution in America's best-known gay community.

Quan Yin is an ancient mother goddess, a compassionate protector and healer who brings good fortune and is associated with prophecy and questioning. But the legend of Quan Yin is unusual. It is said that she was originally male, a shaman called Avalokitesh-vara. He attained enlightenment and became a Bodhisattva, remaining on earth to help suffering humanity rather than enjoying the ecstasies of nirvana. And at that time, he adopted female clothes, or took on female form, assuming the name Quan Yin.

During the heady time of the first few years of Gay Liberation, gay men had shared their experiences by meeting in encounter groups, consciousness raising sessions and experimental living arrangements. These endeavors had their problems and their successes, but they constituted a starting point for our entry into society *on our own terms*. By the mid-1970s, these approaches had been eclipsed by the new gay lifestyle. Now, two decades later, all over America, large and small groups of gay men and their loved ones were forming healing and meditation circles, anger workshops, addiction recovery organizations, and spiritual groups. Connections were being taken up again, with a new awareness born of tragic experience.

It was at this point that the Rainbow Flag began to come into its own as a widely used gay symbol, pinned to lapels, flying over activist parades and decorating the walls in gay restaurants.

The movie of L. Frank Baum's magical novel *The Wizard of Oz* has always been a particular favorite of gay men, with 'Somewhere Over the Rainbow' an unofficial gay anthem sung at innumerable piano bars, political rallies and AIDS vigils. References to *The Wizard of Oz* have popped up several times in this narrative.

The protagonist of *The Wizard of Oz* is a girl called Dorothy, an embodiment of a favorite gay archetype, the lost and/or wounded girl, representing the lost, wounded feminine aspect of the self. She meets two witches, one good, one evil. The good witch arrives in what seems to be a large, pink soap-bubble, like a version of the Blessed Virgin (or Quan Yin or any other healing mother goddess). The presence of a familiar for Dorothy, her dog Toto, suggests she may be something of a witch herself (though she doesn't know it).

Dorothy's goal is to go home – that is, to feel at home in the world. But in order to get there, she must undertake a perilous journey into the otherworld of Oz, with the aid of three friends. These friends are so important to the meaning of the tale that at one point 'friends of Dorothy' became a catch-phrase meaning gay men.[70] And as played by Ray Bolger, Bert Lahr and Jack Haley, they certainly seem anything but straight!

The Scarecrow, Lion and Tin Woodsman are searching for human qualities they think they lack – a brain, courage, and a heart. Courage, love and determined reason are the very qualities gay men have always been told we do not have; fear, shame and guilt have always undermined our cause. In the course of helping Dorothy, the three friends discover they really do have the qualities they need – each in his own way. The baubles the Wizard of Oz bestows on them are merely tokens of their self-discovery.

One of the great lessons of Oz is the lesson of self-belief, or self-healing, which is the same thing. When Dorothy returns home, she is in bed, convalescing, with her three friends gathered round. Gay men's self-healing necessary entails a *sexual* self-acceptance, a recognition that our sexuality is not a sickness, a sin or a lifestyle, but an impulse toward love and wholeness.

Unfortunately, we cannot just click our heels together three times and be home. But our response to the catastrophe of AIDS revealed to us the depth and strength of those qualities of love, mind and courage we were told we did not, and could never, possess. For over a century, we have been Dorian Gray and St Sebastian, Narcissus and Frankenstein, leper and clone. Through all our outward and inward guises, the myth of the homosexual has continued to animate our beliefs.

The health crisis revealed the terrible conclusion of the myth, throwing all our old images and ideas into confusion. A new millenium would necessarily question the attitudes, and the science, of the old. The survivors and heirs of the Stonewall Experiment would have to create new myths and alternative images, in anticipation of a time when we would no longer be unnatural or supernatural creatures, fairies or monsters, but simply mortal men, able to love men.

Notes

1. Dennis King, *Lyndon LaRouche and the New American Fascism* (New York: Doubleday, 1989), p. 143.
2. Rev. Charles Angel, 'AIDS and the African-American PWA' [*sic*], *PWA Coalition Newsline*, April 1987, p. 30.
3. Michael Bronski, 'Death and the erotic imagination', in John Preston, ed., *Dispatches: Writers Confront AIDS* (New York: St Martin's Press, 1989), p. 135.
4. David Wojnarowicz, *Close to the Knives: A Memoir of Disintegration* (New York: Vintage, 1991), pp. 228–9.
5. Ralph, in Perry Tilleraas, *Circle of Hope: Our Stories of AIDS, Addiction & Recovery* (New York: Harper & Row, 1990), p. 141.
6. Bruce Eves, 'Reports from the front: a portfolio', *Christopher Street*, 20 October 1991, p. 27.
7. Casper Schmidt, unpublished interview with the author, 1992.
8. *ACTlife*, No. 1, October 1991.
9. Collected as *Poison by Prescription: The AZT Story* (New York: Asklepios, 1990).
10. Peter Duesberg, Introduction to Lauritsen, *Poison by Prescription*, p. 8.
11. In *AZT: Cause for Concern* (Meditel Productions video).
12. 'Wellcome issue raises £2.16 billion', *Globe and Mail*, 28 July 1992.
13. Charles L. Ortleb, 'Nationally syndicated columnist and talk show host Tony Brown urges Magic Johnson to see Duesberg before it's too late: an important voice against AZT', *New York Native*, 9 December 1991. It was also alleged that blood samples from gay men were sometimes specially marked, perhaps to elicit a 'positive' lab result, and thus encourage more 'responsible' sexual behaviour in the future. See Charles Ortleb, 'Nazi science: it's not what you have, it's who you are', *New York Native*, 8 March 1993.
14. Martin Delaney of Project Inform, quoted in Lauritsen, *Poison by Prescription*, p. 27.
15. Celia Farber, 'Sins of omission: the AZT scandal', *SPIN*, November 1989, p. 40.
16. *Ibid.*
17. *Ibid.*, p. 42.
18. 'Wellcome issue raises £2.16 billion', *Globe and Mail*, p. 44.
19. Marc Colter, *PWA Coalition Newsline*, January 1990, p. 9.
20. See, for example, John Lauritsen's report on Burroughs-Wellcome's

financial dealings with the leading British AIDS organization in his 'Something rotten in the British AIDS establishment', *New York Native*, 10 February 1992, p. 20.

21. In *AZT: Cause for Concern*.

22. *Ibid*.

23. Sal Licata, 'Fire Island impressions', *PWA Coalition Newsline*, September 1987, p. 35.

24. See P. T. Cohen, MD, Ph.D, Merle A. Sande, MD, and Paul A. Volberding, MD, eds, *The AIDS Knowledge Base* (Waltham, MA: Medical Publishing Group, 1990); and Jack A. Levy, ed., *AIDS Pathogenesis and Treatment* (New York: Marcel Dekker, 1989).

25. Tilleraas, *Circle of Hope*, pp. 43–4.

26. Rick Davis, Addictive Behavior Specialist for AIDS Project Los Angeles, quoted in Tilleraas, *Circle of Hope*, p. 43.

27. Tilleraas, *Circle of Hope*, p. 11.

28. *Ibid*.

29. See Barbara G. Falz and Scott Madover, 'Treatment of substance abuse in patients with HIV infection', in Larry Siegel, MD, ed., *AIDS and Substance Abuse* (New York: Harrington Park Press, 1988).

30. Chip, quoted in Tilleraas, *Circle of Hope*, p. 303.

31. George Whitmore, 'Bearing witness', *New York Times Magazine*, 31 January 1988, p. 14.

32. George Whitmore, *The Confessions of Danny Slocum or Gay Life in the Big City* (New York: St Martin's Press, 1980), p. 151.

33. Whitmore, 'Bearing witness'.

34. Dr H. Versicolor, 'The psychology of captivity', *DungeonMaster*, March 1980, pp. 1–2.

35. Ian Young, 'Prescription for suicide', *New York Native*, 12 September 1988, p. 18.

36. Steve Rose, 'AZT zombies', *New York Native*, 26 September 1988.

37. In *AZT: Cause for Concern*.

38. Rose, 'AZT zombies'.

39. Quoted in Jason Serinus, ed., *Psychoimmunity and the Healing Process: A Holistic Approach to Immunity and AIDS*, 3rd ed. (Berkeley: Celestial Arts, 1988), p. 54.

40. 'AIDS-Virus Attack', *Time*, 12 August 1985, p. 47.

41. Alternative AIDS Symposium, Amsterdam, 1992, quoted on Canadian Broadcasting Corporation, 'Ideas'.

42. Sanford I. Cohen, 'Voodoo death, the stress response, and AIDS', in T. Peter Bridge, Allan F. Mirsky and Frederick K. Goodwin, eds., *Psychosocial, Neuropsychiatric, and Substance Abuse Aspects of*

AIDS: *Advances in Biochemical Psychopharmacology*, Vol. 44 (New York: Raven Press, 1988).

43. Quoted in 'Pregnant women and newborns', *Body Positive*, December 1989, p. 11.

44. Tracy A. Kion and Geoffrey W. Hoffman, 'Anti-HIV and anti-anti-MHC antibodies in alloimmune and autoimmune mice', *Science*, 253, 6 September 1991.

45. John Maddox, 'AIDS research turned upside down', *Nature*, 353 (6342), 26 September 1991, p. 297.

46. For insights into the significance of Dr Sheldrake's researches and the Labyrinth Experiments, I am indebted to Jarmo Koskinen's *Thoughts-Forms in Time: Is There a New Age Coming?* (Fort Erie, Ont.: Phoenix Rising Publications, 1988), pp. 174–7.

47. Casper Schmidt, unpublished interview with the author, 1992.

48. Larry Kramer, 'Kramer vs . . . gay "leaders",' *Outweek*, 21 January 1990, p. 36.

49. See Eric E. Rofes, 'Gay Lib vs AIDS: averting civil war in the 1990's', *Out/Look*, Spring 1990, p. 8.

50. Walt Odets, Ph.D., 'The secret epidemic', *Out/Look*, Fall 1991, p. 45.

51. Darrel Yates Rist, 'AIDS as apocalypse: the deadly costs of an obsession', *The Nation*, 13 February 1989; reprinted, with readers' comments, *Christopher Street*, No. 132, 1989, p. 11.

52. In 1994, the director of the World Health Organization's Global Program on AIDS announced, 'We will not have a magic potion against AIDS before the year 2000.' 'AIDS cure not seen in near future', *Globe and Mail*, 21 March 1994, p. A14.

53. Steve Sternberg, 'Medical sleuths lack legal weapons in AIDS mystery', *Vancouver Sun*, 7 September 1991.

54. Sean Hosein, 'The pink triangle test', *Xtra!*, 11 August 1989, p. 11.

55. Karl Mannheim, 'The sociological problem of generations', in *Essays on the Sociology of Knowledge*, Paul Kecskemeti, ed. (London: Routledge & Kegan Paul, 1952).

56. Peter Loewenberg, 'The psychohistorical origins of the Nazi Youth cohort', in *Decoding the Past: The Psychohistorical Approach* (New York: Alfred A. Knopf, 1983), p. 247.

57. Gerald Heard, *The Human Venture* (New York: Harper & Bros., 1955), p. 141.

58. Stuart Marshall, 'The contemporary political use of gay history: the Third Reich', in Bad Object Choices, ed., *How Do I Look? Queer Film and Video* (Seattle: Bay Press, 1991), p. 92.

59. Klaus Dumke, *AIDS: The Deadly Seed: An Anthropological and Epidemiological Investigation of a Modern Epidemic* (London: Rudolf Steiner Press, 1991), pp. 126–34.

60.   Arie Bos, *AIDS: Alternative Approaches to the Understanding and the Treatment of Acquired Immune Deficiency Syndrome Based on Anthroposophical Medicine* (Stroud: Hawthorn Press, 1989), p. 54.

61.   The Great War's aftermath included a worldwide pandemic of 'influenza' which killed more people than the war itself. In a pair of unpublished papers, Casper Schmidt details similarities between the symptomatology and epidemiology of this 'epidemic influenza' and AIDS. Casper G. Schmidt, 'Two forms of epidemic influenza' and 'A comparison of the first and second great AIDS epidemics of the twentieth century' (Working Drafts, 1990).

62.   Joachim Fest, *Hitler* (New York: Harcourt, 1974), p. 3.

63.   'F.D.A. steps up effort to control vitamin claims', *New York Times*, 9 August 1992.

64.   Gerald Heard, *The Third Morality* (London: Cassell & Co., 1937), p. 240.

65.   Louise L. Hay, *The AIDS Book: A Positive Approach* (Santa Monica: Hay House, 1988), pp. 3–4.

66.   *Ibid.*, p. 176.

67.   Quoted in Gerald Hannon, 'A people at war', *Xtra!*, 23 February 1990, p. 15.

68.   *Ibid.*

69.   Hay, *The AIDS Book*, p. 115.

70.   When US Navy Security came across this code phrase, they began to search for the mysterious Dorothy: obviously, she was the leader of a vast military-homosexual ring – and she must have *all the names!*

Epilogue: Another Walk

The Life Force is like a juggler; it is always contriving that we shall watch the hand with which the trick is not being done. When we look back, we often discover that it was the symptom we were studying, not the cause. And yet it is hard to learn. Next time we are certain we shall not be deceived; we shall have no preconceptions as to what is important, what negligible. Everything shall be seen steadily and whole. It is of little use. Surprised at our own patience in considering it at all, we dismiss the clue without a misgiving, assured that it is a trifle. We ought to be learning that the very sensation of amusement at our own tolerance should warn us that we are being bamboozled.

Gerald Heard, *Narcissus: An Anatomy of Clothes* (1924)

AS the year 2000 approaches, it is becoming apparent that the gay movement is not, as had been generally assumed, on the margins of contemporary history, but rather at its center, and that Stonewall was, in the words of cultural historian Camille Paglia, 'a central event in cultural history'.[1]

Commentators on the new phenomenon of the homosexual used to refer to us as a 'sport of nature', a kind of false limb on the evolutionary tree. When the faggots at the Stonewall rioted, people were surprised, assuming so bizarre an event to be of little importance. When a generation of young gays began to make America uncomfortable, the nation's response to people it regarded as sick and criminal was to circumscribe the effects of our behavior by franchising us to institutions it regarded as our natural, traditional overseers: the medical profession and the criminal underworld. Our past was marketed back to us, artfully disguised as our future. At the time, it seemed an acceptably liberal solution. But the resulting social experiment turned out to have far-reaching and disastrous consequences. Society projected its collective guilt feelings about sex, drugs and race onto some of its most feared and despised groups, leading them to act out destructive behaviours that reflected its own excesses. Guilt-fantasies of poisoned blood contributed to the mass sacrificial ritual that ensued, with the outcasts succumbing in large numbers to the consequences of the shared belief system.

The modern world has embarked on numerous grand social experiments, often with devastating results for those involved. The earliest use of the word 'experiment' in this sense seems to have been by the English philosopher Jeremy Bentham, writing in 1812 on the wholesale transportation of Britain's 'criminal class' to the penal colonies of Australia. This endeavor, he wrote, 'was indeed a measure of *experiment* . . . but the subject-matter of experiment was, in this case, a peculiarly commodious one; a set of *animae viles*, a sort of excrementitious mass, that could be projected, and accordingly was projected . . . as far out of sight as possible'.[2] Bentham's description recognized that his candidates for transportation were regarded as both troublesome and somehow less than human. The attitude was typical of other grand experiments to come.

The American nation was itself born of social experiment. Its founding principles were slavery, genocide, and the belief that all men are created equal and entitled to the pursuit of happiness. Its attempts to deal with the problems posed by blacks, native peoples, and psychiatric inmates, can all be seen, in the one-way light of history, as gigantic social experiments, with the ghetto, the reservation and the sanitarium as dumping grounds and laboratories, where the various *animae viles* were transported 'as far out of sight as possible' and rendered inert.

In time, we have come to realize that these schemes were cruel and foolish. Yet when they were instituted, genocide and slavery were not deliberated as matters of policy, their every detail meticulously plotted around a polished oak table by conspiratorial cabals of evil men. Rather they reflected unconscious prejudices and assumptions, cloaked in high-minded rhetoric. Quentin Crisp once remarked that 'the atom bomb wasn't built by a wild fanatic, trying to bring the vengeance of an angry god onto a wicked and adulterous generation. No, the bomb was made by a man with a noble forehead and silver hair, sitting in the middle of an American desert and cutting up the atom while saying, "Pity!".[3]

One of the most telling phrases of the modern age is *The Revolution Betrayed*. Trotsky used it as the title of his brilliant, bitter polemic against the way the Bolshevik experiment turned out, but it could serve as epitaph for almost any social upheaval of recent times. Betrayal and apparent failure are the fate of all revolutions, if only in that compromises are inevitable and expectations frustrated. Success comes too of course, for the degree and details of every failure also shape history. The emergence of gay people over the past 125 years constitutes a revolution whose successes have yet to be fully felt. Its failures are recorded every day in the obituaries.

Our civilization is good at imputing blame; it's one of the things we do best. And it is good at guilt and denial. In guilt we accuse and lacerate ourselves, and do not move, and in denial, we whirl around blindly pointing the finger at others. We create angry, clashing armies of victims, persecutors, avengers and scapegoats. And the futility and hatred piles up, blocking our way. There is certainly enough blame to go around, if we want to play the blame game, because almost everyone collaborated in the co-opting of the Stonewall Experiment: government, physicians, pharmaceutical companies, organized crime, the churches, the public – and ourselves.

For a while, the gay men of the AIDS era will probably cling reflexively, self-protectively, to our partial numbness. An analyst of the psychology of warfare has observed that 'during moments of extreme stress, combat soldiers are often called upon to act regardless of how they are feeling. Their survival depends upon their ability to suspend feelings in favor of taking steps to ensure their safety. Unfortunately, the resulting "split" between one's self and one's experience does not heal easily. It does not gradually disappear with the passage of time. Until an active process of healing takes place, the individual continues to experience a constriction of feelings, a decreased ability to recognize which feelings are present, and a persistent sense of being cut off from one's surroundings . . . a condition known as psychic numbing.'[4] As long as the epidemic continues, our partial numbness will continue with it. Preoccupied with taking care of our lovers and friends, we have not yet given full vent to our grief – or our anger.

For the Stonewall and immediate post-Stonewall generations, our health crisis is the central psychic event that will remain
with us and affect us for the rest or our lives. But another generation
of gay men will want its own perspective on events, will need to
know our history – what we sought and what happened to us, as we
tried to make our way 'over the rainbow'.

In his classic study *Understanding Media*, philosopher Marshall McLuhan identified as a central symbol of our modern,
technological society the figure of Narcissus, whose myth inspired
Oscar Wilde to create Dorian Gray.[5] The classic Narcissus myth has
two versions: a heterosexual one, which is well known, and a gay
one, which has been neglected. In the gay version, Narcissus is a city
boy: 'He was very handsome but scorned the joys of love. He was
loved by a young man, Ameinias, but did not love him in return, kept
rejecting him and finally sent him a present of a sword. Ameinias
used the sword to commit suicide in front of Narcissus' door, calling
down curses on Narcissus as he died.' Yet even this terrible tragedy
did not free Narcissus from his trance; he did not take up his staff
and wander into the desert meditating on love, death and immorta-
lity, like Gilgamesh after his companion, the wild man Enkidu,
mysteriously sickened and died. Instead he gazed into a pool, fell –
finally – in love, and, desperate with passion, drowned.[6]

Echos of this appalling tale resonate through many of the gay
myths alluded to in these pages – not so much because there is
anything intrinsically narcissistic about gay men, but because we
find ourselves in a narcissistic society, and because the myth of
Narcissus holds a special danger for us.

Narcissism is the entranced denial of love, and of self.
Whatever our sexuality, if we are too mesmerized by our gadgets,
our materialism, or our image of ourselves, to hear the voice of
Ameinias, or respond to his love, then he will turn away, and when
he returns to us it will be as a victim of the sword we have handed
him. If there is blood on our doorstep and curses in our ears, we
should at least consider the reasons.

The gay version of the Narcissus tragedy is a prototype of the
myth of the homosexual – a myth that has pervaded our history, and
whose most insidious aspect has been our unconsciousness of it.

Beliefs have consequences – and unconscious beliefs are no exception.

It is said that the Reformation and the concomitant decline of orthodox religion led to a drastic drop in the use of church candles, and consequently, in the demand for beeswax. Less beeswax meant less honey, which led to a demand for a substitute – sugar. And the rising demand for sugar was one of the chief motives for the development of slavery in the West Indies. The new attitudes being ushered in by religious reform included eloquent ideological justifications for the enslavement of non-Europeans on sugar plantations.

Recent newspaper reports tell of a tribe of Indians in the desert of the American Southwest, living in shacks with no electricity or running water. A few yards above them run the power lines upon which the white man's cities depend. Living directly under the power grid, the Indian children have an extraordinarily high incidence of leukemia, and the community is blighted with other cancers.

No cabals issued edicts to suppress honey, or put Indian villagers to death. Thoughts and beliefs ('The only good Indian is a dead Indian') manifest themselves nonetheless.

The idea of buggery was literally a heresy, a theological error practiced by Bulgars, Bogomils, bugger boys and boogey men. It was 'the abominable crime not to be mentioned among Christians'. At Oscar Wilde's trial, the judge reminded him that 'there is no greater crime' than the one he had committed! It takes longer than a mere century for such long-established sentiments to vanish. At best they become covert, unconsciously retained. They go underground, and remain the deeply held beliefs of a society, affecting all its members.

As long as those beliefs were couched in theological terms, the penalty for male/male sex remained death by execution, or some substitute for it. When the anathematization began to be viewed in terms of the new, medical paradigm, Homeros became medicalized, as an illness, a contagion, a baccillus, a virus. A virus that kills. Grafitti proclaimed: AIDS = Anally Injected Death Sentence. Millenia of belief had finally come true. The fear had manifested. The rejected god had reappeared as a disease, and his followers now moved about as though in a trance.

Gay men were caught in a mythic system which led to their own premature deaths. As William Burroughs said of his own characters, 'None of [them] are free. If they were free, they would not still be conditioned in the mythological system, that is, the cycle of conditioned action.'[7]

Even after the riots under the full moon at Stonewall broke the trance, gay men continued to respond to posthypnotic suggestions buried in our myths and reinforced by repeated messages, some overt, some subliminal.

Future generations will need to shed some of these old myths and replace them with other, gentler myths of healing and reconciliation, myths explored and articulated by a lineage of gay teachers, writers, philosophers and prophets, from Socrates onward: among them, the myth of the shaman, who is the wounded healer, and the myth of the androgyne, who is the embodiment of a more evolved, more harmonious stage of human evolution.

In the early days of Gay Liberation, Gary Alinder wrote a piece called 'My gay soul', in which he said: 'I need to be together with other Gay men. We have not been together – we've not had enough self respect for that. Isolated sex and then look for another partner. Enough of that, that's where we've been. Let's go somewhere where we value each other as more than a hunk of meat. We need to recognize one another wherever we are, start talking to each other. We need to say "Hi, Brother!" when we see each other on the street . . . Our Gay souls have nearly been stomped to death here in that desert called America. If we are to bloom, we can only do it together. I need you, brother, because you are all I have.'[8]

That loving need has to be rediscovered by every generation of gay men. We must learn that the Gay Spirit is not something that can be oppressed without incurring terrible consequences. We have to learn that we are not just a 'sport of nature' but a force of history.

In the spring of 1992, I made another excursion to New York. Though I had made several return trips since my walk through a depopulated Christopher Street five years before, nothing I had seen had displaced those desolate images from my memory. This trip was different.

I was with Jamie – the first time we'd been in the city together since 1980 – and the gay community that we found in the New York of 1992 was a community in recovery. Many of the friends and acquaintances I spent time with were, in different ways, coming to understand and heal the wounds of the past. Some were recovering from alcohol and drug addictions or other compulsive behaviors. Some were dealing with the consequences of familial abuse and rejection. Some had taken up spiritual disciplines or were volunteers in community programs.

My friend Joe Kadlec took me to lunch with a group where he helped to cook meals once or twice a week, the Manhattan Center for Living, an organization of people experiencing 'life-challenging' illness of any kind, including AIDS and cancer. Joe took me to the Center's cheery third-floor dining room in their headquarters on Broadway in Lower Manhattan. We took our places at one of the large round tables set for lunch and were served tasty organic vegetarian food in an atmosphere of relaxed friendliness which had a slightly manic, excited undertone, contributing to an aura of good-humored expectancy. One of our fellow diners explained to me that many of the people in the room were on various sorts of medications which rendered them temporarily hyper, uncoordinated or semi-comatose. They seemed no different from any other group of restaurant patrons.

As Joe chatted with an elderly woman friend (they were comparing last night's dreams) I looked at the list of available workshops posted on the bulletin board: Shiatsu; Dating for HIV+ Gay Men; Divine Dance; Recovery – a Personal Journey to Health; Healing Shame; Sex, Love and Intimacy; Introduction to Iridology; Men's Bereavement Group; and, one that particularly caught my eye: Healing False Beliefs. And, next to it, someone had pinned up something Mother Teresa had said when she was asked about PWAs: 'They are all Jesus Christ, in a distressing disguise.' We were back with Sebastian, and the sacrificial son.

What struck me most of about the Center was its unselfconscious mix of people, regardless of sexuality, age, background or personal style. These things remained interesting and significant, but were no longer important, a big deal. We were all in the same boat, and staying afloat meant the chains that weighed us down had to be tossed overboard.

The changed atmosphere in the city seemed to support what the statistics were suggesting. Though the health crisis was by no means over (we would lose many more friends and lovers before the big party we were already planning for New Year's Eve 1999: 'WE SURVIVED THE TWENTIETH CENTURY!') we were finally beginning to regain control of the experiment.[9]

That night after I returned to Toronto, I went to visit some friends and decided to walk home along one of my favorite streets, Danforth Avenue, the broad main street of the city's large Greek community. One side of the street had been cordoned off and was crowded with pedestrians, and I soon found myself walking slowly and deliberately with them, as part of the funeral procession of a young Greek man, a popular entertainer.

At the head of the procession were six young women strewing flower petals. Next came a single man carrying, propped against his chest, a framed portrait of the deceased. A few feet behind walked the mourning family and close friends, dressed in black. Then a row of musicians singing slow, dance-like dirges accompanied by bouzouki, accordion, triangle and drum. Finally, the slow lines of the other mourners, and the growing crowd. It occurred to me that this solemn, dignified ritual was very ancient – far predating Christianity. It had survived, virtually unchanged, for thousands of years, and travelled half way around the world.

I walked with the gathering procession for many blocks, eventually absorbed by the emotional crowd, in tears along with them. In mourning for this young man I did not know, I was mourning for all the dead young men I had known, many of whom were given no such public ceremony to honour them and mark their passing.

When I slipped away from the funeral march and headed into the subway, a memory flashed into my mind – of a gay man, an actor and a friend of Joe's, whom I'd met briefly at the Center for Living. He was helping out in the kitchen, dressed in his cook's apron and a T-shirt with a picture on it of a dancing lizard, which looked rather like an antic version of the lizard sent to Oscar Wilde during his trial. The man came over to tell us about a marvellous new show he was in, based on the works of Edward Gorey. The show was apparently gory in other ways too, with lots of spectacular on-stage deaths. Joe's friend beamed and his hands made an expansive gesture. 'Lots of death!' he informed us gleefully; 'Lots of death! I'm getting it all out of my system!'

*

As this book neared completion, Jamie died – on 1 December, World AIDS Day, 1993. He was thirty-two.

One of the first things the Sorcerer (that was my name for him) ever said to me was, 'Life is Magic!' One of the last things he said to me was, 'It's all mental'. What he taught me in between enabled me to write this book, which he never read, but whose existence he knew of. He is with many of his brothers now, some of whose names appear in my Acknowledgements. His gay spirit lives on. The experiment continues.

Notes

1. Camille Paglia, 'Camille Paglia defends her rotten record', *Advocate*, 22 September 1992, p. 96.
2. Quoted in Robert Hughes, *The Fatal Shore: The Epic of Australia's Founding* (New York: Alfred A. Knopf, 1987), p. 2. Bentham was the first English writer to break with the traditional view of homosexuality, though his writings on the subject were not published during his lifetime.
3. *An Evening with Quentin Crisp* (videotape).
4. T. L. Cermak, quoted in Charles L. Whitfield, *Healing the Child Within: Discovery and Recovery for Adult Children of Dysfunctional Families* (Deerfield Beach, FL: Health Communications, 1989), p. 57.
5. Marshall McLuhan, *Understanding Media: The Extensions of Man* (New York: Mentor, 1964), p. 57.
6. This version of the tale is adapted from Pierre Grimal, *The Concise Dictionary of Classical Mythology*, ed. Stephen Kershaw (London: Basil Blackwell, 1990), p. 286.
7. Quoted in Eric Mottram, *Blood on the Nash Ambassador: Investigations in American Culture* (London: Hutchinson Radius, n.d.), p. 30.
8. Gay Alinder, 'My gay soul', *Gay Sunshine*, September 1970.
9. Nevertheless, even as these recoveries were going on, poppers were making a comeback, sold as 'video head cleaner' or 'polish remover' to be used 'just like the old days'. Bathhouses had returned, and in some of them poppers, alcohol, crack cocaine and unsafe sex were readily available.

Bibliography

ACTLife, No. 1, October 1991.

Adams, Jad. *AIDS: The HIV Myth*. New York: St Martin's Press, 1989.

Adams, Stephen. *The Homosexual as Hero in Contemporary Fiction*. London: Vision Press, 1980.

Adkins, Barry. 'Looking at AIDS in totality: a conversation with Joseph Sonnabend', *New York Native*, 7–13 October 1985.

The AIDS Catch. Meditel Productions, 1990. Videotape.

'AIDS cure not seen in near future', *Globe and Mail*, 21 March 1994.

'AIDS virus attack', *Time*, 12 August 1985.

'AIDS virus causes cancer, research shows', *Globe and Mail*, 8 April 1994.

Alinder, Gary. 'My gay soul', *Gay Sunshine*, September 1970.

'Amebiasis treatment protested: lawsuit against university medical clinic', *Alternate*, January 1981.

Angel, Rev Charles. 'AIDS and the AAfrican-American [*sic*] PWA', *PWA Coalition Newsline*, April 1987.

'Are you sick enough for hospital?', *Folsom*, No. 3, 1981.

AZT: cause for concern. Meditel Productions, 1992. Videotape.

Bach, Edward. *Heal Thyself: An Explanation of the Real Cause and Cure of Disease*. Saffron Walden: C. W. Daniel Co., 1931.

Backgrounder for Editors and Writers of the Globe and Mail. Toronto: Globe and Mail, n.d.

Bad Object Choices. *How Do I Look? Queer Film and Video*. Seattle: Bay Press, 1991.

Badgley, Laurence. *Choose to Live: The Four Fold Path. An AIDS Healing Companion*. San Bruno, CA: Human Energy Press, 1987.

Badgley, Laurence. *Healing AIDS Naturally: Natural Therapies for the Immune System*. San Bruno, CA: Human Energy Press, 1987.

Baldwin, James. *The Evidence of Things Not Seen*. New York: Holt, Rinehart & Winston, 1985.

Baldwin, James, *Notes of a Native Son*. Boston: Beacon Press, 1955.

Baldwin, James, and Richard Avedon. *Nothing Personal*. New York: Dell, 1965.

Bamforth, Nick. *AIDS and the Healer Within*. New York: Amethyst Books, 1987.

Bayer, R. *Homosexuality and American Psychiatry*. New York: Basic Books, 1981.

Bearden, Thomas E. *AIDS Biological Warfare*. Greenville, TX: Tesla Book Co., 1988.

Bell, Arthur. *Dancing the Gay Lib Blues: A Year in the Gay Liberation Movement*. New York: Simon & Schuster, 1971.

Benson, R. O. D. *In Defense of Homosexuality: A Rational Evaluation of Social Prejudice*. New York: Julian Press, 1965.

Bentley, Eric Russell. *A Century of Hero Worship*. Philadelphia: J. B. Lippincott, 1944.

Berkowitz, Richard. 'Joseph Sonnabend', *Christopher Street*, No. 68, 1982.

Berkowitz, Richard, and Michael Callen. *How to Have Sex in an Epidemic: One Approach*. New York: News from the Front Publications, 1983.

Berubé, Allen. *Coming Out Under Fire: The History of Gay Men and Women in World War II*. New York: The Free Press, 1990.

Birdstone, Alabama. *Queer Free*. New York: Calamus Books, 1981.

Blake, Robin. *Mind Over Medicine: Can the Mind Kill or Cure?* London: Aurum Press, 1987.

Blake, William. *Complete Writings*, ed. Geoffrey Keynes. London: Oxford University Press, 1966.

Blake, William. *Songs of Innocence and Experience by William Blake. Tuned by Allen Ginsberg*. MGM Records, 1969.

Blanchard, Steven G. P. Letter in *Body Politic*, July–August 1982.

Bos, Arie. *AIDS: Alternative Approaches to the Understanding and the Treatment of Acquired Immune Deficiency Syndrome Based on Anthroposophical Medicine*. Stroud: Hawthorn Press, 1989.

Boyd, Malcolm. 'Roy Cohn in Heaven?', *Advocate*, 21 June 1988.

Bridge, T. Peter, Allan F. Mirsky and Frederick K. Goodwin, eds. *Psychosocial, Neuropsychiatric and Substance Abuse Aspects of AIDS: Advances in Biochemical Psychopharmacology, Vol. 44*. New York: Raven Press, 1988.

Burroughs, William S. *Blade Runner: A Movie*. Berkeley, CA: Blue Wind, 1979.

Burroughs, William S. *Naked Lunch*. New York: Grove Press, 1959.

Caiazza, Stephen S. *AIDS: One Doctor's Personal Struggle*. Highland Park, NY: 1990.

Califia, Pat. *The Advocate Adviser*. Boston: Alyson Publications, 1991.

Callen, Michael. *Surviving AIDS*. New York: HarperCollins, 1990.

Cantwell, Alan, Jr., MD. *AIDS and the Doctors of Death: An Inquiry Into the Origins of the AIDS Epidemic*. Los Angeles: Aries Rising Press, 1988.

Cantwell, Alan, Jr., MD. *The Cancer Microbe*. Los Angeles: Aries Rising Press, 1990.

Carpenter, Edward. *The Intermediate Sex: A Study of Some Transitional Types of Men and Women*. London: George Allen & Unwin, 1908.

Carpenter, Edward. *Intermediate Types Among Primitive Folk: A Study of Social Evolution*. London: George Allen & Unwin, 1919.

Carpenter, Edward. *My Days and Dreams*. London: George Allen & Unwin, 1916.

Carpenter, Edward, Rev. *Edward Carpenter 1944–1929. Democratic Author and Poet: A Restatement and Reappraisal*. London: Dr Williams Trust, 1970.

Carter, Erica, and Simon Watney. *Taking Liberties: AIDS and Cultural Politics*. London: Serpent's Tail, 1989.

Centola, Jimmy. *The Divas of Sheridan Square*. New York: The Divas of Sheridan Square, n.d.

Chaitow, Leon, and Simon Martin. *A World Without AIDS: The Controversial Holistic Health Plan*. Wellingborough: Thorsons, 1988.

Chan, Ching-Chee. *An Alternative Approach to AIDS and Other Problems*. Mississauga, Ont.: Egret Publishing, 1992.

Chirimuuta, Richard, and Rosalind Chirimuuta. *AIDS, Africa and Racism*. London: Free Association Books, 1989.

Chomsky, Noam. *What Uncle Sam Really Wants*. Berkeley: Odonian Press, 1992.

'Clams dying of "AIDS" ', *Toronto Sun*, 19 September 1989.

Clark, Matt, and Mariana Gosnell. 'Diseases that plague gays', *Newsweek*, 21 December 1981.

Cohen, Leonard. *Beautiful Losers*. New York: Viking, 1966.

Cohen, P. T., Merle A. Sands and Paul A. Volberding, eds. *The AIDS Knowledge Base*. Waltham, MA: Medical Publishing Group, 1990.

Collier, Peter, and David Horowitz. *The Kennedys: An American Drama*. New York: Warner Books, 1985.

Colter, Marc. 'To the PWA Newsline', *PWA Coalition Newsline*, No. 51, January 1990.

Congdon, Kirby. *Dream-Work*. New York: Cycle Press, 1970.

Congdon, Kirby. *Fantoccini: A Little Book of Memories*. Los Angeles: Little Caesar Press, 1980.

Coulter, Harris J. *AIDS and Syphilis: The Hidden Link*. Berkeley, CA: North Atlantic Books/Wehawken Book Co., 1987.

Crewdson, John. 'The great AIDS quest', *Chicago Tribune*, 19 November 1989.

Crichton, Michael. *The Andromeda Strain*. New York: Alfred A. Knopf, 1969.

Crimp, Douglas, ed. *AIDS: Cultural Analysis, Cultural Activism*. Cambridge, MA: MIT Press, 1987.

Crimp, Douglas, and Adam Rolston. *AIDS Demo Graphics*. Seattle: Bay Press, 1990.

Crisp, Quentin. *How to Go to the Movies*. New York: St Martin's Press, 1991.

Croft-Cooke, Rupert. *Feasting With Panthers: A New Consideration of Some Late Victorian Writers*. London: W. H. Allen, 1967.

Crowley, Mart. *The Boys in the Band*. New York: Noonday, 1968.

Culbert, Michael. *AIDS: Hope, Hoax and Hoopla*. Chula Vista, CA: The Bradford Foundation, 1989.

Cunningham, Barry, *Gay Power: The Homosexual Revolt*. New York: Tower Publications, 1971.

Curzon, Daniel. *Something You Do In the Dark*. New York: Lancer Books, 1971.

D'Adesky, Anne-Christine, 'The man who invented safer sex returns', *Out*, No. 1, 1992.

Davis, Christopher. *Valley of the Shadow*. New York: St Martin's Press, 1988.

Davis, John H. *Mafia Kingfish: Carlos Marcello and the Assassination of John F. Kennedy*. New York: Signet, 1989.

Delany, Samuel R. *The Mad Man*. New York: A Richard Kasak Book, 1994.

DeMause, Lloyd. *Reagan's America*. New York: Creative Roots, 1984.

De Witt, Philip Elmer. 'Invasion of the data snatchers', *Time*, 26 September 1988.

Dlugos, Tim. 'Larry Kramer', *Christopher Street*, February 1979.

Dorman, Michael. *Payoff*. New York: Berkeley, 1972.

Duesberg, Peter. 'A challenge to the AIDS establishment', *Bio/Technology*, November 1987.

Duesberg, Peter. 'Human immunodeficiency virus and acquired immunodeficiency syndrome: correlation but not causation', *Proceedings of the National Academy of Sciences*, February 1989.

Duesberg, Peter. 'Retroviruses as carcinogens and pathogens: expectations and reality', *Cancer Research*, March 1987.

Duesberg, Peter, and Bryan J. Ellison. 'Is the AIDS virus a science fiction?', *Policy Review*, Summer 1990.

Dumke, Klaus. *AIDS: The Deadly Seed: An Anthropological and Epidemiological Investigation of a Modern Epidemic*. London: Rudolf Steiner Press, 1991.

Dynes, Wayne. *Homolexus: A Historical and Cultural Lexicon of Homosexuality*. New York: Gai Saber Monographs, 1985.

Ellman, Richard. *Oscar Wilde*. London: Penguin, 1988.

Evans, Arthur. 'Poppers: an ugly side of gay business', *Coming Up!*, November 1981.

Eves, Bruce. 'Reports from the front: a portfolio', *Christopher Street*, 20 October 1991.

Farber, Celia. 'AIDS: words from the front', *SPIN*, April 1990.

Farber, Celia. 'Sins of omission: the AZT scandal', *SPIN*, November 1989.

Fernbach, David. *The Spiral Path: A Gay Contribution to Human Survival*. London: Gay Men's Press, 1981.

Fest, Joachim. *Hitler*. New York: Harcourt, 1974.

Fiedler, Leslie. *An End to Innocence*. Chelsea, MI: Scarborough House, 1972.

Fiedler, Leslie. *Love and Death in the American Novel*. New York: Criterion Books, 1960.

Field, Edward. *Variety Photoplays*. New York: Grove Press, 1967.

Fisher, Peter. *Dreamlovers*. New York: Sea Horse Press, 1979.

Fisher, Peter. *The Gay Mystique*. New York: Stein & Day, 1972.

Fitzgerald, Edward. *Euphranor: A Dialogue on Youth*. Privately printed, 1851.

Flood, Gregory. *I'm Looking for Mr. Right But I'll Settle for Mr. Right Away: AIDS, True Love, the Perils of Safe Sex, and Other Spiritual Concerns of the Gay Male*, 2nd edn. Atlanta: Brob House Books, 1987.

Fone, Byrne R. S. *Hidden Heritage: History and the Gay Imagination*. New York: Irvington, 1981.

Forster, E. M. *Maurice*. London: Edward Arnold, 1971.

Fournier, R. A. *The Intelligent Man's Guide to Handball (The Sexual Sport)*. New York: R. A. Fournier, 1983.

Fox, Emmet. *The Sermon on the Mount*. New York: Harper & Row, 1934.

Freedman, Mark. *Homosexuality and Psychological Functioning*. Belmont, CA: Brooks/Cole, 1971.

Friedman-Kien, Alvin E. *et al.* 'Kaposi's sarcoma in HIV-negative homosexual men', *The Lancet*, Vol. 335, No. 8682, 20 January 1990.

Fritscher, Jack. *Some Dance to Remember*. Stamford, CT: Knights Press, 1990.

Gallo, Robert. 'The first human retrovirus', *Scientific American*, December 1986.

Gentry, Curt. *J. Edgar Hoover: The Man and the Secrets*. New York: Plume, 1991.

Gold, Michael. *A Conspiracy of Cells: One Woman's Immortal Legacy and the Medical Scandal It Caused*. Albany: State University of New York Press, 1986.

Grahn, Judy. *Another Mother Tongue: Gay Words, Gay Worlds*. Boston: Beacon Press, 1984.

Greer, Germaine. *Sex and Destiny: The Politics of Human Fertility*. London: Secker & Warburg, 1984.

Grimal, Pierre. *The Concise Dictionary of Classical Mythology*, ed. Stephen Kershaw. London: Basil Blackwell, 1990.

Grochmal, Chuck. 'Deadly decisions', *Xtra!*, 14 July 1989.

Grof, Stanislav. *Beyond the Brain: Birth, Death and Transcendence in Psychology*. Albany: State University of New York Press, 1985.

Gruen, John. *Keith Haring: The Authorized Biography*. New York Prentice-Hall, 1991.

Grzesiak, Rich. 'Plunging into the dark with Dreamlovers' Pete Fisher', *Gay News* (Philadelphia), 31 March 1983.

Halberstam, David. *The Fifties*. New York: Villard Books, 1993.

Hall, Lyn, and Thomas Modl, eds. *AIDS: Opposing Viewpoints*. St Paul, MN: Greenhaven Press, 1988.

Hamilton, Wallace, *Christopher and Gay: A Partisan's View of the Greenwich Village Homosexual Scene*. New York: Saturday Review Press, 1973.

Hannon, Gerald. 'How gay society is blazing a trail for the future', *Globe and Mail*, 27 June 1992.

Hannon, Gerald. 'A people at war', *Xtra!*, 23 February 1990.

Hatch, Richard. 'Cancer warfare', *CovertAction Bulletin*, Winter 1991.

Hay, Louise L. *The AIDS Book: Creating a Positive Approach*. Santa Monica, CA: Hay House, 1988.

Hay, Louise, *You Can Heal Your Life*, 2nd edn. Santa Monica, CA: Hay House, 1987.

HEAL: An AIDS Information Packet on Alternative & Holistic Therapies. New York: HEAL, n.d.

Heard, Gerald. *The Five Ages of Man: The Psychology of Human History*. New York: The Julian Press, 1963.

Heard, Gerald. *Narcissus: An Anatomy of Clothes*. New York: E. P. Dutton, 1924.

Heard, Gerald. *The Third Morality*. London: Cassell & Co., 1937.

Heard, Gerald. *Training for the Life of the Spirit*. Blauvelt, NY: Steinerbooks, 1975.

Hendler, Sheldon Saul, MD, Ph.D. *The Oxygen Breakthrough: 30 Days to an Illness-Free Life – The Natural Program*. New York: William Morrow, 1989.

Hillman, James, ed. *The Puer Papers*. Dallas: Spring Publications, 1987.

Hinckle, Warren. *Gayslayer! The Story of How Dan White Killed Harvey Milk and George Moscone and Got Away With Murder*. Virginia City, NV: Silver Dollar, 1985.

Hollier, Denis. *Against Architecture: The Writings of Georges Bataille*. Cambridge, MA: The MIT Press, 1989.

Holmes, Ernest. *The Science of Mind*, rev. ed. New York: G. P. Putnam's Sons, 1988.

Hong, Guang-Guo, Robert Gallo *et al.* 'Sequence analysis of original HIV-1', *Nature*, Vol. 349, No. 6312, 28 February 1991.

Hopke, Drew. 'AIDS in Africa: is it a myth?', *CityWeek*, 10 October 1988.

Hosein, Sean. 'The pink triangle test', *Xtra!*, 11 August 1989.

Hughes, Robert. *The Fatal Shore: The Epic of Australia's Founding*. New York: Alfred A. Knopf, 1987.

I Promise You This: A Collection of Poems for Harvey Milk. San Francisco: privately printed, 1979.

Illich, Ivan. *Medical Nemesis: The Expropriation of Health*. London:
Calder & Boyars, 1975.

Isherwood, Christopher, ed. *Vedanta for Modern Man*. New York:
Collier Books, 1962.

Itkin, Bishop Mikhail. *The Radical Jesus and Gay Consciousness: Notes
for a Theology of Gay Liberation*. Long Beach, CA:
Communiversity West, 1972.

Jay, Karla, and Allen Young, eds. *After You're Out: Personal Experiences
of Gay Men and Lesbian Women*. New York: Link Books, 1975.

Jay, Karla, and Allen Young, eds. *Lavender Culture*. New York: Jove
Books, 1979.

Jay, Karla, and Allen Young, eds. *Out of the Closets: Voices of Gay
Liberation*. New York: Douglas Books, 1972.

Jones, Colman. *AIDS and Syphilis: What Is the Connection? Has the
Great Masquerader Made a Deadly Comeback?* Toronto:
privately printed, 1991.

Jones, James H. *Bad Blood: The Tuskegee Syphilis Experiment*. New
York: The Free Press, 1981.

Judell, Brandon. 'The Saint says goodbye', *Advocate*, 5 July 1988.

Judge, John. *The Black Hole of Guiana: The Untold Story of the
Jonestown Massacre*. Santa Barbara, CA: Prevailing Winds
Research, n.d.

Jung, Carl G. *Psyche and Symbol: A Selection from the Writings of
C. G. Jung*, ed. Violet S. de Laszlo. Garden City, NY: Doubleday
Anchor, 1958.

Kantrowicz, Arnie. *Under the Rainbow: Growing Up Gay*. New York:
Pocket Books, 1977.

Kellner, Aaron. 'Reflections on Wolf Szmuness', *Proceedings In Clinical
and Biological Research*, No. 182, 1985.

King, Dennis. *Lyndon LaRouche and the New American Fascism*. New
York: Doubleday, 1989.

Kion, Tracy A., and Geoffrey M. Hoffman. 'Anti-HIV and anti-anti-
MHC antibodies in alloimmune and autoimmune mice', *Science*,
Vol. 253, 6 September 1991.

Kleinberg, Seymour. *Alienated Affections: Being Gay in America*. New
York: Warner Books, 1980.

Klinghoffer, Max. 'AIDS: a viral Pearl Harbor', *Journal of Civil Defense*,
April 1987.

Koskinen, Jarmo. *Thought-Forms in Time: Is There a New Age Coming?*
Fort Erie, Ont.: Phoenix Rising Publications, 1988.

Kramer, Larry. *Faggots*. New York: Warner Books, 1979.

Kramer, Larry. 'Kramer vs . . . Our gay "leaders"' *Outweek*, 21 January
1990.

Lambert, Royston. *Beloved and God: The Story of Hadrian and
Antinous*. New York: Viking, 1984.

Landes, Ruth. *The Prairie Potawatomi*. Madison, WI: University of
Wisconsin Press, 1970.

Lappé, Marc. *When Antibiotics Fail: Restoring the Ecology of the Body.* Berkeley, CA: North Atlantic Books, 1986.

Larkin, Purusha. *A Holistic Health Preventive Approach to Life-Threatening Ilness.* San Diego: Sanctuary Press, 1983.

Larkin, Purusha. *The Divine Androgyne According to Purusha.* San Diego, CA: Sanctuary Press, 1981.

Lauritsen, John. *The AIDS War: Propaganda, Profiteering and Genocide from the Medical-Industrial Complex.* New York: Asklepios, 1993.

Lauritsen, John. *Poison by Prescription: The AZT Story.* New York: Asklepios, 1990.

Lauritsen, John. 'Political-economic construction of gay male clone identities', *Journal of Homosexuality*, Vol. 24, Nos. 3–4, 1993.

Lauritsen, John. 'Something rotten in the British AIDS establishment', *New York Native*, 10 February 1992.

Lauritsen, John, and David Thorstad. *The Early Homosexual Rights Movement (1864–1935).* New York: Times Change Press, 1965.

Lauritsen, John, and Hank Wilson. *Death Rush: Poppers and AIDS.* New York: Pagan Press, 1986.

Lee, John Allan. *Getting Sex.* Toronto: Musson, 1978.

Levy, Jack A. *AIDS Pathogenesis and Treatment.* New York: Marcel Dekker, 1989.

Lewes, Kenneth, *The Psychoanalytic Theory of Male Homosexuality.* New York: Simon & Schuster, 1988.

Lewis, David. 'G.M.S.M.A. clarification', *Gay News* (Philadelphia), 8 September 1983.

Leyland, Winston, ed. *Gay Sunshine Interviews, Vol. I.* San Francisco: Gay Sunshine Press, 1978.

Licata, Sal. 'Fire Island impressions', *PWA Coalition Newsline*, September 1987.

Lipsius, Ellen and Derek Mackie. 'AIDS: the medical dilemma and solutions', *Canadian Tribune*, 11 July 1988.

Liversidge, Anthony, 'AIDS: words from the front', *SPIN*, March 1989.

Liversidge, Anthony, and Celia Farber, 'AIDS: words from the front', *SPIN*, September 1990.

Livesay, Bruce, and Ellen Lipsius. 'AIDS: modern medicine's Achilles heel', *Canadian Dimension*, October 1989.

Loewenberg, Peter. *Decoding the Past: The Psychohistorical Approach.* New York: Alfred A. Knopf, 1983.

Lotringer, Sylvére, (ed.) *Foucault Live (Interviews 1966–84).* New York: Semiotext(e), 1989.

Louis, James. 'Where angels tread', *Numbers*, February 1983.

Lowry, T. P., and G. R. Williams. 'Brachiopractic Eroticism', *British Journal of Sexual Medicine*, January 1981.

McKenzie, Angus, 'Lust with a very proper stranger', *Body Politic*, April 1982.

McLuhan, Marshall. *Understanding Media: The Extensions of Man.* New York: Mentor, 1964.

Maddox, John. 'AIDS research turned upside down', *Nature*, Vol. 353, No. 6342, 26 September 1991.

Maickel, Roger P. Interview in *Moneysworth*, January 1982.

Mains, Geoff. *Urban Aboriginals: A Celebration of Leathersexuality.* San Francisco: Gay Sunshine Press, 1984.

Malcolm X and Alex Hailey. *The Autobiography of Malcolm X.* New York: Ballantine Books, 1965.

Mann, Thomas. *Death in Venice and Seven Other Stories*, translated by H. T. Lowe-Porter. New York: Vintage, 1954.

Mannheim, Karl. *Essays on the Sociology of Knowledge*, ed. Paul Kecskemeti. London: Routledge & Kegan Paul, 1952.

Marotta, Toby. *The Politics of Homosexuality.* Boston: Houghton Mifflin, 1981.

Martin, Robert K. *The Homosexual Tradition in American Poetry.* Austin: University of Texas Press, 1979.

Mayer, Kenneth, and James d'Eramo. 'Poppers: a storm warning', *Christopher Street*, No. 78, n.d.

Mellors, Bob. 'Gay liberation', *LSE Magazine*, Summer 1990.

Melton, George, with Wil Garcia. *Beyond AIDS: A Journey Into Healing.* Beverly Hills: Brotherhood Press, 1988.

Melville, Herman. *Billy Budd.* New York: Pocket Books, 1972.

Mertin, J. *et al.* 'Nutrition and immunity: the immunoregulatory effect of n-6 essential fatty acids is mediated through prostaglandin E', *International Archives of Allergy and Applied Immunology*, No. 77, 1985.

Meyers, Jeffrey. *Homosexuality and Literature 1890–1930.* London: Athlone Press, 1977.

Miles, Barry. *Ginsberg: A Biography.* New York: Simon & Schuster, 1989.

Miller, James. *The Passion of Michel Foucault.* New York: Anchor Books, 1993.

Monte, Tom. *The Way of Hope: Michio Kuchi's Anti-AIDS Program: The Drug-Free Way to Strengthen the Immune System Through Macrobiotics.* New York: Warner Books, 1989.

Morin, Jack. *Anal Pleasure and Health: A Guide for Men and Women.* Burlinghame, CA: Down There Press, 1981.

Mosse, George L. *Nationalism and Sexuality: Respectability and Abnormal Sexuality in Modern Europe.* New York: Howard Fertig, 1985.

Mottram, Eric. *Blood on the Nash Ambassador: Investigations in American Culture.* London: Hutchinson Radius, n.d.

Nassaney, Louie, with Glenn Kolb. *I Am Not a Victim.* Santa Monica: Hay House, 1990.

Nelson, Emmanuel S., ed. *Critical Essays: Gay and Lesbian Writers of Color.* New York: Harrington Park Press, 1993.

Nelson, James B. *The Intimate Connection: Male Sexuality, Masculine Spirituality*. Philadelphia: Westminster Press, 1988.

Norton, Rictor. *The Homosexual Literary Tradition: An Interpretation*. New York: Revisionist Press, 1974.

Nussbaum, Bruce. *Good Intentions: How Big Business and the Medical Establishment Are Corrupting the Fight Against AIDS*. New York: Atlantic Monthly Press, 1990.

Odets, Walt. 'The secret epidemic', *Out/Look*, Fall 1991.

Ortleb, Charles. 'Nationally syndicated columnist and talk show host Tony Brown urges Magic Johnson to see Duesberg before it's too late', *New York Native*, 9 December 1991.

Ortleb, Charles. 'Nazi science: it's not what you have, it's who you are', *New York Native*, 8 March 1993.

Paglia, Camille. 'Camille Paglia defends her lousy record', *Advocate*, 22 September 1992.

Paris, Orlando. *The Short Happy Sex Life of Stud Sorrell and 69 Other Flights of Fancy*. San Diego: Greenleaf Classics, 1968.

Paxman, Jeremy, and Robert Harris. *A Higher Form of Killing: The Secret Story of Gas and Germ Warfare*. New York: Hill & Wang, 1983.

Pennick, Nigel. *Hitler's Secret Sciences*. Subdury, Suffolk: Neville Spearman, 1981.

Pereyra, Armand, MD, and Richard L. Voller, MD. 'A graphic guide for clinical management of latent syphilis', *California Medicine*, May 1970.

'Pins and needles: the painful art of piercing', *Dungeonmaster*, November 1980.

Plant, Richard. *The Pink Triangle: The Nazi War Against Homosexuals*. New York: Henry Holt & Co., 1986.

Plummer, Kenneth, ed. *The Making of the Modern Homosexual*. New Jersey: Barnes & Noble, 1981.

Popert, Ken. 'Public sexuality and social space', *Body Politic*, July–August, 1982.

'Pregnant women and newborns', *Body Positive*, December 1989.

Preston, John, ed. *Dispatches: Writers Confront AIDS*. New York: St Martin's Press, 1989.

Preston, John. *My Life as a Pornographer & Other Indecent Acts*. New York: A Richard Kasak Book, 1993.

Preston, John. 'The white candles come to New York', *Alternate*, December 1980.

Probst, Volker G. *Arno Breker: 60 Ans de Sculpture*. Paris: Jacques Damase Editeur, 1981.

Rader, Dotson. *Gov't. Inspected Meat and Other Fun Summer Things*. New York: Paperback Library, 1972.

Rappoport, Jon. *AIDS Inc. Scandal of the Century*. San Bruno, CA: Human Energy Press, 1988.

Reade, Brian. *Sexual Heretics: Male Homosexuality in English Literature from 1850 to 1900*. London: Routledge & Kegan Paul, 1970.

Rechy, John. *City of Night*. New York: Ballantine Books, 1973.

Rechy, John. *Numbers*. New York: Evergreen Black Cat Editions, 1968.

Rechy, John. *Rushes*. New York: Grove Press, 1979.

Rechy, John. *The Sexual Outlaw*. New York: Dell, 1977.

Reed, David. 'The multimillion-dollar mystery high', *Christopher Street*, February 1979.

Rees, David. *Not For Your Hands: An Autobiography*. Exeter: Third House, 1992.

Reich, Wilhelm. *The Cancer Biopathy*. New York: Farrar, Straus & Giroux, 1973.

Richmond, Len, and Gary Noguera, eds. *The Gay Liberation Book*. San Francisco: Ramparts Press, 1973.

Rist, Darrell Yates. 'AIDS as apocalypse: the deadly cost of an obsession', *Christopher Street*, No. 132, 1989.

Roberts, Seth. 'Lab rat', *Spy*, July 1990.

Rofes, Eric E. 'Gay Lib *vs* AIDS: averting civil war in the 1990's', *Out/Look*, Spring 1990.

Root-Bernstein, Robert S. 'Do we know the cause(s) of AIDS', *Perspectives in Biology and Medicine*, Summer 1990.

Root-Bernstein, Robert S. *Rethinking AIDS: The Tragic Cost of Premature Consensus*. New York: The Free Press, 1993.

Rose, Steve. 'AZT zombies', *New York Native*, 26 September 1988.

Rosenfels, Paul, MD. *Homosexuality: The Psychology of the Creative Process*. Roslyn Heights, NY: Libra Publishers, 1971.

Rubini, Dennis. 'Continental Baths revisited', *Gay News* (Philadelphia), September 1976.

Rumaker, Michael. *A Day and a Night at the Baths*. San Francisco: Grey Fox Press, 1981.

Rumaker, Michael. *My First Satyrnalia*. San Francisco: Grey Fox Press, 1981.

Russo, Vito. *The Celluloid Closet: Homosexuality in the Movies*, rev. ed. New York: Harper & Row, 1987.

Rutledge, Leigh. *Unnatural Quotations: A Compendium of Quotations By, For, or About Gay People*. Boston: Alyson Publications, 1988.

Sarotte, Georges-Michel. *Like a Brother, Like a Lover: Male Homosexuality in the American Novel and Theater from Herman Melville to James Baldwin*. Garden City, NY: Anchor Press/Doubleday, 1978.

Saslow, James. 'The tenderest lover: Saint Sebastian in Renaissance painting', *Gai Saber*, Spring 1977.

Scheim, David E. *Contract on America: The Mafia Murder of President John F. Kennedy*. New York: Zebra Books, 1988.

Schmidt, Casper G. 'The group-fantasy origins of AIDS', *The Journal of Psychohistory*, Summer 1984.

Schmidt, Casper G. *Guidelines for the Psychoanalytic Treatment of AIDS*. New York: privately printed, 1993.

Scortia, Thomas N., and Frank M. Robinson. *The Nightmare Factor*. Garden City, NY: Doubleday, 1978.

Senate Subcommittee on Constitutional Rights. *Individual Rights and the Federal Role in Behavior Modification*. Washington, DC: Government Printing Office, 1974.

Serinus, Jason, ed. *Psychoimmunity and the Healing Process: A Holistic Approach to Immunity and AIDS*, 3rd edn. Berkeley, CA: Celestial Arts, 1988.

Shealy, C. Norman, and Carolyn M. Myss. *AIDS: Passageway to Transformation*. Walpole, NH: Stillpoint Publishing, 1987.

Sheehan, Nik. 'Poetic pessimist', *Xtra!*, 23 November 1990.

Sheldrake, Rupert. *A New Science of Life: The Hypothesis of Formative Causation*. London: Blond & Briggs, 1981.

Shenton, Joan. 'AIDS and Africa', *Rethinking AIDS*, May 1993.

Shepard, Leslie, ed. *The Dracula Book of Great Vampire Stories*. Secaucus, NJ: Citadel Press, 1977.

Shilts, Randy. *And the Band Played On*. New York: St Martin's Press, 1987.

Shilts, Randy. *The Mayor of Castro Street: The Life and Times of Harvey Milk*. New York: St Martin's Press, 1982.

Siegel, Bernie S. *Love, Medicine and Miracles: Lessons Learned about Self-Healing from a Surgeon's Experience with Exceptional Patients*, 2nd edn. New York: Harper & Row, 1988.

Sonnabend, Joseph. 'The etiology of AIDS', *AIDS Research*, Vol. I, No. 1, 1984.

Sonnabend, Joseph, and Serge Sadoun. 'The acquired immunodeficiency syndrome: a discussion of etiological development', *AIDS Research*, Vol. I, No. 2, 1985.

Sonnabend, Joseph, *et al.* 'A multifactorial model for the development of AIDS in homosexual men', *Annals of the American Academy of Sciences*, No. 437, 1985.

Special Virus Cancer Project Progress Report. National Cancer Institute, US Department of Health, Education and Welfare, Public Health Service, 1972.

Spence, Christopher. *AIDS: Time to Reclaim Our Power*. London: Lifestory, 1986.

Steakley, James D. *The Homosexual Emancipation Movement in Germany*. New York: Arno Press, 1975.

Sternberg, Steve. 'Medical sleuths lack legal weapons in AIDS mystery', *Vancouver Sun*, 7 September 1991.

Stewart, Walter. Interview in *Omni*, February 1989.

Storm, Flash. 'Notes from aboveground', *Gay Post*, May–June, 1973.

Straus, Stephen. 'Gallo probe shows the race for Nobel is too much sport', *Globe and Mail*, 4 August 1990.

Sturgeon, Theodore. *A Touch of Strange*. New York: Berkeley
　　Medallion, 1965.
Summers, Anthony. *Conspiracy: Who Killed President Kennedy?*
　　London: Fontana Paperbacks, 1980.
Summers, Anthony. *Official and Confidential: The Secret Life of J. Edgar
　　Hoover*. New York: G. P. Putnam's Sons, 1993.
Summers, Montague. *Antinous and Other Poems*. London: Sisley's,
　　[1907].
Symonds, John Addington. *Gabriel*. London: Michael de Hartington,
　　1974.
Symonds, John Addington. *Male Love: A Problem in Greek Ethics and
　　Other Writings*. New York: Pagan Press, 1983.
Szasz, Thomas. *Ceremonial Chemistry: The Ritual Persecution of Drugs,
　　Addicts and Pushers*, rev. ed. Holmes Beach, FL: Learning
　　Publications, 1985.
Szasz, Thomas. *The Manufacture of Madness: A Comparative Study of
　　the Inquisition and the Mental Health Movement*. New York:
　　Harper & Row, 1970.
Szasz, Thomas. *The Therapeutic State: Psychiatry in the Mirror of
　　Current Events*. Buffalo: Prometheus Press, 1984.
Teale, Donn. *The Gay Militants*. New York: Stein & Day, 1971.
Thomas, Gordon. *Journey Into Madness: Medical Torture and the Mind
　　Controllers*. London: Corgi Books, 1989.
Thompson, Mark, ed. *Gay Spirit: Myth and Meaning*. New York: St
　　Martin's Press, 1987.
Thompson, Mark, ed. *Leatherfolk: Radical Sex, People, Politics, and
　　Practice*. Boston: Alyson Publications, 1991.
Tilleraas, Perry. *Circle of Hope: Our Stories of AIDS, Addiction and
　　Recovery*. New York: Harper & Row, 1990.
Tyler, Parker. *Magic and Myth of the Movies*. New York: Simon &
　　Schuster, 1947.
Tyler, Parker. *Screening the Sexes: Homosexuality in the Movies* New
　　York: Anchor Books, 1973.
Valenstein, Elliot S. *Great and Desperate Cures: The Rise and Decline of
　　Psychosurgery and Other Radical Treatments for Mental Illness*.
　　New York: Basic Books, 1986.
Varange, Ulick (Francis Parker Yockey). *Imperium: The Philosophy of
　　History and Politics*. Sausalito, CA: Noontide Press, 1962.
Versi, Anver. 'AIDS: the epidemic that never was', *New Africa*, December
　　1993.
Versicolor, Dr H. 'The psychology of captivity', *DungeonMaster*, March
　　1980.
Vithoulkas, George. *The Science of Homeopathy*. New York: Grove
　　Press, 1980.
Von Hoffman, Nicholas. *Citizen Cohn: The Life and Times of Roy
　　Cohn*. New York: Doubleday, 1988.

Voyant, Clara. 'N.G.T.F.: a profile in absurdity', *Gay Post*, May–June, 1975.

Voyant, Clara. 'N.Y.C. Gay Parade 1975: which direction is it going?', *Gay Post*, May–June, 1975.

Voyant, Clara. 'On the sodomites and the pigs', *Ain't It Da Truth!*, No. 11, 1975.

Waite, Robert G. L. *The Psychopathic God Adolf Hitler*. New York: Mentor, 1978.

Walter, Aubrey, ed. *Come Together – The Years of Gay Liberation 1970–73*. London: Gay Men's Press, 1980.

Warren, Patricia Nell. *The Front Runner*. New York: Morrow, 1974.

Weatherby, W. J. *James Baldwin: Artist On Fire*. New York: Donald I. Fine, 1989.

Webb, James. *The Occult Establishment*. La Salle, IL: Open Court, 1976.

Weinstein, Harvey. *Father, Son and CIA*. Halifax: Goodread Biographies, 1990.

'Wellcome issue raises £2.16 billion', *Globe and Mail*, 28 July 1992.

Welles, Paul O. *Project Lambda*. Port Washington, NY: Ashley Books, 1978.

White, Edmund. *States of Desire: Travels in Gay America*. New York: Dutton, 1980.

Whitman, Walt. *The Complete Poems*. London: Penguin, 1975.

Whitman, Walt. *Democratic Vistas and Other Papers*. Saint Clair Shores, MI: Scholarly Press, 1970.

Whitmore, George. 'After a "career" in suicide: choosing to live', *Advocate*, 3 March 1983.

Whitmore, George. 'Bearing witness', *New York Times Magazine*, 31 January 1988.

Whitmore, George. 'Beer, baloney and champagne', *Body Politic*, September 1978.

Whitmore, George. *The Confessions of Danny Slocum or Gay Life in the Big City*. New York: St Martin's Press, 1980.

Whitmore, George. *Getting Gay in New York*. New York: Free Milk Fund Press, 1976.

Wilde Oscar. *Complete Works of Oscar Wilde*. London: Collins, 1966.

Wilde Oscar. *The Picture of Dorian Gray*. London: Penguin, 1973.

Williams, Tennessee. *Suddenly, Last Summer*. New York: New Directions, 1958.

Williams, Walter L. *The Spirit and the Flesh: Sexual Diversity in American Indian Culture*. Boston: Beacon, 1986.

Willkie, Phil, and Greg Baysans, eds. *The Gay Nineties: An Anthology of Contemporary Gay Fiction*. Freedom, CA: Crossing Press, 1991.

Wojnarowicz, David. *Close to the Knives: A Memoir of Disintegration*. New York: Vintage, 1991.

Wolfe, Tom. 'Brave new world bites the dust', *Globe and Mail*, 14 January 1988.

Woods, Gregory. *Articulate Flesh: Male Homoeroticism in Modern Poetry*. New Haven, CT: Yale University Press, 1987.

Wright, Pearce. 'Smallpox vaccine "triggered AIDS virus" ', *The Times* (London), 11 May 1987.

Wright, Stephen. 'Full stop: the drug scene', *Follow-Up*, Vol. 2, No. 8, 1974.

Yatri. *Unknown Man: The Mysterious Birth of a New Species*. New York: Simon & Schuster, 1988.

Yoni. 'A foolish young circuit queen finds out what it is to be wise', *PWA Coalition Newsline*, October 1987.

Young, Ian. *The AIDS Dissidents: An Annotated Bibliography*. Metuchen, NJ: Scarecrow Press, 1993.

Young, Ian. *Gay Resistance: Homosexuals in the Anti-Nazi Underground*. Toronto: Stubblejumper Press, 1985.

Young, Ian. 'Prescription for suicide', *New York Native*, 12 September 1988.

Young, Ian. *Sex Magick*. Toronto: Stubblejumper Press, 1986.

Young, Ian. 'Touring New York during the AIDS crisis', *Gay News* (Philadelphia), 1–7 July 1983.

Young, Ian, ed. *The Male Muse: A Gay Anthology*. Trumansburg, NY: Crossing Press. 1973.

Young, Perry Deane. *God's Bullies: Native Reflections on Preachers and Politics*. New York: Holt, Rinehart & Winston, 1982.

Ziebold, Dr Thomas O. 'Alcoholism and recovery: gays helping gays', *Christopher Street*, January 1979.

Zoja, Luigi. *Drugs, Addiction and Initiation: The Modern Search for Ritual*. Boston: Sigo Press, 1989.

Index